THE LIVES OF THE POPES

VOL. XVI.

THE
LIVES OF THE POPES
IN THE MIDDLE AGES

BY THE

RT. REV. MONSIGNOR HORACE K. MANN, D.D.

" De gente Anglorum, qui maxime familiares Apostolicæ Sedis semper
existunt" (Gesta Abb. Fontanel., A.D. 747–752, ap. M.G. SS. II. 289).

RECTOR OF THE COLLEGIO BEDA, ROME ; CORRESPONDING MEMBER OF THE ROYAL ACADEMY OF
HISTORY OF SPAIN ; MEMBER OF THE ACCADEMIA D'ARCADIA AND OF THE R. SOCIETÀ ROMANA
DI STORIA PATRIA

AND

JOHANNES HOLLNSTEINER, Ph.D., D.D.

PROFESSOR OF CHURCH HISTORY IN THE UNIVERSITY OF VIENNA.

THE POPES AT THE HEIGHT OF THEIR
TEMPORAL INFLUENCE

INNOCENT II. TO BLESSED BENEDICT XI.
1130–1305

VOL. XVI.

INNOCENT V. TO HONORIUS IV., 1276–1287

LONDON:
KEGAN PAUL, TRENCH, TRUBNER & CO., LTD.
ST. LOUIS, MO.: B. HERDER BOOK CO.
1932

1889

PRINTED IN GREAT BRITAIN BY
STEPHEN AUSTIN AND SONS, LTD. ,HERTFORD

FOREWORD

THE honoured worker whose labours in the field of mediaeval Papal history deserve such recognition did not live to complete his work. Vol. XVI. was completed in manuscript at his death, and almost ready for the printer, in so far as the Pontificates from Innocent V. to Nicholas III. (1276–1280) were concerned. All that was necessary was a trifling matter of arrangement for printing. Perhaps the author might have developed some small point here or there when giving his work its final touches, but respect for him obviously requires that the manuscript should be printed unaltered, as it left his hands.

With regard to the Pontificates of Martin IV. and Honorius IV. the situation is different. No preliminary work had been done on this period, with the exception of an unimportant extract from Potthast's *Regesta*. Original monographs had to be prepared regarding these two Popes.

This distinction is shown outwardly by the division of the volume into two parts, the first comprising the Pontificates from 1276 to 1280, treated by Monsignor Mann, while the second covers the Pontificates treated by the undersigned, those from 1281 to 1287. This division is also justified by the material itself, since Martin IV. followed methods and policies altogether different from those of his predecessor Nicholas III. and often opposed to those of the latter. I alone am responsible for the treatment of the second part.

JOHANNES HOLLNSTEINER.

VIENNA,

Feast of St. Augustine, 1931.

A LIST OF THE PRINCIPAL ABBREVIATIONS
USED IN THIS VOLUME

Potthast . . . = *Regesta Pontificum Romanorum*, ed. A. Potthast, 2 vols., Berlin, 1874.

Reg. . . = One of the volumes of the *Registres des Papes* in course of publication by the French Schools of Athens and of Rome, ed. Fontemoing, Paris.

L. P. . . . = *Liber Pontificalis*, 2 vols., ed. L. Duchesne, Paris, 1886.

M. G. H. or Pertz . = *Monumenta Germaniae Historica*, either *Scriptores* (M. G. SS.), or *Epistolae* (M. G. Epp.), or *Poetae* (M. G. PP.).

P. G. . . . = *Patrologia Graeca*, ed. Migne, Paris.

P. L. . . . = *Patrologia Latina*, ed. Migne, Paris.

R. I. SS. . . . = *Rerum Italicarum Scriptores*, ed. Muratori, Milan, 1723 ff., or the new ed. in course of publication.

R. F. SS. . . . = *Recueil des Historiens des Gaules*, ed. Bouquet and others, Paris, 1738 ff.

R. S., following an edition of a book. = The edition of the Chronicles, etc., of Great Britain and Ireland, published under the direction of the Master of the Rolls.

Rymer or Foedera . = *Foedera, Literae, etc., ab anno* 1101 *ad nostra usque tempora*, accurante T. Rymer. Unless the contrary is stated, we quote from the original ed., London, 1704 ff.

Other abbreviations will be readily understood by reference to the *Sources* prefixed to each biography.

The sign † placed before a date indicates that the date in question is the year of the death of the person after whose name the sign and date are placed. The sign * placed before the title of a book indicates that the author of these volumes has seen the book in question favourably mentioned, but has not examined it himself.

TABLE OF CONTENTS

ix

INNOCENT V.

A.D. 1276.

Sources.—As we have no contemporary biography of this short-lived Pope, we have to fall back on the short *lives* of him left us by B. Guidonis, ap. *R. I. SS.*, iii, p. 605, and Amalric Augerius, ap. *ib.*, pt. ii, p. 426, and on scattered notices in different chronicles. Unfortunately, like those of Celestine IV. and V., the Registers of Innocent V. are lost, so that only a score or two of his letters have come down to us. They have been collected to the number of fifty-one by " un religieux " (R. P. Mothon), and they are also to be found scattered in a great variety of books.

Modern Works.—The fullest and most important modern biography of Innocent is the work of " a religious of the same Order " as that of the Pope, namely a Dominican, R. P. Mothon, *Vie du bienheureux Innocent V.*, Rome, 1896. It was written with a view "to obtaining from the Holy See recognition of the cult which from time immemorial has been offered to Blessed Innocent V." Then, also very useful, is " the historical dissertation " of Mgr. L. Carboni, *De Innocentio V.*, *R. P.*, Rome, 1894. Of much less importance is the *Panégyrique du B. Innocent V.*, Nancy, 1900, by Mgr. Turinaz, bishop of that city. It is followed by a study on the birthplace, works, and sermons of the Pope whom he styles : " Un pape savoisien." But this last-named little book must be read with caution. In his able and amusingly written pamphlet of 16 pages (*Pierre de Tarentaise d'après son dernier panégyriste*, Paris, 1901), E. Missel has shown that the bishop has made some astounding mistakes in his laudable anxiety to make the most of his distinguished compatriot. To show that Pierre had written even on land-surveying, he wanted to attribute to " Innocentius V. P." (to Pope Innocent V.) a work of a comparatively well-known fourth century lawyer whom he had seen described as " Innocentius V. P.," i.e. Innocentius " Vir Prudentissimus ! " He also attributed to Innocent V. sixty-three sermons which Innocent III. had sent to Arnauld I., abbot of Citeaux. Two sermons of his, however, preached before he became Pope, have come down to us. *Cf.* Hauréau on MS. 14952

ap. *Notices et extraits des MSS.*, t. xxxii, pt. ii, p. 312 f. The
Dominican, Father Bourgeois, has given us in his *B. Innocent V.*,
Paris, n.d. (1898), a brief study, " inspired by the festival of his
Beatification," on " his mission in the Church ".

From the year 1883 onwards, Canon J. P. Béthaz issued a
succession of pamphlets to try to prove that Innocent was an
Italian of Aosta ; e.g. *Le P. I. V. est-il français ou italien* ?
Aoste, 1883, another in 1888, and then *Pierre des Cours de la
Salle, Aoste, pape sous le nom d'Innocent V.*, Aosta, 1891. His
pamphlets were replied to by the Abbé J. E. Borrel, *Patrie du
P. I. V.*, 1890, and 1892, 1894 Moutiers. He would appear to
have proved that Innocent was a Frenchman.[1] See also L. Galle,
Un Archevêque de Lyon, Lyon, 1898, and *Notice sur le sceau
d'Innocent V., ib.*, and the notice of " Pierre de Tarentaise " by
Petit-Radel in *Hist. litt. de la France*, vol. xix, p. 316 ff.

[1] On the same subject see E. Pascalien, *Origines du P. I. V.*, Annecy,
1889. This work was never put upon the market, and I have not
seen it.

CONTEMPORARY SOVEREIGNS.

(See under Gregory X.)

CHAPTER I.

EARLY CAREER OF PETER OF TARENTAISE ; HIS ELECTION

AS POPE.

PIERRE OF TARENTAISE, born it would appear about the year 1225, was, despite all that has been written to confuse the point, a Savoyard. He was born in the district of Tarentaise, probably at Moûtiers. He is called a Burgundian, because Tarentaise, then under the count of Savoy, formed part of the old kingdom of Burgundy.[1] The idea that he was born in the district of Aosta appears to have originated in a confusion between the Dominican Peter, and canon Peter who became archbishop of Tarentaise in 1272. The latter was born at La Salle, near Aosta, and was of the family of the Grossi of Chatelard (Castelar), which was allied to that of the Cours. Hence, by certain authors, these facts concerning the canon are connected with the friar. *[Birthplace of Pierre.]*

From a discourse delivered by Innocent himself on his death-bed, we learn that he was of noble birth, and endowed not only with beauty of body, but with the goods of this life, and with a keen mind which enabled him to garner stores of knowledge.[2] According to Mothon, he was entrusted for his education when a mere child to an uncle, Francis Bermond or Bernard, canon of the cathedral of Tarentaise (1230) ; and the friar adds that going to Paris when only a boy of some 10 years of age, he was *[Joins the Order of St. Dominic, c. 1241 (?).]*

[1] Geoffroy de Courlon, *Chron.*, an. 1273 ; Rishanger, *Chron.*, pp. 87–8, *R. S.* ; B. Guidonis, ap. *R. I. SS.*, iii, p. 605 ; I : " natione burgundus de Tarantasia Sabaudiæ."

[2] See the account of this Pope given by Ambrose Taegio, a Dominican writer of the fifteenth to sixteenth century who has preserved much valuable material of earlier ages, cited by Mothon, p. 22 f.

3

received into the Dominican Order in the great Dominican College of St. Jacques.[1] That he was received into the Order when young is certain not only from Martinus Polonus and Bernard Guidonis, but from Innocent himself.[2] But it is perhaps more likely that, as the *Annals of Basle* say, he was admitted when he was 16.[3]

One of a hundred and fifty religious from all parts of Europe in the College of St. Jacques, where he remained for thirty years, the youthful Peter seems to have had as professors, Hugh of St. Cher, the first Dominican cardinal, and St. Albert the Great ; and, as one of his fellow students, Nicholas of Hanapes, whom, when Pope, he summoned to Rome to be his Penitentiary.

Master and writer.

He made such progress in his studies that he became a Master in Theology, and " wrote on the Sentences, and on the Epistles of the Apostles ".[4] When precisely he became a Master is not known ; but he was certainly teaching along with St. Thomas Aquinas in 1259 ; for with that Saint and three other Masters he was appointed

[1] *Vie*, pp. 2–4.

[2] M. P. " Hic a pueritia sua in Ordine Fratrum Prædicatorum existens." Ap. *M. G. SS.*, xxii, 442. Writing (ep. ap. Ripoll, *Bullar. O. P.*, i, 543) to the General Chapter of the Order assembled at *Pisa* (not Paris as in Potthast, n. 21124) he says that God : " Nos intra gregem vestrum a tenera ætate vocare dignatus."

[3] Ap. *M. G. SS.*, xvii, 200. " Decimo sexto anno ætatis ordinem Prædicatorum ingressus, 30 annis in eodem mansit." With that statement squares the one in *Cont. IV Chron. Min. Erford* : " Juvenis ordinem fratrum Prædicatorum ingressus," p. 689, ed. Holder-Egger.

[4] Gilberti, *Chron. Pont. et Imp.*, contin. v, ap. *M. G. SS.*, xxiv, p. 138. *Cf. Chron. Erford, l.c.*, and *Flores Temp.*, ap. *ib.*, p. 249, " Postillas super quosdam libros biblie fecit, et scripsit notabilia super 4 libros sentenciarum." In the Vatican Library, *Cod. Ottobon.*, nn. 963–70, there may be seen his *Postilla super epp. D. Pauli* in 8 vols. As a friar preacher, he treated St. Paul's epistles to some extent as material for sermon purposes. Mandonnet's criticism on Peter's *Commentaries on the Sentences* is that he " n'a pas une doctrine personnelle bien caractérisée," *Des écrits authentiques de S. Thomas d'Aquin*, p. 125.

by the General Chapter of the Order at Valenciennes in Flanders to draw up regulations for the promotion of the studies of the Order.[1] The works published by Peter whilst a Master came to be officially ranked with those of St. Thomas and St. Albert the Great,[2] and were evidently popular. In one of the interesting documents published by Denifle in his *Chartulary* of the University of Paris, there is a list of charges which the University authorities allowed booksellers to make for the loan of books to students. After the writings of Brother Thomas " de Aquino " come the list of those of Brother Peter " de Tarentasia ". His *Commentaries* on each of the four books of the *Sentences* could be had separately at prices varying from eighteen to twenty-seven denarii. His *Postille* on St. Paul's Epistles, containing seventy quires (peciæ), cost three soldi and six denarii, and those on St. Luke, with thirty-two quires, cost eighteen denarii for hire.[3] Many manuscripts of his *Commentaries* on the *Sentences* still exist in different libraries of Europe. Dedicated to Innocent X., they were published in 1652.[4]

He is also with good reason credited with writing Commentaries on the Pentateuch and other books of the Bible, and pamphlets on special philosophical problems, as, e.g., one on " The understanding and the will " (*De intellectu et voluntate*).[5]

---

[1] *Cf.* the " statuta de studiis " drawn up by our hero, St. Thomas, Albertus Magnus, etc., ap. Denifle, *Chartular. Univers. Paris.*, i, p. 385. According to the *Annals of Basle*, cited above, he taught theology for twelve years.

[2] The works of all three Masters were imposed on Dominican students by the Provincial Chapter of Toulouse in 1316. *Cf.* Mortier, *Les Maîtres gén.*, iii, p. 10, n.

[3] This document, issued between 1275 and 1286, is to be found on p. 644 ff.   [4] Mothon, *Vie*, p. 32.

[5] *Ib.*, p. 33. Echard, *Script. Ord. Præd.*, i, p. 353, believes that the *Commentaries* on St. Paul often edited under the name of Nicholas de Goran are really the work of Peter of Tarentaise.

As he had given evidence when teaching that he possessed a power of governing men, he was, probably in 1262, chosen Prior Provincial of France, and Vicar-General of the Order.[1] It was in visiting the fifty houses of his Order in France, and in holding Provincial Chapters, that Peter gave proof of that piety, prudence, and learning for which our English annalists specially praise him.[2] No doubt, too, it was whilst he held this office of Provincial, that he acquired that experience which enabled him when Pope to give valuable advice to the whole Order. In 1276 the General Chapter of the Order was held in Pisa at Whitsuntide. To it Innocent directed a letter on May 10. Among other things, he urged the Order not to be in a hurry to multiply foundations. Such action would lead to a too great dispersion of the brethren. The foundations, moreover, should be made in the great centres of population. Small convents would lead to slackness, and would be a source of anxiety to the Superiors. He also recommended greater care in the selection of novices, and that faults should not be passed over for fear that impunity would cause their multiplication.[3]

At the General Chapter held in Bologna at Whitsuntide, 1267, Peter was relieved for a brief space of his duties as Provincial, in order that he might return to the University to complete, so says Echard,[4] the three years' teaching required of each Master. During the latter of the two scholastic years which he then passed at the University, we find him again associated with St. Thomas

---

[1] *Chron. Erford., l.c.*; Rishanger, *Chron.*, pp. 87–8, *R. S.* For the date see Mothon, p. 36 f. On the subject of the Vicar-General of the Order, see *ib.*, p. 47 f.

[2] Rishanger, *l.c.* ; Nich. Trivet, *Ann.*, 1276, p. 294 : " Vir religionis eximiæ, expertæque prudentiæ." *Annals of Osney*, " Vir magnæ literaturæ," iv, p. 268, *R. S.*

[3] Ep. given in full by Mothon, p. 42 or p. 299.

[4] Ap. *ib.*, p. 52.

Aquinas on a commission. This time the commission was named to resolve certain practical theological problems that came up for discussion before the General Chapter of May 12, 1269.[1]

No sooner were his two years' teaching completed than he was again elected Provincial of France. Whilst still teaching in the University, Master Peter, in response to a request of the students, drew up what we may call a volume of " Sermon Aids ", but which he called an " Alphabet to the Art of Preaching ". It was a sort of repertory of texts and commentaries, useful for sermons, arranged in alphabetical order of subjects. It is regarded as one of the best works of its kind written during the Middle Ages,[2] and was revised by its author after he became cardinal. The students were led to ask him to draw up the *Aids* for them, as they had been impressed by the sermons which he had addressed to them. Some of these discourses have been preserved, as well as others, some of which he preached at Lyons " before the Roman Court ", during the Council of Lyons.[3]

Again Provincial, 1269–72.

Peter also compiled another useful repertory. This was an abridged collection of the Canons. It was mentioned by Nicholas Trivet, and pronounced by him " most useful ", and is still to be found in manuscript in Paris.[4]

Master Peter must have been either an original thinker, or occasionally at least have failed to express himself

---

[1] See a MS. of the *Opuscula* of St. Thomas cited by Echard, *ib.*, p. 53.

[2] *Cf.* Lecoy de la Marche, *La Chaire française au moyen âge*, pp. 131 and 288. It was la Marche who called attention to this still inedited " Alphabetum in artem sermocinandi a Magistro Petro ". *Cf.* Mothon, *Vie*, pp. 55–6.

[3] Mothon, p. 56 ff., gives a list of the sermons of Peter which he had been able to find in the Bibliothèque Nationale at Paris and elsewhere, e.g. in the Ambrosian library of Milan.

[4] *Annales*, p. 294. " Decretaque, abbreviatione perutili et fideli, in summam parvulam coartavit."

clearly ; for, according to cardinal Bellarmine in his *De Scriptoribus Ecclesiasticis*,[1] more than a hundred propositions extracted from his Commentaries on the Master of the Sentences were attacked. Their defence, however, was undertaken at the command of John of Vercelli, the Master-General of the Order, by an author at one time thought to be St. Thomas Aquinas ; and, as appears from the author's pamphlet, triumphantly vindicated.

Archbishop of Lyons, 1272.

After the resignation of Philip of Savoy, the mere nominal archbishop of Lyons (1267), there had been great trouble in the city owing to violent disputes between the Canons of the Cathedral and the citizens. In the hope of making peace, Pope Gregory resolved to appoint to the vacant archbishopric his old master, the Provincial Peter, of whom, as he said in his letter of nomination, he had long had a high opinion. Because, said the Pontiff, he found the Provincial possessed of virtues and gifts which made him acceptable to God and pleasing to men, he had taken the very first opportunity to draw him from comparative obscurity, and to place him where the flaming light of his character would illumine all who entered God's house. He had, accordingly, with the advice of his brethren, nominated him to the archbishopric of Lyons. He begged him not to be affrighted at the sight of the difficulties of the position, but to realize that his nomination was a command from God.

---

[1] Ad an. 1265, cited by G. J. Eggs, *Vit. Pont. Rom.*, p. 474, ed. Cologne, 1718. *Cf.* Hurter, *Nomenclator*, iv, p. 307. The *Responsio* of St. Thomas or of the unknown author is to be found among the *Opuscula* attributed to St. Thomas, No. 9, vol. xvii, ed. Rome, 1570. P. Mandonnet, *Des écrits authentiques de S. Thomas d'Aquin*, p. 123 ff., Fribourg (Suisse), 1910, believes that we should hold to the statement of the MS. that the reply was really the work of St. Thomas : " Explanatio dubiorum de dictis cujusdam edita a Fratre Thoma de Aquino." Sometimes " St. Thomas " allows that Brother Peter has expressed himself badly, but at other times he declares the criticisms merely malicious.

He must, therefore, without delay betake himself to the Church of Lyons, and trust in God's help, and in the support of the Holy See.[1] Other letters, written about the same time, informed the clergy and people of Peter's appointment,[2] and urged the latter to put a curb on their hostile attitude to the authorities of their Church.

Taking possession of his See in the summer of 1272, the new archbishop applied himself at once to settling the violent and long-standing quarrel between his chapter and the citizens of Lyons. Through his exertions, the matters in dispute, as we learn from a bull of Nicholas III.,[3] were referred to Pope Gregory X. By his award, the sentences of excommunication and interdict against the city and its people were to be removed, and the citizens were to pay for damage done to certain buildings, and not to do anything to interfere with the temporal rights of the archbishop and his chapter over their city.[4] The new archbishop knew also how to defend his rights against the King of France as well as against the citizens of Lyons. The metropolitan Church of Lyons had feudal rights over lands in different localities which it held on a variety of tenures. Of some of these lands " the Primate elect of the Church of Lyons " took possession without waiting to take the oath of fealty to the King of France. Protest was at once made in the Sovereign's behalf. But the archbishop

Peace with its citizens.

[1] Ep. of the beginning of April, 1272. Ap. Mothon, p. 71 ff.

[2] Epp. of April 10 and June 6, ap. *ib.*, pp. 72 and 74. In the latter letter addressed to Peter himself, Gregory says that in selecting him he chose a man after his own heart : " Excitati ut eidem ecclesiæ secundum cor nostrum personam preficeremus ydoneam . . . te prefate Lugdunensi ecclesiæ . . . in archiepiscopum prefecimus et pastorem." *Reg. Greg.*, n. 37.

[3] Ep. of March 23, 1279, ap. *Reg. Nic. III.*, n. 528.

[4] *Cf.* ep. just cited. The peace was not final ; and, at length, archbishop Peter of Savoy, worsted by the citizens, gave up his temporal sovereignty into the hands of the King of France (1312). *Cf.* L. Galle, *Un Arch. de Lyon*, Lyon, 1897, p. 20.

declared that, with regard to the lands on the other side of the Saone, his predecessors had always taken possession of them without reference to the King of France. This he was able to prove ; but he agreed to the proposition that his action should not prejudice any fresh document which the King might be able to allege in the future on behalf of his claim.[1]

Made cardinal, 1273.

But Peter had no time to develop a policy as archbishop of Lyons. That city was on April 13, 1273, proclaimed to the world by Pope Gregory X. as the place which he had selected for the holding of the ecumenical council of 1274. In the following month Peter was, in the first creation of cardinals made by Gregory, named cardinal-bishop of Ostia.[2] When the Pope reached Lyons (Nov., 1273), he himself consecrated Peter bishop ; and, until April, 1274, left the cardinal in charge of the See of Lyons as Apostolic Administrator.[3]

Work in the General Council, 1274.

In the ecumenical council of 1274, the cardinal of Ostia took a prominent part ; and in connection with the Union between the Eastern and the Western Churches, taking for his text : " Lift up thine eyes round about, and see ; all these are gathered together, they are come to thee," [4] he pointed out its advantages to Christendom.[5] Along with St. Bonaventure, he took a very considerable share in the deliberations of the Council, especially in the matter of the reunion of the Churches. As he told the Emperor Michael Paleologus, he was, so to speak, a fellow worker in the affair along with the Pope.[6] Cardinal

---

[1] Document of Dec. 2, 1272, ap. Mothon, p. 89 ff.

[2] *Cf. supra*, Vol. XV, p. 363, and *Chron. Erford.*, p. 689. " A quo (the archbishopric of Lyons) breviter per eundem papam absolutus assumitur in cardinalem et in episcopum Hostiensem."

[3] Mothon, p. 100 f., and the document cited p. 101, n.

[4] Isaias, xlix, 18.   [5] *Cf. supra*, Vol. XV, p. 415.

[6] Ep. May 23, 1276, ap. Mothon, pp. 158 and 318. " Quem (Peter) tunc de fratrum collegio existentem quasi cooperatorem hujusmodi salubre negotium contingebat."

Peter preached also at the fourth session (July 6), and he delivered the panegyric on St. Bonaventure. With the text, " I grieve for thee, my brother Jonathan," (2 Kings, i, 26) he reduced many of his audience to tears. During the fifth session (July 16) he baptized one of the Tartar envoys, who, according to Glassberger, was a son of the Great Khan,[1] and two of his suite.

The influence exercised by the fathers of the Dominican and Franciscan Orders[2] during this Council did not tend to lessen the irritation felt towards them by the secular clergy at large. Mingled, no doubt, with some real reasons for this irritation was a certain jealousy of their success. However that may be, the murmuring against them reached the ears of the Holy Father before the close of the Council. Gregory therefore begged the Dominican General Chapter to make such regulations as would tend to allay the irritated feelings of the seculars.[3]

Accordingly a number of conciliatory decrees were passed, which, on " Nov. 2, 1274, after the General Council of the Lord Pope Gregory X." were sent to all the Domincan Provincials with an injunction that they should be scrupulously obeyed. The friars by these regulations agreed, for instance, not to exercise any parochial functions, such as hearing confessions, without the permission of the local bishop, that they would promptly refer to him cases which he had reserved to his own absolution, etc.

---

[1] *Chron.*, p. 87. He also says that the Pope acted as godfather. *Cf.* Hefele, *Hist. des conc.*, vi, pt. i, p. 180, new ed.

[2] Glassberger, *Chron.*, p. 85, quotes a jibe which was in circulation at the time of the Council against three distinguished Franciscans :

" Rothomagensis anus (Rigaldi, archbishop of Rouen) et Præsul
    Tripolitanus
Et Bonaventura tractant papalia jura
Ordinis immemores, qui tales spernit honores."

[3] Sebastian of Olmedo, ap. Mortier, *Les Maîtres généraux*, ii, p. 98.

These decrees had been previously submitted to Pope Gregory by cardinal Peter, who was one of the cardinals originally commissioned to act with the friars. To the decrees as he received them, Peter added himself a clause to the effect that, if the Pope thought fit to prescribe anything further, the friars were prepared to submit to his wishes. The Master-General informed the Provincials that the Pope was so satisfied with their resolutions that, if they kept them, they would not be in difficulties again.[1]

During the progress of the Council, the cardinal of Ostia was much helped by the advice and prayers of his brethren who, in General Chapter assembled, ordered that all the priests of the Order should offer up a Mass for his benefit.[2] He, on the other hand, showed his esteem for them by refusing to allow the Master-General of the Order to show him special honour, saying to him : " Do not act thus, my well-beloved Master. With you, I am a fellow servant of the brethren." [3]

Leaves Lyons with Gregory, 1275.

Cardinal Peter left Lyons with the Pope (April, 1275), and on the journey towards Italy received another mark of the Pope's favour. By becoming a friar, Brother Peter had renounced the goods of this world. As a cardinal, however, his position required that he should again become a master of some of them ; and, by a special bull, Pope Gregory empowered him to dispose of them by will as he thought fit.[4]

Rudolf and Charles anxious about the new Pope.

In less than six months after this, Gregory had breathed his last, and it became necessary to elect a successor.

[1] See the letter of the Master-General, John of Vercelli, to the Dominican Provincials, ap. Mortier, l.c., p. 99 ff., from Reichert, Lit. Encyc.

[2] Mothon, p. 125, quoting from the Acta of the General Chapter of 1274.

[3] Sebast. de Olmedo, Chron., ap. ib., p. 124.

[4] Ep. Aug. 18, 1275, ap. Ripoll, Bullar., i, p. 532.

Rudolf, the emperor-elect, at once wrote to the cardinals bewailing the death of the Pope. If Greeks and Latins, and particularly those who had taken the Cross, were, he said, all distressed at the premature demise of Gregory, he more than all others regretted the death of one who had raised his throne above Kings and Kingdoms, and who whilst he lived had cherished him with such paternal affection.[1] Though his pierced heart will perhaps never be healed, he consoles himself with the hope that, as God raised up a worthy successor to Moses who completed the work which He did not suffer Moses himself to accomplish, so He will raise up a worthy successor to Gregory who will finish the work he began. "Wherefore we implore you, you columns and hinges (cardines—cardinals) of the Universal Church, put aside all occasions of contention, and with all speed give a ruler to the headless world."[2]

As for himself, he was getting ready to come for the imperial crown when the sad news of the Pope's death reached him. Now he has suspended his preparations for the journey ; but he hopes that God will bring about the election of a Pope after his heart, and he will await his instructions.

Charles of Anjou also was hoping for a Pope after his own heart. Gregory had asked him to meet him in Rome, and Charles had ordered his Barons to meet him "in magnificent array". On the news of the death of the Pope, he, nevertheless, proceeded to Rome, and we find him writing from there (Jan. 13, 1276) for money, because he would have to remain there a long time for

---

[1] Ep. Jan., 1276, ap. Gerbert, *Cod. Epist. Rud.*, p. 102 ff. We are more grieved at his death than all princes "eo quod idem Pater Sanctissimus thronum nostrum super reges et regna constituens, nos dum viveret . . . paterno favore stipabat".

[2] "Applicate ut . . . ocyus mundo acephalo Præsul necessarius erigatur."

the creation of the new Pope, and would have to incur great expense.[1]

At the time of the death of Gregory X. at Arezzo (Jan. 10, 1276), there were only three cardinals in his company.[2]   But, without even being convoked, the thirteen members who then composed the sacred College soon assembled at Arezzo, and on the eve of the feast of St. Agnes, " in all submission and of their own accord," entered the palace in which Gregory had resided. On the feast itself (Jan. 21), after the celebration of the Mass of the Holy Ghost, all the cardinals agreed to proceed immediately to the election, and to employ for the purpose the customary method of scrutiny. On the very first scrutiny, the cardinal of Ostia was unanimously elected.[3]

The humble Dominican felt overwhelmed by the burden he was called upon to shoulder ; but he animated himself by the thought that his being elected in less than an hour was a clear proof that the burden had been laid upon him directly by God.[4]

Four days after his election, Peter, who had taken the name of Innocent,[5] and for his motto, " My eyes are ever towards the Lord " (Psalms, xxiv, 15), notified his election to the Catholic world in the letter from which we have extracted the circumstances of that election. He

---

[1] C. M. Riccio, *La Dominaz. Angioina*, p. 12.

[2] The details in connection with the election of Innocent are taken from his letter announcing his election, ap. the *Register* of archbishop Giffard, p. 291 ff., or Mothon, pp. 134 ff. and 261 ff.

[3] Ep. *ib.*   " In humilitatem nostram . . . iidem fratres, nullo discordante, unanimiter concordarunt."

[4] *Ib.*   " Ecce id, non interjecto quasi horæ unius interstitio perfecisti (God) ad quod alias persepe diffusi temporis spatium vix profecit."

[5] As our historian Wykes notes, though he changed his name of Peter, he yet succeeded him in his high apostolic dignity : " mutato Petri nomine cui successit in celsitudinem dignitatis apostolicæ," *Chron.*, p. 268.

concluded his encyclical by expressing a hope that God would protect the Pope whom He had Himself made.

In due course he received a letter of congratulation on his election from our King Edward I., "his humble servant devoutly kissing his sacred feet." The news of the election had brought joy, wrote Edward, not only to the King of England, but to all Kings, to the universal Church. For "the King of Kings, . . . pouring his precious Blood over the Church so that the clear light of faith might never grow dim therein, has set you on its highest pinnacle (*in lacuna sublimiori*) like a lamp full of the sweet oil of learning and a good life ". The King thanked God for so soon setting him over men and over his holy Mount of Sion. Finally, he assured Innocent that his sweet eloquence had inspired him more than ever with a desire to help the Holy Land, and he expressed his satisfaction that the "lofty apostolic Cedar" condescending to the hyssop of his lowliness, had invited him, in the interests of his regal authority, to have recourse thereto.[1]

[1] Ap. Rymer, *Fœdera*, ii, p. 63.

CHAPTER II.

INNOCENT'S WORK AS POPE. HIS DEATH, 1276.

Peace among the Genoese. BEFORE he was crowned and before leaving Arezzo, Innocent began his work for peace. For the same reason as in other parts of North Italy, there was civil war in Genoa. On one side stood the partisans of Charles of Anjou. In this case, they were the kinsmen of " our dear son Ottoboni, cardinal-deacon of St. Hadrian ", as the Pope expressed it, and a number of other nobles. Opposed to them were the Podestà, the Captains, and, in general, the Commune of Genoa. After setting forth that peace was the one desire of his heart, and that nothing was worse than civil war, the Pope begged the civic authorities to send immediately to him as plenipotentiaries men who were of a conciliatory disposition, so that peace might be made between Charles and his opponents. He told the Podestà that he was sending to him the Dominican, Brother Hugo Ubertini, a man distinguished both for learning and piety, and that he hoped for the best, as in times past Genoa had always been so respectful to the Holy See.[1] From the only document assigned to Hadrian V. by Potthast,[2] which gives us that Pope's confirmation of the agreement made

---

[1] Ep. of Jan. 26, ap. Mothon, p. 138 f. and p. 259 f. His translation on p. 138 f. is not quite accurate. In conclusion Innocent said that the civic authorities must not be astonished that the bulla appended to his letter did not bear his name, as it was not the custom for the Popes to put their names on the bulla before their consecration. For the *date* see Carboni, p. 7.

[2] N. 21149, July 20, 1276. Had. V. had been card. Ottoboni. *Cf. Chron. de Rebus (Ann. Placent. Gib.)*, p. 354, according to which peace was made on June 18. *Cf.* James de Varagine, *Chron. Jan.*, c. 7

by the contending parties, we learn that the mediation of Innocent was successful. Peace was signed at Rome on June 18. War was to cease between the republic and Charles who was to be acknowledged King of Sicily. Prisoners were to be released, and both parties were to combine against the Mediterranean pirates. Innocent was lying on his bed of death, when word was brought to him that peace had been agreed to. At first he indicated his joy only by signs. But presently he contrived to sit up in bed, and raising his hands to heaven and giving thanks to God, he imparted his blessing. Then without another word he lay down and died.[1]

Soon after dispatching the letter to Genoa, Innocent left Arezzo for Rome. When he reached Viterbo, he sent for " his things " which he had left in charge of the Franciscans of Assisi.[2] Presumably having received them, he continued his journey to Rome, and was consecrated bishop and crowned in St. Peter's (Feb. 22). Then he betook himself to the papal residence at the Lateran, though not before saying Mass in St. Peter's— a function which had not been performed there by a Pope for thirty years.[3]

Crowned and consecrated, 1276.

When Innocent had settled down in his official residence, he must have been profoundly distressed at the difficult position in which he was placed. Charles of Anjou who had met him at Viterbo (Feb. 9), and had preceded him to Rome, was still in the city.[4] He was its Senator, and was still Vicar of Tuscany which in the vacancy of the

Tacit consent to the position of Charles.

---

[1] Albertus Stanco, *Ann. Genuen.*, ap. *R. I. SS.*, vi, 565.

[2] Potthast, n. 21100, Feb. 7.

[3] *Annales Admunt. & S. Rudb.*, ap. *M. G. SS.*, xvi, pp. 706 and 801. These authorities say " in summa ecclesia " at Rome. Under the circumstances, it is difficult to say whether St. Peter's, the Lateran Basilica, or St. Mary Major's is meant.

[4] He was to remain in it practically during the whole of the brief pontificate of Innocent. See his *Itinerary* in Durrieu, *Les Archives Angev.*, ii, p. 179.

Empire he had long ruled by papal nomination, first as
Pacifier (Paciarius—Servator pacis, 1267), and then as
Vicar. With his ambitious views, he was not disposed to
give up his position as Vicar, though conditions had
changed by Gregory's recognition of the claims of Rudolf
to the Empire. Feeling that the Emperor-elect would
probably not be prepared to recognize Charles as Vicar,
and yet unwilling or afraid to offend the King, Innocent,
on March 2, addressed to Charles a vague document in
which he declared that, by holding the positions of Senator
and Vicar, he had not and would not contravene the
conditions on which he had been granted the crown of the
two Sicilies.[1] He then turned his attention to Rudolf.

Communica- The King of the Romans had immediately, on receiving
tions with the news of Innocent's election, written to congratulate
Rudolf. him. He answered him that the sadness of the Church
caused by the death of Gregory had been turned into joy,
when it became known that one so distinguished by his
merits had been chosen to succeed him.[2] He begged the
new Pope to confer his favour on one who was ever ready
to second his wishes and those of the Church : and " by
virtue of the power given to him from above ", to fulfil
in him the work begun by Gregory.[3] He brought his
letter to a close by recommending to the Pope his envoy
Henry, bishop of Basle.[4]

To this friendly communication, Innocent replied with

---

[1] Ap. Theiner, *Cod. Diplom.*, i, n. 349. *Cf.* another document of
March 2, also addressed to Charles, in which besides repeating the
above declaration, Innocent officially recorded that Charles had done
homage for the two Sicilies. Potthast, n. 21104. Mothon gives the
two documents in full, p. 266 ff.

[2] "Meritorum candore conspicuum, et virtutem præstantia
luminosum," *Ep. Rud.*, ap. Gerbert, p. 108 f.

[3] " In sinum gratiæ vestræ colligite . . . filium singularem, vestris
et Matris ecclesiæ beneplacitis semper in omni spiritus promptitudine
pariturum, opus Dei benigne perficientes in nobis, ex tradita vobis
desuper potestate," *ib.*, or *Mon. Germ. LL.*, iv, p. 96.

[4] *Cf. re* Henry also ep. 37 *Rud.*, ap. Gerb., p. 107.

caution in two letters of March 9 and 17. He was anxious, he said, that everything connected with the King's visit to Rome should pass off well and peacefully. He accordingly begged Rudolf not to enter Italy until a complete understanding had been arrived at between them, and until the King had reconfirmed his pact with Gregory, especially as to the papal rights in the Romagna.[1] Both Rudolf himself and his predecessors, continued the Pope, had acknowledged that dominion over that province belonged to the Holy See.[2] In his name, however, but, no doubt, without his knowledge, his officials had been receiving oaths of fidelity. Innocent, therefore, begged the King to make it known that this action had been taken by mistake[3]; and he also begged the archbishops of Embrun, Cologne, and other ecclesiastics, and Louis, duke of Bavaria and other Princes, to use their influence with Rudolf to induce him to stand by his promises.[4]

The King of the Romans, however, found it too hard to give up without a struggle provinces which he declared to be a garden of the Empire.[5] He accordingly proceeded to temporize, and meanwhile sent to them, as their Rector, his kinsman and chancellor, Henry, count of Fürstenberg.[6] It was not till the days of Nicholas III. that he resigned his pretensions to them.[7]

[1] "Expedit tractatus eosdem (commenced by Gregory) ante tuum adventum in Italiam debita firmitate vallari." Ep. of March 9, ap. Gerbert, p. 107, or *M. G. LL.*, iv, p. 97.

[2] "Et quidem habet notoria veritas et tam ipsorum principum ac specialiter . . . Ottonis IV et Frederici II, quam tua etiam monimenta testantur, exarchatum Ravenne ac Penthapolim ad jus et proprietatem ecclesiæ R. spectare." Ep. of March 17, ap. *M. G. LL.*, p. 98.

[3] *Ib.*

[4] Ep. ap. Mothon, n. 7, p. 275.

[5] "Bona, et fertilis ac populosa," *Mem. Pot. Reg., R. I. SS.*, viii, p. 1151.

[6] Epp. nn. 40–2, ap. Gerbert, p. 111 ff.

[7] See Coxe, *Hist. of the House of Austria*, i, p. 44. *Cf.* Potthast, n. 21180 for the action of John XXI.

Help for Spain. Meanwhile the absence from his kingdom of Alfonso X., the quondam rival of Rudolf for the imperial crown, had exposed his realm to attacks from the Moors. Mohammed VI. of Granada, obtaining the assistance of Aben Yussef, King of Morocco, invaded Castile, ravaged the country and advanced on Seville and Cordova (1275). But Alfonso was back in his dominions in the very beginning of the following year, and Innocent bade the archbishop of Seville preach the Cross in Aragon in order that that kingdom might assist Alfonso,[1] and the bishop of Oviedo to be instant in collecting the ecclesiastical tenth granted the King by Pope Gregory X.[2] The result of the efforts of the archbishop was satisfactory. The " haughty Saracens " were unable to face the united kingdoms and especially the valour of the King's second son don Sancho. They sued for peace.

The cause of Margaret. During his brief pontificate, Innocent did not forget the Order to which he owed everything. He urged his former brethren ever to aim higher and higher,[3] and he pushed on the cause for the beatification of the Dominicaness Margaret, daughter of Bela IV., King of Hungary, who died on Jan. 28, 1271. She was, however, never canonized ; but her cult in Hungary itself was authorized by Pope Pius II.[4]

Remaining acts of Innocent. As the reign of Innocent only lasted five months, we cannot devote more space to his pontificate. It, therefore, only remains to be said that, if he removed the interdict from Florence,[5] peace did not immediately result therefrom, as the Florentines continued to fight against Pisa,

[1] Ep. ap. Raynaldus, an. 1276, nn. 20-2.
[2] See ep. ap. Mothon, p. 340 ff.
[3] Ripoll, *Bullar. O. P.*, i, p. 543, n. 3.
[4] *Acta SS.*, Jan. 28, ii, 900 ; Mothon, pp. 193 ff., 334, and 343. Butler, *Lives of the Saints*, i, p. 345.
[5] It is so asserted by the late writer Leonardo Bruni († 1444), *Hist. Florent.*, iii, p. 65, ap. *R. I. SS.*, t. xix, pt. iii, new ed. See also the following note.

nominally for the Guelf cause, and really for their commercial interests. However, by the influence of the
Dominican, Blessed Ambrose Sansedoni of Siena (through
whom the interdict had been removed), peace was
concluded after the defeat of the Pisans, in presence of
the papal legate, Velasco, bishop of Idauna (Guarda)
(June 13), a few days before the Pope died.[1] Further,
a glance through the *Regesta* of Potthast will show the
bishops whom Innocent consecrated, the monasteries
which he took under his protection, and other details of
Church government. Reference to the biography of
Gregory X. will show Innocent's wise share in connection
with the Union of the Greek and Latin Churches effected
at the Council of Lyons, and his work for the Crusade
which, like his predecessor, he had greatly at heart.[2]

Unfortunately, in the very midst of all the splendid
work which he was so successfully carrying out,[3] Innocent
fell ill. After a short time, feeling that his end was nigh,
he summoned the Cardinals to his bedside, and, from the
example of his own career, showed them the emptiness
of this life, and the need we have of fixing our thoughts
on the next. God, he said, had given him high birth,
riches, learning, and exceptional beauty of person. How
little did they avail him now, he asked ; and, baring his
breast he showed his body, all wasted away like that of

Death of Innocent.

[1] *Cf. Vit. Ambros.*, c. 40, ap. *Acta SS.*, 20 Mart., iii, p. 189 ; Villani,
Chron., vii, 50. The contemporary, Guido de Corvaria, *Hist. Pisan.*,
ap. *R. I. SS.*, xxiv, p. 685, states that the envoys of the Pope and of
King Charles entered Pisa to make peace on June 6. *Cf.* Ptolemy of
Lucca, *H. E.*, xxiii, 18 ; and document in Mothon, pp. 181, 311. *Cf.*
F. T. Perrens, *Hist. de Florence*, ii, pp. 182–4.

[2] See particularly his letter to Philip of France approving the resolve
of the French to set out against the Saracens on the feast of St. John
the Baptist, 1278, ap. Mothon, pp. 176, 276. He expressed his profound
joy at the King's generous determination to succour the oppressed
Christians.

[3] " Hic licet multa facere proposuisset, morte preventus non potuit
adimplere," B. Guidonis, in *Vit.*

Lazarus just risen from the grave.[1] As usual in the Middle Ages, in the case of anything like a sudden death, some historians, writing at a distance from the place where the event occurred or long after it, ascribed his death to poison or the dagger, and to the instigation of Charles of Anjou or " the Emperor ".[2]

Reaffirming that all his contemporaries[3] praise the learning and piety of Innocent, it only remains for us to state that he died regretted,[4] and that he was honourably buried in the Lateran in the presence of Charles of Anjou,[5] that he soon came to be regarded as a saint, and as a worker of miracles,[6] and that he is now recognized by the Catholic Church as Blessed.

---

[1] This at least is the substance of the address assigned to Innocent by a writer who lived in the fifteenth and sixteenth centuries, friar Ambrose Tægius, *De Insigniis Ord. Præd.*, dist. ii, cited by Mothon, pp. 22–4, and 196 f.

[2] Cf. *Ann. S. Rudbert.*, ap. *M. G. SS.*, ix, p. 801, and Mothon, p. 195 f.

[3] See, e.g., Jac. de Varag., *Chron. Jan.*, ap. *R. I. SS.*, ix, p. 52.

[4] Writing to our King his envoys at the Curia report to him : " Pope Innocent V. is dead, which information we convey to your Highness with grief," *Cal. of Close Rolls* (1272–9), p. 349.

[5] Ptolemy of Lucca, *H. E.*, lib. xxiii, c. 17.

[6] See the frescoes of Thomas of Modena and Fra Angelico with their inscriptions described by Mothon, pp. 217–19, and painted in 1352 and 1440 respectively. Mothon describes eighteen pictures of Innocent dating from the fourteenth to the nineteenth century.

HADRIAN V.

A.D. 1276

Sources.—For this Pope, who reigned only a little over a month, we have to rely on Guidonis and Amalric (see under Innocent V.).

Modern Works.—Natalie Schöpp, *Papst Hadrian V.*, Heidelberg, 1916.

CONTEMPORARY SOVEREIGNS.

(See under Gregory X.)

OTTOBONI FIESCHI,[1] the successor of Innocent V., was of the Genoese family of the counts of Lavagna which took its name :— *Family of Hadrian.*

> " . . . from that stream
> That twixt Chiaveri and Siestri draws
> His limpid waters through the lowly glen." [2]

He was the son of Thedisius de Flisco, and was a nephew of Pope Innocent IV., by whom he was made cardinal-deacon of S. Adriano.[3] He was connected with the royal family of England, for which reason Henry III. confirmed to him when he was cardinal the donation which Innocent IV. had already made to him of property in the kingdom of Sicily that had once belonged to the

---

[1] Or Ottobono di Flisco.

[2] Dante, *Purg.*, xix, v. 98 ff. *Cf.* Jac. de Varag., *Chron. Jan.*, c. 7 ; Theod. de Vaucouleur, *Vit. Urb. IV.*, p. 17.

[3] Guidonis, *Vita* ; Carbio, *Vit. Inn. IV.*, c. 31.

famous Peter della Vigna.[1] Charles of Anjou speaks of
him, not merely as his most dear friend, but also as
his godfather (compater).[2] Documents connected with
England let us know that he had at least two brothers,
Perceval [3] and Frederick,[4] and that they held livings in
our country. His cousin, Tedisius de Camilla, also held
benefices in England.[5] Moreover, from the Canto of
Dante just cited, we learn that he had a niece, Alagia,
whom he seemed to regard as the only virtuous member
of his family.

> " I have on earth a kinswoman (*nipote*) ; her name
>   Alagia, worthy in herself, so ill
>   Example of our house corrupt her not.
>   And she is all remaineth of me there." [6]

According to Benvenuto da Imola, in his Commentary
on this Canto, the last verse (*E questa sola m'è di là rimasa*)
does not imply that she was the last of his relatives left
on earth, but that by her prayers alone did the suffering
pontiff hope for release from his purgatorial pains. The
rest of his relations shared the family and Genoese vice
of avarice.[7] Alagia is said to have been the daughter of
Hadrian's brother, Niccolo. Before leaving Hadrian's

---

[1] " Cum nepotes vestri filiis nostris linea consanguinitatis sunt
conjuncti, etc." Ep. of Henry to him, ap. Rymer, *Fœd.*, i, p. 588.
See also a letter of Alexander IV. (Dec. 21, 1255), in which he confirms
to Ottoboni the property which Granata, Peter della Vigna's sister,
freely made over to him. *Reg. Alex.*, n. 796. *Cf.* C. M. Riccio, *Nuovi
Studi rig. la dominaz. Angioina*, p. 1, where Charles of Anjou orders an
inventory to be made of the property which the late Pope Hadrian
had held in his dominions. *Cf. ib. Della Dominaz. Ang. nel Reame di
Sicilia*, p. 38 f.

[2] Riccio, *Della* of the last note.

[3] *Cal. of Papal Reg.*, i, pp. 512 and 524.

[4] He received grants from Henry III. *Cf. Patent Rolls*, v, pp. 60,
624, and 676. Their names appear also in the Register of Charles of
Anjou, ap. Riccio, *Il Regno di Carlo I.*, an. 1276, p. 45. Perceval was
his " beloved counsellor ".

[5] *Cal.*, *l.c.*, pp. 450–1.   [6] Cary's translation.

[7] Vol. ii, p. 385 ff. of Tamburini's Italian version of the *Comment*.

family, we may add that Obizzo of Este, who according to that gossip, Salimbene, was stained with every vice,[1] was so great a friend of Hadrian that he married a near kinswoman of the Pope (Jacobina or Jacomina de Flisco).[2] Their eldest child, Azzo,[3] married Joanna Orsini, a relation of Pope Nicholas III.[4]

Among other positions held by Ottoboni was that of chaplain to his uncle Innocent IV. He was also canon, chancellor, and archdeacon of Rheims, for we know that, as such, he had a dispute with its archbishop as to the rights of the archdeacon.[5] He was also canon of Notre Dame at Paris and archdeacon of Parma.[6] Whilst holding the two archdeaconries, he was empowered by his uncle to hold other ecclesiastical dignities and benefices even with the cure of souls attached to them.[7] He was made cardinal-deacon of S. Adriano by the same Pope Innocent IV. in December, 1251, and was frequently employed by his uncle in the transaction of various ecclesiastical affairs. Innocent's *Register* also shows that he was constantly " providing " benefices for his nephews (*capellani*), of whom he would appear to have had a considerable number.[8]

Early career of Hadrian.

Though Alexander IV., the successor of Innocent IV., speaks of Ottoboni as one of his " zealous co-operators ",[9] it does not appear from his *Register* that he employed

---

[1] Even from Salimbene, we learn that not all Hadrian's friends were wicked. *Cf.* p. 420.

[2] Salimbene, p. 168 ; Riccobaldi of Ferrara, *Hist. Imp.*, ap. *R. I. SS.*, ix, 135 ; *Mon. Patav. Chron.*, an. 1263, ap. *R. I. SS.*, viii, p. 718.

[3] *Cf.* Dante, *Hell*, Cantos xii and xviii.

[4] Salimbene, *l.c.*

[5] *Cf. Reg.* Inn. IV., n. 7200, Jan. 13, 1254. *Cf.* nn. 7211, 7222. Canon and Chancellor, n. 222.

[6] *Ib.*, n. 3935 ; Guérard, *Cart. de N. Dame*, cited by Potthast, p. 1710.   [7] *Ib.*, n. 4924, Oct. 15, 1250.

[8] *Cf.*, e.g., nn. 6726, 6742, 7081, 7083. Benefices were " provided " for them in every European country.

[9] *Reg. Alex.*, n. 796.

him very much except in the ordinary way as one of his advisers.[1] The same almost may be said of Ottoboni's relations with the next Pope, Urban IV., and with Gregory X. Apart from using him as one of the preachers of the crusade against Manfred,[2] Urban also appears to have retained him " in curia " for the most part.[3] His name hardly appears at all in the short *Register* of Gregory X. But Ottoboni stood high with Clement IV., as the letters of that Pontiff show ; and he sent him on the delicate mission of making peace between Henry III. and the barons of England. We have seen how extraordinarily well he accomplished the task entrusted to him (1265–8), and, incidentally, what little credit he has received from our historians.[4] On leaving England, Ottoboni appears to have gone to Spain, and preached the Crusade in that country.[5]

An accusation of avarice.

We have also noted that some of the chroniclers of the time who favoured the baronial party accused him of avarice.[6] Dante brings the same accusation against him ; and, if he is not relying on English sources, there may have been some grounds for the charge. The poet found him in the fifth *circle* of Purgatory among those :
" all downward lying prone and weeping sore."

" ' My soul hath cleaved to the dust,' I heard
    With sighs so deep, they well nigh choked the words."

---

[1] *Cf. ib.*, nn. 30242. In the former letter he reverses a decision of Ottoboni whom he declares to have been " circumvented ".

[2] *Reg.* Urb. IV., n. 860.

[3] See, however, *ib.*, nn. 1169, 1429, 1766, 2594, whence we see that Ottoboni was occasionally entrusted with unimportant commissions away from the *Curia*. Urban also stood by him in a dispute which he had with the Chapter of Rheims. *Cf.* Georges, *Vie d'Urbain IV.*, p. 218.

[4] Even Stubbs, *The Constitutional Hist. of England*, ii, p. 95, merely says that card. O. " was sent out to punish the bishops who had acted against the King ", and, on p. 97, that the earl of Gloucester could not hold out " under the joint pressure of the King and the legate ".

[5] La Fuente, *Hist. ecles. de España*, iv, 581.

[6] *Supra*, Vol. XV, pp. 318, 327.

Dante then took his stand :—

> " Over that shade whose words I late had marked.
> And ' Spirit ! ' I said, ' in whom repentant tears
> ' Mature that blessed hour when thou with God
> Shall find acceptance . . .
> Say who thou wast '."

The spirit told him that he was the successor of
Peter, and then added :—

> " A month and little more by proof I learnt,
> With what a weight that robe of sovereignty
> Upon his shoulder rests who from the mire
> Would guard it . . .
> Late, alas !
> Was my conversion : but when I became
> Rome's pastor, I discerned at once the dream
> And cozenage of life, saw that the heart
> Rested not there, and yet no prouder height
> Lured on the climber : Wherefore, of that life
> No more enamoured, in my bosom love
> Of purer being kindled. For till then
> I was a soul in misery, alienate
> From God, and covetous of all earthly things." [1]

Supposing it to be the fact that at one period of his
life Ottoboni was addicted to avarice, we may say that
Dante's language is here, as usual, however beautiful, not
sufficiently temperate for the purposes of history. For
the Ghibelline Dante, it was enough that the Fieschi
family was Guelf,[2] and that one of its members, a special
friend of Charles of Anjou, " Messer Prinzivalle dal Fiesco
de' Conti da Lavagna," as Imperial Vicar of Rudolf,
quarrelled with the Florentines, and, in the days of Pope
Honorius IV., fined them sixty thousand marks.[3]

Within three weeks from the death of Innocent V., Election of
Ottoboni was elected Pope (July 11) in the Lateran Hadrian, 1276.

---

[1] *Purgat.*, Cant. xix. *Cf.* Bishop Casartelli, *The Popes in the Divina Commedia*, p. 33 ff.

[2] Villani, *Chron.*, vii, n. 111, " di sua progenie (he is speaking of a member of the Fieschi) gli antichi suoi erano stati Guelfi."

[3] *Ib. Cf.* Riccio, *Il Regno di C.*, an. 1276, p. 45.

palace [1] ; and, without ever being made priest or bishop or being crowned, he died at Viterbo (Aug. 18), whither he had retired to avoid the summer heats.

According to Saba,[2] when speaking of this election, Charles of Anjou, as Senator of Rome, proceeded to apply the conclave laws of Gregory X. in a needlessly drastic manner. The cardinals were shut up in the Lateran palace. Against the will " of the larger and more discreet (sanioris) section " of the sacred college, he even walled up every nook and cranny, including the most lofty windows, through which " even if left open ", says the chronicler we are citing, " only creatures with wings could enter the conclave." Moreover, he was generally so unnecessarily harsh in his conduct on this occasion, that he made enemies of a number of the cardinals.[3] Perchance, continues Saba, he acted in this manner in the hope of securing a Pope after his own heart.[4] Further, after the conclave had lasted eight days, he ordered, in accordance with the Constitution of Gregory X., that only bread and water should be supplied to the cardinals. But, also according to Saba, he took good care that the French cardinals were secretly well supplied with abundance of appetizing food. When the French cardinals had learnt, quite illegally,[5] that Ottoboni would be acceptable to Charles, that cardinal was unanimously elected, and took the name of Hadrian.

[1] Ptolemy of Lucca, *H. E.*, xxiii, c. 20 ; *Ann. Placent. Gib.*, ap. *M. G. SS.*, xviii, p. 563, etc.

[2] vi, 6 ; and *cf.* c. 12.

[3] Saba, *ib.*, names especially John Gaetano and his party—John whom Saba calls " Argus et argutus in Ecclesia Dei . . . contra . . . Karolum *non immerito* causam . . . conceperunt odii ".

[4] " Credens per coërctionem hujusmodi habere summum pontificem forsitan sicut vellet." *Ib.*

[5] Saba, *ib.* " Consulto prius rege a cardinalibus gallicis præter jus et consuetudinem."

Very naturally irritated at the way in which Charles Hadrian
of Anjou had carried out the " conclave decree " of $\begin{smallmatrix}\text{suspends the}\\\text{" conclave}\end{smallmatrix}$
Gregory X., the new Pope at once suspended it. He had $\begin{smallmatrix}\text{constitu-}\\\text{tion ".}\end{smallmatrix}$
no thought of abolishing it altogether, but he intended
so to amend it that it would not be in the power of anyone
to treat the cardinals as Charles had done.[1] Yet he was
a great friend of the King, who had given him a life
interest in a good deal of prosperity.[2]

Unfortunately the health of Hadrian had long been Ill-health of
unsatisfactory. When going to England he had Hadrian.
complained of the state of his health,[3] and, when in the
country, he had uttered similar complaints.[4] The trials
of the conclave had so aggravated his infirmities that,
when his relatives came to congratulate him on his
accession, he said : " Why are you glad ? A live cardinal
could do more for you than a dead Pope ! " [5]

Despite his short pontificate, he had time, according Help for the
to Sanudo, not only to set aside twelve thousand pounds Holy Land.
" of Tours " for the Patriarch of Jerusalem to build
warships or to use for any other purpose more useful at
the moment for the benefit of the Holy Land, but to
send letters to encourage its inhabitants.[6]

Not long after his election, Hadrian went to Viterbo. Retires to
This he did, according to Saba,[7] to avoid the noxious $\begin{smallmatrix}\text{Viterbo and}\\\text{dies.}\end{smallmatrix}$

---

[1] Cf. B. Guidonis ; Ptolemy of Lucca, H. E., xxiii, c. 20 ; Geoffroy
de Courbon, Chron., ad an. 1273. Both Rishanger (p. 88, R. S.) and
Nic. Trivet, Annales, p. 295, also add that the Pope had in mind
" aliter ordinare ". John XXI. definitely abrogated it. Cf. Bullar.
Rom., vol. iv, p. 37, n. 1, ed. Turin. Most modern historians, without
as much as mentioning the conduct of Charles, simply record Hadrian's
suspension of the conclave decree, and then some proceed to censure him.

[2] Riccio, Il Regno di Carlo, 1876, p. 45.

[3] Ep. ap. Eng. Hist. Rev., 1900, p. 89.

[4] He complains of : " labores corporis graves." See his letter to the
clergy of the north of England, ap. Northern Registers, p. 15, R. S.

[5] Jac. de Varag., Chron., c. 7.

[6] Sanudo, lib. iii, pt. 12, c. 15. Cf. Reg. Hon. IV., n. 183, ed. Prou,
p. 141.   [7] L.c.

summer heat of Rome, but according to some modern
historians, to be free from pressure from Charles of
Anjou. However that may be, not even the air of Viterbo
was able to restore the Pope to health. He died in the
house of the Franciscans on August 18, and was buried
as he had wished, in the church of St. Francis in Viterbo.[1]
Charles of Anjou had left Rome for the north on July 20,
no doubt to be on the spot in the event of another
conclave. He was at Vetralla, a few miles to the south-
west of Viterbo,[2] when Hadrian died ; but, as we shall
see, he did not put in an appearance in that city till after
the election of John XXI. That he was not present in
person at the funeral of Hadrian nor at the subsequent
conclave shows that he was not popular with the cardinals.

Hadrian is praised by his fellow countryman, James of
Voragine, for his great wisdom, and is set down by him
as a man of experience.[3] One of our chroniclers cites a
quaint poem in his praise. Playing on his name (often
spelt Octo-bonus), the poet declared that he was worth
not merely eight (octo) good men (bonus), but a thousand.
Honour and life are, however, fleeting. Scarcely having
had time to bear the name of Pope Hadrian, the lofty
Cedar of Lebanon was levelled to the ground. But may
his goodness now receive its reward, and may he be
glorified, praying before God, his benefactor.[4]

---

[1] Ptolemy of Lucca, *H. E.*, xxiii, 20. " Qui (Hadrian) ex maximo
dilectionis affectu cum fratribus habere voluit sepulturam." *Catal.
Gen. Minist. O. F. M.*, ap. *M. G. SS.*, t. xxxii, p. 666. Of course some
historians writing at a distance attribute his death to poison by
" envious cardinals ", *Ann. Lubicenses*, ap. *M. G. SS.*, xvi, p. 414.

[2] See his *Itinerary*.

[3] *Chron. Jan.*, c. 7.

[4] *Annales de Wintonia*, ii, p. 122, *R.S.*

> " Mortuus est Octobonus, ille valens simul octo,
>   Immo mille bonos. Heu ! cito transit honos ! etc."

JOHN XXI.

A.D. 1276–1277.

Sources.—To the papal biographers already quoted for John's immediate predecessors and to the Chroniclers of his age, add his short *Register* of 165 documents, ed. E. Cadier, Paris, 1898.

Works.—Considering the very short duration of John's pontificate quite a considerable amount of literature has gathered round his name. I have not seen the work of his first modern biographer, Köhler, *Vollständige Nachricht von P. Johann XXI.*, Göttingen, 1760. Cristofori in his *Tombe dei Papi in Viterbo*, p. 317 ff., has collected a good deal of material about Papa Giovanni XXI., but the one who has in recent years done most for his memory is R. Stapper, chaplain of the bishop of Münster in Westphalia. In 1897 he published a paper, " Die Summulae Logicales des Petrus Hispanus und ihr Verhältniss zu Michael Psellus," in *Festschrift zum Elfhundertjährigen Jubiläum des Deutschen Campo Santo in Rom*, Freiburg im Breisgau, 1897. In this he proved, against Prantl and others, that a Greek MS. on Aristotle's Logic still preserved in Munich and assigned to Michael Psellus, who lived two hundred years before Peter of Spain, is really a translation of the latter's *Summulæ*. C. Thurot, *De la Logique de Pierre d'Espagne* (an extract from the *Rev. Archéol.*), comes to the same conclusion. In 1898 Stapper published a monograph on *Papst Johannes XXI.*, Münster i. W., and in 1899 a short paper : " Pietro Hispano (P. Giov. XXI.) ed il suo soggiorno in Siena " in the *Bullet. Senese di Storia Patria*. In the same year and in the same periodical. L. Zdekauer wrote a short note : " A Proposito di una recente biog. di P. Giov. XXI." and Dr. G. Petella a valuable paper : " Sull' identità di P. Ispano medico in Siena e poi Papa col filosofo Dantesco." In his article Dr. Petella proves his thesis, despite the silence of Jacopo della Lana, Benvenuto da Imola, Francesco da Buti and other early commentators of Dante. Dr. J. L. Walsh in his *The Popes and Science*, New York, 1908, and in an article : " John XXI.— Philosopher, Physician, Pope " in the *American Ecclesiastical*

Review, Oct., 1908, treats of John XXI. from a medical point of view. See also Daunou, " Pierre d'Espagne " in *Hist. Lit. de la France*, vol. xix, p. 322 ff.

CONTEMPORARY SOVEREIGNS.

(See under Gregory X.)

Nationality of John.

To two short-lived Popes there succeeded a third, " he of Spain in his twelve volumes shining," [1] the only Pope whom the Ghibelline Dante has placed in his *Paradise*.

Born, it is conjectured, about the year 1215, in Lisbon, he is the only Portuguese [2] who, up to this, has ever sat on the Chair of Peter. His father, a physician who may have been of noble blood, was certainly called Julian, and possibly also Rebolo ; and so his son " Petrus Hispanus " is often called " Petrus Juliani ".[3] From his earliest years, as he tells us himself,[4] Peter studied Dialectics and

---

[1] Dante, *Par.*, c. xii, vv. 134–5. The " volumes " are his *Summulæ*.

[2] B. Guidonis, *Vita*. " Natione Hispanus Portugalensis." An addition to Martinus Polonus (*Chron.*, ap. *M. G. SS.*, xxii, p. 443) has, after " nacione Hyspanus ", " de civitate Ulixbonensi ". Jordanus (or Paulinus) O. F. M., in his *Chron.*, ap. Muratori, *Antiq. Ital.*, iv, p. 1008 ; " natione Ulissiponensis." See especially John's letter to Alfonso III., King of Portugal, in which, declaring himself to have been once his subject, he begged him to have greater regard to the freedom of ecclesiastical elections. Ep. ap. Raynald., *Ann.*, 1277, nn. 12–13. This letter is wrongly referred by Potthast (n. 21272 = n. 21249) to Nicholas III.

[3] *Cf.* Ptolemy of Lucca, *H. E.*, xxiii, c. 21 ; and Cristofori, *Le Tombe*, p. 338 ; Stapper, pp. 2–3. A letter of Honorius IV. mentions one Giles Martin, a papal chaplain and relative of Pope John XXI. *Cf. Reg. Hon. IV.*, n. 675, p. 486, ed. Prou.

[4] " Ab annis teneris diucius observati variis scienciis inibi (Paris) studiose vacavimus, et per annos plurimos secus decursus sedentes ipsius, sapidissima eorum libamina gustavimus." Ap. *Dictamina Berardi, Cod. Vat. Lat.*, 3977, f. 170. *Cf.* Petella, pp. 25–7.

Medicine in Paris ; and in a list of doctors of medicine of the year 1260, published by Chomel, figures the name of Peter of Portugal.[1] When he later became Pope, Peter declared that his " very soul was embittered " when he heard that heretical teaching had broken out " where the strong spring of wholesome wisdom had poured forth in abundance its clear waters carrying the Catholic faith to the ends of the earth ". He would have the bishop of Paris (Stephen) send him with all speed particulars of the alleged heretical teaching.[2]

The young Portuguese soon acquired a great reputation for learning, and was known to Salimbene as a " great sophist, logician, disputer, and theologian ".[3] It was no doubt at the University that he made the acquaintance of the famous Franciscan, John of Parma. As John was a man with tastes similar to his own, Peter conceived a great affection for him, and when he became Pope sent for him, because he wished to have him ever at his side. He had, according to Salimbene,[4] even resolved to make him a cardinal, and was only prevented by death from carrying out his intention. One of Peter's masters at Paris was the Englishman, William Sherwood, who in friar Bacon's opinion was an abler man than St. Albertus Magnus himself.[5]

Perhaps owing to some publications on medicine and philosophy, Peter's reputation spread to Siena. In their anxiety to increase their small University, its Municipality invited Peter in 1247 to teach there. From a document in the archives of Siena,[6] it appears that, on his arrival, the new professor of medicine was in want of money.

Professor at Siena, 1247.

[1] *Hist. Lit. de la France*, t. xix, p. 322.

[2] Ep. Jan. 18, 1277, ap. Denifle, *Chart. U. P.*, i, p. 541, or *Reg.*, n. 160. The " heretical teaching ", largely pantheistic philosophy, was duly condemned by the bishop. *Cf.* Crevier, *Hist. de l'U. de Paris*, ii, p. 76 ff.

[3] *Cron.*, p. 304.   [4] *Ib.*

[5] *Op. tertium*, c. ii, p. 14.

[6] Published by Stapper, *Pietro Hispano*, p. 7.

He not only had to lodge in a poor part of the city, in Valle Piatta, but had to sell his Bible. It was, as the deed of sale informs us, a fine volume in parchment, written in large characters (*de littera grossa*) with the initial letters in red, and bound in boards. It was bought by the prior of Selva del Lago which belonged to the monks of Lecceto, for the sum of " seven pounds of *denarii minuti* ".[1] Perhaps Peter's want of money did not last long after his arrival in Siena. At any rate, we find the " Great Master ",[2] three years after his coming to Siena, in receipt of ten pounds from the Commune for the month of May.[3] Further, from the *Libri di Bicherna*, it appears that with two other medical men, he received twenty solidi for testifying (April, 1250), that a certain Piercivalle was suffering from an infectious disease.[4] At the request of one Fantino, " a surgeon of Siena," Peter, modestly declaring that he had " but little knowledge and understanding ", wrote a work on the diet to be given to men suffering from serious wounds.[5]

Peter's *Liber de Oculo.*

A great many works are, on greater or less authority, assigned to Petrus Yspanus [6] ; and, if they were ever written by him, their composition may be assigned to

[1] *Ib.* " Pro pretio VII. lib. den. minutorum." On the convent of the Augustinian hermits, S. Salvatore di Lecceto, " a blessed place where the most High chose to work so many wonders," see E. G. Gardner, *Siena*, p. 304 ff., for a sweet narrative.

[2] " Magnus magister," as he is called by Riccobaldi of Ferrara, *Hist. RR. PP.*, p. 181.

[3] Petella, *Identità*, p. 6.

[4] Cited, *ib.*, p. 5. This is one of the very rare documents of the Middle Ages, which proves that certain municipalities at any rate took an enlightened care of the public health. On the " Provveditori of the Bicherna " who presided over the Sienese finances, see Gardner, *l.c.*, pp. 269–70, etc. On the *Studium Generale* of Siena see Rashdall, *Universities of Europe*, ii, pt. i, p. 31 ff.

[5] Petella, *l.c.*, pp. 6–7, and Stapper, *l.c.*, p. 3. The latter says that a fragment of Peter's work on *Dietetics* is to be found in Rome in the Biblioteca Casanatense (*Cod. Lat.*, 1382, f. 28).

[6] See a list in Cristofori, p. 332, or in Eggs, *Vitæ RR. PP.*, p. 480.

the period of his sojourn at Siena. Among the works which are attributed to him on good authority is the *Liber de Oculo*, which Mr. A. M. Berger published with a German translation.[1] Again, with modest professions, Peter declared that he wrote this book " as the very least of physicians ", but as a " searcher after truth ", and that it was founded on " reason and experience ". It was compiled at the request of his pupil, Fabian of Salerno.

Having laid it down that the human body is subject to the planets, he enumerates and describes the diseases to which the eye is subject. He then gives certain remedies, often appealing throughout to his own experience.[2] Some of his remedies are extraordinary, as " the blood of a tortoise " ; some we should now even consider disgusting, and others too curious to be set down here. On the other hand, many of his remedies are now recognized as good, well known, and still in use. Later writers often speak of a famous lotion of his : " aqua magistri Petri de hispania." [3]

In dealing with the causes of eye trouble,[4] Peter observes that in all eye-diseases, " fasting is dangerous," though in some cases he prescribes abstinence from certain kinds of food.[5]

The book consists only of ninety-three short chapters of about fifteen lines each.

---

[1] Munich, 1899.

[2] " Vide ego semel." " Ego satis fui usus." " Hoc manibus meis experimentavi." " Audivimus quod valet ad guttam calidam, sed scio bene quod numquam curatur." N. 70.

[3] *Ib.*, p. 128.

[4] As general causes he gives : " Fumus, venus (*ausschweifung*, notes the German editor), legumina, caseus, calciate dormire, jejunium, fames."

[5] E.g. when treating " De pediculis in palpebris oculi ", he says that one must abstain from certain foods such as figs, chestnuts, cheese, etc., which engender " pediculos ". Dr. Walsh in his *John XXI.* naturally gives (p. 390 ff.) a more scientific analysis of the treatise than I have attempted.

Before parting from Peter the Scientist, we may mention the *Treasure of the Poor*, which is generally ascribed to him,[1] and, as Dr. Petella writes, if it was not altogether his, it was probably made for the benefit of the poor by his chief physician under his direction when he was Pope. This work has been translated into different languages, among others into English. Such a translation was "imprinted at London by Rob. Stoughten, dwellynge wythin Ludgate at the sygne of the Bishoppes Myter" in 1550.[2] In English the book was entitled: "The treasury of healthe conteynyng many profitable medycines gathered out of Hypocrates, Galen, and Auycen (Avicenna) by one Petrus Hyspanus, and translated into Englysch by Humfre Lloyds who hath added thereunto the causes and sygnes of every dysease, etc."

The book begins with the *Heare*, and gives remedies against its "fallyng". Then follows: "To take awaye heare." After that complaints of the head are dealt with, and remedies, mostly herbal, are prescribed. Speaking of the "Fallyng evyll", the author has the following highly quaint remark: "Certain men say that a rosted mous eaten doth heal Franticke persons." The section on "al diseases in the eyes" is taken from Peter's treatise *On the Eye*, and "al diseases" are treated in this order: e.g. "Of wartes." The causes. "Grosse and colde melancholy of Flegme." The signs. "Every man knoweth a wart." The remedies.

---

[1] Ptolemy of Lucca, *H. E.*, xxiii, c. 21. "Hic generalis clericus fuit, præcipue in medicinis; unde et quædam experimenta scripsit ad curas hominum, et librum composuit qui Thesaurus pauperum vocatur."

[2] There was another ed. in 1585. Neuburger and Pagel, *Handbuch der Gesch. der Medezin*, Jena, 1902, i, 82, doubt whether John XXI. is the author of the *Thesaurus P.* Apart from the *T. P.*, and a *Trattato dei Veleni* by a Maestro Pietro, nineteen treatises on different medical subjects are with good reason assigned to our Peter of Spain. Petella, p. 45. See also, *Hist. Lit. de la France*, xix, p. 327 ff.

Speaking of Petrus Hispanus in his preface, our translator says that " although hee chaunced in a barbarous and rude time, he was a man of great knowledge and long practice ".

But " Petrus Phisicus ", as an old Bavarian chronicle styles him,[1] was not only a scientist, he was also a logician,[2] and his *Summulæ Logicales*,[3] which " contains the substance of the Logic of Aristotle and Boëthius ", was for centuries the Grammar of formal logic.[4] It was translated into Greek and Hebrew, and in the century after the invention of printing no fewer than forty-eight editions of it were printed.[5] Even in the fifteenth century it had to be read for three months for the bachelor's degree.[6]

Summulæ Logicales.

At some period before 1262, Peter Julian became " dean of Lisbon "; for, on Jan. 26, 1262, his name appears with the title " decanus Ulixbonensis " in a deed to be found in the *Register* of Urban IV.[7] When, exactly, Peter became attached to the papal court, and became one of the Pope's *Capellani*, is not clear. But in the *Register* of Urban IV. there is a document in which it is stated that, on Aug. 28, 1263, " Master Petrus Yspanus, chaplain of the lord Pope," engaged to leave the Curia as soon as he obtained peaceful possession (*pacificam*

Ecclesiastical career of Peter.

---

[1] *Chron. Imp. et Pont. Bavar.*, ap. *M. G. SS.*, xxiv, p. 225.

[2] Ptolemy of Lucca in his *Annales*, ap. *R. I. SS.*, xi, 1291, says he was " magnus in Philosophia ".

[3] " Qui tractatus in logica composuit," says Riccobaldi, *Hist. RR. PP.*, ap. *R. I. SS.*, ix, p. 181. " Fecit et librum de problematibus juxta modum et formam libri Aristotelis " is the way Ptol. of L., *l.c.*, expresses the fact of Peter's writing a work on Logic. In the early days of printing quite a number of commentaries were written on Peter's works ; e.g. *Thesaurus Sophismatum circa Tractatus P. Hispani*, Cologne, 1495, in British Museum.

[4] *Cf.* Sandys, *A History of Classical Scholarship*, p. 578 ; Saintsbury, *The Flourishing of Romance*, p. 18 ; and § 2 of Stapper.

[5] Petella, p. 45.

[6] *Cf.* Seybolt, *Manuale Scholarium*, pp. 34 n., and 113.

[7] *Reg.*, vol. ii, p. 16 ff., n. 49.

provisionem) of the See of Mondonedo, a suffragan See of Braga. He had been granted a provision of the See by Matthew, archbishop of Lisbon.[1] He never occupied that See, but in the same year he was named prior of Mafra in the archdiocese of Lisbon, through the patronage of the King of Portugal (July 20, 1263).[2] He also became a canon, even dean, of the cathedral chapter of Lisbon,[3] prior of Guimarães, and archdeacon of Braga.[4]

Elected archbishop of Braga, 1272.

In 1272 Gregory X. is said to have made him his chief physician (*archiater*),[5] and about the same time Peter is also said to have exchanged his deanery of Lisbon for the archdiaconate of Vermuy in the archdiocese of Braga.[6] However all that may be, he was certainly elected archbishop of Braga (1272), after the death of Martinus Giraldes (Sept. 1, 1271). This we know from a letter of Gregory X. in which " by the plenitude of apostolic power " he nominated one Ordonius to the archdiocese of Braga, vacant because Peter, archdeacon of Vermuy, who had been chosen archbishop, had since been made cardinal-bishop of Tusculum.[7] Peter had been promoted

---

[1] *Reg. Urb. IV.*, n. 353, vol. ii, p. 169.

[2] " Præsentavit dnus. Rex Mag. Petrum Physicum, etc.," ap. Cristofori, p. 338. *Cf.* Stapper, p. 30.

[3] Documents in Cristofori, *ib.*

[4] *Ib.*, p. 339, quoting a letter of Clement IV. to the bishop of Ciudad Rodrigo (Civitatensis), dated Viterbo, July 29, 1268. *Reg. Vatic.* " constitutus in præsentia nra. dilectus filius Petrus Julianus, Archidiaconus Bracarensis, prior secularis ecclesiæ S. Mariæ Vimarensis (Guimarães)."

[5] Marini, *Degli Archiatri Pont.*, i, 17, Rome, 1784. John's own physician was a Spaniard, Master Roderick Fernandi, as we see from an appointment granted him by Charles of Anjou : " Mag. Roderico Fernandi (Hispano) de Sto. Jacobo in Galitia medicus qm. Joannis P. XXI. privilegium Regentis in medicina in Studio Neapolitano." *Reg.*, 1276, A. n. 25, fol. 138 t., ap. Ricci, *Nuovi Studii Rig. la Dominaz. Angioina*, p. 29.   [6] Stapper, p. 29.

[7] *Reg. Greg. X.*, n. 607, ep. May 23, 1275. Gregory says that Peter had been elected " unanimiter et concorditer ". *Cf. ib.*, n. 307 of April 13, 1273. It is addressed among others to " electo Bracarensi ".

to the College of Cardinals along with St. Bonaventure
and Peter of Tarentaise on June 3, 1273, and became
one of Gregory's chief advisers.[1] He received episcopal
consecration at Lyons at the beginning of the year 1274,[2]
and was responsible for the archdiocese of Braga until
the nomination of Ordonius.[3]

After the solemn obsequies of Hadrian V. had been Election of
accomplished, the cardinals assembled in the episcopal card. Peter.
palace at Viterbo to elect his successor.[4] The people at
once wanted to apply the regulations of Pope Gregory X.
as to conclaves. The cardinals attempted to resist. Some
of their number, they pointed out, were ill.[5] They also
urged that Hadrian in solemn consistory had suspended
Gregory's decree and that on his death the cardinals had
unanimously borne testimony to that suspension. The
Viterbese, however, affected not to believe the cardinals,
ill-treated their delegates,[6] and shut them up, after a delay
" of some days ".[7] This treatment, superadded to the
divergency of views between the French and the Italian

---

[1] Ricobaldi, *Hist. Imp.*, ap. *R. I. SS.*, ix, p. 140. *Cf. Reg. Hon. IV.*,
n. 6.

[2] *Cf.* Potthast, *Regesta*, ii, p. 1703.

[3] *Cf.* Cristofori, p. 340.

[4] Ep. of John, Oct. 7, ap. *Reg. J. XXI.*, n. 1.

[5] Vicedominus (Visconti) card.-bp. of Præneste, ill at the time when
Hadrian VI. suspended the " conclave " decree, died on Sept. 6. Hence
John speaks of him : " bonæ memoriæ." Ep. Sept. 30, 1276, ap. *Bullar.
Rom. Pont.*, iv, p. 37, ed. Turin. Eubel, *Hierarch. Cath. Med. Ævi*,
p. 49, states that Hubert de Coconato, card.-deac. of S. Eustachio,
died July 13, 1276 ; but this cannot be correct as he was evidently
alive at the date of the last-cited letter, as he is *not* qualified " bonæ
mem.".

[6] Ep. just cited in which John confirmed Hadrian's suspension.
Cf. ep. of Sept. 30, 1276, ap. Ripoll, *Bullar.*, i, 548.

[7] Epp. of John, Sept. 30, ap. Raynaldus, 1276, nn. 31–3, and Oct. 7,
ap. *Reg.*, n. 1, or *Bullar.*, iv, p. 38. " Licet diebus aliquibus per
importunitatem Viterbiensium civium tractatui electionis instantis
nec dare possemus initium, postquam, etc." *Cf.* Saba, vi, 6 :
" Cardinales reducti more solito in palatio sub conclavi."

cardinals, made the members of the conclave anything but disposed to come to a speedy decision. The Viterbese, however, or some of them at any rate, endeavoured to apply the rules of the conclave strictly, and by Sept. 9 (" in crastino nativitatis B. V. M."),[1] the cardinals had already endured five days of a " bread, wine, and water " diet, and had not elected a Pope. Moreover, as in the case of the preceding conclave, a certain amount of fraud was practised in supplying some at least of the cardinals with a more nourishing diet, and so "all the clergy" expected a long vacancy.[2]

There were probably not more than the following nine cardinals in the conclave. Petrus Juliani ; Simon Paltineri, card.-priest of S. Martino († 1277) ; Giovanni Gaetano Orsini, card. of St. Nicholas in Carcere, afterwards Nicholas III. ; James Savelli, card.-deac. of Sta. Maria in Cosmedin, afterwards Honorius IV. ; Godfrey of Alatro, card.-d. of St. George in Velabro († 1287) ; Matteo Rubeus Orsini, card.-d. of Sta. Maria in Portico († 1305). Of the above, all, except Peter " of Spain " were Italians. The remaining three were Frenchmen : Bertrand of S. Martin, card.-bp. of Sabina († 1277) ; Ancher Pantaleon, card.-d. of Sta. Prassede († 1286) ; William de Brajo, card.-p. of St. Mark († 1282).

Simon de Brion, card.-p. of St. Cecily, was absent in France ; and it is perhaps unlikely that the sick cardinals, Visconti and Hubert de Coconato, entered the conclave.

Fortunately the prognostications of a long conclave were falsified, and that, according to Saba and Ptolemy

---

[1] See a letter to King Edward from his agent at the Curia, published by Kern, *Acta Imperii*, n. 8. From this document it is clear that the date of Sept. 8 accepted by Duchesne, Potthast, etc., as the day of John's election cannot be correct.

[2] " Set quia in artatione predicta fraus fit legi, de vacatione diutina merito dubitat totus clerus." *Ib. Cf.* Saba, vi, 6. From what the same author says, vi, c. 12, it may perhaps be inferred that Charles of Anjou continued his intrigues, as far as he could, for a French Pope.

of Lucca,[1] by the "zeal and sagacity" of cardinal
Giovanni Gaetano. He succeeded in uniting the votes
of the cardinals on cardinal Peter Juliani, neither an
Italian nor a Frenchman. This was in the week between
Sunday, Sept. 13, [2] and Sunday, Sept. 20, probably on
the fifteenth or sixteenth.[3] The new Pope, who was
solemnly crowned on Sept. 20 in the cathedral of
St. Lawrence,[4] took the name of John XXI.[5] He did
not forget cardinal Giovanni Orsini. He made him
archpriest of St. Peter's ; and, as we shall see in Giovanni's
(Nicholas III.) biography, supported the cardinal's
efforts to reform the services in that basilica.[6]

It was not till October 7 that John notified his election
to the bishops and princes of the Catholic world, and
begged their prayers to enable him to bear the great
burden he had neither expected nor desired.[7] In his
letter to the Princes, he urged them, our own Edward I.
for instance, ever to be just and merciful, and to respect
the Church and its ministers.[8]

John notifies his election to the world, 1276.

[1] *Ll.cc.*

[2] On that day it seems from the acts of a council at Bourges, that
the See was still vacant, though Hefele, *Conc.*, vi, pt. i, p. 233, new ed.,
believes that John was elected on Sept. 13.

[3] Hadrian V. died on Aug. 18, and we are told by Ptolemy and
B. Guidonis that the vacancy of the Holy See lasted 28 days. As
Charles of Anjou was in Viterbo on Sept. 15, we may suppose that
John was elected early that day. *Cf.* Durrieu, *Itin.*, p. 180.

[4] Potthast, p. 1711.

[5] Strictly speaking, " Peter of Spain " was John XX. ; but, because
in certain chronicles of the twelfth and thirteenth centuries, John XV.
had been turned into two Popes, it was believed that Peter was the
twenty-first John. His number had nothing to do with the fable of
Pope Joan. *Cf.* Duchesne, *L. P.*, ii, 457, n.

[6] Potthast, nn. 21171–2, 21230, 21234.

[7] Ap. *Bullar.*, iv, p. 38.

[8] Ep. ap. Rymer, ii, p. 66 ; or *Reg.*, nn. 1–2. Potthast notes, p. 1718,
that no motto is found on any of the bulls of John XXI., nor any
signatures of cardinals, and that only once does the name of the
vice-chancellor, Peter of Milan, occur.

Gregory's election decree quashed.

On the following day, "with great scandal" says a chronicler, John, following in this matter, as in many others, so it is said,[1] the advice of cardinal Orsini, formally revoked the conclave decrees of Gregory X.[2] He had already (Sept. 30) ratified their suspension by Hadrian V,[3] and at the same time had publicly denounced the insolence of a number of inferior prelates, "writers" and others attached to the papal court, who in the late papal election had encouraged and assisted the violence of the citizens of Viterbo, and had even assailed the authority of the cardinals.[4] John announced his intention of punishing this insubordination, and ordered his vice-chancellor, Peter of Milan, and others to search out the offenders, but promised milder treatment to such as came forward and confessed their guilt. Had the violence of the Viterbese and their clerical abettors been more generally known, the "great scandal" said to have been caused by John's action would probably have been much less. It is, however, none the less a pity that John did not rather suitably modify than wholly abolish the election decrees of Gregory.[5]

Charles renews the oath of vassalage, 1276.

Whether or not Charles of Anjou had worked against the election of John,[6] he went to Viterbo, and on October 7,

---

[1] Ptolemy of Lucca, *H. E.*, xxiii, c. 21.

[2] The *Contin. Sanblas.* of Otto of Freising, ap. *M. G. SS.*, xx, 337.

[3] Ep. Sept. 30, ap. *Bull.*, iv, p. 37.

[4] Ep. "Crescit facile", ap. Ripoll, *Bullar.*, i, p. 548 f. "Dicti prælati et alii, non solum ad nostra et ipsorum fratrum pericula, quibus durius angebamur, compassionis non habuerunt effectum . . . in superiores suos crudeliter sævientes, etc."

[5] *Cf.* Saba, vi, c. 12, ed. G. del Re. The ed. in Muratori ends with chap. 7 of book vi. "Violati igitur per actus contrarios constitutione prædicta, rediviva fratrum discordia solito fortius obstinationis ferreæ recidivat in morbum."

[6] From Saba, *l.c.*, it would appear that at every election Charles worked to secure a French Pope: ". . . Gallicis, quibus rex præfatus hactenus (to the election of Nicholas III.) in electione summi pontificis favit."

took the customary oath of allegiance to the Pope for his kingdom. He swore, as usual, that he would protect the rights of the Pope, the " regalia S. Petri " in the two Sicilies or wherever else they were to be found ; and that neither he nor his would consent to become Emperor or ruler of Lombardy or Tuscany, or the greater part of either of those territories, or would ever unite Sicily to the Empire.[1] The original of this document, which is of considerable length, and bears the stamp of the Sicilian chancellary, is still to be found in the Vatican archives.[2] Charles remained with the Pope at Viterbo till the end of January (1277), and so we may perhaps presume that he was *persona grata* to the Pope. In any case, he had much to arrange with him, so that, already in the middle of November, he realized that he would have to stop at the papal court some time longer. Accordingly, at that date, we find him applying to his justiciars for money and food to enable him to do so.[3]

Charles' daughter, Isabella, had married the King of Hungary, the dissolute Ladislaus IV. (1272–90), known as the Cuman or Kun[4] ; and about the same time (c. 1270) his son, Charles II., had married Mary Arpad— a marriage fraught with profound consequences both to Italy and to Hungary. At the period at which we have now arrived, Ladislaus had not reached the depth of degradation to which he subsequently sank, and was engaged in combating the ambition of Ottocar II., King of Bohemia. That monarch was endeavouring to extend his power at the expense of Rudolf of Hapsburg on the West and Ladislaus on the East. But, though the efforts of Charles and of the Pope also failed to check

John works for peace between (a) Hungary and Bohemia.

[1] *Reg.*, n. 163.
[2] *Ib.*, p. 55, n.
[3] *Cf.* M. Riccio, *Il Regno*, an. 1276, p. 48 and pp. 49–50, from the Angevin archives. *Cf. ib.*, an. 1277, for his demand for money for the papal tribute.
[4] The last of the Arpad line.

Ottocar,[1] the joint attack of Rudolf and Ladislaus against him proved more than he could cope with. The Bohemian King was defeated and slain (Aug. 26, 1278).

(b) Charles and Lombardy.
There was also the perpetual question of Charles' relations with the rest of Italy to be discussed. Finally, yielding to John's pressure, Charles agreed to accept him as arbitrator between himself and the cities and nobles of Piedmont and Lombardy.[2] Unfortunately, however, the death of the Pope and of one of the plenipotentiaries of the cities caused the negotiations to break down for the time,[3] and Charles continued to hold the smaller towns of Piedmont. Besides this influence in Piedmont, and his control of the two Sicilies and of Rome as its Senator, he was at this time also " through the Roman Church Vicar-General of the Roman Empire in Tuscany ".[4] Further, by being able in the interests of the Guelf cause to impose on Bologna a Podestà of his own choosing, he became the head of the Guelf cities of the Romagna [5] ; and, as the ally and protector of the Marquis Obizzo († 1293) of the powerful house of Este, he had great influence in the Trevisan Marches.[6]

Finally it was during the Pontificate of John XXI. that Charles purchased from the " damoiselle Marie ", daughter of Bohemond IV., prince of Antioch, her rights to the crown of Jerusalem (Dec., 1276). Despite the

---

[1] Riccio, l.c., pp. 41, 43, and 49. See the " Legatio ad P. Johannem XII." of Rudolf (Sept. 1276) ap. Rud. Constit., p. 111. " Fortiter accingimur ad debellandum . . . regem Boemie, nostrum et sacri Romani imperii unicum contemptorem."

[2] April 27, 1277.

[3] Riccio, ib., an. 1277, pp. 15, 43.

[4] So he inscribes himself in a letter, ib., p. 45, Sept., 1277.

[5] Cf. Chron. Bonon., ad an. 1276, vol. ii, p. 193, new ed., and Cantinelli, Chron., p. 12, ib.

[6] Cf. Chron. Estense, p. 42 and n. 1 ap. ib. This alliance between the houses of Anjou and Este was further strengthened in 1305 by the marriage of Beatrice, daughter of Charles II. of Naples, and Azzo VIII. of Este.

declaration of her rival, the King of Cyprus, that the
decision as to the rightful claimant to the crown did
not rest with the Roman Curia, but with the barons of
the kingdom, and her acceptance of his contention, the
" damoiselle " made over to Charles her rights. And
as these had been recognized by Rome, and by the jurists
generally, the deed of donation was signed by a number
of cardinals and prelates. Thus, concludes Sanudo, " the
right to the kingdom of Jerusalem devolved on King
Charles (1277)." Nor did he delay to exercise his rights.
In his name, and with the aid of the Templars, Count
Roger of San Severino took possession of Acre.[1] The
power of Charles of Anjou had certainly not suffered during
the pontificates of the short-lived successors of Gregory X.

Alfonso X. of Castile had two sons, Ferdinand and
Sancho. The former, the elder of the two, had married
Blanche, the daughter of St. Louis IX., and the sister
of the reigning King of France, Philip III., the Bold
(Hardi). French authorities assert that, when Blanche
married, it was agreed that her eldest son should succeed
to the throne of Castile, notwithstanding any claim which
Sancho the younger brother might urge [2]—in accordance
with the law of the Visigoths. Unfortunately, Ferdinand
died in 1275, leaving his widow with two sons, Alfonso
and Ferdinand, known as the " infants of Cerda ".
According to William of Nangis, Alfonso X. promptly
deprived the children of their rights, and sent their
mother back to France without her children, or her
dowry.[3] But it is perhaps nearer the truth to say that

(c) France and Castile.

[1] Maria's right as " hæres legitimus regni Jerusalem ", " pluries
ostensum . . . fuerat per judices dominos legum, Magistros decretorum, advocatos et sapientes ". Sanudo, *Secret. Fidel.*, lib. iii, p. xii,
c. 15. *Cf. Les Gestes des Chiprois.* Maria " avoit guaignié le royaume
de Jerusalem par la sentence de la cour de Rome ", n. 398. *Cf.* nn. 375
and 418.   [2] Will. of Nangis, ad an. 1269.

[3] *Chron.*, ad an. 1276, and especially *Hist. Satirica* (of Paulinus
Minorita) ap. *RR. FF. SS.*, t. xxii, p. 14.

Sancho, who was able and popular, succeeded in inducing the Spanish nobles to recognize him as heir-apparent instead of a helpless child. However that may be, Philip took up the cause of his sister, and prepared for war. On hearing this, Pope John at once wrote to Philip, telling him how horrified he was that, in such a case, appeal was made to arms instead of to law, and that the Holy Land was looking for help to those great Christian Kings, and, therefore, that in order to make peace he was sending to him two most distinguished men, John of Vercelli, the Master of the Friars Preachers, and Jerome of Ascoli, the Minister of the Friars Minor. Finally he assured the King that the Apostolic See itself was ready, without sparing any trouble, to devote its energies to the cause of peace between the two Kings.[1] As this letter did not prevent the continuance of warlike preparations, the Pope wrote to cardinal Simon de Brion, the legate of the Apostolic See in France, bidding him, in the interests of the Holy Land which was suffering so much, enforce by excommunication and interdict, if necessary, the peace enjoined on all Christian Princes by the recent General Council of Lyons.[2] John's efforts at pacifying the indignation of Philip were continued after his death by the College of Cardinals.[3] But, if it be the fact that the representations of John had caused Philip to give up his projected invasion of Castile towards the close of the year 1276,[4] they did not prevent him from

---

[1] Ep. of Oct. 15, 1276, ap. Ripoll, *Bullar. O. P.*, i, p. 549. *Cf. ib.*, p. 551, for the Pope's message to the two envoys. Raynaldus also gives the letters, ap. *Annal.*, 1276, n. 47, and 1277, n. 5. The legates were actually dispatched by Nicholas III., Dec. 2, 1277. *Cf.* Ripoll, pp. 553–4.

[2] Ep. of March 3, 1277, ap. Raynaldus, *ib.*, nn. 3–4.

[3] Ep. ap. *ib.*, n. 47.

[4] Such is the assertion of a not very reliable chronicler, Jean d'Outremeuse († *c.* 1400), *Chron.*, v, 423, cited by Langlois, *Philippe III.*, p. 107.

continuing to espouse the cause of the Infants of Cerda,
and to involve Castile in difficulties. The interests of
Alfonso of Cerda and his brother became involved with
others. Pope after Pope took up their claims. Charles,
Prince of Salerno, and our own King Edward also
tried to mediate on their behalf. Alfonso X. himself
finished by declaring Sancho disinherited. Sancho,
however, succeeded to the throne, and his children after
him, despite the later warlike efforts of Alfonso of Cerda
in his own behalf. It was not till the time of Alfonso XI.
(1312–50) that there was peace in Castile on the subject
of the " Infants of Cerda ". Mariana tells us that when
that monarch was once returning from Badajoz after an
interview with Elizabeth, Queen of Portugal, he was
met unexpectedly by Alfonso of Cerda " who kissed his
hand in token of submission ". The King was extremely
pleased and assigned him lands to live upon.[1]

These and other efforts [2] which John made to promote Crusade.
peace were made largely in view of the interests of the
Holy Land, to which, like his immediate predecessors,
he was devoted. He declared that, in his anxiety to
provide a remedy for the dire needs of the Holy Land,
it was his wish especially to favour all who were working
for it.[3] Hence he granted intending crusaders sums of
money from the tenth ordered to be collected by the
Council of Lyons,[4] and gave no little attention to the
collection of the said tenths. He regulated the local
centres to which the money collected had to be sent,[5]

---

[1] *Hist. of Spain*, lib. xvi, c. 1. Mariana is here following the *Cronicas
de los Reyes de Castilla*, " Don Alfonso el Onceno," c. 92, ed. Rosell,
p. 228. " Et aquí fizo D. Alfonso carta di conoscimiento en que
renunció . . . alguna voz ó derecho si avia en los regnos de Castiella
et de Leon ; et besolé las manos otra vez al Rey . . . Et al Rey dióle
parte de las rentas del suo regno con que se mantoviese."

[2] *Cf.* Potthast, n. 21228, *re* peace between Perugia and Assisi.

[3] *Cf. Reg.*, n. 4.   [4] *Ib.*, and nn. 11, 27, 143, 162.

[5] Potthast, nn. 21225–6.

and the salaries of the collectors.[1] While on the one hand forbidding bishops to defend Crusaders who, through their own fault, had not fulfilled their obligations from the fines (*tallias*) exacted by their liege lords,[2] he protected from oppression by the collectors certain bishops whose dioceses were too poor to contribute.[3] He also made special regulations with regard to certain countries,[4] and among them it is very interesting to specify distant Greenland. As the difficulties of the sea, said the Pope, were so great that one could hardly go from the metropolitan See of Nidaros Drontheim (in Norway) to Gardar [5] and back in five years, the archbishop was empowered to send thither suitable persons to collect in his place.[6] Speaking to the archbishop of Norway itself, the Pope begs him to convert the tenth, before forwarding it, into gold or silver, as the local money of Norway is so bad that it has no value outside the country.[7]

Complaints about the levying of the Saracen tithe. John had also to deal with the complaints which had come from England about the way in which the tenth for the Holy Land was being levied.[8] Kilwardby, archbishop of Canterbury, and all the clergy of the province of Canterbury had written to Pope Innocent V. to protest against the oppressive methods by which the collectors were raising the tenth in England.[9] They declare that the clergy of the English Church are being crushed by

---

[1] E.g. the collector in the S.E. of France had to receive 14 solidi "of Tours" a day. *Reg.*, n. 133.

[2] Raynaldus, an. 1276, n. 46.

[3] *Reg.*, n. 35 ; Potthast, n. 21202, 21219.

[4] E.g. the tenth raised in Aragon was to go to defend it against the Moors. Pott., nn. 21242–3.

[5] The episcopal see of Greenland.

[6] Pott., n. 21192, citing Lange, *Dipl. Norveg.*, VI, i, 35, n., 36. *Cf.* Pott., nn. 21193–7. *Cf.* similar regulations and others of Nicholas III., *ib.*, nn. 21524–50.

[7] *Reg.*, n. 96.

[8] *Cf. supra*, Vol. XV, p. 483.

[9] Ep. ap. *The Register of Walter Giffard*, p. 314 ff., ed. Surtees.

the financial burdens imposed upon them. By not accepting the received valuation of ecclesiastical property,[1] the collectors were by most high-handed methods striving to raise extravagant sums. Through disputes as to the valuation of property, the clergy were being involved in sentences of interdict, suspension, and excommunication to the great scandal of the laity. The clergy, therefore, beg " the Holy Apostolic See which is wont to be gracious to its lowly subjects " to order the acceptance by the collectors of the Norwich valuation. In the case of a general tax such as this for the Holy Land which has been imposed " for the common good (*pro communi salute* ", and from which " not even the King's household is exempt (*nec domus etiam principis habetur immunis*) ", men will be more ready to pay if the customary valuation is adhered to.

From the replies of the Pope,[2] it is clear that the province of York had joined in this protest, and that other grievances also regarding the collection were complained of.[3] John took up the matter vigorously. The head collector, Master Arditio, " Primicerius of the Church of Milan and our chaplain," was ordered to examine into the alleged complaints, and to absolve from all sentences of excommunication, etc., but, where there was guilt, to impose some other suitable penance. All the collectors were ordered to proceed to London, and in public to take an oath to exercise their duties justly, to refrain from exactions by imposing taxes above the true value of the benefices, or by demanding anything for themselves above the salary fixed for them by the

---

[1] " Ab eisdem etiam estimatoribus genus mirabile taxandi mirabile reperitur." *Ib.*

[2] *Reg.*, nn. 103–6, Feb. 12–15, 1277 ; *Calendar of Papal Registers*, i, pp. 452–3.

[3] Taxing lazar houses, hospitals, very small benefices and employing various devices for taxing the same property twice over.

Apostolic See.[1]   The bishops were informed of the
steps which had been taken.   John assured them of his
special affection for the English Church, and declared
that their grievances, as against his desires, were grievous
to him also.   With regard to the valuation of the property,
he said that he did not wish any particular valuation to
be followed, but it must be one with which the bishops
were content ;   so that, on the one hand, there should
be no injustice, and on the other the tenths due should
be paid.   In conclusion, he begged the bishops so to act
as to show that they were really in earnest about doing
all they could to effect the deliverance of the Holy Land.[2]

Peter's
Pence and
the annual
tribute
(cess) from
England.

Speaking of England, we may add that, whilst raising
money for the general good, John could not afford to
neglect his own private affairs.   Accordingly, Master
Geoffrey de Veçano was sent by him (1276) to collect
Peter's Pence and other papal dues in England, Ireland,
Scotland, and Wales, and was continued in this duty
by Popes Nicholas IV. and Boniface VIII.[3]   Later on,
we find him described as canon of Cambray and papal
nuncio.[4]   As we learn from a letter of John to King
Edward, Master Geoffrey was commissioned to apply
for the arrears of the tribute which England owed to the
Holy See.   The annual tribute of a thousand marks was
seven years in arrears, and the King was asked to pay the

[1] Master A. was to be allowed 8 shillings a day, and John of
Darlington 3s. 6d.
[2] *Reg.*, n. 105.   " Sic itaque super ipsius præstatione decime pie
liberalitatis officio vos gerere studeatis, ut Terre memorate negotium,
immo Christi, specialibus favoribus prosequi, et liberationem ipsius
plenis videamini desideriis affectare."   A noble appeal to generosity !
[3] Ep. of Boniface VIII. of May 15, 1296, ap. *Cal. of Papal Letters*,
i, p. 564.
[4] *Ib.*, 467.   In 1292 we find him, as " Nuncius in Anglia ", with the
bishops and nobles of England judging of the claims of Bruce and Baliol
to the Scottish crown, though we find it parenthetically stated that
" he was ignorant of the laws of England and Scotland ".   *Cf. Ann.
Reg. Scotiæ*, pp. 225, 260, *R. S.*

arrears and the sum for the current year in three instalments. But apparently Master Geoffrey was authorized
to make a compromise about the payment, should it be
necessary.[1] However Edward paid up in full, as we
learn from the final receipt which was granted by
Nicholas III., as John had died in the meantime.[2]

Though John reigned such a short time, he had other Edward asks
relations with Edward. On May 1, 1277, the English the Pope for
an exemp-
King, writing to the Pope with the usual expressions of tion.
profound reverence,[3] begs that his liegeman, the viscount
de Ventodoro, be not compelled at the moment to join
the Crusade, as he is doing work for him, and he is ready,
without any compulsion, to obey the commands of the
Roman Church in due course.

On his side, John begs the King to support the collation The Pope
of three benefices in the dioceses of York and Lincoln to asks for the
support of
Simon Paltinieri, cardinal-priest of St. Martin, against the King.
certain nobles who are putting forward rights of patronage.
John declares that the said cardinal, whose deeds have
shed great lustre on the Church, is, considering his
position, in real need, and, as he justly adds, it is not
becoming that the cardinals, who are the support of the
Holy See,[4] and with us laboriously watch over the general
good, should be in straitened circumstances.[5]

John followed the policy of his predecessor in the The Empire.

---

[1] Ep. Dec. 18, 1276, ap. Rymer, ii, 77.

[2] Ib., Feb. 23, 1278, p. 107. The Pope reminded the King that he
should pay annually.

[3] Ib., p. 82. " Cum omni reverentia et honore se totum ad pedum
oscula . . . sanctissimæ paternitati vestræ duximus supplicandum."
Cf. the following letter.

[4] Ib., p. 76, Dec. 13, 1276. In allusion to the cardinals being often
legates a latere (from the Pope's side), John speaks of the cardinals
" in quorum electæ maturitatis industria nostra et Apostolicæ Sedis
latera requiescunt ".

[5] The Pope points out too that he is only asking for the benefices
held by " Tedisius de Camilla, our chaplain, who has freely resigned
them into my hands ".

matter of Rudolf and the Empire.[1] At the very beginning
of his pontificate, he had received a letter of congratulation from Rudolf on his accession to " the highest rank
of the apostleship " to which he had been raised " for
the reformation of the Empire and the good of the Holy
Land ".[2] It is John's merits that have brought him to
his present position, and on the strength of them Rudolf
entrusts to him " his person, his wife, his children, and
all he has ". He wished the Pope to be " his ruler in the
Empire, so that between them there might be an identity
of thought and an inseparable union of will ".[3] Finally,
he assured the Pope that, with the exception of the
King of the Bohemians, all the Princes of the Empire
were with him, and with their aid he was preparing to
subdue him, " the only one who despised his rights and
unjustly held many principalities."

With the support of the Princes and his own valour,
Rudolf proved too strong for the Bohemian sovereign,
and in a letter, written about Nov. 19, 1276, the archbishop of Salzburg and his suffragans informed the Pope
of the fact.[4] They first thank God for having placed on
high " his most holy Paternity ", so that shining forth
on the world as from a beacon tower, he may illuminate
God's people. Then they set forth how, on their return
from the Council of Lyons, Ottocar would not allow them
to raise the Holy Land tithe in his dominions, and by
threats wished to force them to oppose both the Holy
See and the Roman Empire in the interests of his
candidature. But Rudolf, entering Austria about the

---

[1] *Cf.* Vol. XV, pp. 456 ff., and *supra*, p. 18.

[2] Ep. *Rud.* ap. *Constitutiones*, p. 111. " Quippe ad supreme dignitatis
apicem, summum ac sanctissimum apostolatus gradum, vobis ad
reformacionem quidem imperii et salutem Terre Sancte . . . divinitus
elevatis, eadem s. mater Ecclesia . . . gratulatur."

[3] " In regno vos rectorem habere volumus, sic ut inter nos ydemptitas
mencium et inseparabilis unio voluntatum." *Ib.*

[4] Ap. Gerbert, *Cod. Rud.*, p. 134 ff.

feast of All Saints, had terrified Ottocar into submission. They accordingly begged the Pope to receive Rudolf into his favour.

This John was only too ready to do, as he wished Rudolf, who had taken the Cross,[1] to lead the Crusade on which his heart was set. But, at the same time, he was anxious that the rights of the Holy See in Romagna should be duly acknowledged. Accordingly he asked Rudolf to declare that his agents had, " in error," acted beyond the terms of their commission in demanding from the cities in Romagna oaths of fidelity to the Empire. He also urged him to fulfil the promises he had made to Innocent V. regarding the exarchate of Ravenna and the Pentapolis [2] ; and not to enter Italy until he had confirmed his pact with Gregory X. and Innocent.[3] The Pope cannot refrain from expressing his astonishment that Rudolf has not already fulfilled his undertakings.[4] Thus appealed to by John, and by the cardinals during the vacancy of the Holy See on John's death,[5] Rudolf, as we shall see, fulfilled his promises in the days of Pope Nicholas III.

Of other acts of John XXI., such as his relations with the Greek Church,[6] and with the Tartars,[7] some have already been treated of, and others will be discussed under " Nicholas III."[8] and " Nicholas IV." [9] It only remains

Death of John.

---

[1] *Cf. supra*, Vol. XV, p. 461.

[2] Ep. Nov. 16, 1276, ap. Theiner, *Cod. Dip.*, i, n. 353, p. 198.

[3] *Ib.*, n. 354. *Cf.* n. 355, where he asks Wernen, archbishop of Mayence, to help his legate, the Franciscan Bernard of Amelia, in these negotiations. The last letter was written Nov. 20, the others, Nov. 16.

[4] " Nec premissis ejusdem predecess. Inn. monitionibus . . . est paritum in hac parte ; de quo non indigne admirationis causa suboritur." *Ib.*, n. 353.   [5] *Ib.*, n. 356.

[6] Raynaldus, 1276, n. 45, ep. of Nov. 20. *Cf.* Vol. XV, pp. 427 ff.

[7] *Cf.* Salimbene, *Chron.*, p. 210.

[8] His negotiations with Edward I. for the release of the de Montforts ; *infra*, p. 140.   [9] The Tartar question.

for us to speak of his tragic death, and of the story of his tomb, and to say a few words about contemporary statements as to his character.

In order to have a quiet place wherein to continue his studies, or to observe the stars,[1] John added a new chamber to the papal palace at Viterbo. This suddenly collapsed when he was working in it at night by himself. Terribly crushed by the falling beams, he lived long enough to receive the last Sacraments; and, " keeping his memory and mind clear," died on the sixth day after the accident (May 20, 1277).[2]

He was buried in the adjoining cathedral of St. Lawrence, near the high altar. His body was originally enclosed in a sarcophagus of porphyry; then on the restoration of the Church in the sixteenth century, it was put in a stone coffin, and finally in 1886 it was transferred to a marble mausoleum.[3]

Legends about John's death.

In the garden of the present episcopal palace at Viterbo traces of John's *observatory* can still be seen. No attempt was made to rebuild it, but on the foundations of his sudden death and alleged little love for the religious,[4] certain

---

[1] A fourteenth century French chronicle, after telling us that he was " moult excellent clerc ", and that he had learnt from the stars that he was to have a long life, speaks of " une maison qu'il fasoit pour regarder ès estoiles ". Ap. *RR. FF. SS.*, t. xxi, p. 127.

[2] Rishanger, *Chron.*, p. 89; *Ann. Mantuani*, ap. *M. G. SS.*, xix, p. 28, and a number of other testimonies, ap. Raynaldus, an. 1277, n. 19; Potthast, ii, p. 1718. " Licet medicus, non tamen seipsum curavit," says the Lanercost chronicler, ad an. 1276. " Habendo memoriam et mentem sanam." *Cont. Mart. Pol.*, ap. *M. G. SS.*, xxx, 711.

[3] See the present author's *The Early and Mediæval Tombs and Portraits of the Popes.*

[4] " Religiosorum non satis amicus." See a chronicle ap. *M. G. SS.*, xxx, p. 711 ; " Religiosis infestus," *Ann. Colmar.*, ap. Böhmer, *Fontes*, ii, p. 11 ; Full of Spanish spirit, " exosos habuit religiosos," Ptolemy of Lucca, *Annales*, ap. *R. I. SS.*, xi, p. 1291. Daunou in the *Hist. Litt. de la France*, xix, p. 327, from the way in which John employed Franciscans and Dominicans, shows how groundless is the assertion of his enmity towards the religious.

monastic writers have erected numerous legends. Even
the Dominican, Ptolemy of Lucca, who is ordinarily a
sober historian, ventures to express the belief that John's
house fell upon him whilst exulting in his own powers,
and because he was unfavourably disposed towards the
religious.[1] Later, however, legends grew up about him
as they did about the scientific Pope Sylvester II. He
was set down as a " magician ",[2] was declared to have
been crushed whilst dictating a wicked and heretical
book, and died exclaiming : " What will become of my
book, who will finish it ? "[3] Villani, also, gives us weird
details about his death on the strength of a nightmare
or second sight or crazy imagination of one Berto Forgetti,
" one of our Florentine merchants of the guild of
Apothecaries." This man, says Villani,[4] had a wandering
fancy, and often, when really asleep, he would sit up in
bed, and tell strange stories and even give rational
answers about them when questioned. It happened, on
the night when Pope John died, that the said worthy
merchant was on board ship going to Acre. Suddenly
his companions were aroused by hearing him cry out :
" I see a black giant with a great club about to break
down a pillar which supports a roof." Then, after a
moment or two, he cried out again : " He has done it,
and he is dead." " Who is dead ? " asked his friends.
" The Pope," was the reply. When the ship reached
Acre, and the news of John's death reached the city, it
was found to have occurred at the very time of the
merchant's dream. " And I the writer," adds Villani,
" heard of this from the companions of Berto who were
with him when the vision took place. They were men of

[1] *Annales, l.c.*, and *H. E.*

[2] *Ann. Colmar., l.c.*

[3] *Cf.* Siffridus, *Epitomes*, lib. ii, ad an. 1276, ap. Struvius, *Rer.
Germ. SS.*, i, pp. 1047–8.

[4] *Chron.*, vii, c. 49, al. 50.

great authority and worthy of belief, and the fame of this spread throughout all our city." [1]

John's devotion to learning and scientific pursuits, combined, we may suppose, with a critical attitude towards some of the religious Orders, caused it to be asserted by some historians, whose assertions were copied by others,[2] that John XXI. was a " wise fool " like his contemporary Alfonso X., " el Sabio." Hence our historian, Rishanger,[3] following Martinus Polonus,[4] says that, though John was famous for much that he did, still he spoilt " the fine flower of science " (which presumably ought to be the outcome of a well-balanced mind), as well as " the pontifical dignity with a certain stupidity and want of energy ". What John accomplished during his brief pontificate [5] is more than enough to show how ill-founded is such a criticism on his conduct.[6]

Rishanger, however, and practically all John's other mediaeval critics, acknowledge that he was praiseworthy in this, that he was accessible to the poor as well as to the rich, and that, a student himself, he gave benefices to many poor scholars. Accordingly, a modern local historian calls him " a democratic and reforming Pope, one of the most remarkable personages of the thirteenth century ".[7]

---

[1] *L.c.* The merchants " i quali erano huomini di grande autoritade degni di fede, e la fama di ciò fu per tutta la nostra Città ".

[2] Perhaps Ptolemy of Lucca is the ultimately responsible authority.

[3] *Chron.*, p. 88, *R. S.*

[4] Ap. *M. G. SS.*, xxii, 443.

[5] For further signs of his energy note his rebuke of the immorality of the King of Portugal, and of his attack on the Church (Raynaldus, an. 1277, n. 12), and his prompt proceedings against the Count of Savoy, etc., for acts of violence. Potthast, nn. 21234 and 21175.

[6] Hence the strong language of Gregorovius, *Rome*, vol. v, pt. ii, p. 476, against John's critics is almost justified.

[7] Signorelli, *Viterbo nella Storia della Chiesa*, p. 279.

NICHOLAS III.

A.D. 1277–1280.

Sources.—For ancient biographers we are dependent on Amalricus and B. Guidonis.[1] The biography of the latter is rather longer than usual ; but this is simply due to the insertion of doings in France, e.g., the finding of the body of St. Mary Magdalen, as Bernard had often heard accounts of the matter from those who had been present at it.

Unfortunately up till now (Nov., 1923), the *Registers* of Nicholas III. have not been completely published. Mons. J. Gay has edited his " common and curial letters " only to Dec. 9, 1279 (Paris, 1898–1916).

To the chronicles already cited for previous biographies, we may add a number of Italian, Roman, and English brief continuations of the chronicle of Martinus Polonus, ap. *M. G. SS.*, xxx, p. 711 ff.[2] To these continuations add the Roman one, ap. *ib.*, xxii, p. 475 ff. They have preserved some useful items of information.

More than a hundred documents of Nicholas III. are printed in Kaltenbrunner's *Actenstücke . . . unter Rudolf I.*, Vienna, 1889, and a few in O. Redlich's *Briefsammlung*, Vienna, 1894, both drawn from the Vatican Archives.

The *Introiti ed esiti di P. Niccolò III.*, edited by G. Palmieri, Rome, 1889, is said to be the oldest document in Italian. In any case it is the oldest extant papal account book (running from May 1, 1279, to May 1, 1280), and the only one written in Italian. It gives the receipts and expenditure for the year ; but Palmieri has not printed an addition in Latin which is found in the original

---

[1] *Vide supra* under Innocent V., p. 1.

[2] Ptolemy of Lucca often quotes the *Roman Continuation*, e.g. *ib.*, p. 712, " ut Scriptores Historiæ tradunt," in his *H. E.*, xxiii, 29. Grimaldi, *De Archipp.*, p. 55 in *Cod. Vat. Lat.*, n. 6196, mentions a certain Bernadino Toni da Fabriano as having written about Nicholas III. I have completely failed to trace this author.

and which gives the Pope's charities or the Vatican's "system of poor relief ". The receipts are mostly from rents or fines of one sort or another, and are reckoned in pounds (*libbre* de ravignani), shillings (*soldi*, twenty to the pound), and pence (*denari*, twelve to the shilling). The expenditure is mostly for legal items, such as salaries of judges, payments for advocates, serving legal notices, etc.

It is to be noted that very often indeed notices occur in this document of exactions lessened " on account of poverty : lascia-mogli il soperchio per povertade ". This furnishes ano her argument as to how little credit is to be attached to Dante's accusations of avarice levelled at Nicholas III.[1]   Incidentally too the document shows the civil power of the Popes in the Romagna.[2]

Modern Works.—The fullest good modern biography is *Papst Nikolaus III.*, by A. Demski, Münster i. W., 1903.   A very full account of the cardinalitial career of Nicholas III. has been written by R. Sternfeld, *Der Kardinal Johann G. Orsini*, Berlin, 1905.

Of great importance is F. Savio's *Niccolò III.* in *La Civiltà Cattolica*, serie xv and xvi (1894–5).   It is an apology, but one that was needed, and that does not go too far.

Of papers on special items of the doings of Nicholas we may mention F. Savio's on *La Pretesa Inimicizia di P. N. III. contro il re Carlo I d'Angiò*, Palermo, 1903 ;   V. Maggiani, *De relatione scriptorum quorundam S. Bonaventuræ ad Bullam " Exiit "* (1279), Quaracchi, 1912 ; and V. Vitale, *Il Dominio della parte Guelfa in Bologna* (1280–1327), Bologna, 1901.   L. Leclère, *Les rapports de la Papauté et de la France sous Philippe III.*, Brussels, 1889, if not always accurate, is useful.   So also for all this period is R. Morghen, " Il card. M. Rosso Orsini," in *Archivio Rom.*, 1924.

---

[1] *Inf.*, xix, 71–2. Palmieri has calculated that out of dues amounting to £2,462, no less than £1,468 and 5 pence were remitted " owing to poverty ". *Cf.* p. 109.

[2] On this interesting document see *English Hist. Rev.*, July, 1889, vol. iv, p. 560 f. ; Aloisi, " Gli Introiti, etc.," in *Atti della R. Deputat. di Storia delle Marche*, Nuova serie, ii, 1, and Palmieri's introduction.

CONTEMPORARY SOVEREIGNS.

(See under Gregory X.)

CHAPTER I.

ON the death of John XXI., it seems that there were only The
seven or eight cardinals, and of these Simon de Brion Conclave.
was in France, and perhaps did not take part in the
election of John's successor.[1] The others who certainly
took part in the election were the two French cardinal-
priests, Ancher Pantaleonis and William de Braio, and
the four Italian cardinal-deacons, James Savelli, Matteo
Rosso Orsini, Godfrey of Alatri, and Giovanni Gaetani
Orsini, who was to be Nicholas III. Finally, while it
is certain that another French cardinal, Bernard, or
Bertrand, of St. Martin, cardinal-bishop of Sabina, died
in 1277, it is not certain in what month he died. On the
whole, therefore, it would appear best to follow the
Chronicle of Piacenza, and to assert that seven cardinals
took part in the election, and, in his list of the seven
cardinals, to replace Simon de Brion, as we have no
record of his having left France at that time, by Godfrey
of Alatri. According then to the Ghibelline Chronicler,
cardinals Orsini, Savelli, and Matteo Rosso, and
presumably Godfrey of Alatri, formed one party, and
cardinals Ancher and William de Braio the other. The
remaining Frenchman, the cardinal of Sabina, according
to him, favoured neither party.

---

[1] The *Chron. Parmense*, an. 1277, would imply that seven took
part in the election. The author of the *Chron. de Rebus* (*Chron. Placent.*),
p. 366, also speaks of seven taking part in the election, but he introduces
the cardinal-bishop of Sabina, and in place of Godfrey of Alatri, he
gives " Symonus de Tursso ", i.e. Simon de Brion.

Election of Nicholas.

However all this may be, it is clear that the cardinals could not agree, so that, after no little time had been passed in idle discussions to the great distress of Christendom,[1] the Commune of Viterbo shut up the electors in the communal palace.[2] But even this action would not appear to have at once produced the desired effect.[3] At any rate, at length, through " the constancy of cardinal Savelli ", according to Saba,[4] cardinal Orsini was duly and unanimously elected on Nov. 25, 1277.[5]

Action of the cardinals in the interregnum.

During the vacancy of the Holy See, the cardinals were called upon to act on several important matters. Following the policy of Innocent V. and John XXI., they begged Rudolf not to enter Italy until the Romagna question had been settled,[6] and they exhorted the papal envoys, John of Vercelli and Jerome of Ascoli (Nicholas IV.), not to cease their exertions to keep the peace between the Kings of France and Castile.[7] Taking advantage of the vacancy of the Holy See, several of the Communes tried to encroach on papal rights or to pursue a course of aggrandisement.

The cardinals, accordingly, had to urge the doge of Venice, James Contarini, and his Council to cease their

[1] See Rudolf's letter to the cardinals, ap. *M. G. LL.*, iii, pt. i, p. 148. " Nostra precordia . . . vicini presaga discriminis, ex Romanæ sedis vacatione diutina, irreparabilia christianitatis excidia reformidant."

[2] *Chron. Parmens.*, p. 33, ap. *R. I. SS.*, ix, pt. ix, new ed. On Sept. 25 the cardinals had sent a letter to the Rectors of the Roman Fraternity, begging the prayers of the City for a speedy election. Ap. Raynaldus, an. 1277, n. 53.

[3] At least Nicholas notes that " clausura diutina non leviter molesta (cardinales) vexarat ". Ep. of Dec. 12, 1277, ap. Theiner, *Cod. Dip.*, i, p. 223, there wrongly dated.

[4] *Chron.*, vi, 12.

[5] *Ib., Annal. de Rebus*, and *Reg.*, ep. 1. " Demum in die b. Katerine . . . per viam scrutinii . . . nos . . . unanimiter elegerunt."

[6] Ep. of July 27, 1277, ap. Raynaldus, *Ann.*, 1277, nn. 48–52.

[7] Ep. ap. *ib.*, n. 47. *Cf.* Mortier, *Hist. des Maîtres-Généraux*, ii, p. 149 ff.

attacks on Ancona,[1] and had to blame the people of
Parma for attacking Monte S. Angelo.[2] Others who
availed themselves " of the widowhood " of the Church
were " the perfidious people of Ascoli ". The cardinals
had to command them to raise the siege of Castrum
Scaletta which belonged to the Holy See, and to make
satisfaction for the harm they had done.[3]

At length, however, " the widowhood " of the Church Giovanni
was, as we have seen, brought to an end on November 25 Orsini, 1277.
by the election of Giovanni Gaetani Orsini; and so, if
Charles of Anjou had been working for a French Pope,[4] he
was disappointed. But, if it is true that Orsini was a
Roman of the Romans, there is no reason for believing
that he was animated throughout most of his pontificate by
hatred of Charles, still less that the cause of it was the
King's refusal to give one of his grandsons in marriage to
a niece of Nicholas. This assertion is made with most
picturesqueness by Villani. He tells us that Nicholas
quarrelled with Charles because the latter had refused
a matrimonial alliance with the Pope's family, saying :
" Although he wears red buskins, his lineage is not fit
to mix with ours, and his lordship will not be hereditary." [5]

[1] Ep. ap. Ray., n. 43.

[2] Ib., n. 46. Cf. Potthast, n. 21225.

[3] Ib., n. 45 or Potthast, n. 21254.

[4] Ciacconius, De Vit. RR. PP., i, p. 759, says that, as is no doubt
probable, he did work for that end. However, if he did, he must
have ceased to take a very active interest in the work, as he was very
ill at the time of the election. Cf. ep. of Nicholas to him of Nov. 26
printed in full in Sternfeld, pp. 356–7. Cf. the two following letters.
Perhaps Ciacconius was relying on the authority of Bonincontrius
(fl. c. 1475) in his Hist. Siciliæ, cited by Vitale, Senatori di Roma,
i, p. 175.

[5] " Perch' egli habbia il calzamento rosso, suo lignaggio non è degno
di mischiarsi col nostro, e sua signoria non era retaggio." Chron.,
vii, 53 (al. 54). Cf. Lu Rebellamentu di Sichilla, n. 10. The anonymous
author of this Chronicle or romance simply says that Charles rejected
the proffered matrimonial alliance and tore up the Pope's letter relating
to it.

But, supposing it to be true that Charles wanted a more distinguished match for his then baby grandson,[1] it is nothing short of absurd to suppose that he would have made any insulting reply to any proposal coming from a Pope. If Charles was anything, he was at least respectful to all the Popes with whom he came in contact. Besides, even if the Orsini family was not royal, facts show that royal families did not disdain matrimonial alliances with it[2]; and one cannot help believing that, with Charles's eagerness for influence with the Popes and with the Roman people, he would have been glad to ally his family with the Orsini. However, whether Villani's story is true or not, we believe that the story of the life of Nicholas will show that, if he received "the retort direct" from Charles, it did not cause him any permanent annoyance. On the other hand we believe that the same story will show that, if Charles was grievously disappointed at the election of an Italian Pope, his relations with Nicholas were always friendly.

The Orsini.
At this period the Guelf family of the Orsini, which we met before at the time of the first Orsini Pope, Celestine III.,[3] was perhaps the most powerful in Rome. For their headquarters they had the castle of St. Angelo; and they were further strong in the possession of a great fortified palace on Monte Giordano,[4] an artificial mound once known as Monte Johannis de Roncionibus, but afterwards, from cardinal Giordano Orsini († 1287), known by the name it now bears. Further increasing the Orsini grip on that part of Rome was their possession of the

---

[1] Cf. Savio, *Pretesa Inimicizia*, p. 6 f.

[2] *Ib.*, p. 7 f.

[3] Cf. *supra*, vol. x, p. 385 f. According to Villani, *Chron.*, vii, 53 (54), it was Nicholas III. himself who gave the Castle of S. Angelo to his nephew, Orso Orsini.

[4] It is well shown in the plan of Rome of 1474 (Tav. iv in De Rossi's *Piante di Roma*). With it and the Castle of S. Angelo, the approaches to St. Peter's were completely in the hands of the Orsini.

Arpacata tower in the Campo di Fiore, built from the ruins of the great theatre of Pompey, which had so captivated the imagination of Theodoric the Goth.[1]

Giovanni Gaetani, of whom modern Romans, shaking off the spell of Dante, have begun to form a more just estimate,[2] would appear to have been born about the year 1217,[3] in Rome. His father, Matteo Rosso, made Senator of Rome by Gregory IX. in 1241, was thrice married, and Giovanni was the son of Perna Gaetani, his first wife. In a document addressed to the Chapter of St. Peter's,[4] Nicholas himself, in arranging about anniversary Masses for them, makes express mention of his father Matteo Rosso, of his mother Perna, of his uncle James, and two brothers Gentilis and Napoleon. From writers on the families of Italy,[5] and from Matteo's will, we gather that Nicholas had seven other brothers and sisters or half brothers and sisters.[6]

Whilst Giovanni was still a boy, his father who was a great admirer of St. Francis, and was a member of his

Birth and family of G. Gaetani.

---

[1] Cf. Rodocanachi, *Monuments de Rome*, p. 18; Fedele, "Aspetti di Roma nel trecento," p. 110, ap. *Roma*, Apr., 1923; and Gregorovius, *Rome*, v, pt. ii, pp. 661 and 441, n. Savio, *N. III.*, n. 12, has shown that Saba's words as to the complete destruction of the Arpacata after the battle of Tagliacozzo must not be taken too literally.

[2] Fedele, *ib.*, "N. III. per altezza di mente e vastità di disegni politici, fu uno dei più grandi papi del Medio Evo, non ostante che l'Alighieri, etc."

[3] Savio, *Nic. III.*, p. 1, n. Nicholas tells us himself that he was born in Rome. "Ad ipsam Urbem quæ naturalem nobis originem prebuit." Ep. ap. Theiner, *Codex*, i, p. 215. Cf. *Chron. Parmense*, l.c., "De Ursinis de Roma."

[4] March 25, 1279, ap. *Bullar. Basilic. Vat.*, i, pp. 198 and 200. He laid it down that, out of the common Chapter fund, the canons and *Beneficiati* were to receive every year on their anniversaries, "40 solidi of Provins of the Senate."

[5] Gamurrini, *Famiglie Toscane ed Umbre*, ii, pp. 24–5, Florence; Litta, *Famiglie Celebri d'Italia*, 15 vols., 1819–88. Gamurrini is wrong in identifying our Giovanni Gaetani with a man of the same name who was already abbot of St. Paul's in 1208!

[6] Savio, ch. i, p. 1, n.

" Third Order ", offered him to the Saint. Whereupon Francis, looking at the child, declared that in habit he would never be a Franciscan, but that he would be the protector of his Order, and the Lord of the World.[1]

Of the youth and early manhood of Giovanni Gaetani up to the year 1244, nothing is known except that he was a handsome cleric, of literary tastes and of a good character.[2] In that year (May 28) he was made cardinal-deacon of S. Niccolò in Carcere by Innocent IV., and appears to have remained always attached to the Curia during his pontificate and during that of his successor, Alexander IV. His signature is attached to dozens of their bulls.[3] Before that, when he was simply " a sub-deacon and our chaplain ", he had been given benefices in France (Laon and Soissons), and a canonry in York by Innocent himself or by one of his predecessors.[4] We further find Innocent granting favours to Giovanni's dependents,[5] and defending his rights, for instance, as executor to certain wills.[6] Giovanni had also the administration of the churches of S. Crisogono and S. Lorenzo in Damaso.[7] Previous biographies in this series have shown him executing various missions for the Holy See. He accompanied Innocent IV. in his retreat to Lyons (1244), and as " one of the distinguished members " of the Church of God was sent by him to try to make peace at Florence (1252).[8] We have seen [9]

[1] With the *Catalogus Generalium Minist. O. F. M.*, p. 667, *cf.* Philip de Perusio, *Ep. de Card. Protect.*, p. 681, both ap. *M. G. SS.*, xxxii.

[2] Alb. Miliolus, *Lib. de Temp., Addit.*, " Pulcher clericus fuit, nobilis, literatus et bonus." Ap. *ib.*, xxxi, 549.

[3] *Cf.* Potthast, *Reg.*, ii, pp. 1285 and 1473.

[4] *Cf. Reg. Inn. IV.*, n. 369, where the Pope protects his rights. For the canonry of York, etc., see Nicholas' own *Reg.*, nn. 215, 217, and 298–9, and Raynaldus, 1277, nn. 53–4.

[5] *Reg. Inn.*, nn. 4759 and 6258.

[6] *Ib.*, 7180, 7981. [7] Raynaldus, *l.c.*, n. 53.

[8] *Epp. Sæc. XIII.*, vol. iii, p. 135 n., 158, ed. *M. G. Epp.*

[9] *Supra* under *Alexander IV.*, Vol. XV, p. 97.

how, in 1258, at the request of St. Louis, he was specially chosen to ratify the peace between England and France.

According to Ciacconius,[1] it was through the exertions of the cardinal of St. Nicholas that the long vacancy after the death of Alexander IV. was brought to a close by the election of Urban IV. (1261). At any rate, Urban named him the temporal governor, or *rector*, of the Sabina,[2] and also Protector of the Order of St. Francis, as that Saint had declared would happen.[3] Our cardinal was one of the four delegated by Clement IV. to invest Charles of Anjou with the Kingdom of the two Sicilies (1265). He was also, as we have seen, one of those who brought about the election of Gregory X. (1271) ; and, from documents in Wadding, we see that he had been named " Inquisitor General ", perhaps the first to hold that title, during the long interval that preceded that election (June 20, 1270).[4] By the short-lived pontiff, Hadrian V., he had been nominated, with two other cardinals, to negotiate between Rudolf and Charles of Anjou (1276).[5] A little later in placing upon " his robust shoulders " the dignity and cares of archpriest of St. Peter's, which, said the Pope, should in every way be a model to all the other churches, John XXI. declared that the greatness of Giovanni's virtue was well known to him, and not indeed unknown to the world. He added that his abilities, which had increased with his years,

---

[1] In *Vit. Urb. IV.*, i, p. 715.

[2] *Cf.* Posse, n. 301, document of Oct. 31, 1263. See also *Mem. Pot. Reg.*, ap. *R. I. SS.*, viii, 1141. " Habebat curam super Inquisitores hæreticæ pravitatis." *Cf.* also Potthast, n. 19747.

[3] Bull of Urban, June 22, 1261 (?), ap. Eubel, *Bullar. Francisc.*, n. 1150. The Pope names Giovanni protector at the request of the General of the Franciscans. *Cf. Catal. Gen. Minist.*, p. 667, and Philip of Perugia, Ep., p. 681, ap. *M. G. SS.*, xxxii.

[4] *Annal. Min.*, v, p. 446. For the date see Pagi, *Vit. RR. PP.*, pp. 362–3. *Cf. Mem. Potest.*, ap. *R. I. SS.*, viii, 1141.

[5] See a document of Nicholas himself, ap. Theiner, *Cod. Diplom.*, i, p. 224.

enabled him " to sum up the past, prudently to dispose
the present and to forecast the future ".[1] With the author
of the *Memoriale* of the Podestàs of Roggio,[2] it may be
said then that Giovanni passed through his career as
Cardinal with distinct credit ; and during all the period,
as the same contemporary declares, he never accepted
any presents.   He did not even do as the English Cistercian
cardinal (John Tolet), who accepted them and then gave
them all to the poor.   Giovanni would not accept them
at all, but always lived on his own patrimony.[3]   No doubt
he was the more easily able to do this seeing that his
nephew, Bertold, not, as he said, in view of his great
cardinalitial dignity, but simply moved by affection, had
granted him (June 30, 1267) all the houses, towers, etc.,
which he possessed in Rome, except such as were situated
on Monte Roncione.[4]

Further material for the activities of cardinal Giovanni
must be gathered from preceding biographies or from the
lengthy account of Sternfeld.

Nicholas announces his election. Whilst still " bishop elect ", Nicholas informally
announced to many his election, for which his long and
varied experience, just summarily stated, had so well
prepared him.   His first letter was to Charles of Anjou,[5]
and was written all the more affectionately that he

---

[1] Ep. of Oct. 18, 1276, ap. *Bullar. Basilic. Vat.*, i, p. 154 f. The Pope
names Nicholas archpriest notwithstanding his possession of Laon, etc.,
and notwithstanding that the cure of souls may be attached to some
of his benefices, and that he is not bound to take priest's orders. *Cf.*
the three following letters of John XXI. about the appointment or
the reform of the services, etc., at St. Peter's effected by Nicholas.
The cardinal is highly praised in the third letter for the work of spiritual
and temporal reform which by March 15, 1277 (the date of the third
letter) he had already accomplished.   The third *Letter* is a long document
setting forth the number, stipends, habitation, and duties of the canons
of St. Peter's.

[2] Ap. *R. I. SS.*, viii, p. 1141, " Bene multis annis steterat Cardinalis."

[3] This does not look like Dante's Nicholas.

[4] " In regione Pontis." *Cf.* a Vatican MS. cited by Savio, n. xii, p. 43.

[5] Dated Nov. 26, 1277, ap. Sternfeld, pp. 356–7.

had heard that the King was stricken with fever.[1] He tells him that he has been elected his father and the father of all, and trusts that his messenger will soon return to relieve " the anxious mind " of a father as to the King's health. This letter was followed some days later by two others, one to Charles himself, and the other to his son, Charles, Prince of Salerno. He assured the King how grieved he was that he had had a relapse, and begged him to send him immediate news of the recovery which the physicians were reported to expect. Charles must meanwhile not worry about business, but must rest assured that his interest will be cared for by him.[2] In his letter to the King's son, he said that, desirous as both of them were to see each other, it was his duty to remain for the time being by the side of his sick father.[3] From the other letters which Nicholas dispatched to announce his election and which have come down to us, we may select the one which he wrote " to his dearest son, the illustrious King of England ". It is in substance the same document that was sent to other important personages, and is a proof among other things that great indignation had been expressed all over the Catholic world at the long vacancy of the Holy See. The letter ascribes the delay to the force of circumstances, and to the desire of the electors to choose the right person, and not to their negligence, and it proceeds to blame presumptuous criticism.[4]

[1] " Ad nos siquidem perlato rumore de febrili discrasia, que te diebus aliquibus dicitur molestasse."

[2] Ep. of the beginning of December. Nicholas had been told " te vexatum pluribus terciane accessionibus ". This letter is also printed by Sternfeld, pp. 357–8.

[3] Ap. *ib.*, p. 359.

[4] " Nichilominus tamen vacationis prolixitatem ingerit, occurrentium casuum qualitas, aliarumque circumstantiarum, non instantium negligentia vel voluntas . . . O ! igitur præsumptuosa judicia murmurantium in Ecclesiæ provisione, quam sæpe indigne arguunt tarditatem." Ep. of Jan. 15, 1278 ap. Rymer, ii, 98 f.

However, it continues, by the secret dispensation of God, sometimes, as in the present case, the one who ought to be rejected is chosen, and so in conclave " by way of scrutiny ", the writer was unanimously elected, and the great mantle [1] literally forced upon him. The letter concluded by imploring the King to govern those well who by God were set under his rule, so that the writer's task of governing them spiritually might be lightened.

Efforts for peace.

Like his predecessors, whilst still " bishop elect ", Nicholas did not fail, whilst announcing his election in various quarters, to do what he could to promote the sacred cause of peace.

France and Castile.

He not only directed letters to Philip of France and Alfonso X. of Castile exhorting them to keep the peace on the subject of the claims of the " Infants of Cerda ", but dispatched the Franciscan, brother Benvenuto, to aid the prodigious efforts for peace which were being made by John of Vircelli and Jerome of Ascoli.[2] The work of the papal envoys must have been very wearying, as it dragged endlessly along. Now they might succeed in extracting a conditional promise from Philip to the effect that he would give a guarantee to " his Apostolic Father " to refrain from hostilities for a given time, if Alfonso would do the same.[3] Now they might contrive

[1] Which he describes as " vestem poderis universum orbis ambitum continentem." Cf. Potthast, 21263, to Philip le Hardi.

[2] Cf. supra, p. 46, and the letters of Nicholas, Dec. 2, 1277, ap. Wadding, Ann. Min., v, 437 ff. Langlois, Philippe III., speaks " des efforts continus, et des prodiges d'habilité " made by the Curia Romana to prevent hostilities (p. 111).

[3] Writing to the Governor of Navarre, Philip declared : " Pour ce que nous avons autroé a nostre père l'Apoustole que nous nous soufrerons de feire guerre au réaume de Castele juques au primier jour de may prochein à venir, se il n'estoit ainsi qui leu nos feist guerre dou réaume de Castele." Aug. 23, 1278, from Arch. Munic. de Pampelune, Cart. del rei D. Felipe, f. 17. We have borrowed this interesting note from Langlois, ib., p. 112.

to patch up a truce for some brief period ; and were ever presenting to the two Kings papal letters full of threats, but more of entreaties.[1] In July, 1278, a cardinal, Gerard of the title of the Holy Apostles, was added by Nicholas to the existing legation.[2] Cardinal Simon de Brion, who had been papal legate in France for so long, was also ordered to co-operate in the good work,[3] and some four months before his death, Nicholas sent to Alfonso one of the Masters of the Knights Templars, just returned from the Holy Land, in the hope that the story he had to tell of the conditions of the Christians there would move him to definite peace.[4] Although, later on, there was war between Alfonso and his rebellious son, Sancho, Nicholas at least succeeded in warding off actual fighting between Philip and the impractical " El Sabio ". It must, however, be confessed first that, in the last letter which he wrote on this subject,[5] he showed that, broken-hearted at the way in which the quarrel was ruining the prospects of the Crusade, and was gradually involving other princes in its meshes, he had almost given up all hope of doing any good, though he had called back his legates to work out with them another plan of campaign. It must next be noted that others also strove to heal the unhappy

[1] Epp. of April 4, 1278. Potthast, 12294–5 ; April 23, *ib.*, 21310–11.
[2] *Ib.*, 21359.
[3] *Ib.*, 21381, Aug. 3, 1278. *Cf. ib.*, n. 21389, Aug. 9, 1278 ; 21488–90, Nov. 29, 1278 ; 21598, June 9, 1279.
[4] *Ib.*, 21683, Feb. 20, 1280. *Cf.* 21684 of the same date, addressed to the archbishop of Tours and his suffragans.
[5] The latter letter of the preceding note. It is given in full in Raynaldus, 1280, n. 13, and sums up all the Pope's work for this peace. In the course of the letter Nicholas recalled how he had begun his pontifical work with this peace effort, and how he sought to add remedy to remedy with feverish energy. " Quasi ponentes viarum nostrarum initium opus pacis . . . remedia remediis quæsitis adjecimus, ad executionem illorum nuntios multiplicantes et litteras, monita monitis, preces precibus, et exhortationes exhortationibus addentes."

dissension, our own King Edward, and especially Charles of Anjou. But with regard to the latter it is urged, no doubt with reason, that he was working for his own ends. Always in dread of Peter of Aragon, he wished to free his nephew Philip from the Castilian complications in order that he might be free to turn his arms, not to save the Holy Land from the Mameluke, but Sicily from the clutches of the ambitious Aragonese. If then after the overthrow of the Caliph of Bagdad (1258) by the Tartars, and their checks by the Mamelukes Kotuz and Kilawun at Ain-Jalût (1260) and Hims (1281), the Holy Land was not rescued from the infidel, it was because Charles, in 1269, induced first St. Louis to go to Tunis instead of to Palestine, and then, later, his nephew to lead his armies against Peter of Aragon instead of allying himself with the Mongol Abaga of Persia, and with him attacking the Moslem Mamelukes of Egypt.[1]

Coronation of Nicholas, 1277. After Nicholas had got well under way the negotiations to urge Philip not to turn " the mighty sword of Gaul " to the shedding of Christian blood,[2] he left Viterbo for Rome; and, after being ordained priest, was on Sunday, Dec. 26, 1277, consecrated bishop, and solemnly crowned in St. Peter's.[3]

Soon after (Jan. 15, 1278), he formally made known to the world that the long vacancy of the Holy See had ended by his unanimous election.[4] At the close of the letter in which he made this announcement, he gave an indication that he was bent on the reform of abuses. He bade the various recipients of his circular

---

[1] *Cf.* on all the negotiations between Philip and Alfonso, Langlois, *Philippe III.*, pp. 99–117 ; and Burke, *A Hist. of Spain*, i, 267. Many of the Pope's letters on this affair are given in full in his *Register*, nn. 222–5, Dec. 2, 1277 ; nn. 239–43, April, 1278 ; nn. 385–7, Nov. 29, 1278.

[2] *Reg.*, n. 222.

[3] B. Guidonis, *In Vit.*, ap. *R. I. SS.*, iii, p. 606.

[4] *Cf. supra*, p. 66.

letter not to allow themselves to be bullied or cajoled by the bearers of it ; but merely to give them the bare necessities, as he has set them forth in detail for their inspection.[1]

[1] Ep. ap. *Bullar.*, iv, 39 ff., or reproduced in the contemporary registers of various bishops, e.g. that of Thos. of Cantilupe, bp. of Hereford, *Reg.*, p. 5 ff. " Necessaria, per alias eis (portitoribus) sub certa forma literas, quas vobis exhiberi mandamus."

CHAPTER II.

The
Chancery.

FROM a little known document published by Cardinal Pitra,[1] it appears that one of the first things to which Nicholas gave his attention was the papal chancery. His Eminence prefaced his publication with the statement that John XXI. was, if learned, brusque and peculiar even in his death, as he was crushed by the fall of a building which he had himself designed. He must, concluded the Cardinal, have left a good deal of disorder behind him in the papal chancery. It was for the new Pope to reassert the pontifical dignity. Without pausing to point out how unfounded is this estimate of John XXI., and how wanting in evidence is the conclusion that he *must have caused* confusion in the chancery, we will simply observe that all that can be gathered from the preamble of the document is that the habit which the Pontiffs, in the course of the *fourteenth* century, had evolved of conforming to the existing chancery rules, or promulgating new ones at the beginning of their pontificate,[2] began before that period. The preamble which we are discussing sets forth that " On Jan. 21, A.D. 1278, in the first year of the pontificate of the Lord Pope Nicholas III., there was presented to the said Lord by the vice-chancellor a schedule containing the subjoined forms of

---

[1] *De Epp. RR. PP.*, p. 162 ff.

[2] E. von Ottenthal has published the chancery regulations, *Regulæ Cancellariæ Apostolicæ*, from John XXII. to Nicholas V. inclusive, Innsbruck, 1888.

the apostolic letters. After the said forms had been duly considered in the presence of the vice-chancellor and certain notaries, the said Lord set forth certain regulations which he wished to be observed with reference to the said forms till such time as he should see fit to prescribe others ".

The regulations of Nicholas left untouched a considerable number of the chancery rules. They said nothing of the *Petitions* which were presented to the Holy See, of those who had to put them in proper form, or who had to correct them, or to reject or present them as the case might be, or of the manner of fixing the *Bulla*.[1] Nor do his regulations touch the question of the actual drawing up of " letters of Grace " or of the " Mandates " or " letters of justice ". The rules governing the form and engrossing of these letters have fortunately been preserved for us in a formulary from the *Audientia Litterarum Contradictarum*, a department of the chancery where certain letters were discussed or examined before being dispatched. This formulary dates from the close of the thirteenth century, but it treats of the practice long anterior to itself. It gives, as we have said, the details to be observed in the actual preparation of the documents which were to leave the papal chancery. It lays down when the name of the Pope has to be written in letters bigger than those used for any other word ; when capital letters have to be employed, and when certain letters have to be joined together. The formulary also treats of the perfection of the parchment, and especially of the difference in form to be observed between letters whose *Bullæ* were attached with silk,

---

[1] These points are dealt with in a poem by Henry of Würzburg (1280), edited by H. Granert, who supposes it was written during the pontificate of Urban IV. Passages describing the chancery are printed by Mr. R. L. Poole, *The Papal Chancery*, p. 162 ff., Cambridge, 1915.

and those to which the leaden seals (*Bullæ*) were attached with hemp.[1]

Cardinal Pitra's formulary, however, enumerates the type of letters which could be dispatched without discussion, and those which had to be considered by the Pope himself or by the vice-chancellor before they were issued. In other words, this formulary sets forth the sort of subjects which could be dealt with by the notaries themselves by means of the stereotyped forms in their possession, by letters "in" or "sub forma communi", such, for instance, as ordinary licences, dispensations, etc. In general, on the contrary, the *debatable* letters, the *litteræ legendæ*, " contained new or disputable matter, a definition of law or a statement of policy," [2] and had to be examined by the Pope himself or the vice-chancellor before issue.

Cardinal Pitra sums up *his* formulary thus : " He (Nicholas) distinguished between the letters which could be issued without reference to consistory (*sans lecture d'audience*), and those which had to be referred back (*passer par l'audience*) ; he prescribed those which had to be given to the parties in person, those which had to be read by the vice-chancellor alone, by the vice-chancellor and a notary, or by a notary alone, those which required further discussion, and those which required a reference to the *ordinary*, those which, given out of hand to clerics, had to be read by bishops and princes, those in which account had to be taken of patronage, of the cure of souls, or residence, those which could be issued according to a prescribed form, those which dealt with the *exempt* and the *non-exempt*, etc."

Further, from reference to the regulations of certain

[1] This formulary has also been printed by Poole, *ib.*, p. 188 ff. It is a pity that Mr. Poole, whose valuable work we have used freely, did not also deal with the formulary printed by Pitra. *Cf. supra*, Vol. XI, pp. 316–29, and Vol. XII, pp. 49 f. and 53.

[2] Poole, p. 118.

of his predecessors whom he names, we may conclude that Gregory X. had given no little attention to the chancery rules; that they had been amended by Urban IV. and Clement IV. before him; and that some regulations had only been changed towards the close of the pontificate of John XXI.[1]

The document printed by Pitra begins: " The following is a list of the letters which are ordinarily issued without any discussion (*sine lectione*), and of those which have to be discussed (*quæ transeunt per audientiam*)." Then follows a brief description of some ninety letters, some of which had to be submitted to examination and some of which had not. The list finishes with the statement that all other varieties of letters had to be weighed and considered.[2] From this list we see that, " on the petition of religious," a letter may at once, without further ado, be dispatched to the diocesan forbidding him to introduce into the enclosure (*in claustra*) more than two or three seculars from his cathedral.[3] On the other hand, documents renewing privileges of exemption had to be read over by the vice-chancellor and notaries. Even a grant of an indulgence of ten days had to be revised by the vice-chancellor and a notary. General denunciations of such as imposed new tolls could be issued out of hand; but, if they were directed against specified persons, they were to be read by a notary. In fine, it may be noted that these regulations of Nicholas prove that experience showed that matters which at one time could be dealt with by stereotyped forms, at another required particular treatment. As Nicholas himself was a very keen worker,[4] and as, following the

---

[1] " Ad dies fere ultimos D. Johannis PP.," p. 163.

[2] " Cætera omnia sunt legenda," *ib.*, p. 167. [3] *Ib.*, p. 164.

[4] " Multum erat morosus homo ad expediendum aliquos de negotiis suis." *Mem. Potest. Reg.*, ap. *R. I. SS.*, viii, p. 1141. *Cf. Mart. Pol. Contin. III. Romana*, ap. *M. G. SS.*, xxx, 712. " In omnibus agendis suis cum maturitate processit."

example of Gregory X. and John XXI., he would not
listen to the pleadings of notaries, he was able to fill
up vacant churches more quickly than any of his
predecessors. Moreover, when he was at Suriano, he
caused the preliminary chancery work to be done at
Viterbo.[1] But he kept by him the officials who had
affixed the bullæ (the *bullatores*), and so dated the letters
from Suriano (*datam Suriani*), leaving the money side
to be dealt with at Viterbo.[2]

Depôt at
Assisi.

It would appear that for some quarter of a century
before the election of Nicholas, property of the papal
chancery, and also perhaps of the papal treasury, had
been preserved at the friary at Assisi. It is thought
to have been deposited there by Innocent IV. on his
return from the Council of Lyons (1254).[3] At any rate,
his successor, Alexander IV., wrote to the *guardian*
at Assisi instructing him to hand over to his treasurer,
Peter, the *books* and certain other things which, on
behalf of Innocent IV., had been deposited there by
Laurence, afterwards bishop of Antivari.[4] In 1273 we
find Gregory X. ordering the guardian to hand over
to the Pope's messenger two muniment chests (*scrinia*)
and articles lodged in their friary.[5] Similarly Nicholas,
a few days after his coronation, instructed the guardian
to hand over to Andrew of Nevers, a member of his

---

[1] "Audientiam fieri fecit in Viterbio." *Cont., l.c.*

[2] Still it appears that many were dated at Viterbo. *Ib.*, n. 6. We
must refer the reader for further information on this interesting subject
of the methods of the mediaeval papal chancery to Poole (where a
bibliography will be found) and to Pitra.

[3] Pitra, *l.c.*, p. 270.

[4] Potthast, n. 16021, Sept. 24, 1255. The articles were "in the
sacristy of the Church of St. Francis". *Cf. ib.*, n. 20312, April 6, 1268,
where Clement forbids interference with goods deposited there by
the bishop of Paphos (Baffo in Cyprus).

[5] *Ib.*, n. 20749, June 20. In n. 21100, Feb. 7, 1276, we see Innocent V.
bidding the guardian hand over to his servant John his property
which had been deposited with the friars.

household, his property which had been left with them.[1]
A month or two later he sent further instructions to him
regarding goods preserved at Assisi[2]; and on the same
date of the following year (1279) he bade him hand over
to the bishop of Gubbio, collector of the Saracen tithe,
certain documents which concerned his work and which
had been left in the sacristy of the friary on the death of
the archdeacon of Spoleto.[3]

After Nicholas had settled the procedure of his chancery
he turned to an even more important branch of papal
administration—to the College of Cardinals. On
March 12, 1278, about the time in the morning (nine
o'clock) when central Italy was shaken by an earthquake,
Nicholas more than doubled the number of cardinals,
by adding nine new ones to their depleted ranks.[4] He
had, he said, been greatly distressed at the harm the
Church had suffered from the fall of so many of its
important columns.[5]

The College of Cardinals.

In choosing the Cardinals, Nicholas would appear
to have acted with great prudence and justice. If he
made two Franciscan cardinals, he also made two

---

[1] *Ib.*, n. 21262, Jan. 1, 1278.

[2] *Ib.*, n. 21278, March 11, 1278.

[3] *Ib.*, n. 21544. Hence, in 1366, we find mention " of the Archives of
the treasure of the Roman Church in the house of the Friars Minor at
Assisi ". *Cf.* an Avignon catalogue, ap. Muratori, *Antiq. Med. Ævi*, vi,
p. 90. See also the inventory of papal registers found in certain coffers
" in camera que est prope sacristiam superiorem fratrum Minorum in
Assisio in loco ubi conservatur thesaurus Rom. Ecclesiæ ", in the
year 1339. Denifle, *Die Päpstlichen Registerbände*, p. 71, Berlin, 1886.

[4] *Cf. Mem. Potest. Reg.*, ap. *R. I. SS.*, viii, 1141. Salimbene, *Chron.*,
pp. 500–1, and others speak of a greater earthquake in 1279. They
assign it to April 30 and May 1. A note to the *Cron. S. Petri Erford.
Mod.* says that the earthquake was felt at Rome. Nicholas was dining
at the time, "and the table and the whole palace were wonderfully
shaken." Pp. 206–7, n., ed. Holder-Egger.

[5] See his letter to brother Jerome of Ascoli (then absent in France)
notifying him of his appointment as cardinal. Ep. of April 23, 1278,
ap. Wadding, *Annal.*, v, p. 48.

Dominican cardinals; and, as Savio has pointed out, he filled up the five vacant suburbicarian Sees with men of the same nationality or the same religious order as their previous occupants. Thus to the See of Ostia he promoted his nephew the Dominican, Latino Malabranca,[1] in succession to the Dominican, Pierre de Tarentaise; to the See of Albano, in succession to the Italian Franciscan, St. Bonaventure, he named the Italian Franciscan, Brother Bentevenga; the Portuguese Ordogno followed Peter of Spain in the See of Tusculum; in the See of Porto, the English Dominican Robert Kilwardby succeeded the English Cistercian, John Tolet; and to fill the See of Palestrina, vacant by the death of Vicedomini, archbishop of Aix in France, Nicholas called Erard de Lessines from the See of Auxerre. The remaining four were the protonotary, Gerard Branio of the title of the Dodici Apostoli; the General of the Franciscans, Jerome Masci of Ascoli (afterwards Nicholas IV.) of the title of S. Pudenziana; Giordano Orsini, of S. Eustachio (deacon); one of the Pope's brothers; and his cousin, James Colonna (deacon) of S. Maria in Via Lata, destined for a very stormy career.[2] This list deserves close study by such as

[1] Unfortunately to appoint his nephew he had to set aside a regulation of Gregory IX. that no one of any distinguished Roman family should be made a cardinal—if such is the meaning of the words of Ptolemy of Lucca, *H. E.*, xxiii, 35 : "Ordinabit nullum de genere quodam Urbis promoveri debere ad statum Cardinalatus."

[2] On cardinal James Colonna, and his grand-uncle card. John Colonna († 1245), see the bull of Boniface VIII., May 10, 1297, in which he excommunicated James C., and his nephew Peter C., ap. Raynaldus, *Ann.*, 1297, n. 27. He says that James though "rather young and ignorant" was made cardinal because he contrived to cover his faults by the cloak of hypocrisy. Ptolemy of Lucca, *H. E.*, xxiii, c. 26, speaking of the creation of these cardinals, says that card. James was "a man of experience (*maturitatis*) and innocence and a friend of religious". Perhaps the truth is that Boniface somewhat exaggerated the faults of an enemy, and the Dominican Ptolemy overpraised the

wish to keep free from the mistakes and exaggerations
of Salimbene, Villani, Gregorovius, and other historians
ancient and modern. Moreover, if we consider its members
as a whole, we may follow the judgment of the English
continuator of Martinus Polonus, who says that " they
were all men of distinguished character ".[1]

With his zeal for improvements there is no doubt The Canons
that, had he lived longer, Nicholas would have still of St. Peter.
further increased the numbers of the College of Cardinals.
However that may be, the College of Cardinals was
not the only ecclesiastical body which Nicholas improved.
As we have already seen, he began to better the status
of the Canons of St. Peter's even before he was Pope.
Originally it appears that the Canons of St. Peter's
had been monks ; but that, owing to the decay of the
monastic spirit in the twelfth century, the monks had
been replaced by secular canons. By degrees, too, the
secular canons got into difficulties partly owing to the
smallness of their numbers, and partly to the insufficiency
of their revenues. The first difficulty had to some extent
been brought about by the fact that a number of them
were employed on diplomatic missions by the Popes.
Hence too few were left in residence to bear the burden
of the daily public recitation of the Divine Office. The
other chief difficulty was largely brought about by the
same causes that had brought financial trouble on other
institutions at Rome at this period—on the *Schola
Anglorum*, for instance. Pilgrims with their offerings
were kept away from Rome to no inconsiderable degree
by the disturbances caused by the friction between
the rights of the Popes over the city of Rome and the

virtue of " a friend of religious ". On this promotion of cardinals see
also B. Guidonis, *In Vit. N. III.* Villani assures us that Nicholas
made Colonna a cardinal in order to please his family, so that they
would help the Orsini against the Anibaldeschi, lib. vii, c. 54 (al. 53).

[1] " Omni honestate conspicuos." Ap. *M. G. SS.*, xxx, 713, or
xxiv, 254.

claims of its new Republic, and by the fierce struggle between the Popes and the Emperors.

A reform of the personnel of the first basilica of Christendom became therefore necessary. It was, as we have seen, begun by Pope John XXI., who put the matter into the hands of cardinal Giovanni Orsini whom he nominated archpriest of St. Peter's.[1] On his appointment, the cardinal wrote from Viterbo, where he was then staying, a letter to his new subordinates. It was truly paternal in tone, kind but firm, pointing out the absolute need of improving the standard of Divine Service in St. Peter's which unfortunately had greatly deteriorated.[2] The new archpriest threw himself with great earnestness into the work which had been entrusted to him, and had already accomplished much when, at his instigation, Pope John issued his bull *Vineam Domini* for the reform of the Chapter of St. Peter's (March 15, 1277).[3] When he became Pope, Nicholas completed his work of reform. He declared that from the time when he had reached the years of discretion [4] he had ever loved " the glorious Prince of the Apostles and his venerable basilica, built by Divine dispensation in the City of Cities ". This love had grown with his growth, and with the honours which had been given to him.[5] It filled him with the greatest zeal for the beauty and decorum of that special house of God. On February 3, 1279, he issued a very lengthy bull on the status and duties of the canons and beneficiati of the basilica.[6] He had

[1] *Cf. supra*, p. 41.

[2] Ap. Grimaldi, *Gli Archipreti*, p. 49, cited by Martorelli, *Storia del Clero Vaticano*, p. 154, Rome, 1792, whom I am here following.

[3] *Bullar. Basil. Vat.*, i, p. 157 ff. *Cf.* the bull of Nicholas, *ib.*, p. 177.

[4] Ep. to all Christians, June 11, 1279, ap. *ib.*, p. 202. " Ab eo tempore, quo ætatem discretivam attigimus."

[5] His love " semper cum promoto majus incrementum habuit, semper cum crescente plus crevit." *Ib.*

[6] *Ib.*, pp. 177-98.

found, he said, when archpriest that there were only ten residential canons attached to St. Peter's, and that they were for the most part hopelessly infirm. To improve this state of things, he continued, he had induced Pope John XXI. and others to give some thousands of pounds for the benefit of the Chapter ; and he had himself also contributed to the fund for it. Now that he was Pope, he felt that he must do more for it. Consequently, besides other monies, he gave to the basilica " for the good of his soul and those of his relatives, benefactors and other faithful departed " five thousand pounds of Provins, and moreover five hundred marks sterling [1] to purchase property to bring in a regular income. All this, asserted Nicholas, he set forth not to obtain the praise of men, but that all may understand the present financial situation, and may in the future be moved to strengthen it. He had already named his nephew, cardinal Matteo Rosso, archpriest,[2] and he trusted that under him and his successors the new order would be maintained. He decided that, apart from the archpriest, the treasurer and the guardian of the *Meta*,[3] there were to be at least twenty-two canons, but that in future there might be as many as thirty. To help in the choir but not to rank as canons, he prescribed the institution of thirty beneficiati.[4]

The rest of the bull, signed by " Nicholas, bishop of the most holy Catholic Church " and ten cardinals, is taken up with settling the relations between the canons and the beneficiati, with their stipends, etc., and cannot

---

[1] Estimated in 1747 to be worth 1,350 scudi.

[2] Of S. Maria in Portico.

[3] The pyramid that stood on the site of the present Church of S. Maria Transpontina. It appears at times to have been used as a sort of outwork of the Castle of St. Angelo. *Cf.* the Diary of Antoninus Petri, ad ann. 1409 and 1414, ap. *R. I. SS.*, xxiv, pp. 1005 and 1041.

[4] They were to be called " Beneficiati chori basilicæ S. Petri ". Page 180 of this bull : *Civitatem Sanctam.*

detain us further. The grateful canons at once resolved to say " for ever " certain Masses for the Pope, his father, mother, uncle, and two brothers.[1]

Altar of St. Nicholas. But Nicholas was not content with raising the standard of Divine Service in the basilica. He loved its very fabric and took steps to render it more beautiful. Under the patronage of the Popes and the skill of the *Cosmati*, there was, as elsewhere in Europe, a great development of artistic production in Rome during the thirteenth century, and especially during its second half. In this latter period, Nicholas III. was one of the most distinguished of the promoters of art. If it be true that, at this time particularly, the churches of Rome were superior to all others in the richness of their pictorial decorations ;   if it be true that advances in artistic work, notably " in the sacerdotal mosaic and the monumental fresco ", were first made in Rome whence they spread to other parts of Italy,[2] it is equally true that Nicholas III., by his splendid encouragement of every branch of art, was one of the causes of this glorious development.

We have said that Nicholas loved the basilica of St. Peter, for as he declared with great enthusiasm : " This is the House of God, built on the rock (*supra petram*), wherein most honourably rests the sacred body

---

[1] *Cf.* bull of March 25, 1279, confirming this resolution of the canons. Ap. *Bullar. B. V.*, i, 198 ff. It appears that cardinal Matteo Rosso was, on his death in 1305, followed as archpriest by another Orsini, his cousin, cardinal Napoleone Orsini. According to A. Huyskens these Orsini archpriests filled up the canonical vacancies with their relations or dependents, thereby causing a decline in the ecclesiastical life of the Chapter. However, as the same author gives the statutes of reform which cardinal N. O. drew up in 1337, one is disposed to believe that the causes of the decline may have been other than those given by Huyskens. *Cf.* " Das Kapitel von S. Peter unter dem Einflusse der Orsini " in the *Historisches Jahrbuch*, 2° trim., 1906 ; and the amendments to that article by Sägmüller in the following number.

[2] Venturi, *La Pittura del Trecento*, pp. 123 and 141.

of that very rock (*ipsius Petri*).[1] This is the divine Tabernacle dear to the choirs of heaven, venerated by all the world. This is the place specially attached to the Roman Pontiff, the Vicar of Jesus Christ." [2] He went on to say that his mind ever turned to it when overwhelmed by the turmoil and anxieties of worldly business. Then, after recalling the fact that he had formed a worthy Chapter for it which he had suitably endowed, and that he had improved very many other things in connection with it, he proclaimed that he had not forgotten his patron saint, Nicholas of Myra. In his honour and to add to the beauty of the basilica, he had set up a new marble altar, and had decorated it with arabesque designs in iron, and with beautiful carvings [3] and frescoes. [4] With his own hands had he consecrated it in presence of a great concourse of people. Wherefore, to encourage piety in connection with the altar and its saint, " by the mercy of Almighty God, and relying on the authority of the Prince of the Apostles and his co-apostle Blessed Paul, to all who are truly penitent and have confessed their sins, and who for piety's sake shall visit the said altar on the anniversary of its consecration or on the feast of St. Nicholas, we mercifully remit a year and forty days of the penance assigned to them." [5]

Nicholas was not, however, satisfied with minor works in connection with the basilica. According to Ptolemy of Lucca, he renovated practically the whole of it, and continued in it, as well as in the basilicas of St. John

General restoration of St. Peter's.

---

[1] Need we remind our readers that Nicholas can play thus on these words because the name Peter means Rock ?

[2] Ep. Sept. 17, 1279, to all Christians. Ap. *Bullar. B. V.*, i, 202.

[3] " Fecimus altare . . . construi marmorea structura fulcitum, cratibus munitum hinc inde ferreis, et aliis decentibus cælaturis ornatum." *Ib.*

[4] Above the altar he caused to be painted St. Nicholas ascending to heaven helped by St. Francis. *Chron. de Lanercost*, an. 1277.

[5] Ep., *ib.*

Lateran and St. Paul's-outside-the-walls, the series of papal portrait medallions which had been begun seemingly by Pope St. Leo I. (440–61),[1] and continued by Pope Formosus at least. The custom of adorning cathedral churches with the portraits of their bishops in mosaic or fresco is believed to date from Merocles († 315), archbishop of Milan, and so from the end of the third or the beginning of the fourth century.[2] A mosaic pavement recently discovered at Aquileia, and shown by a dated inscription to belong to the time of bishop Theodore (fl. 314), presents four mosaic portraits.[3] Moreover, from this period, at least, these representations were real likenesses. Agnellus of Ravenna, after giving a description of the personal appearance of bishop Exuperantius (c. 425–30), says : " Should you ask me where I have learnt what I have written concerning the visages of the bishops, I reply that it is art (pictura) which has given me the information, because at this period it was the custom to delineate the portraits from life." [4]

Portraiture was essentially a Roman art ; and so, had we no direct evidence on the subject, we could have safely concluded that the churches of Rome were very early decorated with papal portraits. At first the medallions, showing half figures, were in fresco in the style of the imperial portraits in Byzantium, which we know from St. John Chrysostom were painted in white on a blue background.[5] It was not indeed till some

---

[1] H. E., l. xxiii, c. 28.   Cf. R. van Marle, La Peinture Romaine au Moyen Age, p. 19, Strasbourg, 1921.

[2] Garrucci, Storia Dell'arte Crist., i, 437.

[3] Nuovo Bullet. di Arch. Crist., 1910, pp. 162–5. Cf. C. Constantini, Aquileia e Grado, pp. 11, 30–4.

[4] Vit. Pont., p. 297, ed. Mon. Germ. Hist. " Quia semper fiebant imagines suis temporibus ad illorum similitudinem."

[5] 1 Cor., x, 1, ap. Migne, P. G., iii, 247. " Εἶδες πολλάκις εἰκόνα βασιλικὴν κυανῳ κατακεχρωσμένην χρώματι, εἶτα τὸν ζωγράφον λευκὰς περιάγοντα γράμμας, etc."

centuries even after Nicholas III. that these medallions were executed in indestructible mosaic. Still, had it not been for the regrettable destruction of old St. Peter's, we should, through the work of Nicholas, be in possession of authentic portraits of most of the great Popes of the thirteenth century.[1]

To enhance the beauty of the services in St. Peter's, and especially at the altar which he had built, we learn from an ancient necrology, still preserved in the archives of the basilica, that Nicholas presented to the basilica a number of gifts " of special magnificence and artistic value ". The gifts in metal which he gave to his altar, comprising silver crosses, candelabra, vases, chalices, etc., weighed twenty-eight marks seven ounces of silver. He also presented to it a number of silk vestments, among which we may notice two chasubles " of white samite with English embroidery ". For the general use of the basilica he gave similar gifts in metal and silk, among others " a most precious cope woven with figures of saints of English workmanship ".[2] He also gave " a silver tabernacle with a gold pyx " for the sepulchre on the feast of Maundy Thursday, or, as the catalogue expresses it, " to keep the body of Christ on the feast of the supper of the Lord " ; also a pyx (or ciborium) to hold the hosts, and a silver *reed* by means of which the supreme Pontiff receives the Precious Blood in the Mass. The document further adds that " with

Gifts to St. Peter's.

---

[1] On this subject of " the Portraits of the Popes " see my paper, bearing that title, in vol. ix of the *Papers of the British School at Rome*, o my later *The Early and Mediæval Tombs and Portraits of the Popes.*

[2] " Item duas planetas de samite albo frisco anglicano . . . item contulit hic unum pretiosissimum pluviale ad imagines sanctorum contextum de opere anglicano." This list is printed ap. *Bullar. Basil. Vat.*, i, 196 n. Mgr. Barbier de Montault is said to have given an incomplete French translation of this list of benefactions in the *Revue de l'art Chrétien*, 1888, n. 3.

his own money ", and with moneys which he had collected, Nicholas purchased houses and other real property for the basilica ; and at the same time he protected property which already belonged to it and which was being wrested from it.[1]

When Grimaldi wrote about old St. Peter's,[2] there was, he says, still to be seen in its sacristy a very beautiful pallium belonging to the Orsini altar of S. Maria de Cancellis which had been given by Pope Nicholas III. It was embellished with portraits of St. Anthony of Padua and St. Francis taken from life, and like to those in the mosaic of the apse of the Lateran and to those in the Church of St. Francis in the *Ripæ* region.[3]

The Vatican palace.

Nicholas next turned his attention to the Vatican palace, in which, as a Roman chronicler correctly noted, he always passed the winter.[4] Nicholas preferred the Vatican to the Lateran palace, not only in order that he might be nearer his beloved basilica, but also, no doubt, that he might be further removed from the baronial brawls that often rendered Rome proper unbearable. Accordingly he greatly increased the Vatican palace, as both chronicles and an inscription tell us. The latter states that it was in the first year of his pontificate that the Pope undertook the work of enlarging the Vatican palace.[5] His additions included " a noble chapel, wonderfully painted ",[6] and a great hall. To-day his

---

[1] See his letter to the Commune of Castrum S. Sepulcro, warning them to cease cutting down and carrying off trees from the Massa Trabaria which were the property of the Basilica of St. Peter. Ep. of Apr. 28, 1278, ap. *ib.*, p. 175. *Cf. Reg.*, nn. 246-8.

[2] *Cathalogus Archipresbyterorum*, Rome, 1685, ap. *Cod. Barb. Lat.*, n. 2719 in the Vatican Archives.

[3] They are no longer extant in that Church.

[4] *A Roman Contin. of the Chron. of Mart. Polonus*, ap. *M. G. SS.*, xxx, p. 712.

[5] This inscription is given by Duchesne, *L. Pont.*, ii, 458 n.

[6] " Capellam nobilem, mirabiliter picturatam." See the Roman continuation of *M. P.* just quoted. The *Chron. S. Petri Erford Mod.*, an. 1277, adds that the erection was made " ex proprio domate ".

work and that of his immediate successors in connection with the palace is represented by the oldest portions of the buildings round the Cortiles of the Maresciallo and the Papagallo.

Around the palace, too, Nicholas erected a considerable number of buildings for the officials of the curia, especially for the penitentiaries, whom for the first time he would appear to have formed into a college or bureau.[1] This text, so important for the history of the papal penitentiary, would appear to be very little known. It escaped the notice even of Haskins, who, in his paper on the penitentiary, truly remarked that the said history has so far been but very imperfectly investigated.[2] Chiefly from him will a brief notice of the story of the papal penitentiary be here given.[3]

The papal penitentiary.

[1] Ptolemy of L., *H. E.*, xxiii, c. 28. "Multas novitates fecit . . . ædificavit palatium . . . ubi mandavit fieri domum pro omnibus officialibus suis, sed præcipue pro omnibus pœnitentiariis, qui claudebantur sub uno cancello." *Cf. Cont. R. of M. P.*, etc.

[2] The subject is not as much as mentioned, e.g., either in the *Catholic Encyclopædia* or in the *Catholic Dictionary*.

[3] *The Sources of the Hist. of the P. Penitentiary*, by C. H. Haskins, ap. *The American Journal of Theology*, July, 1905, p. 421 ff. Another work in English on the subject which I have examined is the introduction by H. C. Lea to his edition of *A Formulary of the Papal Penitentiary in the Thirteenth Century*, Philadelphia, 1892 ; but the editor has found it easier to abuse the institution than to enlighten one as to its origin and history. The following example must suffice to show how far Mr. Lea was qualified to write on the penitentiary. Presumably not understanding the fundamental difference between the forgiveness or pardon or absolution of the *guilt* of sin, and the pardon of the satisfaction which may remain due after the forgiveness of the guilt, he writes (p. x) : Pius III. in 1536 sanctioned the assertion "that it is perfectly legitimate to receive money for the pardon of sins ". The authority he quotes for this says the *direct opposite*. It states : "Quod *non* pro concessione gratiæ, *neque* pro *absolutione* sed pro *peccati satisfactione* possit imponi mulcta pecuniaria, etc." This formulary, dating from the days of Gregory IX., is probably the first of its kind. Benedict XII. issued another important one (1338), and in the days of Urban VI., Walter of Strasburg issued another. *Cf.* Haskins, *l.c.*, p. 437.

In connection with the penitential system of the early Church, we find special " penitentiary priests ", whose business it was " to facilitate and promote the exercise of public discipline by acquainting men what sins the laws of the church required to be expiated by public penance, and how they were to behave themselves in the performance of it ; and only to appoint private penance for such private crimes as were not proper to be brought upon the public stage ".[1] In the Greek Church the system of public penance for secret sins was abolished in the fourth century, and with it the office of penitentiary priests ; but in the Latin Church the system was maintained for many centuries after, and the office of penitentiaries still exists in it. Sozomen, the Greek historian, who tells us of the suppression by the patriarch Nectarius of the system of public penance for secret sins, also avers that it was still " observed with great vigour by the Western Churches, particularly at Rome ".[2] In fact, in the west, it appears that public penance for secret sins was only abolished about the seventh century, and for sins in general about the twelfth century.[3]

If, then, ultimately the Latins also abolished public penance, they did not abolish the office of penitentiary priests. But when special priests, with the title of *penitentiaries*, were appointed by the Pope to deal with

[1] Bingham, *The Antiquities of the Christian Church*, lib. xviii, c. 3, vol. ii, p. 1072, London, 1878. *Cf.* Pelliccia, *The Polity of the Christian Church*, p. 436 ; Thomassin, *Ancienne et Nouvelle Discipline de l'Église*, i, pp. 368 ff. and 381 ff., Paris, 1864 ; Duchesne, *Les Origines du Culte Chrétien*, c. xiv.

[2] *H. E.*, vii, 16. Further on in the same chapter he says that " the Roman priests have carefully observed this custom (of public penance) from the beginning to the present time ". *Cf.* Socrates, *H. E.*, v, 19, who tells us that it was instituted at the time of the Decian persecution in order that those who after baptism " had lapsed " should confess their crime to a priest specially appointed for the purpose.

[3] Thomassin, *l.c.*, p. 369.

matters in connection with the Sacrament of Penance is not certain. If public penance was suppressed " about the twelfth century ", it would appear that " penitentiaries ", i.e. " officials of the Apostolic See appointed for the business connected with penance ",[1] were nominated about the same time, as they are said to be mentioned in the *Registers* of Innocent III. (1198–1216).[2] Writing in 1338, Pope Benedict XII. declared, on the authority " of an ancient book ", that " the office of the penitentiaries " used at one time to be performed by the cardinal priests, but that, as the business of the Church grew, they could not find the time to hear confessions. Accordingly penitentiaries were instituted " who occupy an important position (*priorem locum*) like the cardinal priests, and are in a sense prelates of the world ".[3]

Where there was question of dealing with cases of conscience by correspondence, we may suppose that at first the penitentiaries would act as a department of the chancery. Then, as their work grew with the reservation to Rome during the twelfth and thirteenth centuries of more and more cases for absolution, they were, as we have seen, cut off from the chancery, and formed into a separate bureau by Nicholas III. Like the apostolic camera (treasury), the penitentiary was a daughter of the chancery. It had a seal of its own [4]; and, at least with its establishment as an independent bureau, it began to register its documents.

Bentevenga's Formulary for the use of the penitentiary.

---

[1] " Officiales apud Sedem Apostolicam officio pœnitentiæ deputati." *Formulary*, n. xvii, p. 28, ed. Lea.

[2] Haskins says, p. 423, that the earliest original document of a papal penitentiary that he has noted is a letter of the year 1217 issued under the seal of the penitentiary, Nicholas of Casarnari, ap. Teulet, *Layettes du Trésor des Chartes*, vol. i, p. 450, n. 1241.

[3] See the original from which we have translated in Haskins, p. 446, n.

[4] Cf. *Formulary*, xxvii, n. 1, " Sub sigillo nostro "; xxx, n. 3, etc., ed. Lea.

At any rate, we have a formulary for the use of the
bureau drawn up by one of Nicholas' cardinals,
the learned Franciscan, Bentevenga, Grand Penitentiary
(*Pœnitentiarius Major*).[1] But the fact that Alexander IV.,
when Pope, could quote a document which, under his
orders when cardinal, " brother Egidius, the penitentiary
of the lord Pope " had issued,[2] may perhaps go to
prove that documents issued by the penitentiaries were
registered by them from the early days of their institution.

The various officials of the bureau learnt their duties
from a manual, the *Liber Penitentiarie*, of which three
principal editions are known. The first was issued on
April 8, 1338, by order " of our most holy lord, the lord
Benedict " who had reorganized the bureau ; the second
in 1449 by that of Eugenius IV., and the third by that
of Julius II. in 1552. From this constitution of Benedict,
we may no doubt infer, with sufficient certainty, the
working of the bureau as it was established by
Nicholas III.

In his preamble to his constitution " In agro dominico ",
which was issued in conjunction with the *Liber P.*,[3]
Benedict, with great earnestness, exhorts the Grand
Penitentiary, the Minor Penitentiary, the scribes
(*scriptores*), the keepers of the seal (*sigillatores*), the
correctors and the other officials of the bureau to do their
work neatly, honestly, and promptly, for to them " as
to physicians of souls " men come from all parts of the

---

[1] Edited by Eubel : " Der Registerband des Cardinalgrosspöni-
tentiars Bentevenga," ap. *Archiv für Kathol. Kirchenrecht*, vol. xliv,
1890. P. Lecacheux has published " Un formulaire de la Penitencerie
apostolique au temps du card. Albornoz (1357–8), ap. *Mélanges d'Archéol.*,
vol. xviii, 1898. The region of the activities of the different grades of
the penitentiaries was fixed by a document of Nicholas IV., 1291,
known as the *Summa*. Haskins, p. 426.

[2] Ep. of Jan. 2, 1255, ap. *Reg. Alex.*, n. 25.

[3] See Haskins, pp. 426–7. The bull of Benedict (" In agro dominico ")
is printed in full in the *Bullar. Rom.*, iv, p. 415 ff., and in Guerra,
Pontif. Constit. Epit., i, 402, in short.

world.[1] For the quick dispatch of doubtful cases, the Grand Penitentiary must have an expert canonist at his side with whom he must take counsel ; and another expert to pick out what must be referred to him, and what could be dealt with in the ordinary way. Special scribes must be chosen to correct the letters before they are presented to be sealed. Till their dispatch, they were to be carefully locked up in the house of the Grand Penitentiary. No petition was to be presented for the personal examination of the Pope without the express knowledge of the same official. The hours at which the penitentiaries had to be in Church for confessional purposes were also prescribed, as also the gentle manner in which penitents were to be received, and the places in which alone the confessions of women could be heard. The scribes (*scriptores*) were to use good parchment which had to be ample and of proper shape, and free from any erasure which might give rise to suspicion of alteration. They were, moreover, forbidden to write in " a cursory hand ", and had to observe a number of rules as to the amount of the parchment they were to leave blank. They were also strictly charged to attend to the petitions of the poor before those from which they were to receive pay, " for it is better to serve God in His poor, than men for gain."

Generally the regulations of Benedict XII. were framed with a view to avoiding delays,[2] to preserving secrecy,[3] to serving the interests of the poor, and, with the last-named end in view, to prescribing that certain work was to be done gratuitously, and that on no account was any fee beyond the fixed tax ever to be charged.[4]

---

[1] Especially on account of reserved cases : " præsertim in casibus eidem Sedi specialiter reservatis."

[2] *Cf. ib.*, nn. 5, 6, 7, 14, 19, 21.

[3] *Ib.*, nn. 5, 10, 12.

[4] *Ib.*, nn. 4, 7, 10, 16, 18, 20.

The *Liber* closed with the forms of the oaths which the different members of the bureau had to take.

By degrees the penitentiary began to extend its jurisdiction from private matters of conscience, from the *Forum Internum*, to matters of public notoriety, i.e. to the *Forum Externum*. Though this caused great complaint, the action of the penitentiary was upheld by Sixtus IV.[1] As, however, the inconveniences of the mixed jurisdiction of this tribunal continued to be felt, Pius IV. in 1562 and Pius V. in 1569 made drastic reductions in the faculties and personnel of the penitentiary and restricted its action to the forum of conscience.[2] These decrees were subsequently somewhat modified ; but in our own time Pius X. again restricted the jurisdiction of the tribunal to the *Forum Internum*.

As there is no space here for lengthy treatment of the tribunal of the penitentiary, further information with regard to it must be sought in some of the volumes we have cited or elsewhere.[3]

Returning to the work entered upon by Nicholas for developing and improving the neighbourhood of St. Peter's, we find him continuing work begun during the vacancy that preceded his election. In that interval, Master Albert, canon of St. Peter's, bought, "in behalf of the lord Pope and his treasury," certain properties on the

---

[1] Bull of May 9, 1584, "Quoniam nonnulli," ap. Guerra, *l.c.*, p. 403. It was argued that the authority of the Grand Penitentiary "ad forum conscientiæ tantum se extendit ".

[2] Bull of P. IV. "In sublimi b. Petri " of May 4, 1562, and bulls of St. Pius V. of 1569 "In omnibus rebus " and "In earum rerum " of May 18 and 19 respectively. Guerra, *l.c.*, pp. 403–5, or F. Cherubini, *Compend. Bullar.*, ii, 15, 58, and 59, give epitomes of these bulls. As it is not our province to give a complete account of the penitentiary, we have said nothing about its *tax-lists* or fees charged for its different kinds of letters. See Haskins, page 444.

[3] E.g. F. X. Wernz, *Jus Decretalium*, Prati, 1915, vol. ii, p. 439 ff. ; B. Ojetti, *Synopsis Rerum Moralium*, Rome, 1912, pp. 3019–26.

street which led to the papal palace.[1] Nicholas completed
the purchase so that the approach to the palace could be
widened.[2] Then, to make a garden by the palace, he
authorized the buying of a number of vineyards which
are described as situated outside the Porta Aurea (Porta
S. Pancrazio), or the Porta Viridaria (of the garden—
Porta Angelica), at the foot of Montis Mali,[3] or on Monte
Geretulo or Gereculo, so called from the Circus (or theatre
of Nero).[4] Some of the agreements of sale declare that
if the property sold should really be worth more than the
agreed price, the owners forego the difference " on
account of the reverence and devotion which they have
for the Pope ". The agreements are dated, at times,
" in the office of the treasurer," at others, " on the steps
of the basilica of St. Peter " or " at the windows " or
" balconies of the papal palace ".[5] Then, to ensure that
no property was unjustly enclosed in the new garden,
" the town crier of the City," during the term of office
" of the magnificent man, the lord Matteo Rosso of the
Orsini, illustrious Senator ", thrice on three successive
days proclaimed that any unsatisfied claims relative to
land in the new walled enclosure should be presented to
canon Albert within four days.[6] The land thus acquired,
which we are told was " of considerable extent ", was
well planted with trees, provided with a fountain, and,
" as though it were a city, surrounded by a high strong
wall of brick, well fortified with towers." [7]

[1] Cf. Lib. Censuum, vol. ii, nn. 27–8, p. 57 f., ed. Fabre.

[2] Ib., n. 29, Feb. 2, 1278. [3] Cf. supra, vol. viii, p. 48 f.

[4] Cf. De Rossi, Piante di Roma, p. 83 and Tav. 1, Rome, 1879.
An inscription now in the Capitol tells of all this work. See Gregorovius,
v, p. 632, n.

[5] See the collection of documents, nn. 1–31, ap. L. Cens., l.c., p. 43 ff.,
Feb. to June, 1278, and ap. Fedele in Archivio Rom. di Storia, vol. xxxiv,
1911, p. 515 ff. [6] Ib., n. 23.

[7] Ptolemy, H. E., xxiii, c. 28 ; and Annales, ap. R. I. SS., xi, p. 1292 ;
Cont. Rom. M. P., and Cont. Ital.

Writers on the Castle of St. Angelo are agreed in stating that it was Nicholas III. who connected the Vatican Palace with that stronghold by means of the fortified covered way which exists to this day. The Castle had come into the hands of his family, not, it would seem, by gift of the Pope himself to his nephew Orso Orsini, after he had alienated it from the Church, but by inheritance.[1] However this may be, the way proved on occasion a means of personal safety for more than one Pope. Nicholas is also said to have built the central tower of the Castle, and to have restored the chapel dedicated to St. Michael at its summit.

With all his love for St. Peter's, Nicholas did not neglect the Lateran, still the official administrative centre of the Holy See. First of all, he completed the renovation of the Lateran palace which had been begun by Hadrian V.,[2] and, as already noted, decorated the basilica.

But his chief work at the Lateran, work which has endured in its beauty to this day, was in connection with the oratory known as the Sancta Sanctorum. The first mention of this famous sanctuary, dedicated to St. Lawrence, occurs in the eighth century.[3] It was the papal private oratory of the Lateran palace, and was hence known as " S. Laurentius in Palatio ". Later on, from the number of important relics deposited therein, it came to be known as the " Sancta Sanctorum ",

[1] Such is the assertion of Villani, *Chron.*, vii, 53 (54). But *cf*. Savio, *Niccolo III.*, n. viii : " La donazione di Castel S. Angelo." See also Pagliucchi, *I Castellani del C. S. A.*, i, p. 13 ff. ; Rodocanachi, *Le Château S. Ange*, pp. 28 and 36. It is the so-called *Anonymus Magliabecchianus* (*c*. 1410) who tells us " decursum fecit (Nich. III.) a palatio suo usque ad castrum predictum, quod *nunc* Joannes XXIII. restauravit ", ap. Urlichs, *Cod. Topog.*, p. 149.

[2] *Cont. Rom. M. P.*, p. 712, ap. *M. G. SS.*, xxx. *Cf*. the other *C. R. M. P.*, ap. *ib.*, xxii, p. 476.

[3] *L. P.*, under Stephen III., i, p. 469. " In oratorio S. Laurentii intra eundem patriarchium."

and, as such, is said to have been renewed by
Honorius III.[1] An inscription testifies, too, that he made
one of the reliquaries for it which have been preserved
to this day.[2] A list of a number of the most famous of
the relics of " S. Lawrence in the Palace " has been given
us by John the Deacon in his *Story of the Lateran Church*
which, mostly from a very ancient book which he had
found in the archives of the basilica, he had dedicated
to Alexander III. He tells us, moreover, that some
of the principal ones, such as the relic of the true Cross,
and the sandals of Our Lord, were preserved in caskets
which were enclosed in a chest or ambry of cypress
wood made by Leo III.[3] This precious ambry and its
contents were found intact when the Sancta Sanctorum
was finally opened at the instance of Father Grisar, by
permission of Pius X., in June, 1905.[4] It bore the inscription " Leo indignus tertius episcopus Dei famulus fecit ".[5]

When the Lateran palace, much damaged during the
residence of the Popes at Avignon, was destroyed by
Sixtus V., he left undisturbed the sanctuary of the Sancta
Sanctorum ; and, from his day till our own, it was
not touched. In 1900, Ph. Lauer obtained permission

[1] *Ib.*, ii, 453. " Basilicam quæ Sancta Sanctorum dicitur renovavit."

[2] On the cover of a silver casket may be read : " ✠ Honorius PP. III.
fieri fecit pro capite beate Agnetis." *Cf.* Grisar, *Il S. Sanctorum*,
p. 138, Rome, 1907.

[3] *De Eccles. Lat.*, n. 14, ap. *Pat. Lat.*, t. lxxviii, p. 1389, or ap. *ib.*,
t. cxciv.

[4] See his *Il Sancta Sanctorum*, pp. 3–4. After the opening of the
enclosure where the relics had been contained, they were removed to
the Vatican.

[5] " Leo III., unworthily bishop, God's servant, made this chest."
See illustrations of this wonderful chest (now more than a thousand
years old), shut and open, in Lauer, *Le Trésor du S. S.*, pp. 33 and 35,
and in Grisar, *l.c.*, p. 70. Another article, a silver coffer of cruciform
shape covered with figures, also belonging to this historic treasure,
bears the inscription : " Paschalis Plebi Dei episcopus fieri fecit."
See Lauer, 62 ff. and plate ix. The work was probably of Paschal I.
(817–24).

to make some excavations in its massive substructures. Among other interesting discoveries then made, apart from damaged frescoes of unknown Popes,[1] was a fairly well-preserved fresco of a man (St. Augustine ?) reading, which served to fix the site of the archives (*scrinium*) of the old palace.

The little sanctuary, as we now see it, is due to the work of Innocent III., Honorius III., and chiefly of Nicholas III. Inscriptions on the bronze door of the face of the altar[2] and elsewhere attest the work of Innocent and Nicholas. The name of Innocent III., for instance, appears at the foot of the elaborate silver work with which he covered the famous picture of Our Lord, known as the " Acheropita " or " not painted by the hand of man ". The inscription giving his name is to the same effect as the one on the door, i.e., " Innocent III., Pope, caused this work to be executed." [3] Often carried in procession, and so exposed to the weather, this ancient picture had stood in need of restoration even before his time. From a note on the back of it,[4] it appears that

[1] To one of them was, however, attached an inscription which apparently should read " S. Stephanus PP." *Cf.* Lauer, " Les fouilles du S. Sanctorum," pp. 266–7, ap. *Mélanges d'Archéol.*, 1900, Rome.

[2] " Hoc opus fecit fieri dns. Innocentius PP. III." on one leaf of the door which enclosed the relics, and on the other, " Nicolaus Papa III. hanc basilicam a fundamentis renovavit et altare fieri fecit ipsumque et eandem basilicam consecravit." Grisar, *l.c.*, pp. 68–9. *Cf. Contin. Rom. M. P.*, ap. *M. G. SS.*, xxx, 712.

[3] " Innocentius PP. III. hoc opus fieri fecit." This fine incised silver plaque of Innocent (with the two *wings* added to the picture to cover it, which were made seemingly at the expense of James the son of Teolo in the beginning of the fifteenth century) can be studied better in the engraving of it in Marangoni, *Istoria dell' Oratorio di S. Sanct.*, p. 92, Rome, 1747, or in Galletti, *Inscriptiones Romanæ*, i, p. 92, than in the photographic reproductions of Grisar or Lauer.

[4] " Hanc (i)conam decimus renovavit Joannes." Stanislao, *La Cappella Papale di S. Sanct.*, Grottaferrata, 1919, p. 231. The picture is painted on canvas stretched over a board. *Cf. supra*, vol. i, pt. ii, p. 294, for a notice of this picture being carried by Stephen III.

John X. (915–28), was the first to take steps for its preservation. In this matter he was followed by Alexander III.[1] and Innocent III., and in our own days by Benedict XV. (1919)—a distich setting forth that this icon was renewed by John X. and ten centuries later by Benedict XV.[2]

But the ornamentation of the chapel itself, with its mosaic roof, its arcading with its twisted columns, and its frescoes, is the work of Nicholas III. To carry out his design, he employed Cosmati, as is testified by the inscription " ✠ Magister Cosmatus fecit hoc opus ".[3] Many of the frescoes are so well done that it is thought that they must be due to the famous Roman Master, Pietro Cavallini and his school. However that may be, the most interesting of the frescoes, as far as we are concerned, is one of those over the altar which shows Pope Nicholas III., wearing his tiara, and kneeling between SS. Peter and Paul by whom he is being presented to Our Lord seated on a throne. As far as the somewhat faded condition of this attractive fresco enables one to judge, it is the model of his chapel which the Pope appears to be holding in his hand and presenting to Our Lord. Before leaving this graceful little Gothic Chapel, we may note that one of the coffers found in its reliquary was fastened by a cord which bore a seal, which in turn showed a child fishing with a hook. It is " the seal of the Fisherman ", and is believed to be its oldest known specimen.[4]

---

[1] *Cf.* Gervase of Tilbury, *Otia Imperialia*, Decis. iii, c. 25, ap. Leibnitz, *SS. RR. Bruns.*, i, p. 968. This restoration was done " in our time ", he says.

[2] " Iconam hanc decimus renovavit Joannes Sæcula postque decem cumulat Benedictus honore." Ap. Stanislao, p. 247.

[3] *Cf.* Venturi, *Pittura nel Trecento*, p. 189, who identifies this Cosmas with the family of Lorenzo, and L. Filippini, *Scultura nel Trecento*, who supposes him to have been a member of the Mellini family.

[4] *Cf.* Stanislao, *l.c.*, p. 137, and Lauer, *l.c.*, plate xi.

Before his work of the renovation of the sanctuary was begun, Nicholas himself by night transported the most precious relics to another part of the Lateran palace, and confided them to the care of trustworthy religious. When the work of restoration was complete, he exhibited the reliquaries to an enormous number of people, enclosed them in the altar of the sanctuary, and then consecrated it (June 4, 1279).[1]

A palace by the Lateran. Just as by St. Peter's Nicholas had built residences for some of his officials, so he did in the neighbourhood of the Lateran. His erection was quite a large fortress, as it is described as " a city, urbs, strongly fortified with walls and towers ". The notice is given to us by the chronicle of Erfurt ; and, as originally printed, the chronicle stated that the fortress was made for the Pope's friends among the *cardinals*.[2] But a later edition of the chronicle gives an alternative reading which would make us conclude that Nicholas built the place for his relations.[3] However, as his friends among the cardinals might well be his relations, we may accept either reading as giving the same sense.

S. Maria sopra Minerva. Nicholas was not content to employ local talent only. The magnificent Gothic piles which were springing up at this time on the other side of the Alps could not but produce an effect upon Italy. The *Cosmati* were powerfully influenced by Gothic art ; but were not masters of it on a large scale,[4] so that when the Pope, urged by the Dominicans, who found the existing church too small, wished to build a large church in that style, he had to summon architects from elsewhere. He brought to Rome the Dominican friars, Fra Sisto and Fra Ristori,

[1] *Cont. Rom. M. P.*, ap. *M. G. SS.*, xxx, 712.

[2] " Amator amicorum suorum *Cardinalium*, construxit eis, etc.," ap. *M. G. SS.*, xxiv, p. 212.

[3] Ed. Holder-Egger, p. 689. " Amicorum suorum *Carnalium*."

[4] *Cf.* Parker, *Mosaic Pictures in Rome,* p. 98 ff.

who had just begun the church of S. Maria Novella
in Florence [1] ; and they are always credited with having
designed the only Gothic church in Rome, S. Maria
sopra Minerva. [2] As a Gothic Church, it cannot be called
a great success, and is by no means equal to its model the
Novella in Florence. It was, however, the only church of
any size erected in Rome for a long period, [3] and was built
largely out of funds provided by the Roman Municipality. [4]

Our account of the artistic work accomplished by
Nicholas may be closed by noting that he had an
opportunity of indulging his taste for building even before
he became Pope. Peter Capocci, cardinal-deacon of
St. George in Velabro († 1259), left it in his will that
his executors should build a hospital by the Church of
St. Anthony which stands near St. Mary Major's. The
hospital, duly built by our cardinal and cardinal Otho,
has disappeared, and the Church of St. Anthony has been
closed since 1870 ; but, above the fine bold round arch
of its principal door still standing, an inscription keeps
alive the memory of their work. [5]

Hospital of St. Anthony.

---

[1] See Vasari's *Life* of Gaddo Gaddi.

[2] On what art owes to the Dominicans, *cf.* Leader Scott, *The Renaissance of Art in Italy*, p. 42.

[3] On S. M. sopra M. see P. M. Masetti, *Mem. di S. M. sopra M.*, Rome, 1885, and Frothingham, *The Monuments of Christian Rome*, p. 189.

[4] See the letter of Nicholas III. of June 24, 1280, to the Senators Colonna and Savelli, saying that the Municipality had promised to help to build a new church " de Minerva ", ap. Ripoll, *Bull. O.P.*, i, p. 571. See the notes to the latter.

[5]   " ✠ D. Petrus Capoccius cardinalis
    Mandavit construi hospitale
        in loco isto
    Et DD. Otho Tusculanus episcopus
    Et Joannes Caietanus cardinalis
    Exequutores ejus fieri fecerunt
        Pro anima
     D. Petri Capocci."

Cf. Ciacconius, i, p. 699 ; Armellini, *Chiese di Roma*, p. 813.

Churches,
etc., of Rome
to be visited.
But Nicholas was not content to see to the improvement merely of the material fabrics of Roman Churches. He who, as he stated, by virtue of his office had " the care of all the churches of the world ", realized that he had a special duty of looking after the general well-being of those churches,[1] monasteries, and hospitals in Rome which were directly dependent upon the Holy See. Accordingly he ordered Philip, bishop of Fermo, count of Casate, archdeacon of Milan, a man in whom he had great confidence, to visit the said churches, etc., in person, and " with God alone before his eyes " to regulate and reform them in their heads and members.[2] Similarly with regard to vacant episcopal sees in any part of the world which were directly dependent upon the Holy See, or were by appeal submitted to it, he decreed that, to avoid the spiritual and temporal losses which followed long vacancies, those nominated to such sees must come to the Apostolic See for the final settlement of their appointment within a month after their nomination.[3]

Settlement
of relations
with the
Senate, 1278.
From the very beginning of his pontificate, Nicholas turned his attention to the civil as well as to the ecclesiastical condition of Rome. Whether because as a Roman he did not care to see in his city the chief officials, the Senator and his staff, in the hands of foreigners, or because he thought that the King of Sicily was too powerful a Senator, he made known to Charles of Anjou that he wished him to resign the senatorial dignity. This Charles at once professed himself ready to do, but said that, as Clement IV. had given him the office for ten years,[4] and as the ten years would be up

[1] Among them certain "archipresbyteral churches which are commonly called papal chapels ". Ep. of March 31, 1278, *Reg.*, n. 231.
[2] *Ib.*
[3] Raynaldus, *Annales*, 1279, n. 44 ; Dec. 13, 1279.
[4] *Cf. supra*, Vol. XV, p. 281.

on September 16, 1278, he would like to retain the office
to that date. To this Nicholas readily agreed,[1] and meanwhile (July 18, 1278) issued a constitution to regulate
the tenor of the office after its resignation by the
Sicilian King. Wrongly ascribing the temporal authority
of the Papacy in Rome " to a pragmatic constitution "
of Constantine, but rightly maintaining that the Pope
and the cardinals must be absolutely free in the exercise
of their sacred duties, he declared that it was his duty
to provide for the welfare of the city. He recalled to mind
what it had had to suffer at the hands of the stranger.[2]
Accordingly he decreed that the senatorial office should
not in future be held by any emperor, king, or powerful
noble, or by any of their near relations ; and that,
without special permission of the Holy See, the office
was not to be held for more than one year. Roman
citizens, or regular inhabitants of Rome or its district,
can be elected provided that they are not in possession
of such power as would put them into the class of
candidates already excluded.

Nicholas' next step was to send cardinals Latinus
and James Colonna to Rome to be ready to take over
the government of the city (July 27).[3] He bade them
see especially to the supply of corn, salt, etc., so that the
people might be happy, and take steps that Charles's
officials should be duly respected during the remainder
of their term of office, and should be allowed to depart

Two cardinals sent to Rome.

[1] All this we learn from a letter of Charles to the Pope, and that
of Nicholas to the King (May 23, 1278), ap. Raynaldus, *ib.*, an. 1278,
nn. 69–72. The King's promise to resign is dated at St. Peter's whither
he had no doubt gone to discuss the matter with the Pope. It was
sealed with a golden bull bearing the effigy of the King (May 24, 1278).
Cf. Chron. de Rebus, p. 370.

[2] " Numquid obduxit oblivio, que Urbi, que incolis nota dispendia
intulerunt hactenus peregrina regimina ? Numquid non hæc destructio
menium, deformatio veniens ex ruinis luce clarius manifestant." The
Constitution, ap. Theiner, *Cod. Diplom.*, i, 217.

[3] N. 370, ap. *ib.*, p. 215.

with honour. " We are desirous that the King and his
subjects should be honoured as our beloved sons." [1]

A few days later the cardinals were instructed to make
it known to the Roman people that, as far as the election
of the new Senator was concerned, the Pope had no
intention of taking any part. The election was, as usual,
to be made by the people.[2]   However, they at once
(Aug. 9) elected Nicholas himself Senator for life,[3] and
he, in turn, chose deputies to represent him. The Senator
who succeeded Charles was Matteo Rosso Orsini, the
Pope's brother.[4]   He was followed (1279) by Giovanni
Colonna and Pandulfo Savelli,[5] as we know from letters
sent by Nicholas to them, to the people of Rome, and
to the two cardinals.[6]   In his letter to the people Nicholas
declared that, both before he became Pope and afterwards,
he was animated with the desire of exalting the name
and honour of the Romans. He therefore exhorted them
to honour and obey the worthy Senators whom he
had chosen for them, or rather to honour him in them.

The new Senators entered into office on the first of
October (1279) ; and, in accordance with the Pope's
directions, took an oath to fulfil their duties properly,
to defend the rights of the Holy See within and without
the City, and to obey the Pope.

---

[1] *Ib.*   He also says that " Charles, through his own distinguished
merits, was dear to him among the other Princes of the earth ".

[2] Ep. " Visis " of Aug. 2, 1278, ap. Kaltenbrunner, *Actenstücke*,
n. 120, p. 134.   *Cf.* Gregorovius, *Rome*, v, p. 485.   " Non intendimus
. . . super hoc aliquod jus seu possessionem acquirere."

[3] " Nobis dispositionem vestri regiminis quoad vixerimus com-
misistis."   Ep. of Sept. 24, 1279, given in full by Vitale, *Senatori*,
i, 181 f.   *Cf.* Guido de Corvaria, *Hist. Pisan.*, ap. *R. I. SS.*, xxiv, p. 687.

[4] A letter of Nicholas of Sept. 26, 1278, shows that M. R. was already
Senator.   *Reg.*, n. 128, p. 42.   The Archives of Todi, ap. Vitale, *ib.*,
p. 179, show that M. R. was still Senator in Sept., 1279.

[5] Brother of Card. Jas. Savelli, afterwards Honorius IV.

[6] Epp. of Sept. 13 and 24, 1279, ap. Onof. Panvinio, *De Gente
Sabella*, p. 45, ed. E. Celani, Rome, 1892, and Vitale, *l.c.*, p. 180 ff.

Besides having to regulate the City of Rome, Nicholas was called upon to regulate his own household. There was trouble between the *Mappularii* and the *Adextratores* " of the City " on the one hand and the *Servientes Nigri* " of the household of the lord Pope " on the other.[1] The former had given trouble in the early part of the century by their habit of extorting gifts from bishops and others who came to Rome to be consecrated,[2] and they now claimed all the *servitia* or dues paid by the said prelates when they were consecrated in Rome by the Pope. Their claim was disputed by the *Servientes Nigri*, and the matter was brought before the Pope. Whether prevented by his early death or not, Nicholas did not settle the dispute. It dragged on till 1288, when it was decided by his namesake, Nicholas IV. The claimants were to have the dues if there was a *Station* at the Church on the day on which the Pope consecrated the prelate ; otherwise the *Servientes Nigri* were to have all the dues.[3]

If Nicholas did not live long enough to settle the

---

[1] The *Adextratores* were guardians of the papal crown; the *Mappularii*, called also *Manipularii*, and no doubt so called from the white trappings of their horses, had to carry carpets and other articles for the use of the Pope in processions, and to take care of his mantle, mitre, etc., when he was celebrating. *Cf. Ordo Romanus XII.*, n. 45. The *Servientes Nigri* were so called not because they were black men, but because they were clad in black. They were contrasted with the *Servientes Albi* ; and, in an *Ordo Romanus* (No. XIV, c. 46) of the period, we read that these latter in processions led the horse on which the Pope rode and carried the case for his mitre, spurs, and umbrellas, hoods, etc., in case of rain ; whereas the *Servientes Nigri* carried on similar occasions different kinds of papal head-gear, faldstools, cushions, and hot and cold water, and towels, etc., for the washing of the Pope's hands. *Cf. supra*, Vol. XI, pp. 44–5.

[2] See a regulation of Innocent III. (1208), ap. Muratori, *Antiq. Med. Ævi*, vi, p. 459.

[3] Ap. *ib.*, p. 461. The decision was based on data from the *Liber Censuum* (rubrica libri censualis), and hence is also given in that document, vol. i, p. 593, ed. Fabre.

pecuniary claims between different bodies of his retainers, he was able about a month before his death to reassert the claim which, like all rulers ancient and modern, Innocent III. had already made to treasure-trove in the papal states.[1]   It had been reported to him that a treasure had been found in Campania.   Accordingly, "lest our right or that of the Roman Church should be lost," he at once commissioned a notary, and his nephew Orso Orsini, who is described as "our marshal (*of justice*)[2] and Rector of the Patrimony of Blessed Peter in Tuscany", to proceed to the spot, and make all enquiries regarding the supposed treasure.   Should it exist, the Commissioners were to use the spiritual and temporal forces necessary to obtain possession of it.[3]

[1] See his letter of May 11, 1199, cited in full, p. 29, by G. G. Bufferli, *La Regalia dei tesori ne' Pontificj Dominj*, Rome, 1778.

[2] Or " of the Curia ".   Orso is called " Marescalcus justitiæ " in a document given by Pinzi, *Viterbo*, vol. ii, p. 361.

[3] Ep. of July 14, 1280, ap. Bufferli, p. 30 f.

CHAPTER III.

THE EMPIRE. THE ROMAGNA AND TUSCANY. CHARLES
OF ANJOU. THE CRUSADES.

ALTHOUGH Dante freely blamed Rudolf and his son Rudolf, and negotiations with Nicholas, 1278. for suffering "Through greediness of yonder realms detained, The garden of the Empire to run to waste ",[1] it was not, at any rate, altogether the fault of that King if he was not at least crowned Emperor.

Within three weeks after his election, and even before the dispatch of the official notice of his election to the King of the Romans, Nicholas wrote Rudolf a long letter (Dec. 12, 1277).[2] He began by assuring the King of the Romans that he was so anxious about certain matters that he could not wait to give either the cardinals or himself the little rest which they badly needed after the trying conclave, nor to observe the ordinary custom of the Roman Church, according to which the formal notices of the election of a new Pope should precede the dispatch of all other kinds of letters. However, he could not, he said, wait for formalities, and so at once discussed the political situation with his brethren. Following their discussions, he earnestly exhorted Rudolf to peace with his dearest son Charles, and, in view of what Gregory X. had done to secure him the kingdom, and of previous negotiations, finally to settle the Romagna question.[3]

---

[1] *Purg.*, vi, 104 ff. *Cf. ib.*, vii, 94 : Rudolf " who might have healed The wounds whereof fair Italy hath died ".

[2] In full ap. Theiner, *Cod. Diplom.*, i, p. 223, n. 382. It is there wrongly assigned to 1278 instead of 1277.

[3] Nicholas summed up all the previous correspondence on the question. *Cf. supra*, pp. 19, 44.

As soon as he had received this letter, and before he could have received the official information of the election of Nicholas, the King nominated Conrad, the provincial Franciscan Minister of Germany, to be his proctor to him. In appointing Conrad, the King declared that, " as a devoted son of the Roman Church," he recognized the favours he had received " from God and His Vicar, the Pope of Rome ". He renewed " to our most holy father the lord Pope Nicholas III." all the concessions and privileges which he and his predecessors had hitherto granted. At the same time, " to clear his conscience," he revoked all that had been done by himself or his agents contrary to the said concessions, and faithfully promised not in any way to interfere with the Pope's agents in dealing with them (Jan. 19, 1278).[1] Then, in commending his envoys to Nicholas, Rudolf declared that they had been commissioned to treat not only about " the principal affair " (of his coronation), but also about terms of friendship with Charles, and all other matters that concern the Christian Commonwealth which have to be promoted by the Pope.[2]

On May 4 (1278) the King's plenipotentiary, Conrad, was received by Nicholas in full consistory at the Vatican palace ; and there in his master's name, in the presence of the Pope and his cardinals, and a number of German and Italian bishops and nobles, Conrad solemnly renewed the oath which Rudolf had sworn at Lausanne to restore the Romagna.[3] Further, some three weeks later, Rudolf, recalling the fact that his predecessors, in gratitude for favours received from the Apostolic See, especially " for transferring to them the Empire from the Greeks ",

[1] " Procuratorium Regis," n. 182, ap. M. G. LL., iii, pt. i, p. 167.

[2] Ep. of Jan. 19, ap. ib., p. 168, or Gerbert, p. 152.

[3] Cf. the documents ap. M. G. LL., l.c., pp. 169–73.

had made donations to it, formally revoked all that had been done by his officials which was in opposition to them.[1] The King of the Romans, still troubled by the opposition of the powerful Ottocar II., had no doubt of the value of the friendship of Nicholas who " had excommunicated all his adversaries, and in Rome had publicly proclaimed him emperor ".[2]

Then, in order, as he said, to avoid the obscurities which generalities are wont to cause, Nicholas requested Rudolf to issue a special document sealed with a golden bulla bearing his image in which, in order to make the extent of the donation clear, express mention should be made of " Ravenna, Emilia, Bobium (Sarsina), Cesena, Forumpopuli (Forli), Faventia (Faenza), Imola, Bologna, Ferrara, Comacchio, Adria and Gabellum, Rimini, Urbino, Montefeltre (now S. Leo, S.W. of S. Marino), and the territory of Balneum (Bagno di Romagna)",[3] and the districts appertaining to the aforesaid places. He was, moreover, requested to confirm the donation by another deed within eight days after his reception of the imperial crown.[4]

At the same time, in order to convince the King that he was not advancing any new claims, Nicholas forwarded to him copies of the donations of Louis, Otho, and Henry, and assured him that he had shown the originals to his envoy, Conrad,[5] whom he exhorted to

Copies of donations sent to Rudolf.

[1] Cf. Rudolf's letter of May 29 to Nicholas " cum filialis obeditionis reverentia, devotissima pedum oscula beatorum ". Ib., p. 177.

[2] Such at least is the language of the Annals of Colmar, an. 1278, ap. Boehmer, Fontes, ii, p. 12.

[3] The " territorium balnense " is south of Forli and almost equally west of San Marino. Cf. Shepherd, Hist. Atlas, map 90 (inset).

[4] Ep. 193, p. 178, ap. ib. In a later letter, ap. ib., n. 196, p. 184, he asks that the confirmation be made on the King's coronation day or on the day after, and that it receive the assent of the lords spiritual and temporal of Germany. Though always hoping to come to Italy (cf. epp. 240, 269, ib.), Rudolf never entered it.

[5] Ep. 194, p. 181, ap. ib.

the greatest care in the conduct of the important negotiations with which he was entrusted.[1]

The first step taken by the King's plenipotentiaries was, at the request of the Pope,[2] to declare null and void all the oaths of allegiance, etc., which the King's chancellor, also called Rudolf, had exacted from the people of Bologna and the Romagna.[3] They next duly obtained from Rudolf the formal confirmation of all that they had done, and of all that he himself had promised at Lausanne (Aug. 29, 1278).[4] By these documents the authority of the Pope was formally recognized over the country from Radicofani to Ceperano, the March of Ancona, the Duchy of Spoleto, the territory of the Countess Matilda, the county of Bertinoro, the exarchate of Ravenna, the Pentapolis, the Massa Trabaria, including Bologna, Imola, etc.

Of course, all the questions, such as that of the Vicariate of Tuscany,[5] that arose in connection with such extensive territories were not settled at once, and negotiations went on about them till the close of September, 1279.[6] In securing the adhesion of the German nobles to the donation, even the language question caused difficulty, and Nicholas had to authorize his envoys to use interpreters.[7]

---

[1] *Ib.*, n. 195, p. 183.   [2] *Ib.*, n. 202, p. 188.

[3] *Ib.*, nn. 200 and 201, p. 186 f.

[4] *Ib.*, nn. 197–9, 206–9.   [5] *Cf. infra*, p. 117.

[6] *Ib.*, nn. 216–31, documents ranging from Nov. 17, 1278, to Sept. 27, 1279.

[7] *Ib.*, n. 219, p. 202. *Cf.* ep. 220, p. 202 f., a letter to the electors who appear as the Marquis of Brandenburg, the Duke of Saxony, the Duke of Bavaria count palatine of the Rhine, and the three arch- bishops of Trier, Cologne, and Mainz. Henry of Wittelsbach, Duke of Lower Bavaria, voted in place of Ottocar, King of Bohemia, who had been aiming at the Empire himself. In 1290 Rudolf decided that the seventh vote for the election of the King of the Romans belonged to the King of Bohemia, and that the dukes of Bavaria and the County Palatine should have but one vote between them.

Rudolf also undertook not to interfere in matters strictly ecclesiastical, such as the election of bishops, the right of free ecclesiastical appeal to Rome, etc., and not to trouble the vassals of the Church, especially " the magnificent Charles, King of Sicily ".[1] Following the example of their head, the Princes of the Empire, in gratitude to the Holy See for giving the imperial dignity to Germany, and proclaiming the Empire " to be that lesser light in the Church militant which is illuminated by the greater, i.e. by Christ's Vicar ", confirmed on their own behalf the grants of their King.[2]

The principle of cordial union between the Empire and the Papacy was at length securely laid down, and was sincerely acted upon by Rudolf. If only that glorious ideal of a universal supreme spiritual power acting in harmony with a universal supreme temporal power had been suffered to expand, what a path would have been opened for the onward march of a real civilization, and what an obstacle would have been erected against the prevalence of the cruel wars among the nations which have brought such ruin to mankind !

On paper, at any rate, Nicholas was lord of the Romagna, " the most delightful and fertile of all the provinces of Italy," according to Dante's commentator, Benvenuto da Imola, but, at the same time, the most

Trouble in enforcing papal rule in the Romagna.

[1] *Ib.*, n. 223, Feb. 14, 1279.

[2] *Ib.*, n. 225, p. 212. " Hic est illud luminare minus in firmamento militantis ecclesie per luminare majus, Christi vicarium, illustratum." *Cf.* n. 226, p. 214, the separate letter of Louis, Duke of Bavaria, March 19, 1279. " Hic (the Empire) est qui materialem gladium ad ipsius nutum excutit et convertit, ut ejus presidio pastorum pastor adjutus oves sibi creditas spirituali gladio communiat, temporali refrenet . . . ad vindicta malefactorum, laudem vero credentium et bonorum."

Bernard Guidonis justly assigns the happy termination of the Romagna restoration to " the prudent management " of Nicholas. *Vit. Nich.*, *l.c.*, p. 606.

restless.[1]　This writer assures us that "after it came
into the hands of the tyrants it had never known rest,
especially after Nicholas caused it to be given to him by
the emperor Rudolf". For its restlessness he assigns
four reasons. First the avarice of its bishops, who
sell now one estate, now another, and favour first one
tyrant and then another, which brings about a constant
change of officials. Then there was the wickedness of
the tyrants themselves who were constantly fighting
and oppressing their subjects. Thirdly, there was the
fertility of the soil which attracted all kinds of adventurers
out for plunder, and, lastly, in the inhabitants themselves
there was a deep-seated envy of one another. In all
this there is much truth, but we may doubt whether the
turmoil in the Romagna increased after it was taken
over by Nicholas, seeing that we are assured by the
strictly contemporary Saba that, in the days of Nicholas,
there was such peace in the world " and especially in Italy,
that it seemed to have been sent directly from heaven ".[2]

Bologna.　　　The chief source of Guelf, and so, more or less, of
ecclesiastical power in the Romagna, was Bologna [3];
and, in Bologna, the party of the Geremei which was
generally in power during a period of about fifty years
(1274–1327). Opposed to the family of the Geremei
was that of the Ghibelline Lambertazzi, led by the famous
count Guido da Montefeltro, who, says Villani, "as a
tyrant lorded it over the province." [4] He was that
" man at arms " whose deeds " less bespake the nature

---

[1] Comment. in Dant., Inf., xxvii, ap. Muratori, Antiq. Med. Ævi,
i, pp. 1102–3, or, ed. Lacaita, ii, p. 301.

[2] Hist., vi, c. 13. "Tanta pax mundo, maxime Italiæ tempore
pontificatus d. Nicolai quasi cœlitus emissa donatur."

[3] The Annals of Bologna thus briefly record the restoration of their
city to the Pope : " Bononienses dederunt (1278) civitatem et comitatus
in perpetuum d. Papæ, salvis honnibus (sic) racionibus quas haberet
communi Bononie in Romagna. Et sic juratum fuit in publico
aremgo." Ap. R. I. SS., t. xviii, pt. i, vol. ii, p. 200, new ed.

[4] Chron., vii, 53 (54).

of the lion than the fox " whom Dante has wrongfully plunged into hell.[1] On June 15, 1278, Nicholas wrote to one of his agents in the Romagna, the Dominican, brother Lawrence of Todi, to say that he had heard that Count Guido with the citizens of Forli,[2] the exiles of Bologna (the Lambertazzi), and others had invaded the district of Ravenna. As such action will prejudice the rights of the Roman Church, and cause injury to the locality, Lawrence must endeavour to persuade the Count to withdraw, using ecclesiastical censures if he should deem it expedient.[3]

But, in dealing with such men as Guido da Montefeltro, Nicholas did not trust altogether to men of peace and spiritual arms. Hence he did not content himself with sending two other ecclesiastics, his chaplain, Geoffrey of Anagni, and the Dominican, John of Viterbo, with letters to the different cities informing them that the Roman Church had re-entered into possession of the Romagna, etc., and calling on them to tender him their allegiance,[4] but he sent as his rector there his nephew Berthold Orsini [5] with troops partly furnished by his vassal, Charles of Anjou.[6] A little later (Sept. 25)

Nicholas sends a rector with troops into the Romagna.

---

[1] *Inf.*, xxvii, 64 ff. *Cf.* the commentary by Benvenuto da Imola, ap. Muratori, *Antiq. Med. Ævi*, i, p. 1109 ff. Dante put Guido in Hell on account of the advice he is *supposed* to have given Boniface VIII. to seize Palestrina, the city of his enemies the Colonna, by treachery.

[2] The *Annals of Forli*, ap. *R. I. SS.*, xxii, pt. ii, p. 30, new ed., call Guido "invictus capitaneus communis Forlivii et generalis Guerre pro parte dicti communis ". *Cf.* Kaltenbrunner, n. 117, for Nicholas' commission to John.

[3] Ep. ap. Theiner, *Cod. Diplom.*, i, p. 212.

[4] Epp. June 20 and 22, 1278, ap. *ib.*, p. 213, nn. 366–7.

[5] Ep. Sept. 24, ap. Theiner, *l.c.*, n. 374.

[6] Ep. of Aug. to Charles, ap. Kaltenbrunner, n. 129, and of Sept. 24, ap. Theiner, *l.c.*, n. 375. *Cf.* the Archives of Charles, ap. Riccio, *Il Regno di C.*, an. 1278, Aug., pp. 48–9. Charles orders Guillaume l'Etendard to take 300 men-at-arms to Romagna for the service of the Pope.

Nicholas appointed another nephew, cardinal Latinus of Ostia, his legate in Tuscany and Romagna,[1] and exhorted him, " whom God had adorned with remarkable gifts," and the rector Berthold to work in harmony —the cardinal presiding and using spiritual arms, and the Rector wielding the power of the sword. Their near relationship, he said, ought to help their united action.[2]

Submission of the Romagna, 1278. As a result of the vigorous action of Nicholas, the people of the Communes of Romagna, called together " by the tolling of the bell and the voice of the herald ", speaking generally, proclaimed themselves " faithful subjects of the Roman Church as they had been before of the Roman Empire ".[3] Even the redoubtable Guido submitted,[4] and Latinus was ordered to absolve him from the sentence of excommunication which he had incurred.[5] Berthold, and, after he fell ill, his son Gentilis,[6] went about all over the Romagna receiving the keys of the cities, taking possession of the fortresses, and appointing loyal podestàs and local rectors. In those cities in which there were factions, deputies were chosen from both sides, and sent to the Pope himself at Viterbo. When their differences had been settled, they returned to their province, and all the males from fourteen to seventy took an oath of fealty to the Pope and the Roman Church. All this we know from the chronicler Peter Cantinelli who took part in these proceedings himself.[7] He also tells us how

---

[1] Ep. ap. Theiner, *l.c.*, n. 379.   *Cf.* ep. 378.

[2] *Ib.*, n. 377. " Ceterum cum sitis tanta sanguinis et specialis sinceritatis idemptitate conjuncti," etc.

[3] *Ib.*, n. 369, July 27, 1278. " Et omnes juraverunt ejus (the Rector's) precepta et Ecclesiæ." *Chron. de Rebus* or *Ann. Placent. Gib.*, p. 369.   [4] Kaltenbrunner, *l.c.*, n. 138.

[5] Theiner, *l.c.*, Sept. 25, 1278.   [6] Kaltenbrunner, n. 138.

[7] *Chron.*, ap. *R. I. SS.*, t. xxviii, pt. ii, p. 28 ff., and the extra authorities there cited in the notes. *Cf. Annal. Foroliv.*, *l.c.*, p. 32 ff., and also the *Chron.* of Marcha di Marco, ap. *R. I. SS.*, t. xvi, pt. iii, p. 14, new ed. Marcha di M. Battagli was a Ghibelline, † between 1370 and 1376.

the work of settlement and pacification of the province was helped by a general assembly (*parlamentum*) before Berthold, and by banquets given by the legate Latinus, at which were present great numbers of clerics and laymen including such magnates as Guido da Montefeltro.[1]

Unfortunately this work of the general pacification of Romagna was to no little extent spoilt by the fierce feuds between the Geremei and Lambertazzi at Bologna. Their quarrels embroiled others, ruffled the temper of Nicholas, and caused a further drain upon his already almost empty treasury.[2]

To further the cause of peace in that important city, Nicholas named Berthold himself its podestà,[3] and on June 29, 1279, the Rector of the Province entered the city with great pomp and was most honourably received.[4] In his efforts to heal the deadly faction between the Geremei and the Lambertazzi, he was powerfully helped by the eloquence of the Dominican, brother Lawrence of Todi.[5] Representatives of the two families met together in the Church of St. Dominic ; and peace was soon after solemnly concluded between the two factions in presence of the podestà, cardinal Latinus, and a number of bishops (Aug. 17, 1279).[6] The terms of this peace, thus happily inaugurated, had been laid down by Nicholas in a long document which he had issued on May 29, 1279. He begins by saluting the city as a "magna parens heroum", especially of those

[1] *Ib.*, p. 30 ; Feb., 1279.

[2] " Cameram quoque nostram ad presens quasi exaustam multis expensis, a debitorum oneribus preservare studemus." Ep. Nov. 16, 1278, ap. Kalt., n. 152.

[3] Ep. of June 1, 1279, ap. *ib.*, n. 158. Berthold was to enter on his duties on June 29. *Cf.* nn. 159, 160.

[4] Cantinelli, *l.c.*, p. 30.

[5] *Cf. Annal. Bonon.*, *l.c.*, pp. 199–200.

[6] Cantinelli, *l.c.*, pp. 30–1. Nicholas had prepared the way for the coming of Latinus by letters of Dec. 13, 1278, and of Jan. 30, 1279, ap. Theiner, *Cod.*, i, nn. 383, 386.

heroes of learning for which it has ever been remarkable.[1]
He then proceeds to decree that the exiled Lambertazzi
must be allowed to return to Bologna, and that for a
time, a year or so, in order that things may settle down,
he will himself take over the management of the city.
For that purpose he will send a representative, with
five judges, seven notaries, three assessors (*socii*), and
a suitable household, for whom the people must provide
a salary of seven thousand pounds of the money of
Bologna for a year. The city must also maintain for
his representative a guard of forty men.[2]

The Lambertazzi return and are again expelled.

As a consequence of the peace, the exiled Lambertazzi
returned with no little honour to Bologna in September,
but, though Berthold did all he could to make their
reception really cordial, many of the Geremei viewed
their return with bitterness.[3] Before the year was out,
the two parties were at one another's throats, and the
Lambertazzi were again expelled (Dec. 22).[4]

Nicholas, we are told, and his letters prove it, was
very indignant with the two chief factions at this speedy
breaking of his peace, and at the excesses perpetrated
during the disturbance.[5] He ordered his legate cardinal

[1] The document is given by Theiner, *l.c.*, n. 389 (see certain amendments in n. 390), and in Cantinelli, *l.c.*, pp. 32–8. " Ipsa quidem civitas, inter alias Italicas speciali prerogativa fecunda, viros eminentis scientie, viros alti consilii, etc. . . . solet . . . propagatione quasi naturali, producere."

[2] " Habeat quoque XL beroarios pedites in expensis communis ejusdem." *Ib.*, p. 36.

[3] " Verumtamen multi et multi de parte Geremiorum non viderunt eos libenter, nec bono animo. D. tamen Bertuldus . . . fecit regimen suum honorifice." *Ib.*, p. 39.

[4] *Ib.*, pp. 40–1. The Chronicle of Este assigns the blame to the Lambertazzi, ap. *R. I. SS.*, t. xv, pt. iii, pp. 43–4, new ed. *Cf.* Guido de Corvaria, *Hist. Pisan.*, p. 688, for dates.

[5] " De quo facto d. papa indignatus est contra Gereminos." *Chron. Placent.*, p. 373. *Cf.* epp. Nich. nn. 202–6, Jan. 16–18, 1280, ap. Kaltenbrunner. " Multos hinc inde patratos nepharios excessus audivimus." Ep. 204.

Latinus to return at once to Bologna, and to co-operate with Berthold in trying to discover which of the parties was responsible for the outbreak.[1] He exhorted the Geremei and the Lambertazzi to submit to the legate, whom he urged to be impartial himself and to strive to induce Berthold to such cautious action as, if possible, not to render himself suspected of leaning to any party.[2]

Latinus was at the moment in Florence trying to make peace there, and had no heart to go back into such a fiery furnace of faction as Bologna. He accordingly begged to be excused. Nicholas, however, insisted on his proceeding to the storm-centre without delay.[3] Again Latinus made excuses. In vain. " In virtue of obedience," wrote the Pope, " you must go as soon as possible " (April 1, 1280).[4] Meanwhile, Nicholas took the preliminary steps to raise an army,[5] and Berthold had commenced to act in the matter on his own account. On January 12 he held a " parliament " of the whole province at Faenza, condemned the party of the Geremei, inflicted fines upon them, and ordered them to appear before him and submit to his decisions.[6] On the arrival of cardinal Latinus in the Romagna (April), he and the Count summoned representatives of the two factions before them at Imola (May 18, 1280). This time, however, the cardinal could effect nothing. Fighting recommenced in the province, and Nicholas died before his energy could provide a remedy (Aug. 22).[7]

Latinus fails to make peace.

[1] Epp. 202–3.

[2] Epp. 204–6. In the instructions sent to Latinus by the auditor " litteram contradictarum " we are told " amaritudine cordis ejusdem domini (the Pope) super facto Bononiensi ".

[3] *Ib.*, n. 210, Jan. 26.   [4] *Ib.*, n. 226.

[5] *Ib.*, nn. 213–14, March 1 and 2. *Cf.* n. 215, where Nicholas tells Latinus that he has asked Charles of Anjou " for a large body of soldiers "; and also n. 216, where, though Berthold is much blamed for what has happened, Nicholas declares his intention of putting down the contumacious by force if necessary.

[6] Cantinelli, *l.c.*, p. 41.   [7] *Ib.*, p. 42.

Berthold the scape-goat (?).

In all this affair, Berthold, at any rate, did not carry out the original instruction of his uncle so to conduct himself as not to appear to be partial to either of the factions. He succeeded in making himself appear partial to both. Nicholas told him that he was the more disturbed about the troubles at Bologna that some ascribed the outbreak to his carelessness or to his having absented himself from the city. He blamed him for cowardly withdrawing his officials immediately after the outbreak, and for the favour which he and his are said to have shown to the Lambertazzi. It is reported, wrote the indignant Pontiff, that you declared that you would only abandon Guido da Montefeltro and his party when Magdalen deserted Christ. There is grave danger of your partiality bringing disgrace on the house of Orsini.[1]

But whilst Nicholas was begging Berthold not to contaminate the solid Orsini body with the leaven of his partiality for the Lambertazzi, Cantinelli assures us that the people of the Romagna were unwilling to obey him " on account of his evil deeds and because he favoured the party of the Geremei ".[2] It would appear that Cantinelli was right. Not only is his testimony supported by that of Salimbene,[3] but Berthold is said to have restored to the Geremei for fifteen thousand pounds the hostages they had given him whilst he carried off to Rome (1281) those that the Lambertazzi had given him.[4]

---

[1] See the grave memorandum addressed to Berthold by Nicholas, ap. Kalt., n. 216.

[2] *L.c.*, p. 43.

[3] *Chron.*, p. 504.

[4] Cantinelli, *ib.*, and *Chron. Bonon.*, *l.c.*, p. 208. On the Bologna affair see also *Chron. Parmense*, ap. *R. I. SS.*, t. ix, pt. ix, p. 36 ; *Ann. Mantuani*, ap. *M. G. SS.*, xix, p. 28 ; the later *Chron. Faventinum*, ap. Mettarelli's add. to Muratori, iii, p. 322 ; *Mem. Potest. Reg.*, ap. *R. I. SS.*, viii, p. 1146.

Whilst these stirring scenes were being enacted in the Romagna, Nicholas had also to fix his attention on the adjoining province on the western side of the Apennines, i.e. on Tuscany. During the vacancy of the Empire, Clement IV., for the sake of order, had nominated Charles of Anjou as the imperial vicar in Tuscany (May, 1268). Now, however, that there was a recognized heir of the Empire, it was felt that even if, through " the territory of the Countess Matilda ", the Pope had considerable rights in Tuscany, the imperial rights therein had to be acknowledged. Indeed, it is said that Nicholas asked Charles to resign his office in Tuscany on the ground that unless he did so negotiations could not be carried on with Rudolf.[1] In any case, Charles had already sworn to resign his office within a month after the notification to him of a new Emperor.[2] We are further told that, when Nicholas first thought of requesting Charles to resign the Senatorship and the Vicariate, he sent a cardinal to sound him on the subject (before May, 1278). On receiving his envoy's report that Charles was loyally prepared to fall in with his wishes, he exclaimed : " Ah ! he has learnt loyalty from his home in France, clearness of intellect from Spain, and care in the use of words by his intercourse with the Roman curia. We may be able to get the better of others, but never of him." [3] However this may be, it is certain that Charles, that " noble arm of the Church ", as the Pope's biographer calls him,[4] did resign his position in

The Vicariate of Tuscany.

---

[1] Cf. Raynaldus, Annal., 1278, n. 67.

[2] " Et si forsan . . . Imperatorem . . . a Sede apostolica approbatum regnare contigerit, aut per Sedem eamdem præfatum nobis officium interdici, nos eodem officio ultra mensem . . . non utemur." Ap. Raynaldus, Ann., 1267, n. 8.

[3] Will. of Nangis, De Gest. Phil. III., i, 25, ap. RR. FF. SS., xx, p. 512. He repeats the story in his Chron., ad an. 1279. See also Paulinus Min., Chron., ap. Muratori, Antiq. Med. Ævi., iv, 1010.

[4] " Nobilem ecclesiæ pugilem." Vit. Nicol., ap. L. P., ii, p. 458.

Tuscany (Sept., 1278).[1] It was not, however, till after the death of Nicholas that Rudolf nominated bishop John von Gurk and his chancellor, Rudolf, his vicars in imperial Tuscany (Jan. 5, 1281).[2] Later, in order to facilitate the division between the imperial rights in Tuscany and those belonging to the Pope in virtue of the donation of Matilda,[3] he nominated the subdeacon, Percival of Lavagna, chaplain of Honorius IV. (Nov. 23, 1285), and then (Feb. 1, 1286) cardinal Matteo Rosso.[4]

Parties in
Florence.

But it was not only the question as to who should hold the highest civil authority in Tuscany that occupied the attention of Nicholas. It was also the position of parties in its chief city, Florence. What that position was can best be stated in the words of the most famous of its historians, Giovanni Villani.[5] " In these times," says the chronicler, " the Guelf magnates of Florence—having rest from their wars with victory and honour, and fattening on the goods of the exiled Ghibellines—began, by reason of pride and envy, to strive among themselves. Whence there arose many quarrels. . . . Among the greater of these was the contest between the house of the Ademari, who were very great and powerful on the one side, and

[1] Raymond de Poncellis was the last of the deputies of Charles in Tuscany. Cf. Reg., nn. 178, 303, 304. Saba, vi, c. 12, " Restituitur dominium Tusciæ Rodulpho."

[2] Cf. Böhmer-Redlich, Regest. Imp., vol. vi, n. 1252.

[3] On her territories ceded to Gregory VII. see her biographer, Donizo (ii, c. 6), Benvenuto da Imola on Dante, Purg., Cant. xxvii, v. 94, and a solemn deed in which the whole people of Piacenza (Sept., 1331) acknowledge " ipsam Civitatem cum toto districtu suo esse et fuisse et esse debere suppositari in dominio . . . temporali S. R. E." Ap. Della Istoria del Domin. Temp. nel Ducato di Parma et Piacenza, p. 291 ff.

[4] Percival is appointed " for the honour of holy mother Church . . . for the honour of the Holy Roman Empire . . . and in order that the way may be properly prepared by which we may go to receive the diadem of the Roman Empire." Cf. M. G. LL., iv, n. 371, p. 353. Cf. n. 378 from M. R.

[5] Chron., vii, 55 (56).

on the other the Tosinghi, the Donati and the Pazzi leagued together. Almost all the city was divided, . . . and the Guelf party was in great peril. Accordingly, the Commonwealth and the Captains of the Guelf party sent their solemn ambassadors to the court of Pope Nicholas in order that he might make peace and prevent the break up of the Guelf party. . . . In like manner the Ghibelline exiles from Florence sent their envoys to him to beg him to enforce the treaty which Pope Gregory X. had made between them and the Guelfs." Nicholas, accordingly, confirmed the treaty, and ordered his legate cardinal Latinus to leave the Romagna and proceed to Florence.[1] It was some time before the cardinal could fulfil this commission as he was in the midst of the troubles on account of which Nicholas had sent him into the Romagna.[2] At length, however, he was free to leave the eastern province, and on October 8, 1279, he entered Florence escorted by three hundred horse. He was received by the Florentines with the greatest honour, and he exerted on them his great oratorical powers " in a very noble speech ". The effect of his words was wonderful. Guelfs and Ghibellines kissed each other " on the mouth ", terms of peace between the two parties were drawn up, and the Ghibellines were allowed to return and receive their property. Latinus also made special terms of peace and amity between the individual citizens, and brought about several marriages between members of the

---

[1] *Ib.* Villani describes Latinus as a man " of great authority and learning, and highly considered by the Pope ". We have for the most part used the translation of Miss R. E. Selfe. *Cf.* the letters of Nicholas to the Florentines (Aug. 28, 1278) and to Latinus (Sept. 25, 1278), ap. Kaltenbrunner, nn. 128 and 131. Both the " intrinseci et extrinseci " of Florence have put their differences in his hands.

[2] Ep. Oct. 18, 1278, ap. Kalt., n. 134. *Cf. ib.,* n. 173, July 14, 1279, where Latinus is reminded of the Pope's wish that he should go to Florence.

different factions.   Although he had for a brief space
to return to the Romagna (April, 1280),[1] Latinus did
his work so well that " the city of Florence abode thereafter long time in peaceful and good and tranquil
state ", and he himself won honour from the people
and the Pope.[2]

Peace
between
Rudolf and
Charles.

Perhaps the most delicate task that Nicholas had to
undertake was to adjust the relations between Rudolf
and Charles of Anjou.   He had to deal with two powerful
men whose respective aims might soon bring them into
a collision which would be fatal to the peace of Europe,
and to any hope of a great combined Crusade.   As emperor,
Rudolf would naturally expect that his influence in
Italy should be paramount.   As restorer and mainstay
of the Guelf power in the peninsula, Charles conceived
that he was its natural overlord.   It is true that when
Nicholas became Pope, Rudolf was hampered by the
strenuous opposition of Ottocar of Bohemia.   But, if
not to the great grief of the Bohemians, at any rate to
the peace of the Empire, their King was defeated and
slain at the terrible battle of Marchfield in the very
first year of Nicholas' pontificate (Aug. 26, 1278).[3]

Though even Rudolf himself praised the great valour
of the " magnificent Ottocar ",[4] it would seem that,

[1] He appears to have been back in Florence in June, 1280. *Cf.* ep.
Nich., June 16, 1280, ap. Kalt., n. 228.

[2] Villani, *ib.*, and ep. Nich., Oct. 10, 1279, ap. Kalt., n. 189. *Cf.*
Ferrens, *Hist. de Florence*, ii, p. 191 ff. ; Villani, *Hist. of Florence*,
i, p. 257 ff., ed. 1901.   " Length of time " of duration of peace at this
period in an Italian city is quite relative, and hence Ptolemy of Lucca,
Annales, ap. *R. I. SS.*, xi, p. 1292, says the cardinal's peace lasted only
" a short time ".

[3] " Bohemia plange !   O Moravia luge, tantum perdidisse honorem
protecta quondam sub clipeo regis Ottokari."   Such are the words of
Henry of Heimburg, *Chron.*, ap. Emler, *Fontes Rer. Bohem.*, iii, p. 316.

[4] See his letter to Nicholas announcing his victory, ap. Gerbert,
n. 15, p. 161.   " Ille rex magnificus cum victoria vitam perdidit."
The most picturesque account of the defeat of O. is given in the *Contin.
of the Chron.* of Magnus, ap. *M. G. SS.*, xvii, p. 533 f.

from the beginning of the pontificate, Nicholas had no doubt as to the ultimate triumph of Rudolf. Hence, as we have seen, his very first request to him was that he should come to an accommodation with King Charles [1]; and he did not rest until, in the last year of his too short pontificate, he saw their differences adjusted. He eased the situation in Italy for Rudolf as against the King of Sicily by seeing to it that Charles resigned the Senatorship of Rome and the Vicariate of Tuscany, and for Charles as against Rudolf by inducing the King of the Romans to increase the papal power by the restoration of the Romagna, etc. This much he was able to effect by reason of the goodwill which both Kings proved by their deeds that they had for the Holy See. But, besides the general question of the relations of both of them to Italy, there remained to be adjusted Charles's position as Count of Provence, etc., in the kingdom of Arles, or Burgundy, over which Rudolf claimed suzerainty. To straighten out differences of aims and ambitions between two such neighbours was not likely to prove an easy task, as Nicholas no doubt gathered from a remark in one of Rudolf's first letters to him. The King of the Romans informed the Pope that he had sent his envoys to arrange terms of peace with the illustrious Charles, according to his recommendations " if they squared with his desires ".[2]

Despite this promise of difficulty, Nicholas braced himself up to continue the efforts for peace between the two potentates which, by command of Hadrian V., he had begun as cardinal (1276). Charles's position as count of Provence was not too easy to deal with,

---

[1] *Cf. supra*, p. 105.

[2] Ep. 9 of Feb. 1, 1278, ap. Gerbert, p. 153. " Amicitia . . . juxta providentiæ vestræ consilium, si hoc voto nostro consideat, solidanda ! " The chief envoy was Conrad Probus, the Franciscan minister-general of Germany.

as it was far from regular. On the one hand, he had, during the interregnum of the Empire, set aside its rights, and on the other he had ignored the claims of his three sisters-in-law, Eleanor, queen of England, Sancia, duchess of Cornwall, and Margaret, widow of St. Louis IX., to rights in Provence. The King of Sicily, therefore, was naturally keen to secure the good offices of the Pope in order to effect a good understanding with Rudolf, and it was not long before the latter was equally ready to avail himself of them. Declaring that he believed in the Pope's complete impartiality and real goodness of heart, he entrusted to him the drawing up of the terms of friendship between Charles and himself. He also yielded to the insistence of the Pope that the friendship should be cemented by a renewal of the marriage-contract between his daughter, Clementia, and Charles Martel, the grandson of Charles of Sicily. This was on Sept. 5, 1278.[1] Negotiations between the two Kings, and between Charles and Margaret of France with the Pope as intermediary, went on till, in the last year of his pontificate, Nicholas was able at any rate to issue the dispensation for the marriage (Jan. 23, 1280).[2] The dispensation was needed, as both Charles and Clementia had meanwhile been betrothed to others.

Nicholas worked with all his accustomed energy to rivet the good understanding between the two sovereigns ; and, that no time might be lost, he on one occasion begged Charles to take up his abode in some place close to the border of his kingdom.[3] At one moment he was

---

[1] Ep. ap. *M. G. LL.*, iv, p. 194. *Cf.* ep. of Dec., 1279, ap. Redlich, *Briefsammlung*, n. 129.

[2] Ap. Kalt., n. 209, p. 207.

[3] Ep. Nov. 22, 1278, ap. *ib.*, n. 139, p. 154, or ap. *M. G. LL.*, iv, p. 200. " Ad hec . . . continuis vigiliis nostra studia convertentes, etc." The documents regarding this treaty are given both by Kalt. and the *Monumenta, l.c.*, p. 222 ff.

trying to soothe Margaret of France [1] ; at another com-
plaining to both Charles and Margaret that they had
sent to him envoys bound by secret instructions instead
of true plenipotentiaries [2] ; then drawing up and dispatching drafts of a treaty that would satisfy all parties [3] ;
and then, to prove to Rudolf his regard for him, urging
the German Princes to active loyalty towards their
King. [4]

Ably seconded in Germany by his envoy Paul, bishop
of Tripoli, and later, at Rudolf's own request, by his
legate cardinal Jerome, [5] and in Sicily with Charles by
cardinal Matteo Rosso (Orsini) and the notary, Benedict
Gaetani, Nicholas had the satisfaction of seeing his
heroic efforts crowned with success. He did not, however,
live to see their complete formal accomplishment. It
was not till March 4, 1281, that Clementia was solemnly
espoused to the young Charles Martel at Bologna [6] ;
and it was not till May 24, 1281, that Martin IV. solemnly
confirmed the treaty between the two Kings, and sent
duly certified copies of it to each of them. [7] By the terms
of the treaty, such claims to Provence as might be held
by Margaret, the widow of St. Louis IX., were practically
put aside, and Rudolf acknowledged Charles as Count
of Provence and Forcalquier. Margaret was not to

[1] Ep. May 7, 1279, ap. K., nn. 156–7.

[2] *Ib.*, nn. 217–19, March 7, 1280.

[3] Ep. June 3, 1279, ap. K., n. 162. *Cf.* n. 208, Jan. 25, 1280, and
nn. 211–12, Feb. 3, 1280.

[4] Ep. June 3, 1279, ap. *ib.*, nn. 166–7.

[5] See the letter of Nicholas to Rudolf of July 6, 1280, ap. Wadding,
Ann., v, p. 478.

[6] Cantinelli, *Chron.*, an. 1281, p. 46. *Cf.* the letter of the cardinals
during the vacancy of the Holy See to the Communes of Tuscany to
receive her well. Ep. Feb. 11, 1281, ap. Kalt., n. 232. See also Saba,
vi, 13 ; *Lib. Reg. Paduæ*, pp. 334–5 ; *Ann. S. Rudbert.*, ap. *M. G. SS.*,
ix, p. 806.

[7] See his solemn act of confirmation enclosing the various articles
of the treaty, ap. Kalt., p. 243 ff.

disturb Charles in the possession of these territories, though she might lay any claims she might have before the imperial court. But in any case the final word on the subject was to be with the Pope.[1] Then, " saving in all things the rights of the Roman pontiff and the Apostolic See," Rudolf recognized the position of Charles in the two Sicilies, and agreed not to help his enemies, except such enemy might be the Holy See. In return, Charles was not to help any enemy of the King of the Romans, unless, again, that enemy might be the Holy See. And if any disagreement were to spring up between them, they were not to have recourse to arms, but were to refer their differences to the Roman pontiff.[2] In concluding his side of the treaty, Rudolf declared that in the matter of the observance of all its articles he freely submitted " spiritually and temporally " to the decisions of the Roman pontiff.[3]

On his side, Charles undertook to respect the King of the Romans and the Empire, and not to help his enemies, and at the same time gave permission to all his subjects to oppose him should he venture to act

[1] " In omnibus autem et singulis supradictis Romano pontifici . . . reservantes ejus . . . declarationem . . . nos servaturos obligamus." *Ib.*, p. 249, in Rudolf's statement to Margaret. *Cf.* E. Boutaric, " Marguerite de Provence " in *Rev. des Quest. Hist.*, 1867, p. 417 ff., from whose charming article it appears that Margaret only got justice after the death of Charles of Anjou in 1285. *Cf.* also P. Fournier, *Le Royaume d'Arles*, p. 229 ff., Paris, 1891. Nicholas, too, in his instructions to his legate Paul of Tripoli as to the articles of the treaty had merely directed that he should require a declaration from Rudolf that, in his recognition of Charles, no prejudice " in jure " was to arise against Queen Margaret. See these instructions (June 7, 1279), ap. *M. G. LL.*, iv, p. 226.

[2] " Quod si, quod absit, aliqua discordia inter nos et Sicilie regem oriretur, unus non movebit propter hoc guerram alii . . . sed nos et dictus rex Sicilie ad Romanum pontificem recurremus, et . . . stabimus dicto . . . Romani P." *Ib.*, p. 259.

[3] *Ib.*

against the King or Emperor. Though, because his son, Charles the Lame, had married May, the daughter of Stephen V. of Hungary, it was to be lawful for him to assist in the defence of Hungary, he was not to be allowed to help any vassal of the French King against Rudolf. He also agreed to submit differences to the Pope in the same manner as Rudolf had done,[1] and to pay to Rudolf the proper dues for Provence and Forcalquier.[2]

It appears that ultimately, with these provinces and others, the old kingdom of Vienne or Arles was to be reconstituted ; and, if Ptolemy of Lucca is to be relied on, to be given to Charles Martel and his wife Clementia. This was to be Clementia's dower which had been left in the hands of Nicholas to fix.[3] This kingdom, more frequently known as the kingdom of Burgundy, situated more or less between the Rhone, the Saône, and the Alps, would, as a vassal state, have been a considerable support to the Empire. It had come into existence in the ninth century, but " for two hundred years and more " had been of no value to the Empire.[4] That state of affairs was not destined to be altered. The new scheme did not mature. The power of France and not of the Empire was to prevail in the " Kingdom of Arles ".

It was, however, the idea of revivifying this kingdom which perhaps inspired the scheme which Ptolemy of Lucca attributed to Nicholas III.[5] It is certain

The kingdom of Arles or Vienne.

[1] *Ib.*, p. 262.

[2] *Ib.*, p. 264.

[3] " Fiat matrimonium olim tractatum per d. Gregorium . . . De dote sit in beneplacito Rom. Pontificis." Instructions of Nicholas to Paul, bishop of Tripoli, June 7, 1279, ap. *M. G. LL.*, iv, p. 229. *Cf.* Ptolemy of Lucca, *H. E.*, xxiii, c. 34, and *Ann.*, p. 1292.

[4] So said " John, Duke of Saxony " in giving his approval to the formation of the new kingdom to be given to Charles Martel and Clementia " in feodum ". Ep. of Sept. 5, 1281, ap. *M. G. LL.*, iv, p. 253.

[5] N. " ut tradunt historiæ, *cum Rodulpho* . . . tractat super novitatibus faciendis in Imperio, ut totum Imperium in quatuor

that before he became Pope the long vacancy of the
Empire and the evils resulting therefrom had set men
thinking. Hence the famous Humbert de Romanis,
in the memoir which he prepared for Gregory X.,
and which we have already cited, wrote as follows :
" Among many peoples (*nationes*) who are subject to
the Empire, such as those who once formed the Kingdom
of Arles, and others, countless evils have arisen from the
want of a sufficient number of overlords (*domini generales*)
to whom they could have recourse. Hence it seems
desirable that some overlord should be created for such
peoples, or that the Emperor, or, when the Empire is
vacant, the Pope, should provide a Vicar for them to
whom they could appeal in grave necessities." Such
are his words as they appear in the edition of his work
printed by Brown.[1] But in the extract from the same
work cited by Raynaldus,[2] we read : " When the Empire
is vacant a vicar should be nominated ; or, in future,
the King of Germany (*Teutonia*) should be constituted
not by election but by succession. Then, content with
Germany, he should allow one or two kings to be elected
for Italy with the consent of the prelates and the communes . . ." From these extracts it is clear that what
Humbert wished to remedy was the abeyance of central
authority in the state. He had evidently no objection
to the Empire as such ; but, if the Empire proved to
be too large to be able to supply adequate authority
to its several great divisions, he wished that a sufficient
number of subordinate central authorities should be

dividatur partes, videlicet in regnum Alamanniæ, quod debebat posteris
Rodulphi perpetuari, in regnum Viennense . . . unum in Lombardia,
aliud vero in Tuscia." He insinuates that the last two kingdoms
were to be given to the relatives of N., ap. *H. E.*, xxiii, c. 34.

[1] *Opusc. Tripartitum*, iii, c. 11, ap. *Fascic. Rerum Expetend.*, vol. ii,
p. 228.

[2] *Annal.*, an. 1273, n. 6, note (1). Demski, *Nikolaus III.*, p. 169, n.,
gives yet another version.

created. The fact is that at this period thinking men were distressed at the evils which they saw were consequent on prolonged vacancies of central authority in the Church and in the State, and wished to provide against such vacancies. It was the sight of these evils that caused Gregory X. to push on the election of Rudolf and to introduce his conclave regulations. If then Nicholas turned his attention to devising a remedy against the disastrous results caused by a long vacancy of the imperial power, it would appear more consonant with papal tradition and practice that he should have thought of the provision of a number of imperial vicars, rather than of a number of independent kingdoms.[1]

In all his incessant and diplomatic efforts to promote peace everywhere, Nicholas had ever in view, as he declared to Philip the Rash of France,[2] the interests of the Holy Land. To push forward the raising of the Saracen tenth ordered by the Council of Lyons, he sent collectors into every country,[3] and urged bishops and others to induce their subjects to leave something in their wills for the cause of the Crusades.[4] He earnestly exhorted the Templars, the Hospitallers, and the Teutonic Knights to be zealous in the performance of their special duties, and to maintain a proper number of fighting

Zeal for the Crusades.

---

[1] Savio, *Niccolo III.*, nn. ix and x, properly relegates Ptolemy's assertion on this matter to the realm of fable.

[2] Ep. Dec. 3, 1278, *Reg.*, n. 392. He speaks of the " compassiones intimas, quas ad Terram ipsam in nostris precordiis tulimus " and of the *continual* thought and labour he had given to the promotion of peace (especially between Philip himself and Alfonso of Castile) in order that help might the more speedily be sent to the Holy Land.

[3] Potthast, n. 21304, April 9, 1278. Into Germany, see *Reg.*, n. 3 ; N. Italy, *ib.*, 14 ; Hungary, Poland, etc., *ib.*, n. 42, or Theiner, *Mon. Hung.*, i, n. 541 ; Portugal, *Reg.*, nn. 480–1, etc.

[4] *Reg.*, nn. 169, 173. See the form of the oath which Nicholas required to be taken by the collectors to fulfil their duties conscientiously. *Reg.*, n. 447, p. 169.

men.[1] In this matter of maintaining fighting men for the Holy Land, Nicholas showed himself less amenable to the requests of sovereigns than many of his predecessors. Rulers had not infrequently represented to the Popes that they were prevented from taking the Cross by some local war. If they had money they could soon clear away the obstacle, and then they would be ready to proceed to the Holy Land. In response to these representations, Popes had at times " stretched a point ", and had, sometimes with scandal, allowed moneys which had been collected for a Crusade to be diverted from that purpose.[2]

Favour refused to Philip of France.

One of those to whom " Crusade money " had been granted in this way was Philip of France ; and, in order to get more of it, he begged the Pope to increase the amount of the grant of indulgences to those who, instead of taking arms against the Moslem, gave money for the cause. This request Nicholas kindly but firmly refused. To grant it, he said, would hurt his conscience. Still, he declared, should circumstances change, or should there arise any prospect of an immediate departure of an expedition to the Holy Land, he might reconsider his decision.[3]

Care of Crusade money.

Nicholas had also to prevent Kings and even bishops from appropriating the moneys that were being collected for the Crusade. Hence, if he could praise Eric, King of Denmark for his zeal in urging on the raising of the tenth,[4] he had to urge Magnus of Sweden to restore Crusade funds which he had taken on pretence of an urgent

---

[1] *Reg.*, n. 167.   [2] Savio, *N. III.*, n. xi, p. 168 ff.

[3] *Reg.*, n. 392, a fine letter. He bewails the prevailing apathy with regard to the Crusades. See a similar letter to our King Edward. He allows him 25,000 marks to prepare for his expedition to the Holy Land, on condition that the sum be refunded should he not set out. Ep. Aug. 1, 1278, ap. Rymer, ii, 119 ; or *Reg.*, nn. 110–12 ; or *Calendar of P. Reg.*, i, p. 455.

[4] Potthast, n. 21578 ; *cf.* 21577.

necessity,[1] and he had severely to blame clerics who had withdrawn to remote parts with the same funds,[2] and people [3] and even a bishop who had forcibly seized them.[4]

Although Nicholas was properly anxious that as much money as possible should be collected, he took care that no oppression or hardship should arise from the collection. Hence communities which devoted all their revenues to the service of the poor were not to be taxed.[5] Similarly, " on account of the malice of the Ocean," he granted various exemptions to Greenland, " rarely visited by ships," to Iceland, and other islands in the North Sea.[6] At the same time he begged the archbishops of Nidaros (Trondhjem) to convert into money such tithes as walrus tusks, hides, etc., as were raised in those remote parts.[7]

However, despite difficulties of every kind, we are assured that he raised a very considerable sum for the benefit of the Holy Land, and that Martin IV. spent it on campaigns in the Romagna, especially against the people of Forli.[8] Whether the amount of money collected by Nicholas was great or small, it was not destined to be used to promote a general crusade organized by the great countries of Europe. The idea of the one Commonwealth of Christendom was dying out, and with it the idea of the necessity of the corporate action of its great members.

---

[1] *Ib.*, 21595. [2] *Ib.*, 21602.

[3] *Ib.*, 21617. [4] Kaltenbrunner, n. 130, p. 144.

[5] *Reg.*, n. 8, and n. 190. *Cf.* n. 16. Many dioceses in Spain, and the military orders there engaged in fighting the Moors, were to be exempted from the tax. *Reg.*, nn. 27–41, and n. 186 ff.

[6] *Reg.*, n. 434.

[7] *Ib.*, n. 435. *Cf.* Potthast, n. 21858, and nn. 21524–6.

[8] *Mem. Potestat. Reg.*, ap. *R. I. SS.*, viii, p. 1141. Such charges as that against Martin are easily made. We have seen similar charges, apparently without reason, brought against Nicholas III. It is not easy to understand how the writer of the *Memoriale* could have known sufficient about the state of the papal exchequer to be able to make a well-founded statement on such a matter.

CHAPTER IV.

THE BRITISH ISLES.

THE relations between Nicholas III. and England were for the most part concerned with the archbishopric of Canterbury. On March 12, 1278, he nominated Kilwardby, then archbishop of Canterbury,[1] cardinal-bishop of Porto and Santa Rufina. The Chronicler of the Monastery of Abingdon is pleased to assert that Nicholas did this " from a desire to show the extent of his power ".[2] Despite this definite assertion as to the mind of Nicholas, we may be permitted to believe that it was the archbishop's piety and learning that inspired the Pope's action.[3] Unfortunately, however, his learning was not destined to be long serviceable to the Curia. He was old and ill when he reached Viterbo, and died about a year and a half after his promotion (Sept. 12, 1279).[4] At any rate, in order, says our chronicler Thomas Wykes, that he might not seem disobedient to the Pope, he exchanged wealth for honour, and, bidding farewell to his own suffragans (about July 24, 1278), set out for the Curia.[5]

His protest
against a
papal
collector.
It appears that, in any case, he would have gone to Rome this year. From an extract of his lost *Register*, preserved in that of John de Pontissara, bishop of

---

[1] *Cf. supra*, p. 78, and *Reg.*, 242.

[2] *Chron. of Ab.*, p. 61, ed. with translation of J. O. Halliwill.

[3] *Cf.* the Pope's letter of appointment, April 4, 1278, *Reg.*, n. 242. He speaks of " personam tuam quam virtutum Dominus multis virtutibus insignivit ".

[4] *Cf.* Ciacconius, *Vitæ RR. PP.*, ii, p. 224, who adds that he was employed by the Pope in writing letters to " the King of the Tartars " urging his conversion.

[5] *Chron.*, p. 277.

Winchester,[1] we find that he was very much annoyed at the action of Master Geoffrey de Veçano, the papal collector of the moneys for the Crusade. In virtue of a mandate from the Apostolic See, the collector claimed, as the archbishop declared, against immemorial custom, not merely the goods of those who died intestate, but, refusing to accept the probate of wills by the local authorities, he demanded that they should be proved by him, and he sequestered the goods of those who died in possession of several benefices. Such action was prejudicial to the rights of all the *Ordinaries* in England. The bishops of England must see to it that the English Church was not oppressed in their time. He himself would arise and go to the Holy Father, the Vicar of Jesus Christ, in behalf of the Clergy of England. Whether Kilwardby prosecuted this appeal as cardinal does not appear to be known. But, perhaps with that end in view, he took away with him " all the registers and judicial records of Canterbury ", so that " to this day its oldest records begin with Peckham's Archbishopric ". This seems all the more likely that Peckham believed that, had he lived longer, he would have returned them.[2]

Edward now made a more determined effort to secure the election of Burnell, bishop of Bath and Wells. Owing to the pressure which he and the Queen put upon the monks, they duly elected the royal candidate.[3] To promote his cause, the King wrote a special letter to the Pope in his behalf,[4] and envoys were sent to Rome by the monks and the King to ask for the confirmation of the election. But, say the Annals of Waverley, they

Election of a successor.

---

[1] Vol. i, p. 356 ff., Dec. 13, 1277. In all cases of taxation it is asked that the Norwich valuation (1254) of Bishop Walter Suffield be accepted. See *supra*.

[2] *Cf. Dict. of Nat. Biog.*, sub Kilwardby.

[3] *Ann. of Waverley*, p. 389, ap. *Ann. Monast.*, ii, *R. S.*

[4] July 10, 1278, ap. Rymer, ii, 118.

could not obtain their request " either by entreaty or by money, *nec prece nec pretio* ".   As we learn from a letter of one of Edward's agents to his master, Nicholas, on being asked (Dec. 26, 1278) to confirm the election, said that, " as he regarded the See of Canterbury as the greatest after that of Rome," [1] he wanted to see the person on whom he was to confer so conspicuous a dignity ; and that unless the candidate presented himself before the first of June (1279), he would himself nominate a suitable person for the See.   He, moreover, declared that it was no use to plead that the country could not get on without Robert.   Another agent of the King, one Francis Accursus, assured him (Jan. 4, 1279) that Robert must put in an appearance by the appointed day.   He believed, however, he wrote, that the confirmation would be accorded, and added that he thought that it was not so much on account of the personality of the candidate that Nicholas wished to see him, but on account of matters connected with the reform of the Church in England.[2]

Nicholas nominates Peckham to Canterbury, 1279.

However, Nicholas apparently soon discovered that Burnell had no intention of risking a cross-questioning at his hands ; and so, on Jan. 25,[3] he nominated the Franciscan, John Peckham, to the vacant See.[4]   When chosen, John was personally known to the Pope, as he was at the moment lecturing in theology in the school of the papal palace, and is hence called by our historians " lector curiæ," or " lector palatii in Romana curia ".[5]

---

[1] " Pronuntiavit (N.) quod, pro eo quod Cantuariensem Ecclesiam in orbe terrarum majorem post Romanam Ecclesiam reputabat, etc." Ep. ap. Langlois, " Nova Curiæ," ap. *Revue Historique*, Jan., 1905, p. 65.

[2] Ep. ap. *ib.*, p. 66.   [3] The date given by Wykes, *l.c.*, p. 279.

[4] See his bull, *Reg.*, n. 415.   It is dated Jan. 28.   *Cf.* Bliss, *Calendar of Pap. Reg.*, i, p. 456.

[5] *Cf.* Rishanger, *Chron.*, pp. 93–4, R. S. ;   *Mon. Francisc.*, pp. 537, 552, R. S. ;   Trivet, *Annales*, p. 300.

He was a man of remarkable learning,[1] very keen about the interests of his Order ; and, if somewhat " pompous in manner ", very kindly in disposition.[2]   In the performance of his duty his vigour was only equalled by his rigour.   To the Franciscans he was the *moon* of their Order, as the Minorite Pope, Nicholas IV., was its *sun*.[3]

Despite his great unwillingness to become a bishop,[4] he was consecrated by the Pope himself on mid-Lent Sunday, and landed in England about June 24.[5]

On his way to this country he reached Amiens (May 21, 1274), and was present at a meeting (May 23) between Philip of France and Edward (who had submitted their differences to the Holy See) [6] to conclude terms of peace. On the following day Peckham wrote to inform the Pope that Edward had " freely for God's sake " renewed the treaty which his father had made with St. Louis IX., although it was greatly against his interests.[7]   He also told the Pope that Edward had given him a remarkable proof of his goodwill.   By some mistake of the notary who had drawn up the papal notification to the King of Peckham's consecration, he had not been asked to bestow the temporalities of his See on the new archbishop. Edward had, however, overlooked this breach of custom, and had at once granted the archbishop the temporalities.

Peace between France and England.

[1] " Supereminentis literaturæ," says Wykes, p. 280.

[2] " Gestus affatusque pompatici, mentis benignæ, et animi admoduin liberalis." Trivet, *ib.* He had a special right to be interested in his Order as the Pope had named him : " Protector of the privileges of the Order of Minorites in England." *Reg.*, n. 246.

[3] Both died the same year (1292). Hence the *Chronicle of Worcester*, p. 511, " Sol obscuratur, sub terra luna moratur."

[4] Wykes, *l.c.*, p. 280 ; *Con. M. Polon.*, ap. *M. G. SS.*, xxiv, p. 254.

[5] *Ann. Wav.*, *l.c.*, p. 391.

[6] " Qui uterque Rex submisit se ordinacioni d. Papæ de injuriis et pace formandis inter eos." Sprott (?), *Chron.*, p. 121, ed. Hearne. The terms of peace, ap. Rymer, ii, 134.

[7] Ep. 2, ap. *Lit. Jo. Peckham*, i, p. 4, *R. S.* *Cf.* ep. 3.

For this act of courtesy Peckham begged the Pope personally to thank the King.[1]

Burnell again, 1280.

Though Nicholas had refused to let Burnell have the See of Canterbury, he had not heard the last of him. On March 21, 1280, the monks of Winchester elected him to the bishopric of that See. When, however, they appeared before Nicholas, they were severely blamed for choosing a man who had already been rejected by the Holy See.[2] Their candidate, he said, had already benefices enough. Permitted ultimately by Nicholas to select another candidate,[3] their second choice was no more successful than their first. They elected (Nov. 6) Richard de la More, archdeacon of Winchester. This time the initial difficulty came from Canterbury. Peckham refused to confirm the election on the ground that the archdeacon, without a dispensation, held two benefices with the cure of souls.[4] More appealed against the archbishop, and set out for Rome (Feb., 1281). His appeal was not listened to by Martin IV., the successor of Nicholas, not because " fearing simony " he had refused to give presents to certain cardinals,[5] but for the same reason as originally influenced Peckham.[6] Ultimately Martin IV. (1282) gave the bishopric to John de Pontissara, archdeacon of Exeter, " Devoniæ," who chanced to be on the spot (Orvieto), and was one of his chaplains.[7] Despite their strong support of Burnell, Edward, after he and his Queen had been given

---

[1] Ep. of May 24, ap. Rymer, ii, 1072.

[2] *Ann. of Waverley*, p. 394.

[3] At first (June 28) he decided to reserve the nomination to himself, but at length (July 7) gave the monks leave to select another candidate. Epp. ap. Bliss, *Calendar*, i, 462.

[4] *Ann. of Waverley*, *l.c.*

[5] As is asserted by the *Ann. of W.*, *l.c.*, p. 399.

[6] *Ann. of Dunstable*, ap. *Ann. Monast.*, iii, 282. *Cf.* Wykes, p. 283, and the Register of Peckham, nn. 206, 219, 277, 281, 1004, 1065–6.

[7] Epp. ap. Bliss, *l.c.*, p. 466, June 15, 1282.

great presents,[1] gave the temporalities to the Pope's nominee.

Peckham's opposition to de la More was part of a campaign which, " on the advice " of Nicholas,[2] he had opened against the abuse of " pluralities ", or the holding of several benefices by one man. Peckham was in the main successful in his righteous efforts to carry out the decrees of the Council of Lyons, and he was able to inform the Pope that the famous Anthony Bek, the King's secretary, had surrendered five benefices having the cure of souls. However, he added, he had left one benefice in Anthony's hands until he had the Pope's instructions, " because it is publicly said to me that the Pope is disposed to grant dispensations to him and to certain other clerics of the court." [3]

Peckham against " pluralities ".

It has been said of Peckham by a modern historian that he attempted " to magnify ecclesiastical authority at the expense of the temporal power ".[4] Bearing in mind the ideas of the age in which he lived, it would perhaps have been more correct if the historian had said that he resisted attempts, whether justifiable or not is

Peckham's discontent with Rome.

---

[1] " Rege ac regina in muneribus amplis salutatis," say the *Waverley Annals*, p. 399.

[2] " Sancta informatione vestra edoctus." Ep. 116 of Peckham, vol. i, p. 137, *R. S.*

[3] *Ib. Cf.* epp. 121–2. He was not so successful with Tedisius de Camilla, a cousin of Pope Hadrian V., who was rector of Wingham, and Terringis, etc. He had plenty of influence in Rome naturally. *Cf.* his Register, nn. 131, 384–7, 598–604, 822. According to Wadding, *Ann.*, v, 82, he grossly deceived the Pope. On him see Bliss, *Calendar*, i, pp. 448, 450–1, 467, 473, and 489. The last is the final decree in favour of Tedisius by Honorius IV., Aug. 19, 1286.

[4] Miss Hilda Johnstone, who has made a special study of Peckham (" Arch. P. and the Council of Lambeth of 1281," ap. A. G. Little and F. M. Powicke, *Essays in Mediæval Hist.*, 1925), denies that he was a blustering prelate " over assertive in words and fearful in action ", and declares that " in the trials of strength between himself and the King, the honours were more evenly divided than has sometimes been supposed ". Pp. 171–3.

beside the question, on the part of the royal authority
to encroach upon what was then generally recognized
as coming under the authority of the Church. We,
accordingly, find him impressing on King Edward that
the Church had been oppressed contrary to the decrees
of Popes and Councils, and that the age-long conflict
between the Church and the State would go on till Kings
acknowledged that their laws were secondary to those
of Christ. Enemies of the Church, he added, may hold
that it is not for the Pope to lay the yoke of laws and
canons of this kind on secular princes. But, he continued,
this we deny and we have with us the saints and the
universal Church.[1]

However, whichever may be the correct view of
Peckham's conduct in the relations of Church and State,
he was far from being always satisfied with the manner
in which he himself was treated by the Church.

When in Rome, in order to meet the expenses connected
with his consecration, he had had to contract a loan
of four thousand marks sterling from certain merchants
at Lucca. On July 1, 1279, he wrote to inform Pope
Nicholas that these merchants had suddenly given him
to understand that, unless he repaid their loan within
a month after the feast of St. Michael, he would incur
the greater excommunication. Owing to the action of
his predecessor and the King, the See of Canterbury was
completely impoverished, and he could not pay back
the money at such short notice. He expressed his conviction to the Pope that the merchants had deceived
both of them. They had certainly hoodwinked him,
as they had promised him time to enable him to repay
the loan. However, under the circumstances, he begged
the Pope to let him have the temporary use of five
thousand marks of the money collected for the Crusade

[1] See his *Reg. Epp.*, vol. i, pp. 239–44, Nov. 2, 1281, *R. S.* *Cf.* Miss H.
Johnstone, *l.c.*, p. 182.

with which he could repay the merchants. Owing to the depreciation of the coinage which was going on in England at the moment, he could not, he declared, get the money in any other way.[1]

Writing in the same connection to Cardinal Ordonius of Tusculum and others, he indignantly assured them that, if he had known how the Curia was going to treat him, "not all the men in the world could have induced him to shoulder the burden of the Church of Canterbury." And he assured the cardinal also that the result of the successive depreciations of the coinage in England was that there was hardly any money in the country.[2]

With all his good qualities, it would appear that Peckham was somewhat small-minded. On Sept. 19, 1279, Nicholas had written to William Wickwane, to the King and others to say that, though he had cancelled the election of William to the See of York on account of certain formalities, he had nevertheless, in virtue of his character and learning, appointed him to that See.[3] Aware too of what Wykes justly calls " the old and frivolous " dispute between the archbishop of York and Canterbury,[4] he wrote a closed letter to Peckham, begging him to refrain from contests regarding the carrying of the cross, and assuring him that his rights were untouched.[5] Despite this request, no sooner had the new archbishop landed in

Quarrel with the Arch-bishop of York, 1279.

---

[1] Ep. 15 of Peckham, vol. i, p. 17 ff. " Nec præ mutatione et decurtatione monetæ quæ instat, a me inveniri valeat mutuum aliunde." It was part of the policy of the Popes at this period to protect the merchant bankers (*mercatores*). This protection did much for the advancement of trade even if at times some hardship resulted to individuals. *Cf. Reg. Nic.*, nn. 64–8.

[2] Ep. 17, ap. *ib.*, p. 21. " Propter enim attonsam monetam Angliæ, et mutationem etiam alterius imminentem, vix pecunia in Anglia invenitur." *Cf.* epp. 27, 43, 45.

[3] *Reg.*, n. 559. The letters in connection with W. W.'s election are also given in his *Register*, p. 305 ff., ed. Surtees Soc., 1907.

[4] P. 281, *R. S.*

[5] Ep. Sept. 20, Bliss, *Cal.*, i, p. 459.

England after his consecration at Viterbo (Sept. 17, 1279),[1] than trouble began. He journeyed through Kent " quietly ", he afterwards declared, but with his cross carried before him. At Rochester, however, an official of Peckham went so far as to smash it, and until he got clear of the archdiocese of Canterbury, he was subjected to various indignities.[2] Calling himself " primate of England ", Wickwane, after diplomatically advancing in his diocese the interests of the Pope's nephew, Napoleone,[3] addressed letters to the Pope and various cardinals to complain of the manner in which he had been treated. Nicholas, however, died before he could move in the matter, and though the King tried to interfere, Peckham[4] behaved in the same way to Wickwane's successor, John Romanus.[5] The quarrel dragged on till 1353, when, at the request of Edward III. and the English nobility, and " induced especially by charity and humility ",[6] John de Thoresby of York came to an understanding on the matter with the archbishop of Canterbury, Simon Islip. He practically agreed to take the second place, and the compromise was duly confirmed by Pope Innocent VI.[7]

Wickwane
and
Nicholas.

The last communication which Wickwane made to Nicholas was penned the day before that Pope died, and concerned the Crusade. Describing himself as " the most devoted little servant (*servulus*) " of the Pope, and thanking God for giving to the Church, " or rather

[1] See the *Introduction*, p. vi, to W. W.'s *Register*.

[2] See his letters to the Pope and various cardinals (April 1, 1280), ap. *Letters from North. Regist.*, p. 60 (*cf.* pp. 59, 82 ff.), R. S., and W. W.'s *Reg.*, p. 178 ff.

[3] W. W.'s *Reg.*, p. 180.

[4] *Close Rolls* (1272–9), p. 582.

[5] W. W.'s *Reg.*, n. 929, p. 338.

[6] So says the historian of York, T. Stubbs, p. 1732, ap. Twysden.

[7] " Pontificatus sui anno tertio ex certa scientia confirmavit." Step. Birchington, *Vitæ Arch. Cant.*, ap. *Anglia Sacra.*, i, p. 44.

to the whole world," such a support as the present Pontiff, he tells him that circumstances have occurred which make it impossible for the King to go to the help of the Holy Land. He therefore advised the Pope to entrust the command of the English to the King's brother Edmund, and to give him the tenth for the Crusade. If he were appointed many would go with him.[1]

Nicholas was also called upon to deal with the remains in England of the De Montfort trouble, complicated with the situation in Wales. Llewelyn of Gwynedd, Prince of North Wales, in his efforts to maintain his independence, allied himself with the enemies of the royal family, and in 1275 married by proxy Eleanor de Montfort, the daughter of the great earl Simon. In the same year (Sept. 11), he appealed to Pope Gregory X. against King Edward. He averred that Edward had broken the peace which had been made between him and Henry III., and which had been sanctioned by the legate Ottoboni. Edward, he went on to say, had taken no notice of the letters which the Pope had written to him to exhort him to keep the peace. For his own part he was ready to take the oath of allegiance whch he had promised to take, if only Edward would name a place to which he could safely go. This, however, the King had not done. Llewelyn, therefore, earnestly begged the Pope to intervene, and meanwhile not to believe that he had acted against the terms of the peace. Finally, he impressed upon Gregory that, as his enemy had command of the sea, he could not readily communicate with him.[2]

How true was the last statement was proved in the following year, when the King's ships captured the

Almaric and Eleanor de Montfort, 1275–1282.

---

[1] Ep. of Aug. 21, 1280, ap. his *Reg.*, p. 185, or *Letters from N. Reg.*, p. 63. Peckham wrote to the same effect to Nicholas (ap. his *Reg.*, n. 118, vol. i, p. 140), and also (April 2, 1281), n. 149, to Martin IV.

[2] Ep. ap. Haddan and Stubbs, *Councils*, i, 506 ; or Rymer, ii, 57.

Prince's spouse as she was being brought to him by her brother, Almaric or Amaury de Montfort.[1] As Amaury was a papal chaplain, Pope John XXI. at once wrote to the bishops of England (Jan. 28, 1277) bidding them try to induce Edward to entrust him to their care till the Pope should decide what should be done in his case.[2] At the same time, in response to an entreaty of Llewelyn, he begged the King to set Eleanor at liberty.[3] As far as Amaury was concerned, the Pope's request appears to have been listened to. He was entrusted to the custody of certain bishops.[4] Eleanor, however, was not released until after peace had been made between her betrothed and the King. The terms of the peace were finally ratified in Nov., 1277,[5] and then she was duly set at liberty and married to Llewelyn in 1278.[6] Amaury was, however, still kept in durance vile ; and Nicholas exerted himself to obtain his freedom (1280).[7] His successor Martin IV. continued the efforts for the chaplain's release,[8] and at length (April 23, 1282), the bishops of England were able to inform him that Amaury had been liberated on condition of quitting the realm, never returning to it, except with the express permission of the Apostolic See.[9]

John of Darlington.

Nicholas also came into contact with another man who had been prominent in English life for many years,

[1] Nic. Trivet, an. 1276, p. 294 ; Walter of Heminburgh, *Chron.*, ii, p. 5.

[2] Bliss, *Cal.*, i, p. 452.

[3] *Ib.*, Jan. 30.

[4] See ep. of Nich. IV., Feb. 17, 1280, ap. Bliss, *l.c.*, 461.

[5] *Cf.* Rymer, ii, 88 and 92.

[6] Rymer, ii, 97.

[7] *Ib.*, 144, 145 ; Bliss, *l.c.*, 461.

[8] *Reg. Mart. IV.*, nn. 18–20.

[9] Rymer, ii, pp. 192–3. *Cf. Ann. of Worcester*, ap. *Annal. Monast.*, iv, p. 483, *R. S.* "P. Martino jubente, archiepiscopus Cantuariæ et suffraganei sui X. Kal. Maii (April 22) Emericum de Montforti de custodia eduxerunt." *Cf.* Blaauw, *The Barons' War*, p. 296 ff.

i.e., the learned Dominican, John of Darlington. He had supported Henry III. against the Barons, and hence was a *persona grata* to his son, for whom, too, he had obtained from Pope Nicholas a grant from the Crusade tenth.[1]

John had already been employed on various commissions in England by Gregory X.,[2] when he commissioned him with Raymond de Nogeriis to collect the tenth for the Crusade ordered by the Council of Lyons (Sept. 20, 1274).[3] Pope John XXI. gave him minute instructions as to the way in which he should proceed in the collection, and allowed him three shillings and sixpence a day for his expenses.[4] John appears to have been over strict in fulfilling his commission, and grievous complaints were sent to Rome about his methods.[5] Accordingly Pope John XXI. ordered him and the other collectors to swear to exact nothing beyond the true value of the benefices,[6] and Nicholas III. sent him several special injunctions not to exact the tenth from various poor hospitals.[7]

However, despite John's excessive zeal in the performance of his duty, Nicholas cut short a disputed election to the See of Dublin of nearly eight years' duration by setting aside the two original candidates and nominating him (Feb. 8, 1279).[8] On July 1, he gave

[1] See epp. of Nich., Aug. 1 and 12, 1278, ap. Bliss, *Cal.*, i, 455 ; *Reg.*, nn. 110–12. John failed, however, to effect any alteration in the conditions of payment of the annual tax of 1,000 marks.

[2] *Cf.* Bliss, *l.c.*, p. 445, 448.

[3] *Ib.*, p. 449.

[4] *Ib.*, p. 452.

[5] *Ib.*, pp. 452–3. *Cf.* John of Oxnead, *Chron.*, p. 231, *R. S.* Rishanger, *Chron.*, p. 89, says that " with all due respect to the Pope " it was against the spirit (*professionem*) of the Order for a Dominican to be a collector of tenths.

[6] Bliss, *ib.*   [7] *Ib.*, pp. 456, 459.

[8] *Ib.*, p. 457. *Cf.* Rishanger, *Chron.*, pl 95, " Ex collatione papali efficitur archiepiscopus Dublinensis." See also *Annals of Waverley,*

him permission to be consecrated by the archbishop of Canterbury or by any other Catholic bishop along with two or three others.[1] After his consecration by archbishop Peckham (Aug. 27), he did not proceed to his See, but remained, says Rishanger, " some years " in England collecting the tenth. From this work he he was relieved by Martin IV., in 1283 ; but, as he died in 1284, he cannot have done much for his archiepiscopal See.[2]

Persons summoned to appear outside the country.

One result of the frequent appeals at this time to Rome, was that a number of persons were summoned to give evidence or for one cause or another outside the country. Complaints on this matter reached the King's ears. Edward accordingly dispatched " to the supreme Pontiff of the universal Church " a letter of protest. He said that he had full confidence that the Pope would listen to petitions, especially to such as were just. Long ago, he declared, the Apostolic See had granted the English the privilege of not being cited for trial to any place outside the country. At the present time especially, he continued, the kingdom was so settled that access to it and departure from it was most easy. He therefore " with all possible affection " implored the Pope to renew their privileges " for our English who are ever devoted

p. 392, *R. S.* The disputed election was due to the fact that two chapters, those of Holy Trinity and St. Patrick's, claimed the right of electing the archbishop. Nicholas settled their respective rights, March 7, 1279. Bliss, *ib.*, p. 458.

[1] Bliss, *ib.*, p. 459.

[2] Sig. E. Re in an article on " La compagnia del Riccardi in Inghilterra ", ap. *Archivio Rom. di Stor. Pat.*, vol. 37, 1914, p. 125, has printed a number of interesting documents on the collection of this tenth in England. From the first it appears that in the first year were collected 22,546 marks, 9s, $5\frac{1}{4}$ (*obolum*) d. *Cf. Reg. Mart. IV.*, Oct. 11, 1283, n. 385. *Cf. ib.*, nn. 421–5, March 1, 1284. During the absence of the archbishop, certain " clerics and laymen " had been burning churches.

to the Roman Church ".[1] We may be sure that this reasonable petition was not presented in vain.

Although the relations of Nicholas III. with Scotland and Ireland do not pass beyond the ordinary details of Church government, we may notice his connection with Tuam in the latter country, as it brings us in touch with a little known writer, Friar Malachy, a Franciscan of Limerick. He was the author of a work *On Poison* (*De Veneno*) which was printed in Paris in 1518, now an excessively rare book. In it he has a number of very interesting remarks about Ireland, which he calls " Greater Scotland, to wit Hibernia ". After assuring us that no poisonous animal is to be found therein, he declares that the poison has been reserved for its people. They are greater liars, thieves, and adulterers than the people of any other country. Like to the Kingdom of Babylon, he adds, that of Ireland came to an end with an impure King, Roderick O'Connor.[2]

On the death of Thomas O'Connor, archbishop of Tuam (June, 1279), there was a disputed election. The majority of the canons appointed to make the election chose Master Nicholas de Machin, one of the canons of Tuam, whereas the dean, the archdeacon, and another canon chose the said Friar Malachy of the Minorite Convent of Limerick.[3] The Primate of Ireland, Nicholas, archbishop of Armagh, espoused the cause of Malachy and begged King Edward I. " to pity the poverty of the Church and to extend the kingly favour to brother Malachy who is in the flower of his youth, and is provident

The Archbishopric of Tuam and brother Malachy, 1279–86.

---

[1] " Beatitudini vestræ cum omni affectione qua possumus, supplicamus quatenus ad Anglicos nostros, Ecclesiæ Romanæ devotos continuantes . . . privilegia . . . conservare eis illibata dignemini." Ep. Feb. 7, 1279, ap. Rymer, ii, 130, or ap. *Close Rolls*, 1272–9, p. 555 ; *cf. ib.*, 1278–88, pp. 347–8.

[2] Fol. 15b–23b, cited in the *Engl. Hist. Rev.*, July, 1918, pp. 360–1.

[3] *Cf.* letters of July 12, 1286, of Honorius IV., ap. Bliss, *Calendar of Papal Letters*, i, pp. 487–8, or Theiner, *Mon. Hib.*, p. 135 f.

and discreet ".[1] The royal assent to Malachy's election was given on April 22, 1280, and then that of the Pope was asked.[2] But the other party prayed Pope Nicholas to confirm the election of Master Nicholas. He handed over the matter to three cardinals, but died soon after. Whereupon brother Malachy, who had meanwhile betaken himself to Rome, without asking anyone's permission, promptly left the eternal city, and would not push his claims any further.[3] Pope Martin IV., however, ordered the examination to be continued. Finally to save further expense, as the cause dragged on, Master Nicholas also gave up his claims, and Honorius IV. sanctioned the translation of Stephen de Fulburn (or Folebourn) from the See of Waterford to that of Tuam (July 12, 1206).[4] On the same date, by the hands of archdeacon Denis, Master Adam de Folebourn and Henry de Foscamp, canon of Tuam, the pallium was sent to Stephen. It had to be conferred upon him by the bishops of Elphin, Killala, and the new bishop of Waterford, who had also to receive from him his oath of fidelity to the Pope and the Roman Church.[5]

[1] Sweetman, *Calendar of Docs. relating to Ireland*, ii, p. 311 f., *R. S.*
[2] *Ib.*, p. 340.   [3] Bliss, *l.c.*
[4] *Ib.*   [5] *Ib.*, p. 488.

CHAPTER V.

ON the death of Alexander IV. who, as Pope, had kept still in his hands the protectorate of the Order of St. Francis which had been entrusted to him as cardinal, St. Bonaventure, then Minister-General of the Order, and the other ministers begged Urban IV. to nominate cardinal Giovanni Gaetani their Protector. Although it is believed that he had had thoughts of appointing his nephew, cardinal Ancherus, Urban granted their request, making Gaetani Protector also of the Poor Clares (1263).[1]

Cardinal Gaetani and St. Clare.

As Protector of the latter Order, he came up against the question of poverty, which had already begun to trouble the Order of St. Francis, and which was destined, through unrestrained fanaticism, to bring increasing trouble on the Order and the Church up to the days of John XXII. In the *Life* of Blessed Agnes of Bohemia, we read that, at the time of the Council of Lyons (1274), cardinal Giovanni, " because the days were evil," wished the Saint to buy some property (*possessiones*) for herself and her sisters. She firmly refused, declaring that she preferred to suffer every kind of want rather than fall away in the very least from the poverty of Christ, who had for our sakes made himself poor.[2] The cardinal,

---

[1] Philip of Perugia (whom Nicholas III. had caused to enter his household, p. 683), *Ep. de Card. Protect.*, pp. 681–2, ap. *M. G. SS.*, xxxii.

[2] C. 5, p. 88, ed. W. W. Seton, *Some New Sources for the Life of Blessed Agnes of Bohemia*, London, 1915.

accordingly, dropped his suggestions, and obtained from Urban IV. the confirmation of their rule of strict poverty.[1]

Nicholas
makes
cardinal
Matteo
Protector of
the Fran-
ciscans.

When cardinal Orsini became Pope, he in turn also confirmed the rule of the Poor Clares,[2] and continued to display remarkable affection for the allied Order of St. Francis. He protected its members,[3] saw to their being properly housed,[4] readily selected bishops from their ranks,[5] and, in accordance with their wishes, gave them as their protector his nephew cardinal Matteo Rosso. This last fact we know through the irrefragable testimony of Philip of Perugia,[6] who, as one who was present, gives us a touching picture of the conferring of this position on cardinal Matteo. In the presence of the minister-general and other ministers of the Franciscans, Nicholas thus addressed his nephew : "Many are the benefits we have conferred upon you ; but no one of them is so nearly a pledge of eternal life as the one we now bestow upon you. For we give you what may well lead you to Paradise, the meritorious prayers of all the holy brethren of this Order. We give you the best we have, our heart's desire, the very apple of our eye." Completely overcome by emotion,[7] he could not continue, but giving his own ring to the cardinal he said : "To thee do we commit the Order of the Friars Minor."

---

[1] Oct. 18, 1263, is the date of Urban's bull, ap. Potthast, n. 18860. *Cf.* the letter of Philip of Perugia : "Qui (Orsini) eis ordinavit regulam quam nunc habent, sub bulla d. Urbani," p. 682.

[2] May 21, 1278, ap. *ib.*, n. 21324.

[3] *Ib.*, n. 21321.

[4] *Reg.*, n. 60.

[5] *Chron. Bavaricum*, ap. *M. G. SS.*, xxiv, p. 225.

[6] "Singulorum votis per privatum scrutinium disquisitis." *L.c.* Hence we must conclude that the author of the *Mem. Potest. Reg.*, ap. *R. I. SS.*, viii, p. 1143, was mistaken when he wrote that Nicholas had appointed M. R. because he was his relation, but that the friars had wanted the Franciscan cardinal, Jerome of Ascoli.

[7] "Me teste qui narro," says Philip, *ib.*, p. 682.

Then for nearly two months, practically neglecting The rule of St. Francis and poverty. everything else, to the great astonishment of the Curia, he devoted himself with certain heads of the Order to the study of the rule of St. Francis,[1] with a view to pronouncing a final interpretation upon it.

Though, as the Saint declared in his Testament,[2] he had written his rule " in a few words and simply ", and " the lord Pope had confirmed it ",[3] and though, in the same Testament, the brethren had been forbidden to have recourse to Rome for privileges, recourse had soon to be made to Rome for authoritative interpretation of the " few words " of the rule.   It had declared that the Minor Brothers were " to observe the Holy Gospel of our Lord Jesus Christ, by living in obedience, without property, and in chastity ". They were not " to receive coins or money either themselves or through a third party ". Nor were they " to appropriate to themselves a house or place (convent) or anything " ; and, according to the addition of the Testament, the " churches and poor dwelling places " which were assigned them should only be such as were " becoming the holy poverty which we have promised in the rule, always dwelling there as strangers and pilgrims ". With the phenomenally rapid spread of the Order, and the varying conditions of times and countries, an absolutely literal observance of the rule and Testament soon became practically impossible.   The rule had to be rendered to some extent at least flexible ; and at once, while there were the sober majority of the friars who wished merely for such modifications of the rule as could make it generally workable, there of course appeared among them such as

[1] *Ib.*, p. 683.

[2] Both the Rule and Testament of St. Francis were given in the *Opuscula S. F.*, pp. 63 ff. and 77 ff., ed. Quaracchi, and in English in Fr. Paschal Robinson's *Writings of St. Francis*, pp. 64 ff. and pp. 81 ff.

[3] Honorius III., Nov. 29, 1223.

wished for a flexibility that would have destroyed the spirit of the Order completely, and such as would have had it made rigid to breaking point. These last were the Spirituals or Zealots, the others were the Conventuals. Already Gregory IX.,[1] in response to an appeal made to him by the superiors of the Order, had called attention to the fact that, in his Testament, St. Francis had forbidden the brethren to seek for letters from the Apostolic See, and had inserted certain points that could not be observed without great difficulty. Accordingly, as one well acquainted, as he justly said, with the mind of the Saint, Gregory, to clear away the difficulties, decided that the Order was not bound by the *Mandate* or Testament. This decision he gave on the ground that what concerned all could not be imposed upon all without the consent of all, especially of the ministers, and that the Saint could not bind his successors. Further, the brothers were only to be bound by those evangelical counsels that were definitely presented in the rule ; and, as they could not possess money, they were to be allowed to buy what was really necessary through a third party who was to be regarded as the agent of the person who had been good enough to supply them with the purchase money.[2] Though, too, they were not to own anything either as an Order or individually, they could have the use of utensils, books, and necessary movables ; but, according to a decision of Innocent, the ownership of everything was to be in the hands of the Holy See.[3]

---

[1] In his bull *Quo Elongati*, Sept. 28, 1230, ap. Sbaralea, *Bullar. Fr.*, i, p. 68 ff., or Sabatier, *Speculum Perfect.*, p. 314 ff.

[2] Innocent IV. extended this permission to things that were useful or convenient. See his Bull *Ordinem vestrum*, Nov. 14, 1245, ap. Wadding, iii, p. 129.

[3] *Ib.* This bull (iii, 519) and the " Quo elongati " (iii, 449) are both in the *Bullar Rom.*, ed. Turin.

These decisions did not put an end to the " Poverty Question ". As the Conventuals got laxer, the Zealots got stricter. Nor were there wanting those outside the Order who condemned the rule of St. Francis with its vow of Poverty altogether. Nicholas had to intervene ; and in a bull, as long as it is famous, justified the rule, and gave solutions to the difficulties regarding the interpretation of the rule of St. Francis which were dividing the Order. His bull, *Exiit qui seminat*, issued Aug. 14, 1279, was, in the main, on the same lines as those of his predecessors, but more detailed, and, perhaps unfortunately as it turned out, more strictly worded.[1] Based upon the teachings of St. Bonaventure, it is regarded as forming, along with the bull *Exivi* of Clement V., the basis of the present Franciscan observance.

The bull *Exiit* of Nicholas III., 1279.

Among those, began the Pope, who received the good seed of the Sower, was St. Francis, and he spread it among his children. However, among them, and over his holy rule, the enemy of mankind has not ceased to try to sow tares, despite the fact that this rule has been approved by several Popes.

As difficulties of interpretation of the rule have arisen, he has decided to treat of them, after having carefully discussed the situation with some of the companions of Francis. It was a question of explaining what exactly was meant when the novice engaged to observe poverty (*sine proprio*), humility, obedience, chastity, and the Holy Gospel of our Lord Jesus Christ.

Distinction must first be made between the precepts and counsels of the Gospel, and then, with regard to the latter, it must be held that the brothers were bound only by those in the rule which were strictly commanded,

---

[1] It may be read in *Lib. VI. Decretal.*, v., tit. 12, c. 3, vol. ii, p. 1109, ed. Freidburg, or *Reg. Nic.*, n. 564.

which were contained in it " preceptorie vel inhibitorie."
Still, with regard to the other counsels, the brothers are
more bound to strive to observe them than are other
Christians.[1]

Their renunciation for God's sake of property whether
held privately or in common (" tam in speciali quam
etiam in communi ") is " meritorious and holy ", as
" Christ confirmed by word and example ".   They are
to live on what is freely offered to them, or by what they
humbly beg, or by what they gain by the labour of their
hands.   They must, indeed, renounce dominion or ownership, but, of course, not the *use* of necessities.   They
were not to have the right to anything, but merely the
use of what was necessary (" usus non juris sed facti ").
The " confessor of Christ " (St. Francis) must have
sanctioned that view of the case, as he ordered, for
instance, clerics to say the divine Office.   For this they
must have the necessary books, etc.   Then, too, as he
ordered that the preaching of the friars must be sound
and useful, the necessity of study, and so of the use of
books, was implied.

Nicholas then went on to approve of the ruling of
Innocent IV. whereby the Holy See was made the
proprietor of all the things which the friars had to use,
except in the case of real property where the original
donor wished to reserve the proprietorship to himself.

Even with regard to necessaries, the friars were not
to have anything that savoured of the superfluous ; and,
though " necessaries " might be allowed to vary with
persons or places, holy poverty was to be obvious
everywhere.

The Pope next proceeded to declare that more fully
than his predecessors did he intend to deal with the

---

[1] " Ad nonnulla vero alia per Evangelium data consilia eo magis
secundum exigentiam sui status tenentur plus quam ceteri Christiani,
quo, etc."

problem of money, which the friars were by their rule forbidden to handle. They were to abstain from raising loans ; but, if alms failed, they could try to induce a third party to pay for the necessities they had had to acquire. Should the person who was to provide the money prefer to act through an agent, the friars could exhort that agent to fulfil his commission justly, but were not to have anything to do with his management of the funds entrusted to him, nor were they to take any action against him if he failed to do his duty. Future needs connected with building or dwelling houses, or with the writing of books or with the buying of them at a distance, etc., may be provided for in a similar manner. But in all cases, the friars must be careful not to ask for any more than is strictly necessary to pay their dues.

After dealing with the way in which the friars may accept legacies, Nicholas decides a number of smaller questions. The superiors of the Order could settle the question of the amount of clothes to be given to the friars by considerations of climate, health, etc. " Labour " need not necessarily be understood as " manual labour ". The Order was not bound to receive into its ranks any but suitable candidates.

Finally, after ruling that the Testament of St. Francis was not binding, he decreed that his Constitution [1] alone was binding, and that it was to be read in the Schools of Canon Law. It was, however, only to be explained *grammatically*. No one was to dare to attack the rule of St. Francis or the Pope's regulations with regard to it, but should any further doubts arise regarding it, they were to be referred to the Apostolic See.

Commenting on this important pronouncement, a

---

[1] See the *Register* of Bishop Richard of Swinfield, p. 23 ff. for an application of this *Constitution* by the Protector of the Franciscans, card. Matteo Rosso.

modern writer[1] has justly observed : " If only the
Conventuals had shown more zeal, and the Zealots more
discretion in their lives, a satisfactory adjustment might
have been made between them on the basis of this
Decretal, and the terrible scandals (which took place
later) might have been averted." Franciscan writers
meanwhile declared that the Pope had defined that their
rule " contained the highest perfection "[2] ; and others
in authority proceeded at once to explain to their subjects
that, by virtue of the decree of Nicholas, they had only
the use of their possessions, and that the ownership of
them was vested in the Pope.[3]

Our account of the relations of Nicholas with the
Franciscans may well be closed with a good story told
against them by a Benedictine.[4] The reader will know
how much credence to attach to it. Wanting what was
against their rule, the Friars Minor, in their anxiety to
exploit (*exploratores*) the whole Church, offered the Pope
forty thousand florins to be allowed to hold property.
When he had got possession of the money, he kept it,
and told the discomfited friars that the rule of St. Francis
was holy, and he would not violate it.

Heretics.

Before he became Pope, Nicholas had been president
of the Congregation of the Inquisition,[5] and consequently
was well aware that in various cities of Italy there were
lurking a number of heretics, most of them, such as the
Cathari, Arnoldists, etc., as dangerous to the State as to
the Catholic faith. He therefore not only renewed the
general excommunication against them, ordering that

[1] Mr. A. G. Ferrers Howell, *St. Bernardino of Siena*, p. 17. I have
made free use of his lucid commentary on this vexed question of
Franciscan " poverty ".

[2] *Contin. Angl. O. M. of Martinus Pol.*, ap. *M. G. SS.*, xxiv, p. 254.

[3] See a letter to the *Guardian* of the Franciscans in London of
Jan. 21, 1280, in the *Register* of John di Pontissara, i, p. 254 ff.

[4] *Chron. Brev.*, ap. *Memorials of St. Edmund's*, iii, p. 293, *R. S.*

[5] Potthast, n. 21307.

when condemned by the Church they should be handed over to the secular arm to be punished,[1] but took special measures against them in different cities.[2]

Even in Viterbo, so often honoured in this age by the presence of the Popes, there were a number of strange heretics, whose beliefs were not infrequently as much based upon Ghibelline or political as upon religious considerations. One set of heretics there taught the very convenient, but decidedly immoral, doctrine that those could not be damned, no matter what crimes they committed, who had once been baptized.[3] Under Clement IV. (1265), a number of the Viterbesi had shown themselves very restive in the matter of the prosecution and punishment of heretics,[4] and consequently Nicholas found it necessary in the beginning of his reign to come to an understanding with them. It was agreed by the people that the papal inquisitors should be allowed to perform their duties without let or hindrance, that the authorities of their city should help them, and that the statutes of the Popes against heretics should be included in the city's by-laws ("in ejusdem Communis capitularibus").[5] Then, about a year later (May 8, 1279), he ordered brother Sinibald de Lacu to take strict measures against the heretics at Viterbo.[6]

Not infrequently the performance of their unpleasant

---

[1] Bull of March 3, 1280, ap. *Bullar. Rom.*, iv, p. 47.

[2] *Reg.*, n. 71, shows that he readily inclined to the side of mercy in dealing with cases of heresy.

[3] *Cf.* the letter of the bishop of Viterbo, Ranierius, printed by I. Ciampi as a note to his ed. of della Tuccia's *Chron. of Viterbo*, p. 326. Some of the teachings of these heretics were so filthy that the editor would not even print them in the original Latin.

[4] See documents *ib.*, p. 327 ; Potthast, n. 19314. *Cf.* Pinzi, *Storia di Viterbo*, ii, pp. 169–71 ; and *Chron. Parmen.*, pp. 35–6, for the trouble caused there by the burning of an heretical woman.

[5] *Istrum* of May 1, 1278, ap. Ciampi, *l.c.*, p. 327.

[6] Wadding, *Ann.*, v, 86, quoting the bull "Qui cuncta solus".

duties brought personal trouble upon the inquisitors. At Parma the house of the Dominicans was plundered; and the brothers themselves were maltreated or even killed,[1] because members of their Order were employed to decide whether or no accused persons were guilty of heresy. Also in the course of the year 1278, when the Dominican, brother Paganus, was in charge of a heretic, Conrad of Venosta in the diocese of Como, his party was attacked by a number of relations and adherents of the prisoner. Conrad was rescued; Paganus and four of his company were slain; and all who were unable to escape were plundered of all they possessed. Nicholas was naturally very indignant, and his letters, addressed to Rudolf, the King of the Romans, and to the various ecclesiastical and civil authorities of the neighbourhood, called upon them to see that the crime did not pass unpunished.[2] For over a year the murderers remained uncaptured.[3] But the whole party, including Conrad, were caught by the people of Bergamo in October, 1279, and the last Nicholas has to say about them is contained in a number of letters, dated Nov. 29, 1279, in which he exhorts the people of Bergamo to guard their prisoners securely.[4]

Jews.

Nicholas was also as eager to spread the faith as to preserve it; and hence it is recorded in the Annals of Colmar that, in the year 1279, a papal letter came to their city ordering the Provincial Prior of the Dominicans to devote himself along with his brethren to preach the faith to the Jews.[5] He had already written to Albert, the Minister of the Friars Minor in Austria, urging him

---

[1] See the *Chron. of Parma*, just quoted, ap. *R. I. SS.*, new ed.

[2] *Reg.*, nn. 76–9, June 1, 1278.

[3] See first bull of Nicholas to the civil authorities in Lombardy, ap. Ripoll, *Bullar. O. P.*, i, p. 567, Sept. 29, 1279.

[4] *Reg.*, nn. 585–7.

[5] Ap. Böhmer, *Fontes*, ii, p. 13.

and other friars by means of special sermons and in other ways to devote themselves to the conversion of the Jews.[1] In writing a touching letter to the same effect to the Provincial Prior of the Friars Preachers in Lombardy, he expresses his wish to toil for the men of Judah, once " sweet shoots (*delectabile germen*) " of the vineyard of the Lord. He exhorts the prior to pick out brothers conspicuous for their upright character, their learning, their prudence, and their experience, and to devote them to the work of putting the Gospel of Christ in the best manner before the Jews. Converts from their ranks are to be specially recommended to the lords spiritual and temporal of their locality, and in no case are they to be allowed to be molested. Finally the prior is urged to keep the Pope frequently informed of the result of his work, and especially about such as may obstinately refuse to listen to the exhortations of the brethren.[2]

Like all his immediate predecessors, Nicholas frequently The East. turned to the East. He hoped to see a Crusade launched from Europe, and, with the aid of the Mongols of Persia, break the power of the Moslem and free Jerusalem. He hoped also to see the Greeks more closely united to the Universal Church. What he did to forward that union we saw in the biography of Gregory X.[3] What correspondence he had with the Ilkhans of Persia we hope to relate on a later page.

Meanwhile we may note that he interested himself The Cumans. also in the conversion of the Comans, Kumans, or Kipchak who dwelt in the great plain north of the Black and Caspian Seas. They had been cruelly treated by the

---

[1] Potthast, 21382, Aug. 4, 1278.

[2] Ep. " Vineam Sorec ", ap. *Bullar. Rom.*, iv, p. 45 ff. " Ut autem de præmissis *Avidis nostris conceptibus*, juxta desideria nostra satisfiat, frequenter nobis intimare studeas, etc." He wrote to others in the same spirit, Potthast, 21383.

[3] *Cf.* Pot., nn. 21463–7 ; 21470–6 ; 21478–9, and 21481 ; *Reg.*, nn. 367–85.

Tartars, and in their country John of Piano Carpini had "found many skulls and bones of dead men lying upon the earth like a dunghill".[1]   Perhaps it was their misfortunes that made them think of Christianity.   At any rate it was reported to Nicholas that they, especially those who had fled from the Tartars into Hungary, were well disposed towards the faith.   He accordingly ordered the Provincial Minister of the Friars Minor in Hungary to send suitable friars to preach to them.   The converts, he decided, could be baptized according to the Roman rite.   At the same time, he wrote to his legate in Hungary, Philip, bishop of Fermo, bidding him make all the necessary inquiries preparatory to the establishment of a bishopric among the Cumans.[2]

The Hungarians, 1278.

Philip had been sent by Nicholas into Hungary (Sept. 22, 1278),[3] as his legate with the fullest powers to see if anything could be done to stop the downward rush of its people into anarchy and paganism.   Its degenerate ruler, Ladislaus IV. (1272–90), with the aid of his at least semi-idolatrous Cuman favourites, gave himself up to the grossest debauchery.   His wife, Isabella, daughter of Charles of Anjou, was disgracefully neglected, and under the influence of his Cuman mistresses, he became more than half a pagan himself.   He, of course, neglected his duties, allowed the royal power to be usurped by powerful nobles, and looked on while the whole country was being torn with civil wars.[4]   But too many followed

---

[1] See his *Liber Tartar.*, c. 23, ed. Beazley.   The Kumans, the Polovtsi of the Russian chronicles, and their language were Turkish.

[2] *Cf.* epp. of Oct. 7, 1278, ap. *Reg.*, 182–3.

[3] See the letter of Nicholas III. naming him legate, ap. Theiner, *Mon. Hung.*, i, p. 327 ff.

[4] In his letter to Philip just quoted Nicholas speaks of the country being rent with disorders, of "bella plus quam civilia . . . ex quibus inter alia . . . graviter solium regale deprimitur, ejusque depresso regimine non solum in Regno ipso vastantur bona fidelium sed jura ecclesiarum . . . in direptionem veniunt, etc."

the example of their king, and, in their degeneracy, let their hair grow and in their dress adopted the fashions of women.[1]

The legate held a council at Ofen (Buda) in the diocese of Vesprim, where sixty-nine canons were issued for the reform of the lives both of the upper and the lower clergy.[2] Ladislaus, however, dispersed the Council by violence, although he had in Philip's presence previously sworn to amend his life, to keep the Catholic faith, and to work for the real conversion of the Cumans (June 23, 1279).[3] The frivolous excuse for his conduct which he sent to Nicholas did not avail him. The Pope sent him a somewhat long and severe letter in which he reproached him for the evil he had done and for the breaking of his oath. Even the Cumans, interjected the Pope, had accepted all the canons except the one about the cutting of their hair. Grievously distressed at his conduct, Nicholas told the King that he earnestly prayed that God would enable him to see clearly the error of his ways. At the same time he told him plainly that he might find it necessary to employ not only spiritual but also temporal methods of correction. He had every hope that the Princes and people of his realm would not tolerate his wrongdoing.[4] At the same time, while urging his legate to have constancy,[5] he urged the people of Hungary, Charles of Anjou, and the King of the Romans to persuade Ladislaus to submit to the legate.[6]

---

[1] " Ritu paganismi disgregatis comis, prolixis crinibus et habitu muliebri conversabantur." *Ann. Aust. Contin. Vindobon.*, ap. *M. G. SS.*, ix, p. 731. This explains Philip's vain attempt to induce the Kumans, when they agreed to become Christians, to cut their hair and alter their style of dress. *Cf.* Katona, *Epit. Rer. Hung.*, i, p. 532.

[2] The canons of the council are given in full by Raynaldus, *Ann.*, after the year 1285, p. 577 ff., ed. 1887. *Cf.* Hefele, *Conc.*, vi, p. 247 ff., new ed.

[3] See his oath ap. Theiner, *Mon. Hung.*, i, p. 339 ff.

[4] Ep. of Dec. 9, 1279, ap. Theiner, *l.c.*, p. 341 ff.

[5] *Ib.*, p. 344.   [6] *Ib.*, pp. 344–5.

For the moment the King of Hungary was touched with repentance. In a proclamation he expressed his regret for the past, and as atonement offered a hundred marks a year for a hospital to be paid by himself and his successors for ever (Aug. 18, 1280).[1] But he soon returned to his evil ways. His mistresses were recalled, his wife imprisoned, and the legate expelled. It required a rising of the people to bring him back once more to the performance of his duty.[2]

Nicholas stands for the rights of the Church.

As a kind of introduction to what we shall have soon to say of the character of Nicholas, we may here give a few more instances of his steady insistence on the rights of the Church in different parts of Christendom. " It was his resolve," says Saba,[3] " that the authority of the Apostolic See should not be diminished." Many times he had to direct letters of protest to Alfonso X el Sabio, of Castile. At one time he is protesting against that foolish monarch's high-handed treatment of the arch-bishop of Compostella,[4] and at another he is sending the bishop of Rieti to lay before him a number of complaints, drawn up under seven heads, against his oppression of the Church in his dominions.[5]

---

[1] Ib., p. 347. Ladislaus declares that he sinned " furore juventutis . . . accensi, et quorundam pravorum depravati ".

[2] Cf. Ann. Aust. Contin. Vindob., ap. M. G. SS., ix, p. 711 ; Ann. S. Rudberti, ib., p. 805 ff., and the somewhat late authority of Thos. Ebendorfer de Haselbach, Chron., ap. Pez., ii, 760, cited by Sayous, Hist. des Hongrois, i, 286. Some of the documents quoted above are also to be found in Endlicher, Rer. Hung. Mon., p. 559 ff.

[3] Lib. vi, c. 12.

[4] Ep. Feb. 13, 1278, ap. Raynaldus, Ann. 1278, n. 32. Cf. his defence of the bishop of Bayeux against Philip of France. Ib., n. 33.

[5] Ep. of March 23, 1279, ap. ib., 1279, n. 27. The seven " complaints " are given, ib., nn. 24–6. Complaints are made, for instance, about interference with ecclesiastical elections : " In primis preces, minaces et impressiones quæ fiunt in electionibus et postu-lationibus Ecclesiarum et magistrorum religionum per regem et suos et mala quæ inde contingunt."

Nearer home, Nicholas had to require of Charles of Anjou to order his Justiciary in the Abruzzi to restore certain properties which he had usurped and which belonged to the Roman Church. They were situated on the north of the river Tronto which was more or less the boundary between the Papal States and the Kingdom of Naples on the Adriatic side.[1]

In any endeavour to make known the real character of Nicholas III., and certain other Popes of his age, the sober historian is often grievously hampered by the poet. It is the sweet music of verse which readily captures the ear and the imagination, and then, by these seductive channels, the mind also. The words of the poet have wings and soon reach every listener. But the words of truth are weighty and slow of foot ; and, if they prevail, it is only after long lapse of time. Shakespeare has enabled many an unworthy character to remain long on a pedestal, and Dante has for ages kept many a hero from his throne.

Character of Nicholas III.

A poet must in any case be a man of the strongest feelings, and these of themselves tend to hurry him in advance of truth ; and when this man of powerful emotions is also a violent partisan, truth is outstripped indeed. Such a poet was Dante ; and it is only in recent times, only after some 600 years, that truth is beginning to overtake him. Nicholas III. and Boniface VIII. are being dragged out of the holes in hell in which he plunged them, and placed much nearer that heavenly mansion which their immortal works have merited.

Let us now look at the hole in which Dante thrust Nicholas, and in which most men have unfortunately seen him ever since. In the third pit of hell is a dark grey

---

[1] *Cf.* epp. to Charles of Anjou and to the Rector of the March of Ancona, May 19, 1280, ap. Pot., n. 21718, and Theiner, *Cod. Diplom.*, i, n. 394.

rock pierced with holes from each of which two legs with soles on fire protrude. One pair is especially violently agitated ; and Dante, bending low, asks the name of the sufferer. From out the hole ascend the words :—

> " Learn
> That in the mighty mantle I was robed,
> And of a she-bear was indeed the son,
> So eager to advance my whelps, that there
> My having in my purse above I stow'd,
> And here myself."

A little later the poet himself thus addresses the unhappy Pontiff :—

> " Abide thou there.
> Thy punishment of right is merited ;
> And look thou well to that ill-gotten coin,
> Which against Charles [1] thy hardihood inspired.

*　　　*　　　*　　　*　　　*

> Your avarice
> O'ercasts the world with mourning, under foot
> Treading the good, and raising bad men up." [2]

Dante's early commentators naturally followed in the footsteps of their master. Nicholas, says Benvenuto da Imola, "was the first Pope publicly denounced for simony " [3]; and he adds that Boniface VIII. was, after him, the next and last to be stained with that vice.[4]

That Nicholas succeeded in improving the temporal power of the Roman Church was quite sufficient to prejudice him in the eyes of the ultra-Ghibelline Dante. Hence he readily accepted what Döllinger justly calls Villani's "improbable accusation " of his having been corrupted by the Byzantine gold—" that ill-gotten coin " —of John of Procida. Dante's estimate then of the

---

[1] Of Anjou.
[2] *Inferno*, Canto xix, l. 71 ff.
[3] *Comment. in Inf.*, xix, vol. ii, p. 37, ed. Lacaita.
[4] *Ib.*, pp. 40 and 47.

character of Nicholas, resting simply on party prejudice and a baseless story, may be at once dismissed.[1]

But Dante is not the only ancient writer who attacks Nicholas. That is true ; but, of all his contemporaries or quasi-contemporaries who blame him, there is not one whose praise does not far outweigh his blame, or who accuses him of anything but nepotism. His character is summed up in two phrases of two anonymous chroniclers : " He was a most honourable and most prudent man," and " He did much in a short time ".[2] Another such annalist assures us that " he surpassed very many of his predecessors in what he accomplished (*potencia*) both in the spiritual and in the temporal order ".[3] Others dwell on the nobility of his birth, on his handsome face and figure, on the beauty of his moral character, and on the clearness of his understanding, and the soundness of his judgment. We are assured that he was an excellent preacher in the vulgar tongue, that he sang beautifully, that he paid great attention to the liturgy and said Mass most devoutly. His doors were open to all, and he gave great alms both in public and in private.[4] His dignified appearance won for him the appellation of " El Composto ".[5]

Those writers, however, who have fault to find with

---

[1] " The judgment of Dante rests only on the unproved and improbable accusation " of Procida's gold. Döllinger, *Hist. of the Church*, iv, p. 75, Eng. trans. See also the reflections to the same effect of Prof. Rocca, quoted by Bishop Casartelli in his useful little paper on *The Popes in the Divina Commedia*, p. 41 f., London, 1922.

[2] " Honestissimus et prudentissimus " says the English Franciscan continuation of Martinus Pol., ap. *M. G. SS.*, xxiv, p. 254. This chronicler is most favourable to Nicholas. " In paucis temporibus multa fecit," *Contin. Mart. P.*, ap. *ib.*, xxx, p. 711.

[3] *Ann. Austriæ Cont. Zwetlen.*, ap. *ib.*, ix, p. 657.

[4] *Contin. Rom. Mart. Pol.*, ap. *ib.*, xxx, p. 712.

[5] Ptolemy of Lucca, *H. E.*, ap. *R. I. SS.*, xi, p. 1179. *Cf.* p. 1182. *Cf. Mem. Potest. Reg.*, ap. *ib.*, vol. viii, p. 1141, " Nobilis literatus, etc."

Nicholas, generally do it in some such terms as those
employed by the Italian continuator of Martinus Polonus.
" He would, it was said, have been without an equal,
if he had not had relations." [1]

In case our narrative has not of itself been sufficient
to convince the reader that Nicholas III. cannot justly
be accused of either simony or nepotism *strictly* so called,
we will quote what has been said on his behalf by the
author of *Italy in the Thirteenth Century*.[2] After con-
demning Dante's " extreme and narrow judgment " of
the " great Pope " Nicholas, and observing that " his
hatred of his own enemy Pope Boniface VIII. extends
backwards and brands Boniface's predecessors ", he
declares that " for impartial persons a good defence has
been made on behalf of Nicholas' nepotism ". " Rome
and the Papal States constituted the necessary base for
the vast fabric of the Church." To keep this territory
steadily loyal, it was necessary for the Pope to have
trustworthy persons in authority. Hence Nicholas made
three of his relations cardinals. But " embittered
Ghibellines believed the popes ready to commit every
crime " and " Friars and monks liked to exaggerate the
contrast between their own secluded lives and the gaudy
naughtiness of the world ". Hence " it would be unfair
to condemn Nicholas for nepotism upon the testimony
of monastic gossip. . . . As to his nephews sent to
Romagna, . . . and charged with the duty of turning
that crop of nettles into a garden, one may say that, if
to give such a task be nepotism, all the specks of
corruption therein have first been washed away ". True
as all this is, one cannot help feeling that, in the matter
of advancing relatives, Nicholas indulged rather freely

---

[1] Ap. *M. G. SS.*, xxx, p. 711. *Cf.* Villani, *Chron.*, vii, 53 ; Ricobaldi
of Ferrara, *Hist. Pont.*, ap. *R. I. SS.*, ix, p. 182, etc.

[2] Sedgwick, vol. ii, p. 101 f.

in a practice which in less careful and conscientious hands was sure to result in abuse.

From his seemingly good constitution, and his temperate mode of life, it was generally expected that Nicholas would have a reign at any rate of more than three years,[1] but he was stricken down on Aug. 21, 1280, with a stroke of apoplexy at Suriano, whither he had gone in the beginning of June. The cardinals from the neighbouring city of Viterbo were at once summoned to his bedside, but they arrived hardly more than in time to see him die (Aug. 22).[2]

Death of Nicholas, 1280.

The body of the late Pope was at once taken to Rome, and buried on the Sunday after his death in the chapel of St. Nicholas which he had built in St. Peter's.[3]

When, says Martin IV., our predecessor Nicholas III. had departed from this life, his body was conveyed to Rome, and with due funeral obsequies solemnly interred in the place he had selected.[4] The spot he had chosen

The tomb of Nicholas III.

---

[1] B. Guidonis, *In Vit.*, p. 607. *Cf.* Ptolemy of Lucca, *Annales*, p. 1292. The comparatively sudden death of Nicholas of course gave rise to silly stories about poison, etc. *Cf. Ann. S. Rudberti,* ap. *M. G. SS.*, ix, p. 806, and *Chron. Bavar.*, ap. *ib.*, xxiv, p. 225. It is to be hoped that his death was not accelerated by his want of faith in doctors. *Cf.* G. Marini, *Degli Archiatri*, i, p. 26, who quotes a letter of Clement IV. to him when he was a cardinal blaming him for not relying on his doctor.

[2] *Mart. Pol. Cont. Rom.*, ap. *M. G. SS.*, xxii, p. 476 ; ep. ap. Redlich, n. 159 ; Saba, vii, 8. *Cf.* for all the authorities on the death of Nicholas, Potthast, ii, pp. 1754–5.

[3] B. Guidonis, *l.c.* ; Ptolemy of Lucca, *H. E.*, xxiii, 35 ; *Reg. Mart. IV.*, n. 1. It is known that his sculptured effigy was once to be seen in the crypt of St. Peter's, and it has been conjectured that the carved figure of a Pope on top of the tomb of Urban VI. is really that of Nicholas III. At any rate, at present there is no recumbent effigy on the sarcophagus of Nicholas III. *Cf.* Ciampini, *De Sacris Ædificiis*, p. 108, Rome, 1693, " Julii II. et Nicolai III. sepulcra hic sunt, quorum etiam imagines cœlatæ cernuntur " ; and L. Filippini, *La Scultura nel Trecento a Roma*, p. 123.

[4] Ep. Mart., " Incomprehensibilis," dated from Orvieto in the first year of his pontificate, ap. *Bullar. Rom.*, iv, p. 49.

was the chapel he had dedicated to St. Nicholas in the basilica of St. Peter (1279), somewhere about the angle formed by the junction of the more northerly aisle of the *Epistle* side with the north transept.[1]   Five years later (May 16, 1285), it was laid to rest in the " most elegant marble " [2] sepulchral monument which had been prepared for it.[3]   During the course of the destruction of old St. Peter's (1620–1), cardinal Alexander Orsini caused to be placed in one absolutely plain unpolished marble sarcophagus, but in separate caskets, the remains of three members of his family—Pope Nicholas III., Rainaldo Orsini, cardinal deacon of St. Hadrian († 1374), and a still earlier cardinal Rainaldo Orsini.[4]   This rude sarcophagus bears the simple inscription : Nicolaus Papa Tertius, Ursinus ;   Rainaldus card. Ursinus ;   Rainaldus Ursinus Sancti Hadriani Diac. Card. Hujus Basil.   Vatic. Archpresb.[5]

The Tombs of the Popes.   We may here perhaps be permitted to insert a paragraph or two on the tombs of the Popes in general, based upon recent researches.[6]   In the year 1915, out of the 264 Popes of the official catalogue, 228 were buried in Rome, mostly in St. Peter's,[7] twenty-six in other Italian

---

[1] *Cf.* Alfarano, *De Basilic. Vat.*, pp. 92–3, ed. Cerrati.

[2] *Ib.*, p. 192.

[3] *Ib.*, and Dionysio, *Crypt. Monument.*, p. 144 (Rome, 1828), and the authorities there quoted.   The work of Dionysio was first published in 1772.

[4] *Cf.* Alf., *l.c.*, pp. 40–1 and 93, quoting a MS. of Grimaldi (Vat. Lat. 6437), which was finished in June, 1622.   See also Dionysio, *l.c.* and Sarti's *Appendix* thereto, Rome, 1840, pp. 60–1, 107, and plate xvii.

[5] By the side of the sarcophagus will be seen three stone fragments bearing the arms of the Orsini family.

[6] Especially upon R. Cecchetelli-Ippoliti, " Le Tombe papali," ap. *Rivista d'Italia*, April, 1925.

[7] For instance, from S. Leo I. († 461) for nearly five centuries they were buried in St. Peter's, some seventy of them.   *Cf.* Duchesne, " Vaticana," ap. *Mélanges d'Archeol.*, 1902, p. 404 ff.   After Leo V. († 903) they were buried in the Lateran for some time, but even during that period many were buried in St. Peter's.

cities, eight in France, and two in Germany. Of all these
tombs only about a hundred still exist. The Popes of the
first two centuries were buried like St. Peter, and around
his body on the Vatican Hill ; but of their tombs we
know practically nothing. The first sepulchral monuments of the Popes on which we can look to-day belong to
the third century, and to those Pontiffs who were buried
in the cemetery of S. Callisto on the Appian Way. These
monuments, because made in the age of the martyrs,
are naturally very simple. They consist of a simple
marble slab bearing the name of the Pope, and his title
of bishop in Greek characters for the most part, e.g.,
ΠΟΝΤΙΑΝΟϹ ΕΠΙϹΚ.[1]   They are some six or seven in
number.

In the early Middle Ages old pagan sarcophagi were
used as papal sepulchral monuments, as we see in the
case of the tombs of Gregory the Great, Boniface IV.,
Leo IX. in the basilica of St. Peter's, and that of
Hadrian IV. in its Crypt. These tombs are of simple
design without the effigy of the deceased person, but
sometimes displaying some rude bas-reliefs or an
inscription.

In the thirteenth century Christian sepulchral art took
a step forward ; and, as in ancient Etruscan and Roman
tombs, the figure of the deceased was represented resting
on the top of the monument, as we see in the case of the
mausoleums of Clement IV., Hadrian V., and John XXI.,
of which we have already spoken. Very often the tomb
with its recumbent figure, not infrequently inclined at an
angle so that it could be the better seen, was placed
beneath a canopy resting against the wall.[2] And as these
canopies were often decorated by Cosmati work the

---

[1] *Cf.* Marucchi, *Epigrafia Cristiana*, p. 187 ff., Milan, 1910, and
Scaglia, *The Catacombs of St. Callistus*, p. 98 ff., Rome, 1911.

[2] E.g., the monuments of Clement IV., Hadrian V., Gregory X., and
Benedict XI.

result was superb. With the Avignon papal tombs what was lost in colour was compensated for by the increased architectural elegance of the canopies that surmounted them.

At least from the time of Hadrian V., the arms of the Popes almost always figure on their sepulchral monuments, now in mosaic, now cut into the stone or marble, and now in terra-cotta as in the case of the tomb of Alexander V. at Bologna. Finally, at times the heraldic figure in the arms serves as the decorative theme of the monument, as does the lion on the mausoleum of Clement VI.

MARTIN IV.

A.D. 1281–1285.

Sources of Information and Bibliography.—Pope Martin IV. is one of the Popes concerning whom we have few original sources of information. The short biographies which appear, as in the case of his predecessors, in the *Liber Pontificalis* or the works of Raynaldus and others, are brief and tell us little. Our principal sources of knowledge are his registers which have been published for his entire reign by the *École française de Rome* in the *Bibliothèque des écoles françaises d'Athènes et de Rome*, Series ii, xvi, 1913 ff. Other sources are the Papal and Imperial *Regesta*, the *Bullaria*, particularly the Franciscan Bullarium, which, of course, is very important in view of Martin's pronounced preference for that order, the relevant volumes of the *Monumenta Germaniæ*, and the works enumerated in the comprehensive list of authorities subjoined. This list also covers the most important literature, but this indeed is not extensive in regard to this Pope, who has not been portrayed by any modern biographer. Works dealing with the Sicilian Vespers and with Rudolf of Habsburg must of course contain references to Martin, but the present is the first account written of his pontificate as such. Concerning his life before his elevation to the Papacy there is a valuable work by N. Backes.

CONTEMPORARY SOVEREIGNS.

HOLY ROMAN EMPIRE.	GREEK EMPIRE.
Rudolf of Habsburg (1273–91).	Michael VIII. (Palaeologus) (1259–82). Andronicus II. (1282–1332).
ENGLAND.	FRANCE.
Edward I. (1272–1307).	Philip III. (1270–85). Philip IV. (1285–1314).

167

Authorities and Literature.[1]

Aktenstücke zur Geschichte des deutschen Reiches unter den Königen Rudolf I. und Albrecht I. Collected by A. Fanta, F. Kaltenbrunner, and E. v. Ottenthal, and communicated by F. Kaltenbrunner (Vienna, 1889. *Archiv für österreichische Geschichte*, vol. vi, pp. 108 ff.)

N. Backes, *Kardinal Simon de Brion* (*Martin IV.*) (Breslau, 1920).

Baronius, *Annales ecclesiastici.*

A. Bellesheim, *Geschichte der kathol. Kirche in Schottland* (Mainz, 1883).

J. Böhmer, *Fontes rerum Germanicarum*, i.

Bullarium Franciscanum Romanorum pontificum. Studio et labore F. Joannis Hyacinthi Sbaraleae, vol. iii (Rome, 1765).

Bullarium ordinis Prædicatorum, i.

Bullarium Romanum, iv.

L. Cardella, *Memorie storiche dei cardinali*, i–ii (Rome, 1792).

O. Cartellieri, *Peter v. Aragon und die sizilianische Vesper* (Heidelberger Abhandlungen zur mittleren und neueren Geschichte. Heft 7, 1904.)

E. Choullier, *Recherches sur la vie du pape Martin IV.* (Revue de Champagne et de Brie, iv, 1878).

Chronicon Florentii Wygorn., ii. Edited Benj. Thorpe (London, 1849).

Ciacconius, *Vitæ et res gestæ pontificum Romanorum et S. R. E. cardinalium ab A. Oldoino recognitæ*, ii (Rome, 1677).

Chartularium universitatis Parisiensis, i. Edited Denifle (Paris, 1889).

Denifle, *Geschichte der Universitaten im Mittelalter*, i (Berlin, 1885).

F. Duchesne, *Histoire de tous les cardinaux françois de naissance* i, (Paris, 1660).

Durrieu, *Les archives Angevines de Naples*, 2 vols., 1265–85 (Paris, 1886).

Festgabe zu Ehren Max Budingers (Innsbruck, 1898).

P. Frizon, *Gallia purpurata* (Paris, 1638).

Geschichtsquellen der Provinz Sachsen, i–ii (Halle, 1870), Th. Fischer, *Nikolaus von Bibra, Carmen Satiricum.*

Giov. del Giudice, *Codice diplomatico di Carlo I. et II. d'Angiò* (Naples, 1863–96).

---

[1] Works referring to a pontificate are cited thereunder.

A. Gottlob, *Die papstlichen Kreuzzugsteuern des* 13. *Jahrhunderts* (Heiligenstadt (Eichsfeld), 1892).

P. Gratien, *Histoire de la fondation et de l'évolution de l'ordre des Frères Mineurs au XIII. siècle* (Paris, 1928).

F. Gregorovius, *Geschichte der Stadt Rom im Mittelalter*, vol. v (1892).

A. Hauck, *Kirchengeschichte Deutschlands*, v (1920).

C. J. Hefele, *Konziliengeschichte*, vi (1890).

J. Heller, *Deutschland und Frankreich in ihren politischen Beziehungen vom Ende des Interregnums bis zum Tode Rudolfs v. Habsburg* (Göttingen, 1874).

Jahresberichte der Geschichtswissenschaft, 1882.

Fr. Kern, *Acta imperii Anglie et Francie*, 1276–1313 (1911).

H. Leo, *Geschichte der italienischen Staaten*, iv (Allg. Staatengeschichte, part i, Italien, 1829).

Liber pontificalis, 2 vols., ed. L. Duchesne (Paris, 1886).

E. Martène–U. Durand, *Thessaurus novus anecdotorum*, vol. ij (Paris, 1717).

E. Martène–U. Durand, *Veterum scriptorum et monumentorum historicorum, dogmaticorum, moralium amplissima collectio* (Paris, 1724–33).

Mitteilungen d. österr. Instituts für Geschichtsforschung, vols. 4, 14, 19, 31.

Monumenta Germaniæ historica : Constitutiones iii, *Scriptores* viii, ix, xvi, xvii, xviii, xix, xxii, xxiv, xxx, xxxii ; *Epistolæ selectæ*.

Monumenta Vaticana Hungarie, Series i, vol. i.

En Ramon Muntaner (German edition by Dr. K. Fr. W. Lang, 1842).

Muratori, *Antiquitates Italiæ medii ævi*, iv (Milan, 1738–42).

Muratori, *Rerum Italicarum scriptores*, vols. iii, vi, viii, ix, x, xi, xii (Milan, 1723 ff.).

W. Norden, *Die Papstgeschichte und Byzanz* (1903).

B. Pawlicki, *Papst Honorius IV.* (1896).

B. Platina, *Vitæ pontificum* (Venice, 1511).

Program des erzbischöflichen Privatgymn. Colleg. Borromäum in Salzburg, 1887.

Raynaldus, *Annales ecclesiastici*.

O. Redlich, *Rudolf von Habsburg* (published 1903).

Regesta Imperii, edited by Böhmer and Redlich, vol. ii (pub. 1898).

Regesta Pontificum Romanorum, edited by A. Potthast, in two volumes (Berlin, 1874). *Cited as* Potthast.

Les Registres d'Honorius IV. (published by Maurice Prou, Paris,
    1888.   Bibliothèque des écoles françaises d'Athènes et
    de Rome. Second Series). *Cited as* Reg.

Les Registres de Martin IV. (published or analysed by members of
    the École française de Rome, Paris, 1913 ff. Bibliothèque
    des écoles françaises d'Athènes et de Rome, Series ii, xvi).
    Cited as Reg.

A. v. Reumont, *Geschichte Roms,* vol. ii (published 1867).

Ricordi e documenti del Vespro Sicil., documenti inediti (pub. 1882).

Salimbene, *Chronicon Parm.,* edited by A. Bertani (Parma, 1857).

J. B. Sägmüller, *Die Tätigkeit und Stellung der Kardinäle bis
    Papst Bonif. VIII.* (1896).

Scriptores Ordinis Prædicatorum, i.

F. Seppelt, *Das Papsttum und Byzanz,* ii (1904).

R. Sternfeld, *Der Kardinal Johann Gaetan Orsini* (Berlin, 1905).

Historische Studien, Heft 52 (Rome, 1863-75).

A. Theiner, *Vetera Monumenta Slavorum meridion.; Vetera
    Monumenta Poloniæ et Lithuaniæ* (Rome, 1860).

Historische Vierteljahrschrift, iii (Freiburg i. Br., 1900).

F. A. Vitale, *Storia diplomatica de Senatori di Roma dalla deca-
    denza dell'Imperio Romano,* i (Rome, 1790).

*Eine Wiener Briefsammlung zur Geschichte des deutschen Reiches
    in der zweiten Hälfte des 13ten Jahrhunderts nach den
    Abschriften von Albert Starzer,* issued by O. Redlich (Mittei-
    lungen aus dem vatikanischen Archiv ii, Vienna, 1894).

Historische Zeitschrift, vols. 25, 55, 80.

Zeitschrift der Savignystiftung Kanon, Abteilung vols. 28, 29.

CHAPTER I.

CONCLAVE. ELECTION. PERSONAL PARTICULARS. CAREER
AND ACTIVITIES UP TO ELECTION.

O<small>N</small> August 22, 1280, Pope Nicholas III. had died of a Disturbances heart attack. His death took place at Castel Soriano, in Rome follow death near Viterbo, which he had bestowed on his nephew of Nicholas III. Orso. When the news reached Rome disorder was let loose. The strong hand of the Pope had enforced peace on the rival noble families of the city, and the Orsini and Colonna had actually formed an alliance. But as soon as the Pope was no longer to be feared, a general uprising took place against the Orsini, whose power had waxed during the papacy of Nicholas. At the head of the opposing party were the Annibaldi, and, with the support of the populace, the senators were overthrown. Nevertheless at the new election both parties had to agree to a compromise which allowed Petrus Conti of the Annibaldi party and Gentile Orsini to share the office of Senator.[1]

The disturbance extended itself to Viterbo, where the At Viterbo, conclave was taking place in the episcopal palace. the scene of Riccardo degli Annibaldi compelled Orso Orsini, who conclave. was detested by the citizens, to renounce the office of Podestà and appointed himself as guardian of the conclave. The story that Charles of Anjou came to Viterbo, as accepted by Reumont,[2] Gregorovius,[3] and others, cannot be established, and is improbable in the light of Charles's itinerary.

Moreover, it was not to his interest to bring about a

---

[1] Cf. Muratori, RR. II. SS., iii, 1, 608.

[2] L.c., ii, 601.

[3] L.c., 470.

speedy election : on the contrary, the longer the papal throne remained unoccupied, the easier was it for him to carry out his own plans. Nor was his presence essential to the exercise of his influence on the election, for his interference could be much more effective if operated through the medium of a third party, and a number of high officials of the Curia—including Benedict of Anagni, later to be Boniface VIII.—were among Charles's partisans. That Benedict was working for the election of Martin IV. is intelligible. His well-known friendship for France would not be a recommendation to an Orsini Pope, who might be expected to endeavour like his predecessor to limit the scope of French influence. But on the other hand, he might well expect that if he worked for a Frenchman, the latter would in due course recognize his services. And, in fact, Benedict was the only Italian cardinal created by Martin, and his elevation took place as early as the first half of April, 1281. That Benedict's connection with Charles was an intimate one so early can be judged from the circumstance that, on April 28, 1281, Charles nominated Benedict as his representative in proceedings to settle a dispute regarding property, a clear proof of the confidential relations which must have existed between Benedict of Anagni and Charles of Anjou. By the agency of men like Benedict, Charles could attain far more than by his personal presence ; and, in addition, he could at any time prove his alibi.

The conclave.

The conclave lasted for about six months in consequence of the abolition by Nicholas III. of the strict conclave procedure of Gregory X. With thirteen electors present, five sufficed to prevent the necessary two-thirds majority from being obtained. The three French electors had little chance of forcing through a francophile Pope, while the family policy of the Orsini had concentrated together all former enemies for the common purpose of preventing the election of an Orsini who seemed chiefly concerned to increase the power of their house. Even Ghibellines and Angevins united when there was question of preventing the election of an Orsini, hated equally by both. On the other hand, the Orsini, although not strong enough to attain the two-thirds majority for their own candidate, were able to prevent any other from reaching it. Those who favoured the French did everything possible to elect a Pope who would be a friend to France, so as to counteract the policy of Nicholas III., which had been directed towards strengthening the Papacy by eliminating the influence of the house of Anjou. This policy of Nicholas had brought considerable triumphs to the Papal State. He had secured Romagna for the church, established peace in Florence and Rome, and indicated a path of compromise to Rudolf of Habsburg and Charles of Anjou, forcing both back within the limits of their respective spheres. More important still, he had driven the Angevins from Italy back into Sicily and had opposed their designs on Constantinople. Beyond all else the Angevins wanted to make good this reverse, and consequently they desired a Pope who would be favourable to themselves and would abandon the Orsini policy.

Although the Ghibellines had been in agreement with the Roman policy of Nicholas III., they hated the Orsini and their ambitions, so they, too, were in opposition. But since the Orsini were strong enough to prevent any other candidate from being elected, the struggle in the conclave continued to be indecisive, until an act of violence effected a change. The Orsini were also unpopular with the people of Viterbo, because Giovanni Gaetani Orsini, as head of the Inquisition in Viterbo in 1265, had carried out his duties with severity, and, in addition, Orso Orsini, appointed Podestà of Viterbo by his uncle Nicholas III., had been far from popular there. Accordingly, it was easy to induce the citizens to

intimidate the Orsini.   On February 2 all the bells of
Viterbo rang out as a signal and the infuriated populace,
under its chosen leader Visconte Rainer Gatti and the
new Podestà Ricciardello, stormed the Bishop's palace
where the conclave was in session, hurling threats against
the cardinals.   But violence was directed against the
Orsini cardinals alone.   Soon the attackers desisted from
their threats against Latino Malabranca, but they carried
off Matteo Rosso and his uncle Giordano Orsini and
imprisoned them in another part of the palace.   Giordano,
having given certain undertakings, was released in three
days, but Matteo remained a prisoner until the election
was over.   At times he was allowed nothing but bread
and water, and even his confessor was refused admission
to him.[1] Twenty days after the attack, on February 22,
the Pope was elected.   With Matteo Rosso the Italian
opposition had lost not only its leader but also the power to
prevent the two-thirds majority from being attained, since
in an assembly reduced to twelve members the opposition
had declined to four, and without the four votes of the
Orsini group, or even against the latter's votes, a two-
thirds majority was obtainable.

In these circumstances the choice was not difficult.
Simon de Brion was the only experienced politician and
skilled diplomat among the cardinals, and to guide the
Church in those days an acute, trained diplomatic mind
was necessary.   The political situation was a complicated
one.   Simon was regarded as a friend of the French royal
house, especially of Charles of Anjou.   For many years
he had been the papal agent in the negotiations with
Charles regarding the annexation of Sicily.   At a moment
when the policy of Nicholas III. was being abandoned,
that policy which aimed at rendering the Papacy

---

[1] Raynaldus, *Ann.*, 1281 ; Jordani, *Chronicon* (in Muratori, *Antiqu.*,
iv, 1012).

independent of temporal influences, it was desirable that the Pope should once more enjoy the protection of powerful dynasties. Only a politically powerful Papacy, such as the Orsini desired, could hope or wish to stand aloof from temporal influences. In the eyes of the electors, who were now turning their backs on the Orsini policy, Simon's friendship with the French dynasty was a recommendation ; and none could have guessed the extent to which he was to favour French interests. So, on February 22, 1218, the cardinal of Santa Cecilia, Simon de Brion, was made Pope. As Pope he chose the name of Martin after the patron saint of Tours, where he held rich benefices. Since the Popes Marinus I. and Marinus II. had been wrongly catalogued under the name Martin in the list of Popes, he became Martin IV., although in fact only one Martin had preceded him (649–53). As his motto he selected a verse from the Psalms (cxli, 6) : *Portio mea Domine, in terra viventium.*[1]

The French who were present at Viterbo rejoiced at Simon's election, and their joy was to be quickly justified, although indeed the Germans also hoped at first that the new Pope would be favourable to them.[2] Since Rudolf of Habsburg had formed an alliance with the Pope's close friend, Charles of Sicily, and had even become a marriage connection of the latter, they could see no reason for any papal unfriendliness towards Rudolf, particularly as he had pleaded Rudolf's cause at the Council of Lyons (1274).

Although elected at Viterbo, Martin did not wish to be crowned there on account of the violence done to the cardinals during the conclave, while a coronation in Rome was out of the question, as the city was in a state of complete disorder. The new Pope went therefore to

Coronation at Orvieto.

[1] Raynaldus, *Ann.*, 1281.
[2] Böhmer-Redlich, *Regesta imperii*, vol. 6/1, 1267.

Orvieto, where he was solemnly crowned [1] on March 23, 1281.

Martin IV. came of the noble family of de Brion, which took its name from the village of Brion in the diocese of Sens, east of Joigny. The commonly expressed [2] opinion that Martin was of humble origin is incorrect, and is contradicted by the fact that the Romans conferred the dignity of Senator on the new Pope on personal grounds, he being descended from a distinguished house. His birthplace was Mainpincien in the parish of Andrezel in the province of Brie. The place no longer exists, but it was in the neighbourhood of Melun and Donnemarie near Provins.[3] It is not possible to establish the date of his birth ; all that can be ascertained is that it fell in the period 1210–20.[4] Our information about his father is also very scanty. Probably his name was Jean de Brion, and he was born in the vicinity of Gugnes, in the present department of Seine-et-Marne, the district where the Pope's birthplace is to be sought. In 1228 he was in the service of the chapter of Saint Martin at Tours, being at once Collector, Administrator, and Ecclesiastical Judge. The future Pope had two brothers and one sister.

Of one of his brothers, Guillaume, we know nothing but the name ; the other, Gilles (or Ægidius), was of some importance at the Parisian court, having a seat in the king's council. Later he became grand-juge-maire of Donnemarie near Provins in Lower Brie, an office which he held until his death, controlling the property there and exercising all the rights attendant on it. These

---

[1] *Liber pontificalis*, p. 459.

[2] By Villani, for example.

[3] Views about the Pope's family history differed widely. *Cf.* Potthast, *Reg. pontif.*, 1765. The only certain facts were that his name was Simon and that he was French. For the details given here we are indebted to the dissertation of N. Backes, pp. 11–24.

[4] *Cf.* Backes, p. 41 ff.

lands belonged to the chancellor of St. Martin at Tours, in virtue of his office, and, at the time, the office was held by his own brother, Simon, the future Pope. Accordingly, Gilles administered his brother's property. The archives also contain references to a sister of Simon who married a man named de Poilechien. There was one son of this marriage, Odo (or Hugo according to some sources). The family of Poilechien was among those which Charles of Anjou had caused to migrate to Lower Italy, where its name became Polliceni or Pelichini. It was one of the more distinguished families in the Angevin realm and enjoyed the favour of its ruler. Charles II. bestowed on Odo the prosperous and peaceful town of Ostuni in the Otranto territory. Thus, in the time of Pope Martin IV. the family possessed a certain eminence, but little influence: before long it disappeared completely. Bishop Simon de Perruché of Chartres (1277–97) is also described in his epitaph as a nephew (*nepos*) of Pope Martin IV. No doubt he was a son of a sister of the Pope.[1]

Martin belongs to that category of historical personages *Character.* concerning whose character opinions differ. He is among the Popes placed by Dante in hell.[2] Certain traits of his character stand forth clearly, in particular his pronounced nationalism. He loved France, and this love was the guiding influence in many of his governing acts as Pope. Beyond all doubt his heart was set on contributing to the growth of his country's glory and influence. On that *Nationalism.* account his work as papal legate to his native country, France, caused him special joy. In that capacity he advanced as far as in him lay the canonization of Louis IX., conducted the negotiations for granting Sicily

[1] Duchesne assumes without foundation that Simon's father also bore the names de Perruchoy or de Perruché and that the relationship was through a brother of the Pope. For this no proofs are available. For family details see Backe's dissertation, pp. 15, 25, 28, 36, 39.

[2] *Divina Commedia, Inf.,* xxiv, 20–4.

in fief to Charles of Anjou, and supported Charles's efforts
to attain the German crown. Even by his contemporaries
this love of France was interpreted as hatred of Germany,
a view that was particularly widespread in Germany
itself. Nicholas of Bibra in his *Carmen satiricum*, written
between 1281 and 1283, reports that on his fourth visit
to Rome at the beginning of Martin's Papacy, he was
told that Martin had expressed the wish that Germany
were a fish-pond and the Germans eels swimming in it
so that he—the Pope was known to have a fondness for
eels—might destroy the whole nation in the way most
pleasing to himself, by eating it. Nicholas replies in
some satirical verses composed in the form of an epitaph
on the Pope, although the latter still lived, in which he
describes Martin as a wolf in sheep's clothing.[1] The
Continuatio Vindobonensis and other sources [2] also take
notice of the Pope's alleged hatred, to which he was said
to have given harsh expression in the words quoted.
But the proof that the Pope's policy was not dictated by
hatred of Germany is to be found to some extent in the
fact that at the Council of Lyons in 1274 he pleaded the
cause of Rudolf of Habsburg. So long as Germany was
not at issue with France, he did not oppose her, but in
all circumstances he endeavoured to advance France's
interests. We can understand the bitterness felt against
the Pope throughout Germany if it is realized that the

[1] *L.c.*, v, 1014–17 :—

> Hic jacet ante chorum submersor Theutonicorum
> Pastor Martinus extra qui totus ovinus
> Et lupus introrsus cui nulla redempcio prorsus
> Sed sit ad inferna detrusus ab arce superna.

[2] *M. G. SS.*, ix, 712, *Ann.* 1284 : " Qui papa in tantum odio habuit
Theutonicos, quod ipse frequenter optabat effici ciconia sub hac forma
quod Theutonici in paludibus essent rane, ut saltem sic eos posset
devorare ; aut in lacu esset lucius et ipsi pisces, quod sic eos posset
deglutire." The *Annales Lubicenses* remark under the year 1281 :
" Creatus est papa Martinus . . . Iste Theutonicos multum invidebat."
(*M. G. SS.*, xvi, 415.)

Germans saw at the head of the Church not a man standing supreme above all nations and states, but a Frenchman and a Frenchman only. Even his contemporaries recognized and censured that fact and the injurious effects of his unlimited love for his native France.

For example, in the *Notitia sæculi*, it is said of him that he disturbed the entire Church by his preference for France.[1] A similar view was expressed incidentally by Jordan of Osnabruck. While he was still a cardinal, Pope John XXII. called him a great zealot for the welfare of the King and the realm of France,[2] while the annals of Genoa testify to his exaggerated favour towards Charles of Anjou.[3] In the *Continuatio Vindobonensis* already mentioned, it is also maintained that he placed the entire wealth of the Church at the disposition of Charles.[4] Another charge laid to the Pope's account was fondness for delicacies ; it was adduced by Dante as a reason for placing him in hell. The Chronicles of Brother Pipin of Bologna mention his passion for eels cooked in milk and wine, and the same authority tells of a book entitled *Incipit initium malorum*, and containing a picture of the Pope holding in his hand an eel at which a bird pecks.[5] In Germany, too, Martin was known as a

Other alleged disedifying attributes.

[1] M. qui ob amorem sue gentis turbavit ecclesiam Dei totam volens totum mundum modo Gallicorum regere. *Cf. Denkschriften der Wiener Akademie*, vi, 108.

[2] Sedulum zelatorem : Raynaldus, *Ann.*, 1277.

[3] Martinus favorabilis erat ultra modum dicto regi Karolo (*M. G. SS.*, xviii, 294).

[4] Anno Domini 1284 rex Aragonum bellum commisit cum Karolo rege . . . Occisis ex utraque parte innumerabili multitudine, tandem rex Arragonum potenter victoriam obtinuit fugato turpiter Karolo de bello, *quamvis papa tota virtute sua cum suis hominibus et pecunia tocius ecclesie ei assisteret.*

[5] *Chronicon fratris Pipini Bononiensis* in Muratori : *RR. II. SS.*, ix, 726 ff. In the same place a lampoon on the Pope is mentioned, viz. *gaudent anguille, quod mortuus est homo ille Qui quasi morte reas excruciebat eas.* The same authority goes so far as to ascribe the Pope's death to an illness resulting from immoderate indulgence in eels.

gourmet, according to an observation of Johann von Viktring.[1] The other observations regarding him to be found in the satire by his contemporary, Nicholas of Bibra, namely, that he has a *cor ovinum* and is the heir of Simon Magus, bearing the name but not possessing the spirit of his patron saint, Martin of Tours (*nomen non tamen omen*), find no justification in history. Martin may be regarded as a man who, without being a genius or a model of sanctity, was far above the average standard

True character. of his time in intellectual and ethical respects. He was distinguished by serenity and selflessness. Nepotism was alien to him, as is illustrated by the following episode related by Antoninus, the saintly Bishop of Florence.[2] Immediately after the Pope's election his brother came to congratulate him, but found his hopes of rich presents and honours bitterly disappointed, for the Pope merely made good his travelling expenses and sent him straight home again, because " the property he owned as Pope belonged to the Church and not to himself ". This story is corroborated by the fact that, according to a papal brief, Martin at this time sent a costly reliquary to the dean and chapter of his native diocese of Sens by his brother Gilles, so that the latter must really have been in Orvieto. Another testimony is that his nephew, Magister Simon de Brion, who was studying in Bologna, was not advanced to any particular spiritual dignity, as was otherwise usual for relatives of the Pope. The reproach of nepotism could in truth never be directed against Pope Martin IV.

Had not sought papal dignity. Martin had not striven for the papal dignity. In the proclamation in which he announced his election he

---

[1] Böhmer, *Fontes rerum Germ.*, i, 316.

[2] *Chronicon Lugduni*, 1512, iii, tit. xx, cap. iv ; Raynaldus, *Ann.*, 1281.

emphasized and stressed his earnest wish not to accept it.[1] Indeed, he struggled so much that the papal robes had to be put on him by force. True, it was regarded in those days as a matter of etiquette not to accept dignities without a struggle, but Martin's conduct went much further than that. His resistance was genuine. Probably he shrank from the responsibility of the burthen which it was proposed to lay upon him. His was no fiery spirit : rather did he avoid deep emotions.

While he had been glad to forward the business of the Church in his own country for the benefit of that country, he had fears when it was a question of guiding the whole Church. Obviously he knew himself sufficiently to realize that he would be unable to resist the pressure of his royal friends ; therefore he would have preferred to avoid altogether the difficult decisions which his mind's

---

[1] *Reg. M. IV*, 1 : " Tanto ex huiusmodi vocacione redditi proinde magis attoniti proposito alieni arbitrati semper, tutioris fore consilii nobis altiora non querere, in domo Domini humiliter habitando de propria salute curare, quam periculose supra universalem omnium curam erigi et ad tanti fastigii sollicitudinem elevari, hinc insufficiencie nostre consideracio contrahebat animum et a tanti assumpcione laboris dexteram retrahebat, suadebat instancius potius tante molis pondus effugere, quam eorundem fratrum instancie consentire, verum in contrarium consciencia suadente non esse vocacioni Domini, quam tanto verisimilius eorundem fratrum adeo unanimis concordia pretendebat, quanto diutius ipsorum fuerant vota discordia contumaciter resistendum, ne ipsa Dei ecclesia eo prolixius viduitatis dispendiis gravaretur, quo alias spes erat incertior de ipsius provisione vicina, tandem variis allegatis excusationibus nec admissis sed ab eisdem fratribus in eo fervore voluntatis anexie importunitatisque multimode obauditis, ut manus ad exuendum nos clamidem, qua tegebamur, extenderint nec ipsius rupture pepercerint, sub spe unigeniti Dei filii Domini Jesu Christi humilitatis nostre colla subjecimus jugo apostolice servitutis, de sua pietate sperantes, quod ipse, qui iuxta evangelicam veritatem quinque panum duorumque piscium paucitatem satietati discumbentis ad jussum ipsius immense multitudinis cum mira fragmentorum superhabundantia coequavit, nostre imbecillitatis insufficienciam sua immensa virtute quali saltem sufficiencie tanti oneris et laboris equabit." To this he adds a request for prayers that God may assist him.

eye foresaw would rest on him when Pope. During his
pontificate the slowness of the Curia became a proverb ;
men spoke of the " leaden feet " (*per pedes plumbeos*) of
the course of matters in the Curia. This no doubt resulted
from the fact that Martin avoided taking decisions as
long as possible. Filled though he was at all times with
a realization of the significance and majesty of the papal
dignity, he never ceased to feel its responsibilities as a
burden.

Authorities [1] also praise his great charity to those
in need. In years of high prices he showed great
prudence in his financial arrangements. Particular praise
is accorded to him for that he always preserved the
property of the Church and did not use it to enrich his
family.

Thus the personality of Martin IV. emerges before us,
as one devoid of heroism no doubt, but filled with the
consciousness of the dignity of the Papacy, and one who
never made bad use of its powers nor wished to do so.
No doubt his deep love of country often led him to
forget that as Pope he must not regard himself as a
Frenchman, but as the universal father and shepherd of
all Christians, but his political attitude can only be
understood correctly in the light of his earlier life.

Studies.

He was a Frenchman through and through. France
was his cradle, and it was in Paris that, in his own words,
he acquired the foundations of a scientific education
(*primaria sciencie elementa*). This must mean at the
very least that he belonged to the faculty of arts there.
For information regarding his subsequent studies we
must fall back on scanty references and assumptions.
He can hardly have studied theology in Paris, for it
would have been out of the question, in view of the

---

[1] Raynaldus, *Ann.*, 1283 ; Potthast, *Reg.*, 22073, 22074 ; Muratori,
RR. II. SS., viii, *Istoria Fiorentina*, 1025, 1044.

language of the period, to have described that training as *primaria elementa sciencie*. Moreover, he would not have kept silence on the point, in view of the importance of the Paris Faculty, seeing that he mentions his introduction to knowledge. He seems to have studied law in Parma whither he was drawn, no doubt, by the lectures of the famous Hubertus of Bobbio, and probably also in Bologna. How he paid for his studies is unknown, but it may be assumed that, like most students, he held some ecclesiastical benefices or cathedral office, the yield of which enabled him to procure his education.

In office we find Simon de Brion for the first time as a priest in Rouen, and he quickly became in turn official, archdeacon, and, finally, chancellor of the chapter. Offices and dignities.

Later on he likes to recall this period [1] and the advancement he experienced during it. Simultaneously he held a canonry of St. Quentin, which he owed to King Louis, the Saint. Soon after 1255 he obtained a canonry of St. Martin at Tours, and indeed the rank of second dignitary of the Church, that of chancellor, a clear testimony that he had carried out his duties in Rouen satisfactorily. The two principal dignitaries were nominated by the King himself, and the nomination of Simon de Brion shows that he had the King's entire confidence. The dignity of chancellor of St. Martin's was no empty one, but carried with it important responsibilities.[2] Simon was aware of these. When a committee of reform, consisting of Bishop Gaufridus of Le Mans and the Cistercian Abbot Philip of Francarmont, decreed in the interests of discipline, without the chancellor being

---

[1] He says in a document addressed to the College of Canons of Rouen : " Non enim sumus immemores, quinimo frequenter ad memoriam revocamus, quod ipsa ecclesia nos, dum in minoribus ageremus, maternis tractavit affectibus, provenit gratiis, beneficiis honoravit."

[2] *Cf.* Backes, *Dissertation*, pp. 56–62.

present, that for the future entrance to and exit from the
monastery should take place only through a guarded
gate, Simon at once protested to Rome. He pleaded
that, by virtue of his ecclesiastical office, the exercise of
justice over Chateauneuf was his prerogative ; a limitation on ingress to and egress from the monastery would
hamper him in the exercise of his freedom of movement
as a judge. In the event the Pope at his request dispensed
him from this regulation.[1]

When the Bishop of Le Puy, Guido Fulcodi, became
Archbishop of Narbonne on October 10, 1259, a majority
of the chapter of Le Puy selected William de la Roue
as the new Bishop. The dean and provost of the chapter
put forward Simon the chancellor of St. Martin's as an
opposition candidate, and the ensuing contest went on
for years. Not until 1263 did Simon renounce the
bishopric, having in the meanwhile advanced to other
spiritual and worldly honours. Louis IX. made him a
member of his council, and there he sat among the most
eminent men in France, including the future Pope
Clement IV., Robert of Sorbonne, etc. During the octave
of Candlemas Day in 1260, and again in 1261, we find
his name mentioned specifically among those present in
parliament. His nomination by the King as chancellor
of France and Keeper of the Great Seal also took place
in 1260. Even though this was a distinction rather than
an office, the position and influence of Simon was
appreciably increased by it. Perhaps it may have been
the factor which moved Pope Urban IV. to take him into
the supreme council of the Church, for on December 24,
1261, the Pope elevated him to the dignity of cardinal-
priest of St. Cecilia.[2] Of course, the main reason for

Enters the
College of
Cardinals.

---

[1] Potthast, *Reg.*, 18913.

[2] Potthast, *Reg.*, 56. For the date *cf. Revue d'histoire et de littérature
religieuses*, v (1900), 326 ff. For the researches which follow regarding

this elevation was the suitability of Simon for the office, and Pope Urban IV. was renowned for the care he exercised in choosing the cardinals, from whom he demanded the highest standards.

Indeed, he caused a succession of distinguished and tried men to enter the College of Cardinals.[1] We have direct evidence of the high regard in which Urban IV. held Simon in the wide powers with which the latter was endowed when legate to France, and also in the letter in which the Pope recommends Simon to the clergy of France, the terms of which go far beyond what is usual. In it the Pope describes Simon as a man distinguished for the depth of his knowledge, the purity of his morals, and the prudence of his counsel.[2] But political considerations also entered into Urban's selections. Obviously he desired to strengthen French influence in the College of Cardinals, for during his reign the number of French cardinals rose to nine, seven of whom were nominated by him. Besides the French, there were eleven Italians, one Englishman, and one Hungarian. In the event of the papal State being threatened from north and south, Urban wished to be sure of aid from France.[3] It was inevitable that the Pope's eye should be directed thither. The whole world was in disorder. Strife, disunion, struggle were everywhere. But France

the activities of Simon as a cardinal, I am indebted to Dr. N. Backes, who with the greatest kindness placed at my disposal the extensive portions of his dissertation which have unfortunately not been printed. For this I wish to thank him here.

[1] According to a letter addressed to Archbishop Guido of Narbonne, the cardinals must be : " viri devotionis immensitate prefulgidi, consilii maturitate conspicui, discretionis honestate decori, magnanimitate sublimes et virtutibus precellentes " (Baluze, *Conc. Gall. Narbonnensis*, Appendix, 167 ff. ; Martène, *Vet. script. ampl. collectio*, iv, 1256).

[2] Martène et Durand, *Thesaurus novus, Epistolæ Urbani IV*, 62 (xxix).

[3] *Cf.* Hampe, *Urban IV. und Manfred* ; Heidemann, *Papst Klemens IV.*, 94.

alone stood strong and at unity under a ruler whom the world contemplated with admiration.

From St. Louis the Pope need fear for the Church neither oppression nor imposition. Even if he were not himself French, he must have turned for aid to France in the first instance, and he could hardly foresee the unhappy consequences of the network of connecting links, particularly when the French kingdom was no longer directed by a saint, but by clear-sighted politicians. If the connection between the Papacy and the French dynasty became too close, Cardinal Simon de Brion contributed powerfully to that end.

On March 22, 1262, Simon bade farewell to the French court and to Paris. Previously, in January, at the request of Louis IX., he had conferred with Archbishop Odo of Rouen, probably in regard to important questions affecting Church and State in France.[1] During his first two years in Italy he remained close to the Pope, but we have no exact information as to his activities at the Curia. Twenty-five months after he reached Rome, Cardinal Simon was given his first important task when he was entrusted with concluding the negotiations with Charles of Anjou and Louis IX. relating to the grant of Sicily as a papal fief.

French Legation.

The importance which this question was to assume once more during Martin's pontificate [2] makes it necessary to go into its earlier history somewhat closely.

The Sicilian question.

On the death of Alexander IV., Manfred was not merely undisputed master of Sicily, but also occupied a pre-dominating position in the Mediterranean. He had

---

[1] *Recueil*, xxi, 586 ; Bonnin, *Regestrum Archiep. Rothomagensis*, p. 420 ff.

[2] The Sicilian Vespers. For this *cf.* Le Nain de Tillemont, *La vie de S. Louis IX.*; R. Sternfeld, *Karl von Anjou als Graf der Provence* (Berlin, 1888) ; K. Hampe, *Urban IV. und Manfred* (Heidelberger Abhandlungen, ii, 1905) ; A. Bergmann, *König Manfred von Sizilien* (Heidelberger Abh. 23, 1909).

himself crowned King in Palermo on August 11, 1258, after having violently suppressed a number of revolts in Sicily which had been supported by the Curia. He was in close contact with the Pallavicini, the chief rulers of Upper Italy, and, in harmony with the traditional Mediterranean policy of the Sicilian Kings, he entered into firm friendly relations with Genoa and Venice. He established matrimonial connections with the King of Aragon and the Prince of Epirus; the kingdom of Torres in Sardinia was in his possession; he had established himself in Illyria; his troops were fighting successfully in Macedonia; shortly before the death of Alexander IV. the Ghibelline party had elected him Senator. When Urban assumed the direction of the papal State, his position was a dubious one. Unable to banish the threatening danger himself, he turned soon after his elevation to France, and offered the crown of Sicily to the younger son of Louis IX. When Louis declined the offer, Urban made a similar proposal to Charles of Anjou, Louis's youngest brother. This was in the spring of 1262. Still Louis hesitated. He was in doubt as to whether the Hohenstaufens had not a hereditary claim to Sicily, and there was also the difficulty that Alexander IV. had conferred Sicily in fief on the English Prince Edmund.

He wished to have these points cleared up. Before long the Pope informed him that negotiations had been in progress with Manfred, but had led, entirely through the latter's fault, to a deeper breach with the Holy See. Hereupon Louis abandoned Manfred. Urban wrote to King Henry of England on July 28, 1263, that the conditions of the infeudation had not been fulfilled, and indeed could not be, wherefore the Pope now found himself obliged in the interests of the Church to make other arrangements regarding Sicily. As soon as these difficulties were surmounted numerous others arose. On behalf of the Curia the negotiations with Charles of

Anjou had been carried on by the skilful notary Albert of Parma, who went to France in March, 1262, to offer the kingdom of Sicily in return for a yearly tribute of 2,000 gold pieces. Just at that time Charles was fully occupied by a revolt in Provence, which, however, he mastered after reducing Marseilles in November. A second hindrance then developed. The Queen of France, Margaret, abhorred her brother-in-law Charles so deeply that she caused her eldest son, the seventeen-year-old Philip, to swear an oath that he would never enter on an alliance with his uncle Charles.[1] As might be expected, she opposed the grant of Sicily to Charles. The Pope set himself to change her mind. Writing to the heir apparent [2] on July 6, 1263, he released the latter from the oath which his mother had caused him to swear, and shortly afterwards [3] he sent the Archbishop of Cosenza, Bartholomew Pignatelli, to France and England to conduct personal negotiations. The Archbishop's chief mission was to procure from the King of England and his son Edmund a written renunciation. In the beginning of August other complications developed when Charles of Anjou by his own efforts had himself elected a Roman senator. An essential point of the treaty to be signed between Charles and Rome was that the wearer of the Sicilian crown should hold no other office in any of the territories of the Church.[4] On the one hand the Pope felt that the actual taking over of Sicily would be made easier for Charles, who was more acceptable to him in that capacity than anyone else, but, on the other hand, he could not hide from himself the dangers of the position. As a way out of the difficulty the Pope desired Charles

[1] Langlois, *Histoire de France*, iii, p. 43 ff.

[2] *Reg. Urban IV.*, n. 273. The letter of recommendation was dated July 25, 1263 (*Reg.*, 298).

[3] Martène et Durand, *Thesaurus novus*, ii. Ep. Urb., n. 12 (26 ff.).

[4] *Reg.*, n. 269.

to declare that he did not wish to hold the dignity of senator for life. If Charles could not bring himself to make a public declaration to this effect he was to swear privately to the Pope's representative, Magister Albert, that he would be prepared, when the Pope desired, to lay down the senatorship. A majority of the Roman Curia agreed to this, although a minority wished to limit the duration of Charles's senatorial rank to three or at most five years.

At the beginning of 1264 the Pope was ready to dispatch cardinals to France to bring the negotiations to a conclusion, but Louis intimated that he did not desire this ; the time seemed to him not yet opportune.[1] In the spring matters moved forward. Charles of Anjou sent a warship from Marseilles to Rome to impress the Pope and to gain new concessions, and almost simultaneously the papal negotiator, the Archbishop of Cosenza, succeeded by his skill in winning over Louis IX. to the Pope's schemes.

Now the time was ripe for the Pope to entrust a cardinal with the task of bringing matters to a head. No person could be more suitable than Simon de Brion, who from the early years of his career had enjoyed the complete confidence both of the King and Charles of Anjou. It was quite in keeping with the facts that the Pope described him in his credentials to France as a zealous protagonist of French interests.[2] On May 3, 1264, Urban IV. nominated him as papal legate to France.[3] His mission was to prepare the treaty with Charles, in complete agreement with the King. An essential point was to induce

Simon goes as legate to France.

Mission and Powers.

---

[1] Martène et Durand, *l.c.* In n. 18 the King again writes to the Pope (January 9, 1264) : "Ex his potes colligere manifeste nondum ad illum statum venisse negotium, de quo agimus, ut destinandi fuerint cardinales, quos pro gravitate non expedit currere in incertum."

[2] *Reg.*, n. 807, 812.

[3] *Reg.*, 802.

Charles to swear privately at least that he would renounce the Roman senatorship if the Pope desired it, and that in general he would recognize the supremacy of the Pope in Rome. But the principal part of the task was to work out the conditions relating to Sicily. Charles had asked the papal negotiator, Albert, for modifications of the papal proposals in certain respects, namely, a reduction of the tribute of 10,000 ounces of gold and an extension beyond what was proposed of the succession to the kingdom of Sicily.

Ecclesiastical punishments should, he suggested, apply to himself or his successors only if they knowingly acquired the greater part of Tuscany or Lombardy : if they did so without full knowledge (*ignoranter*) and if they surrendered the parts in question on the demand of the Curia, no ecclesiastical punishment should be meted out to them. The strength of the Sicilian army must be left to Charles himself to determine. Finally, the Pope would have to be satisfied with an oath of allegiance from Charles and his successors, and should not demand such an oath from the population of Sicily. The secret instructions given to Simon on these points were definite only in regard to the financial question, on which he was directed in no circumstances to go lower than 8,000 ounces. If Charles could not agree to that, then the negotiations were at an end. In everything else Simon had a free hand, but on the final point he was commissioned to stand out determinedly for the maintenance of the oath of fealty from the Sicilian population. If necessary it might be suspended during the reign of Charles, or even during that of his immediate successor, but only if the negotiations were about to break down on this account might the oath be abandoned. As regards the remaining points, the legate was to confer first with King Louis and agree with him on the line of discussion to be followed. As soon as an agreement with Charles should be reached it should be reduced to writing in the King's presence, whereupon Simon might assure Charles of the transfer of Sicily to him by the Pope. Urban reserved to himself the act of investiture.

To carry out the mission Simon was endowed with the usual plenipotentiary powers which in essence had been identical [1] for all legates *a latere* since the struggles against Frederick II., viz. power to transform the crusaders' vow into a vow to fight for Sicily against the Hohenstaufen dynasty; to preach a crusade against Manfred and the Saracens; to grant certain indulgences; to convoke synods; to impose and remit certain ecclesiastical punishments; to make use of Franciscans and Dominicans in legation matters; to grant five dispensations from the matrimonial impediments of blood relationship to the fourth degree and dispensations allowing plurality of benefices; to confer benefices on five of his priests, including canonries in cathedral and collegiate churches if such were vacant.[2] The territory to which he was accredited extended to the entire realm of France, the County of Flanders, the County of Provence with its adjoining territories, and the provinces of Lyons, Vienne, Embrun, Tarentaise, and Besançon, i.e. over practically the whole of modern France. As was customary, officials of the Curia were appointed to assist him. One of these stands out in particular, the young Benedict Gaetani, later Pope Boniface VIII.[3]

Negotiations developed, it seems, slowly, for in two letters of June 19 and July 17 Urban pressed for a conclusion so that Charles might come to his assistance, hard-pressed as he was.[4] In his second letter he represented the emergency as most urgent: the expenses of

---

[1] *Cf.* Guido Levi in *Archivio della società Romana di storia patria,* xiv (1891), p. 235 ff.

[2] *Reg.,* 813–35.   [3] Finke, *Aus den Tagen Bonifaz VIII.,* p. 3.

[4] Martène et Durand, *l.c.,* nn. 55, 56.

the defence amounted already to 200,000 pounds of Siena, and unless Charles arrived by September, it would be impossible to hold Rome, which would have to be given over to Manfred, other arrangements being made for ruling the church. He urged Simon to inform him at once whether Charles of Anjou was coming to Italy, and, if so, when. He also required to know how far generally the discussions had been successful. If he could not tell of any agreement actually reached, at least he should give his personal opinion on the situation, in particular whether he thought it probable that Charles would be in Italy with his army by the autumn. The long delay was due to an illness of Simon and also to the fact that at this time Charles was greatly taken up with English matters. Not until August were successful negotiations begun, successful chiefly for Charles, since Simon gave way on almost all points on which he had not overriding instructions from the Pope. He reduced the tribute to 8,000 ounces and renounced absolutely the oath from the Sicilian subjects, which the Pope had empowered him to do only in the last resort. Only in regard to fixing the strength of the army was the question left over for agreement between Charles and the Pope. Except for this Charles had obtained everything he wished. In addition he demanded the French tithes for three years. The Pope knew the difficulties which the French clergy would feel about this, but nevertheless he sent a letter to the French prelates in which he called on them to support Charles of Anjou, descendant of Charlemagne, so that, like his great ancestor, he might stand by the church. If a truly Catholic prince became King of Sicily, the Curia's financial demands would be lessened.

The Holy Land, too, would benefit greatly by the existence of a Catholic kingdom in Sicily. Accordingly the French prelates should help Charles of Anjou by granting him the tithes so as to make it possible for him to win over Sicily, thus assisting the Church and saving themselves from additional taxation.[1] Simultaneously, the Pope turned to King Louis [2] with the request that he might use his influence to have the tithes granted.

The legate's principal task was, of course, to create an atmosphere favourable to the Sicilian undertaking. To that end he convoked three synods at Paris, Clermont, and Lyons between August 24 and September 25, in which he actually carried the grant of the tithes for three years, carried it, as a matter of fact, unanimously.[3] Although Urban did not live to hear of this success of Simon's— he died at Perugia on October 2—he was quite satisfied with what had been already achieved, despite the great concessions made to Charles. He sent Simon a flattering letter of thanks and entrusted him with the conduct of the affair to a favourable termination.[4]

The Pope's death brought matters to a standstill. Charles of Anjou was in Provence, zealously occupied with fitting out the Roman expedition. Simon was also in the south of France, where the news of the Pope's death probably reached him at Avignon. After an interregnum of four months another Frenchman, Guido Fulcodi, ascended the papal chair, and the possibility of a new Pope adopting an anti-French policy was ended. Scarcely had Clement IV., the new Pope, taken over the conduct of the papal State than he attacked the Sicilian question as one of the most pressing problems. As early as February 26 he bestowed the warmest praise on Simon for his earlier work and ordered him to join Charles in Provence and assist the latter to equip his forces. As regards his attitude on the tithes' question, an envoy would before long convey instructions to him. On

[1] *Reg.*, n. 804, 814.
[2] *Reg.*, n. 806.
[3] Winkelmann, *Acta imperii inedita*, ii, n. 1050.
[4] Martène et Durand, *l.c.*, n. 58.

the same date the Pope declared that any claims which
England might raise regarding Sicily were null and void,
since England had completely failed [1] to carry out its
obligations either to the Church or to Sicily.   The third
document [2] of the same date sets out thirty-five
conditions for the transfer of the kingdom of Sicily to
Charles in fief.   They corresponded to those already agreed
to by Urban, excepting that in the matter of the Roman
senatorship Pope Clement insisted that three years after
his investiture as King of Sicily, Charles must renounce
the dignity of senator and place it at the disposal of
the Pope.   As the date for the transfer of the kingdom
the Feast of Saints Peter and Paul (June 29) was settled.
In the final negotiations with Charles in the latter half
of April, 1265, there took part, in addition to Simon, the
bearers of the papal letters, the Archbishop of Cosenza
and a papal notary.

Since the outstanding questions affecting Sicily
remained as they had been, no difficulties were
encountered.   Reluctantly Charles had to yield on the
point of the Roman senatorship, as otherwise the negotiations would have collapsed.   He, too, had a reason for
wishing the matter concluded and himself at Rome, as
the position of his deputy in the senate had become a
very dubious one.   On May 18 Clement received a
message from his legate Simon that the negotiations were
successfully concluded.[3]   Even though Charles's ingenuity
and his policy of exploiting the Pope's unfavourable
situation had resulted in a number of partial successes,
nevertheless the Papacy had triumphed on the point
which had been the cause of its struggle against the
Hohenstaufens.   Charles was forced to recognize the

---

[1] Lünig, *Codex Italiæ diplomaticus*, ii, n. 42.
[2] Lünig, *l.c.*, n. 43.
[3] Martène et Durand, *l.c.*, ep. Clementis IV., n. 60.

unconditional supremacy of the Pope, to recognize
and testify on oath to the absolute impossibility of
combining his rule over Sicily with ruling any other
territory in Italy or Germany, and finally, to guarantee
the independence of the Church and the clergy from the
secular government.   When the negotiations were at an
end Simon, as papal legate, announced the imminent
transfer of the kingdom of Sicily to Charles of Anjou.
On May 14, 1265 (Ascension Day), Charles set out from
Marseilles to Rome with twenty warships and a large
number of small ships manned by 1,500 men.   On Whitsun
Eve (May 23) he was received in St. Peter's, and on
June 21 he repeated the oath that he would hold the
Roman senatorship for three years at most, and would
lay it down immediately after conquering the greater
part of Sicily.

On the vigil of SS. Peter and Paul (June 28), 1265, the
solemn investiture of Charles took place in the Lateran
Basilica, although the papal Bull was not issued until
November 4.[1]   The delay was due partly to the fact
that the Pope first sent the Bull to France to be signed
by the legate, Simon, a very marked honour and distinction intended to mark his services in bringing about the
agreement.   It was by no means a general practice of
the Curia to send Bulls for signature to cardinals who
happened to be abroad.   The ceremonies concluded with
the coronation and anointing of Charles and his wife,
who had come to Rome at the end of September.   The
coronation took place in St. Peter's on the Feast of the
Epiphany (January 6), 1266.

While all these ceremonies were taking place, Simon
continued to work unremittingly in France.   The treaty
was concluded, and it remained to raise the funds
necessary to carry it out, perhaps the hardest task of all.

Simon preaches the "crusade" against Manfred.

---

[1] Martène et Durand, *l.c.*, n. 174.

To rouse enthusiasm for the undertaking, the papal legate travelled up and down France preaching a " crusade " against Manfred and in favour of Charles of Anjou. Since the wars against the Hohenstaufen every fight of Rome against the enemy of the Church, who was often merely an enemy of the papal State, had been known as a " crusade ". And so Charles of Anjou's campaign was declared a crusade, although beyond doubt it was primarily a personal enterprise dictated by Charles's ambition, which incidentally was to be useful politically to the Pope. But without this ecclesiastical sanction the necessary funds would never have been made available. For that reason Charles had informed the Pope right from the beginning of the negotiations of his wish that his enterprise should carry the prerogatives of a crusade and that all participants in the campaign against Manfred should be granted the same privileges as those who had fought for the liberation of the Holy Land.[1] In fact, the Pope had, on May 4, 1264, entrusted the cardinal legate with the mission of preaching the Crusade in France and explained this step by reference to Manfred's various offences against the Church, among them his alliance with the heathen against Rome. The privileges accruing to the Crusade were communicated to Simon in a special document.[2] They were the indulgences and privileges which Innocent III. had granted the Crusaders at the Fourth Lateran Council. Clement IV. renewed Simon's crusade mission [3] on March 20, 1265, and even granted an indulgence for merely hearing a crusade sermon preached ; he also granted power to compel people under the pain of ecclesiastical displeasure to hear such sermons. On September 19, 1265, he urged Simon to greater zeal in spreading the news of the Crusade ;

[1] Martène et Durand, *l.c.*, ep. Urb., n. 16.
[2] Martène, *l.c.*, n. 44.
[3] Martène, ep. Clem., *l.c.*, nn. 30, 32.

no doubt the tithes were flowing into the papal coffers too sparsely and too slowly. However, it seems to have been difficult to please the Pope, who in the following year blames his legate for excessive zeal in the matter and charges him with having connected his preaching with his mission, rather than his mission with his preaching.[1] We glean some information regarding Simon's preaching of the Crusade from a Hungarian named Andreas [2] who was then in France. Under the year 1265 he sets down that the Bishop of Auxerre, Guido de Mello, had won over for the Cross a number of French noblemen, such as Robert of Flanders, Jean de Soissons, Bocardus de Vendôme, Guido de Lavalle, Marshal Guido de Mirepoix, Henri de Sully, Guillaume and Peter de Beaumont, and many others, all of whom had set out from Lyons to Italy. They entered Charles's army before the decisive battle which gave Charles victory over Manfred at Benevento in February, 1266.

In that battle Manfred himself fell. With his death the threat to Rome seemed past, and the Pope was free to turn to the development of earlier plans which had been thrust into the background by the danger to the papal State. Prominent among those plans was a new crusade. Since the Mameluke Bibars ascended the Egyptian throne in 1260, the situation in the Holy Land had considerably deteriorated. Cæsarea and Arsuf had been captured and destroyed by him, and complaints and cries for help became more and more numerous and pressing. Louis IX., whose plans for a crusade had broken down badly in the first attempt, was moved in particular to resume those plans. Whereupon the Pope

Crusade for the Holy Land.

---

[1] Martène, *l.c.*, ep. Clem., 144, 145, 393. We also get some references to Simon's preaching of the Crusade in Sternfeld, *Kardinal J. G. Orsini*, p. 327 ff.

[2] Andreas Ungarus, *Descriptio victoriæ* in *M. G. SS.*, xxvi, 567. This account is confirmed by the *Chronica Normannorum*.

ordained once more the collection of hundredths. While
comforting the Christians in the Holy Land and holding
out hopes of aid to them, he ordered that a crusade for
the Holy Land should be preached.

Once more Simon was given the task of forwarding
with all his powers the Crusade for the Holy Land and
of collecting hundredths for it.[1]

With all the energy which characterized him, Simon
devoted himself to the Crusade, and even had the honour
of handing the Cross to King Louis himself. The Pope
allowed him to fix the date for the departure of the
Crusade as seemed best to him. An assembly of French
barons and prelates convened by the King took place in
Paris on March 25, 1267, and there both the King and
Simon, speaking as papal legate, urged their hearers to
forward the Crusade. At this meeting Louis himself
and his three sons received the Cross from the hand of
the legate.

Not only the spiritual but also the material preparation
of the great enterprises undertaken by the Church in
France was the care of the cardinal legate. He was
Collector-General, i.e., supreme director of all financial
collections in the territory to which he was accredited.
The campaign against Sicily and the Crusade had to be
financed by the Church, but it was necessary to levy
special taxation for the purpose, since the normal revenue
of the *camera apostolica* was far from sufficing for such
abnormal occurrences. A way to deal with such demands
had already been marked out by that great organizer
Innocent III. At first he had ordered the prelates to
supply troops, or in their place a sum of money in
commutation, but it was not long until he passed from
that to earmarking a specific proportion of the revenue
as a tax for the Holy Land, and the Fourth Lateran

---

[1] Martène, *l.c.*, 110, 367, 266, 300, 339, 348, 397, 401, 420.

Council confirmed his right to do so.[1] This model was followed by the later Popes when their coffers were low, as was usually the case. To collect these grants and taxes was one of the tasks of the legate Simon.[2] Even though the three French synods of Paris, Clermont, and Lyons had conceded the tithes for the Sicilian enterprise, it was not easy to collect them, because the French Church had already been called upon several times for taxes. Accordingly, cardinal Simon had to collect tithes for Charles of Anjou, hundredths for the Holy Land, and, in addition, a three-year tithe for the Crusade of Louis IX. The Curia was pressing for prompt and, if possible, full payment. As Collector-General Simon had adopted a collection procedure new to France. Previously the assessment on which the tax was calculated had been prepared by the taxpayer himself: in the reign of Innocent IV. we hear for the first time of an official assessment made by a person nominated by the Collector-General and in no way connected with the owner of the benefice.[3] Bishop Walter of Norwich in 1253 controlled as Collector-General such an assessment for the Crusade-tithes granted to King Henry III., working through collectors and sub-collectors and including even the smallest benefice holders. Simon now applied this much more fruitful method in France. He caused official taxation lists to be drawn up, and on the basis of these lists the taxes were levied under threat of ecclesiastical punishments which were often applied, and with the assistance of the secular power. Needless to say, this strict method of tax-gathering provoked violent disapproval, but the Collector-General had no choice

---

[1] *Cf.* Potthast, *Reg.*, 915, 922, 923, 934 ; Gottlob, *Kreuzzugsteuern*, p. 23 ff. ; Mansi, *Concil.*, xxii, 1059–63.

[2] Martène, *l.c.*, ep. Urb., 27.

[3] By this method the tax yield was doubled (*cf.* Gottlob, *die Kreuzzugsteuern*, 221).

owing to the persistent pressure of the Curia for quicker
and more ample supplies to cover the cost, first of the
campaign against Manfred [1] and then of the Crusade.
Another hardship caused by the new method was that
the centralization it involved made it much more difficult
to get concessions in cases of misuse of authority or of
hardship.   Formerly the individual Bishops as collectors
had dealt with such cases.   Dissatisfaction with the taxes
and with the Collector-General was, in consequence, all
the greater, as may be understood from a number of
contemporary sources.[2]   The tax-gathering procedure
was laid down by the *Declarationes dubitationum in negotio
decime*.[3]   In the unpublished portion of his dissertation
Backes proves successfully that these declarations in the
main were the work of cardinal Simon.   In support of

[1] The outlay from the papal treasury for Anjou and his army
when he reached Italy amounted alone to 1,000–1,200 pounds a day
(*cf.* Papencordt, *Geschichte der Stadt Rom*, p. 314).

[2] The *Chronicon Maius* of Limoges (Recueil xxi, 770) contains an
important reference both to the new method of assessment and to the
dissatisfaction with the Collector-General.   " Iste Legatus (Simon)
per universas dioeceses misit fideles suos, qui nescientibus et ignorantibus
beneficiatis per personas estraneas faciebant æstimari beneficia et
illam æstimationem tradebant collectoribus, qui per excommunicationem
et regis compulsionem compellebant secundum illam æstimationem ad
solvendum.   Episcopi tantum erant exempti.   Super hoc et hac
æstimatione magnum fuit murmur in ecclesia Gallicana, cum per
iuramentum non crederetur beneficiatis.   Novit Jhesus, si bene fuit
factum.   Et licet iste cardinalis esset nacione Gallicus et fuisset
cancellarius regis Franciæ et thesaurarius Turonensis, bene didicerat
morem Romanum ad bursarum corrosionem exactiones, emunctiones,
compulsiones, que facta fuerant pro ista decima et pro procuratoribus
suis (*sic*) exprimere non novi."   The Italian collectors were the most
feared.   In the treaty between England and Rome of 1289 regarding
a universal crusade and the grant of church tithes for a period of six
years, it is expressly agreed that the tax shall be collected by English-
men only and not by Italians.   A similar form of expression occurs
in the History of Normandy (Duchesne, *Historiæ Normanniæ scriptores*,
1012).

[3] Gottlob, *Kreuzzugsteuern*, p. 261 ff.

his argument he cites certain texts. In the first of these, a letter from Pope Gregory X. to his Cardinal,[1] the Pope mentions the conditions thus : *" declarationes per te factas dum in partibus illis legationis officio fungereris."* Backes also adduces the *Cartulaire de l'église Notre Dame de Paris*,[2] where under the title *" Certae constitutiones Simonis legati "* conditions the same as the *declarationes* are set out. It is also most probable that in issuing regulations for the tax collection a man of Simon's experience would not only be heard on the matter but would be entrusted with its conduct. Particular unpopularity attached to Article 32, which ordained that in a case where a false declaration was suspected, the official assessment alone should be considered and that false statements of means should be punished by excommunication. The principal purpose of the *declarationes* was to make the taxation yield as high as possible, and Simon's activity received recognition from the Pope [3] again and again.

Clement, indeed, went so far as to offer him in the most flattering terms a responsible mission to Germany.[4]

---

[1] *Reg. Greg. X., n.* 208.   [2] Paris, 1850, 367-72.

[3] Martène, ep. Clem., n. 212.

[4] *Reg.*, 1342 : " Exigit siquidem dicta legatio tam prudentem quam fidelem personam, puras habentem manus, communes oculos et apertos, non declinantes ad dextram vel sinistram et nichilominus ea propensius attendentes, que ad statum spectant imperii conservandum absque sedis apostolice scandalo et nequorum periculo vicinorum. Dum enim de legatis mittendis agimus et viros magni nominis de imperio certantes conspicimus, vix aliquem invenimus, quem pars neutra suspecta habeat, quamvis et aliud timendum occurrat, ne videlicet imperii principes sua possint artata potentia perturbari vel laxata licentia carissimis in Christo filiis nostris Francie et Sicilie regibus illustribus durum aliquod valeat preparari. Ad hec igitur omnia te credentes ydoneum, dum tamen voluntarium habeamus, en tertio tibi scribimus multis mirantibus legationem huiusmodi tanto tempore fuisse dilatam. Unde nunc saltem volumus, ut supra hoc nobis rescribas, quid tibi placeat in premissis, cum intentionis nostre non sit, quicquam tibi imponere, quo tuus animus perturbetur . . ."

Incidentally this letter shows that at that time nothing was known of his supposed hostility to Germany, for otherwise he would not have been suitable for the mission.

Nevertheless, even during the reign of Clement IV. he was recalled from France, where he was replaced by the cardinal-bishop of Albano, Raoul de Grosparmi. The grounds of his recall are not very clear, but there is not the least reason for assuming that he had lost the confidence either of the Pope or of the King of France. We know that the legate's health had been poor at times, and the preaching of the Crusade, as well as the office of collector-general, compelled him to make frequent journeys.

Possibly he asked to be relieved of his office for reasons of health. It would not be impossible to reconcile such a request with the fact that the Pope had lately wished to entrust him with a mission to Germany, for such a mission would make far fewer demands on Simon's health and physical vigour. Perhaps it appeared opportune to Simon or to the Curia or the King to sacrifice to the clergy the unpopular collector-general who had introduced strict taxation methods into France, and who had carried them out with determination, thus causing the same clergy to be more generous. But it is also possible that the Pope brought back the legate because his principal task, the conduct of the Sicilian mission, was at an end, and the final preparations for the Crusade constituted an entirely different task for which Clement had perhaps a still more suitable representative in the bishop of Albano. Probably we shall never arrive at absolutely certain reasons for the legate's recall. All we know definitely is that Simon left Paris at the beginning of January, 1269, and that cardinal-archbishop Raoul arrived in the French capital during the course of the same month.[1]

[1] Cf. *Recueil*, xxi, 539, and Belgrano, *Documenti inediti*, 269.

For five years with brief interruptions the cardinal remained at the Curia without taking any special or leading part in any particular matter until on August 1, 1274, he was again sent to France as papal legate by Gregory X.   There he functioned as collector-general until the early years of the pontificate of Nicholas III. His recall on this occasion must have taken place in the second half of 1279, or the beginning of 1280. In a letter to King Philip dated March 31, 1280, Pope Nicholas III. makes mention of it.   During this period, Simon's efforts were based on his earlier activities ; even the assessment lists drawn up during his previous tenure of office were again employed.[1]   If during his first period of office Simon devoted himself to additional problems—foremost among them the reform of the female Franciscan Order— as well as dealing with the Sicilian matter and conducting the financial operations, the same was true to a still greater extent during the period of his second legation. He presided over numerous provincial synods where he busied himself with church reforms.   One of the most important was the Synod of Bourges in 1276.   He worked with special zeal on behalf of the mendicant friars. Repeatedly during both his terms of office he had occasion and opportunity to interfere on the side of discipline in the affairs of the University of Paris.[2]

He was entrusted by Pope John XXI. with an important political mission, that of restraining Philip of France, if necessary under threat of ecclesiastical censure, from waging war against King Alfonso of Castile.   On Pope Nicholas' direction he had also to make representations to Queen Margaret that she should confer with King Charles of Sicily with regard to their rival claims to Provence and Forcalquier.   With the greatest enthusiasm

---

[1] Gottlob, l.c., 223.

[2] H. Denifle, *Chartularium Universitatis Parisiensis*, i.

the legate associated himself with the efforts to bring
about the canonization of the recently deceased King
Louis. But important as these activities were in their
time, none of them had the significance for Martin's
eventual Pontificate of the tasks of his earlier mission.
For then he had brought the Sicilian question to a
solution, for which he was to fight later as Pope with all
the sources at his disposal and with all the might of the
Church. At that time he had himself organized and
largely carried through the financing of costly undertakings, and thus when he himself was called to lead the
Church, he was able to make use of his great experience
in solving financial questions. His activity during his
first period as French legate was a kind of prelude to his
work as Pope. For that reason it has been necessary
to dwell on it to some extent in order to make it possible
to understand his papal policy from its beginnings.
Martin IV. really only continued as Pope the policy which
he had pursued with the greatest enthusiasm as legate.
His legation in France was to him a school for his later
political activity as Pope, and was for those who elected
him an indication and a guarantee of his political inclina-
tions and his considerable political ability.

For the problems solved by the legate Simon de
Brion had not been simple ones, and the manner in
which he solved them should have conveyed a hint of
caution even to the francophile cardinals. For in his
French mission he had gone to the uttermost limit
possible in France's favour, even though he, in doing
so, attempted successfully to exploit the financial resources
of the country. But the papal electors did not worry
about that. They thought only of the cardinal's friendly
personal relations with the French royal house, and
hoped that these relations would result in a generous
and persistent measure of support for the papacy in its
now uncertain position.

An indication of the new Pope's attitude was to be seen in the fact that the first people to be informed of his election were the King of France and the archbishop of his native diocese of Sens.[1] Not until a month later did he send an official intimation to the bishops of the world and the King of England.[2] His first acts of government were concerned with the papal State.

[1] Potthast, *Reg.*, **57** ; *Reg.*, n. 1.
[2] Potthast, *Reg.*, **57**.

CHAPTER II.

ROME, THE PAPAL STATES, AND ITALY GENERALLY
(EXCEPTING THE KINGDOM OF SICILY).

Embassy to Rome.

SCARCELY had the reins of government fallen from the strong hand of the Orsini Pope than disturbances broke out, and the mutual animosities of the various noble factions were resumed. Nevertheless, the newly elected Pope at first considered the question of a coronation in Rome. He sent two cardinals, Latino Malabranca, bishop of Ostia, and Godfrey of Alatri, cardinal-deacon of St. George ad Velum Aureum, as envoys and "messengers of peace" to Rome. In view of the Lenten season, it was felt that the Romans would receive them with suitable respect.[1] Significantly, the Pope notified this embassy by public proclamation not only to the Senate of Rome, but also to Charles of Anjou. But the quelling of the disturbances occupied a longer time than the Pope anticipated, and the Romans refused to receive him. Accordingly, the solemn entry into the city had to be abandoned and the coronation took place at Orvieto.

Senatorial dignity.

In the end, however, the papal legates achieved what their master wished, not because of any friendliness felt by the Roman parties, but because internal dissensions made it impossible and hopeless for them to resist the Pope and Charles of Anjou.

They conferred the dignity of senator for life on the Pope, with power to confer it further on others. By the wish of the popular assembly the existing senators were made electors and it was the latter who elected the Pope as a lifelong senator, not because of his papal dignity,

---

[1] Potthast, *Reg.*, 57 ; Martène et Durand, *l.c.*, ii, 1280.

but on personal grounds.[1]   This reason for the election
was strongly emphasized so that the Romans should
not lose altogether the privilege of electing senators, and
that the office of senator should not be connected
automatically with that of Pope.   The two former
senators proceeded to Orvieto and on their knees presented
the deed of appointment to the Pope.   The latter expressed
no pleasure in the dignity conferred, but dwelt on the
burden it entailed.   He accepted it, of course, nevertheless.

---

[1] Vitale (*l.c.*, 184) gives an authoritative report of these proceedings :
In nomine Patris et Filii . . . Anno Domini 1281 tempore domini
Martini IV. pape die lune decimo Martii none Indictionis.   In presentia
mei Stephani scribe senatus et horum testium ad hoc specialiter
vocatorum et rogatorum congregato magnifico populo Romano ante
palatium Capitolii publice ad sonum campane et voce preconum, ut
moris est, de mandato nobilium virorum dominorum Petri de Comite
et Gentilis de filiis Ursi alme Urbis et illustrium senatorum iidem nobiles
viri domini Gentilis de filiis Ursi et Petrus de Comite senatores electores
ordinati a magnifico populo Romano ex auctoritate et potestate eis
super hoc a prefato populo Romano concessa attendentes sanctitatem,
prudentiam et bonitatem sanctissimi patris nostri domini Martini
pape IV. et dilectionem, quam idem d. papa habet ad Romanam urbem
et Romanum populum et sperantes, quod per ipsius sapientiam et
probitatem expertam bono statui Urbis et populi Romani salubriter
poterit divina favente gratia provideri invocata Spiritus sancti gratia
prefato d. Martino pape IV. *non ratione papatus vel pontificalis dignitatis,
sed ratione sue persone*, que de nobili prosapia traxit originem, unanimiter
et concorditer transtulerunt et plenarium commiserunt regimen
senatus Urbis eiusque territorii et districtus toto tempore vite sue.
Et dederunt sibi plenam et liberam potestatem regendi toto tempore
Urbem eiusque territorium et districtum per se vel per alium seu alios
et eligendi, instituendi seu ponendi senatorem vel senatores unum vel
plures ad tempus seu tempora et ad salarium secundum formam et
modum prout sibi placebit . . .   These powers are then set out in
further detail.   They extend to every act of government, to full control
of the revenues, and to the power of imposing punishments.   Not until
after the Pope's death are these rights to revert to the people of Rome.
Voluerunt quoque predicti electores, quod per predicta vel aliquod
predictorum in nullo diminuatur vel crescat ius populi Romani seu
ecclesie Romane in electione senatus Urbis transacto tempore vite
ipsius domini pape Martini sed ius suum permaneat ex tunc integrum
cuilibet et illesum . . .

To preserve appearances he first sent Petrus de Lavena to Rome to represent him, as senator, but as early as April 30, 1281, he transferred the dignity of Prosenator to Charles of Anjou. By immense exertion Nicholas III. had re-established papal influence in Rome, and had forced Charles with the greatest difficulty from the city. Now Martin handed back to the latter complete power over the city.

French influence—French officials.

One can well imagine the satisfaction felt by Charles when he once more took possession of Rome. After a short interval Frenchmen were again in occupation of the most important offices in the city, and distinguished men, such as Philip de Lavena, Guillaume l'Etendard, and Goffredo de Dragona were Charles's lieutenants. Charles took care to see that those who represented him appeared surrounded with pomp. They were attired like princes in scarlet robes edged with fur, and were accompanied by a stately retinue—a horseman as their deputy, a second horseman as marshal, with a train of forty mounted followers, eight Capitoline judges, twelve notaries, followed by heralds, doorkeepers, trumpeters, a physician, a chaplain, thirty to fifty sentries, a keeper for the lion kept as a symbol in a cage at the Capitol, and various other officers and servants.[1] In addition they dispatched guardians to the various estates belonging to the city such as Barbarano, Vitorclano, Monticello, Riscampano, Civita Vecchia, and Tivoli. Nor was Charles satisfied with his authority over Rome and the surrounding territory; he desired to rule the entire papal State through his trusted knights and followers.

Fighting in Rome.

Charles had never been popular in Rome or in Italy, and he did not become more so under Martin IV. His rule was merely suffered because unity—the only means of shaking him off—was wanting. As soon as it was

---

[1] *Cf.* Vitale, 188.

understood that a successful attempt had been made to liberate Sicily from foreign rule, Charles's power in Rome began to totter also. The Orsini, driven from power by Martin IV. and his French favourites, now began to try to recover their position. All over Italy the Ghibellines began to stir. At first success did not attend their efforts, and they were forced to retire to Palestrina, where their resistance was continued. The Pope also thought it opportune to withdraw to the fortified castle of Montefiascone and from there to endeavour to restore order and regain control. He was clever enough not to drive the Romans to extremities by using force. Rather did he wish to appear as the solicitous father of the country, a rôle for which there was plenty of scope during the famine of 1283.

The Romans sent a delegation to him asking for help in their need ; they were received cordially by the Pope, who supplied them with 5,000 pieces of gold for the purchase of grain in Sicily, and regretted that he could not do more, since the struggle for the rights of the Church was absorbing all his resources. He appointed Albert of Parma, canon of St. Peter, and the hospitaller [1] Johannes Basilius, to carry out the relief measures, and even tried to exercise a moderating influence [2] on the royal vicar at Rome, G. de Dragona. But success was not attained immediately. Unrest increased still more when friends of Peter of Aragon spurred on the Ghibellines and supported them financially in their determined resistance. Once more the Orsini attacked Rome, this time successfully. On January 22, 1284, the Capitol was stormed, the French garrison slaughtered, and the prosenator Goffredo de Dragona taken prisoner. That day was the end of Charles of Anjou's power in Rome. Once

---

[1] Potthast, 22073, 22074 (November 3, 1283) ; Baronius, *Annales*, an. 1283.

[2] Potthast, 22043 (July 3, 1283).

more the people elected their own rulers : Giovanni
Cinthii Malabranca, brother of cardinal Latinus Malabranca, was chosen as *capitaneus urbis*. Martin was
sufficiently adroit to adjust himself to the new conditions.
He dispatched a cordial letter to the Romans, admonishing
them to peace and stating that three cardinals representing
himself would arbitrate on the matters at issue.

He confirmed Giovanni Cinthii—for six months in the
first instance—in the office of prefect of supplies
(*præfectus annonæ*), and confirmed a city council elected
by the craft guilds and a *prosenator* who was to reside in
the Capitol along with the *capitaneus urbis*. Control of
the finances was entrusted to a *camerarius urbis* appointed
for the purpose. Under the banner of liberty the various
factions were reconciled ; even Riccardo Annibaldi did
penance for the violence he had done to the conclave at
Viterbo and reconciled himself to cardinal Matteo. The
Pope was obliged to withdraw formally his appointment
of Charles of Anjou as his deputy in the dignity of Roman
senator. He now sent Pandulf Savelli and Annibaldo,
son of Petrus Annibaldi, to exercise senatorial power in
Rome in his place. Thus, the Romans themselves
compelled a return to the national system of Nicholas III.[1]

Fighting in
Romagna.

Originally Martin IV. had given Charles power not
merely over Rome, but over the entire papal State, the
whole *patrimonium Petri*. Frenchmen or their friends
ruled everywhere. Charles's captain, known to the
Italians as Giovanni de Appia, or d'Epa,[2] became count
of Romagna in place of Berthold Orsini. Opposed to
him were the Ghibellines under Guido de Montefeltro.
With Giovanni were some 800 French mercenaries.[3]

---

[1] Cf. *Liber pontificalis*, p. 460 ff. ; Vitale, 193 ; Baronius, *Annales*,
an. 1284.

[2] Potthast, *Reg.*, 21760.

[3] *Liber pontificalis*, 459.

The Pope sought help for him from the Podestà, Malatesta de Veruculo of Rimini,[1] whom he expressly forbade under penalty of excommunication and loss of privileges to give his daughter in marriage to Guido de Montefeltro. When the desired help was not forthcoming quickly enough, he sent a first dispatch on October 9, 1281, followed in quick succession by another on October 16, and two more on October 28 and 29.[2] On October 29 he was in a position to congratulate Giovanni d'Epa on his first successes.[3] These, however, were not very far-reaching, in consequence, probably, of lack of money, for as early as October 2 the Pope was obliged to suggest to him that he should reduce the numbers of his troops during the winter months.[4] As recompense he increased the papal mercenaries in the spring of 1282 by 300 men placed at the disposition of the Church by the March of Ancona. These men he sent to Romagna under the hospitaller, Fr. Bonaiunta.[5] In spite of numerous fierce engagements,[6] fruitful in casualties to both parties, neither side was able to achieve a decisive victory. This state of affairs can hardly have impressed the Pope with the capacity of his general, and, when the latter began to exceed his powers and take steps on his personal authority which were not approved by the Pope,[7] he was replaced by Guido de Monteforti on May 11, 1283.

On this occasion the Pope laid down clearly in a letter of appointment what were Guido's rights and obligations.[8] Soon the new commander secured the help of the Podestà of Rimini, who was thanked expressly by the Pope.[9] Within a short time he succeeded in restoring peace and

[1] Potthast, *Reg.*, 21799.
[2] Potthast, *Reg.*, 21799, 21800, 21805, 21807, 21809.
[3] Potthast, *Reg.*, 21808. [4] Potthast, *Reg.*, 21792.
[5] Potthast, *Reg.*, 21902. [6] *Liber pontificalis*, 460.
[7] Potthast, *Reg.*, 21997. [8] Potthast, *Reg.*, 22022.
[9] Potthast, *Reg.*, 22027, 22065.

order in Romagna.   Guido de Montefeltro submitted to
him, and undertook on oath to be submissive to the
Church for the future.   Thus, Romagna returned to
obedience to the Pope, Urbino alone maintaining a bitter
resistance for a number of years.[1]   Martin had committed
the Romagna to the spiritual jurisdiction of one of the
most renowned teachers of law of the period, William
Durandus of Provence.[2]   In the March of Ancona,
Tuscany, and Campania, likewise, Frenchmen were
frequently to be found at the head of affairs.[3]   Among
the more prominent of them were Godfrey of Anagni,
formerly *auditor contradictorum* to the papal Curia, and
later rector in spiritual and worldly matters in the
March of Ancona [4]; as well as Andrea Spiliati, former
papal chaplain and canon of Cambrai,[5] who was rector
in spiritualibus et temporalibus in Campania, subject to
bishop Peter of Anagni who exercised spiritual
jurisdiction.[6]

Relations
with Venice.

Martin exerted himself zealously to establish friendly
relations with Venice.   At the very beginning of his reign
he was anxious to detach the city from his bitter opponent,
Guido de Montefeltro, and he begged Venice to dissolve
all treaties which it had concluded with this open enemy
of the Church.   He asked the city especially to abrogate
all treaties relating to the purchase of salt from the salt
mines of Cervia.[7]   Before the decisive battle in Romagna
the Pope thanked Venice for the help it had given him,
and requested that the city might favour the Pope's

---

[1] *Liber Pontificalis*, 461.   [2] Potthast, *Reg.*, 21761.

[3] *Liber Pontificalis*, 459, " . . . Hic electus (*scil.* papa) in senatorem
urbis ad vitam loco sui instituit Karolum regem Sicilie in senatorem et
de domo seu de familia ipsius regis existentis in Urbevetere sumpsit
ipsius regis milites ad regendum tam Patrimonium quam Campaniam,
Marchiam, et Ducatum."

[4] Potthast, *Reg.*, 21903.   [5] Potthast, *Reg.*, 21843.
[6] Potthast, *Reg.*, 21747.   [7] Potthast, *Reg.*, 21756, 21810.

adherents in Romagna by allowing food to be conveyed through its territory and to be exported from it. Bishop Bartholomew de Amelia of Grosseto was entrusted (May 3, 1283) with the negotiations bearing on this matter.[1] The two antagonists in the fight for Sicily—on the one hand, the Pope and Charles of Anjou, on the other hand, Aragon—were each specially eager to secure the assistance of Venice. Although the city was first on the side of Charles, Peter of Aragon succeeded by the representations he made in the spring of 1283 in inducing the Republic to break the alliance and to forbid its citizens to enter foreign military service, whereupon the Pope laid Venice under an interdict.[2] When peace and order had been restored in Romagna and the Pope's dangerous opponent, Guido de Montefeltro, had yielded, the Pope appealed to Venice to allow free export of salt from Cervia to Lombardy and to give it safe conduct[3] (January 6, 1284).

Martin appreciated the importance and the situation of Venice sufficiently to make continuous efforts to gain its adherence. Only when the city prevented even individuals from assisting the Angevins in the struggle between Charles of Anjou and Peter of Aragon did the Pope, feeling that this was an exceedingly unfriendly act towards himself and the papal State, lay Venice under the interdict which was not removed until his successor occupied the chair of St. Peter.

Perugia was a focus of Italian unrest. On February 27 the Pope granted it the privilege that no occupant of the city could be indicted before a court outside the city.[4] But no sooner did the news of the Sicilian Vespers get abroad than the city broke away from the Pope, being

Struggle between Perugia and Foligno. The Pope intervenes.

---

[1] Potthast, *Reg.*, 22016.
[2] Raynaldus, *Annales*, 1285 ; Potthast, *Reg.*, 22031.
[3] Potthast, *Reg.*, 22091.
[4] Potthast, 21855.

among the first to do so.   Indeed, the citizens went so
far as to burn in public straw effigies representing the
Pope and the cardinals.[1]   An attack was made on the
town of Foligno which remained faithful to the Pope.
Martin endeavoured to prevent hostilities from breaking
out.   He sent his chaplain Pandulf de Suburra as an
envoy to suggest that the city should avail itself of the
Pope's mediation.   Perugia yielded so far as to send a
deputation, but the deputation had not full powers, and,
to make matters worse, it took its departure before the
Pope dismissed it, and even went away without taking
farewell of him. Thereupon the Pope threatened anathema,
interdict, and a large indemnity if the city advanced
against Foligno, simultaneously sending out a number
of envoys to prevent help from being given to Perugia.
In fact he demanded mobilization against Perugia if that
city should defy the papal commands and open warfare.
In the event of disobedience he laid down penalties of
exceptional severity.   All papal fiefs were declared forfeit,
the clergy must leave the city, barely sufficient priests
remained to baptize new-born children and hear the
confessions of the dying.   All guilty inhabitants of
Perugia were summoned in November, 1282, by the
papal envoy, the bishop of Bagnorea, to appear before the
papal See before Christmas to give an account of themselves.   Those who did not appear were declared incapable
of holding any office.   So long as they continued in office
despite this declaration the city would be under an
interdict, and all judicial acts (judgments, deeds, etc.)
would be invalid.[2]   But all these threatened punishments
were insufficient to prevent either Perugia or its allies
from fighting against Foligno and laying waste the

---

[1] According to Gregorovius (*l.c.*, p. 445) this popular judicial event
was the first of its kind.

[2] *Reg.*, 280.

territories without that city's walls.[1] A whole series
of cities fell under the ban for aiding Perugia, including
Espello, Assisi, Narni, Città di Castello, and Spoleto.[2]

Not until the year 1283 did the Pope succeed in forcing
Perugia to desist. Even on April 15 in that year he
threatened the city with a fine of 10,000 silver
marks unless it returned to its allegiance within a week
and atoned to Foligno. A similar sentence was issued
against Spoleto,[3] but it was not until December
that the city authorities bound themselves on oath to
resume obedience to the Pope, to desist from the fight
with Foligno, to make good the losses occasioned and,
in addition, to pay the fine imposed. Thereupon the
Pope directed bishop William of Corinth to discharge the
inhabitants of the city from all ecclesiastical punishments,
and to direct the clergy to return to the city and resume
their usual offices. Lætare Sunday [4] was fixed as the
date for the payment of the fines. If the full amount
was not forthcoming by then the ban and interdict
would be enforced again and the clergy would leave the
city once more.[5] On February 4, 1284, the Franciscan
Deotaleve of Perugia was commissioned by the Pope to
discharge from ecclesiastical punishments even those who
for any reason had not received absolution from bishop
William.[6] But the appointed date arrived without the
city having fulfilled its financial obligations. The Pope
showed himself most accommodating and on March 11
extended the period by three further weeks, until Easter
(March 25), without demanding any additional payment.[7]

[1] *Liber pontificalis*, 460.
[2] *Bull. Franc.*, 527, 529, 531 ; *Suppl. Bull. Franc.*, 158 ; *Reg.*, 281,
282, 283, 465 ; Potthast, 21889.
[3] *Reg.*, 463, 464.
[4] The fourth Sunday in Lent, March 5, 1283.
[5] *Reg.*, 485.
[6] *Reg.*, 491 ; *Bull. Franc. Suppl.*, 156.
[7] *Reg.*, 492.

When the fine was paid by the city syndic, who expressed his willingness to make good the damage done to Foligno, the ban was finally raised and the Franciscan Angelo of Perugia was empowered to absolve [1] all citizens of the city who were still under it. That this indicated a complete reconciliation with the Pope is seen from the fact that on October 4, 1284, the Pope entered Perugia and was most cordially received. Perugia's allies were discharged from ecclesiastical punishments during the period between December 21, 1284, and February 28, 1285. [2]

Mediation between Pisa and Genoa.

Another struggle in Italy, in which, however, Rome was not directly concerned, was that between Pisa and Genoa. The Pope exerted himself to mediate in the matter. On January 19, 1283, he invited both cities to send delegations to him with full instructions and as wide powers as possible, as he wished to undertake the office of mediator. [3] Nothing came of it, however, and a very severe struggle ensued which ended eventually with the victory of Genoa. [4]

Revolt against the French in Orvieto.

Hatred against the French showed itself in many places and led in Orvieto to a regular revolt ending in bloodshed. The *Liber Pontificalis* reports that even before the Sicilian Vespers the movement had begun in Orvieto and that the people had turned on the hated oppressors, shouting " Death to the French " (" mortem ad Gallicos "). Many were wounded and many of the people of Orvieto killed, while the French had only one death on their side, which shows with what severity the French garrison acted, proceeding at once to massacre the native population, and this, it would appear, without cause. For, if the people of Orvieto

---

[1] *Bull. Franc.*, 524 ; *Suppl.*, 157.
[2] *Bull. Franc.*, 527, 529, 531 ; *Suppl.*, 158.
[3] *Reg.*, 285 ; Potthast, 21977.
[4] Baronius, *Annales*, an. 1284.

had really made up their minds to kill their oppressors,
undoubtedly there must have been a great many more
deaths among the French. This suppressed hatred of the
French, which blazed up from time to time, should have
been a warning to the French, and also indeed to the
Pope, of the rooted dissatisfaction with which the people
regarded the foreign domination.   Charles of Anjou
thought that he could keep the peace permanently
by force of arms, and the Pope turned a deaf ear to the
voices which urged him to intervene and moderate the
French domination.   And thus occurred the terrible
happenings in Sicily which resulted in the limitation
of the French power in Italy, to the papal fief in Naples,
and in the liberation of Sicily.

The Pope's pronounced interest in politics com- Enlistment
pelled him to maintain an adequate papal army and of mercenaries.
Martin's intervention to suppress the Sicilian revolt
compelled him to recruit mercenaries. Beginning in
May, 1282, we find commissions being issued regularly
for the recruitment of such soldiers, usually in France.
At one time it was Robert de Ricavilla, marshal of the
Curia, who was entrusted with recruiting fresh troops
for the Pope in France and the other countries
north of the Alps, Master Henry, canon of Limoges,
being appointed to assist him.[1] Six months later the Pope
was asking the King of France to assist his representatives
Walter de Fontanis and Petrus de Mollanis in their
work of recruiting mercenaries in France and, above all,
to provide a capable leader. He stated that the suppression of the Sicilian rebellion was a work pleasing
to God, and that in consequence the greatest zeal should
be expended on it.[2] The funds necessary for it would
be drawn from the Crusade-tithes granted to the King of
France for the conduct the Crusade which were in the

---

[1] Potthast, 21905, 21906.   [2] *Reg.*, 271.

custody of the Knights Templars at Paris. The Pope asked the King to open a credit up to 100,000 pounds for his envoy : an exact account should be kept of the sums actually drawn, and a duplicate thereof submitted to the Pope in person.[1] Four months later the Pope was again asking for money, this time for 20,000 pounds of Tours from the same source to pay the papal soldiers in Romagna.[2] At the same time the collectors of the Lyons tithes and of the Peter's Pence of Poland were instructed to push on energetically with their collections. On the pretext that they were not safe in Germany the German tithes were removed to Italy and used likewise for the war against Sicily. While doing this Martin protested against "cunning tongues and poisoned lips" spreading a report in Germany that the tithes intended for the Holy Land were being used for other purposes. He may have regarded this payment from the Crusade-tithes as a loan, although he must have foreseen that he would never be in a position to repay the money to the fund. It strikes one, too, as strange that William Durandus, the *rector in spiritualibus* of Romagna, was connected with matters of a purely military character, such as a purchase of arms on a considerable scale in Ferrara, an increase in the army pay in consequence of a rise in prices, the dispatch of money to the military leaders and the raising of money for military purposes.[3] From this it can be judged that spiritual and very worldly matters were in those days very intimately connected.

Coining in the papal State.

From the beginning of his reign the Pope was resolved to establish order in the papal State. In December, 1282, he took steps to prevent the minting of coins in Roman territory without his permission. He pointed out that without the permission of the

[1] *Reg.*, 273, 274.   [2] Potthast, 22014.
[3] Potthast, 21961 ; Vitale, p. 186 ff.

Apostolic See coins might not be issued, and he required the royal vicar, Philip de Lavenna, to take steps to put a stop immediately to illegal coining. Coins already made might not be used but must be regarded as false money. In other matters, too, he opposed abuses. He attacked the custom by which the bearer of a letter from the Pope was remunerated by the recipient of the letter. He declared that he himself paid his servants adequately and that his messengers were bound on oath to desist from all such practices. If, however, they should forget their oath and endeavour to enrich themselves, nothing should be given them, this being his wish.[1]

In the administration of the Church, Martin IV. made no innovations worthy of mention. Since the days of Innocent III. the papal chancery had been expanding continuously. Even then it had controlled a considerable administrative machine : at the beginning of the fourteenth century the number of *scriptores* had risen to 110. In addition to the chancery there were a number of other administrative departments, each with its own staff. Chief among these were the *Pœnitentiaria*, the chief court in matters of conscience, and the apostolic camera which controlled the papal finances. The chancery was directed under Martin IV. by magister Petrus (Peregrossus) of Milan, who held the same office under Martin's predecessor and successor. As was usual since the time of Honorius III. he bore the title *vicecancellarius*, and it can be authenticated that he was head of the papal chancery in the years 1277–86. The exactness with which chancery usages were followed is worthy of mention, for at the very beginning of Martin's pontificate this policy was emphasized. On the leaden bulls attached to the charters before his consecration and coronation

Papal Officials.

---

[1] *Reg.*, 1.

the Pope's name is missing, and in the text of the document attention is directed specifically to the fact that this was a custom of the papal chancery with bulls engrossed before the consecration of the Pope.[1]

Tabellionate.   One office, which was not exercised within the Curia, was in the gift of the Pope, that of tabellio [2] or public notary. Here it was not a question of a papal *officium*, but through the Pope's nomination the holder of the office became an officer of public justice, *manus publica*. Nominations are fairly frequent : The register contains the names of twenty-nine persons who held the office. Candidates had to submit to an examination before magister Nicholaus de Terracina, *doctor decretorum* and archdeacon of Lisieux, who was appointed by the Pope for the purpose. A fee was charged, as we might expect.

Most of those appointed were Italians, and next in order, according to the numbers appointed, come Frenchmen. From Germany and England only individual entries appear in the register. A large number of those appointed were Franciscans, holders of minor orders, but a number of laymen also appear in the list. Occasionally bishops were given the right to hold examinations and appoint up to three candidates to the office of the tabellionate. They were, in the order of time in which permission was granted : the bishop of Rieti for two persons

[1] Document regarding the reservation of the archiepiscopal throne of Compostella, 1281, Feb. 2, *Reg.*, 2 : " . . . Nec miretur aliquis, quod bulla non exprimens nomen nostrum est appensa presentibus, que ante consecracionis et benedictionis nostre solempnia transmittuntur, quia hii, qui fuerunt hactenus in Romanos electi pontifices, consueverunt in bullandis litteris ante sue consecracionis et benedictionis munus, modum huiusmodi observare. . . ."

[2] The Arenga (introductory formula) of most of the certificates of appointment contains an excellent definition of the office : " Ne contractuum memoria deperiret, inventum est tabellionatus officium, quo contractus legitimi ad cautelam presentium et memoriam futurorum manu publica notarentur." (*Reg.*, 12.)

to assist him in collecting the Crusade-tax [1]; the bishop of Orleans for two [2]; the archbishop of Rheims, one [3]; the bishop of Valence-Dié, two [4]; the archbishop of Vienne, two [5]; the bishop-elect of Gnesen, two [6]; the archbishop of Dublin, three.[7] One man, who was not of the rank of bishop, was given the power to confer the tabellionate on one person.

He was a leading official of the papal chancery, named Gaufridus (or Gifredus) of Anagni,[8] head of the *audientia litterarum contradictarum*, the department to which all papal documents dealing with judicial grants were sent for examination. Later he became rector of the March of Ancona.

In short, it may be said that the Italian policy of Martin IV. does not approach that of his predecessor either in vigour or definiteness. In the main it was limited to protecting the interests of the papal throne and of the papal favourite, Charles of Anjou, when these were threatened. This undertaking it was that involved Martin IV., to an extent greater than the interests of the Church demanded, in one of the greatest tragedies in Italian history, the Sicilian Vespers, and what came of them.

---

[1] *Reg.*, 87 (Oct. 17, 1281).

[2] *Reg.*, 210 (Dec. 28, 1282).

[3] *Reg.*, 338 (June 8, 1283).

[4] *Reg.*, 437 (July 3, 1283).

[5] *Reg.*, 366 (July 8, 1283).

[6] *Reg.*, 446 ; Potthast, 22097 (Jan. 18, 1284).

[7] *Reg.*, 425 (1284, iii) ; incorrectly Potthast, 22109, under date March 6, 1284.

[8] *Reg.*, 213 (Jan. 7, 1283) ; this also proves him to have been auditor as late as 1283, although Bresslau (*Handbuch der Urkundenlehre*, 1^2, p. 284 (1912)) only brings him to 1282.

CHAPTER III.

THE SICILIAN VESPERS.

Political
position of
Charles of
Anjou. FROM the moment when Martin IV. assumed control of papal policy, the star of Charles of Anjou, King of Sicily, was in the ascendant. The previous occupant of the papal throne, Nicholas III., had succeeded after a severe struggle in checking the unjustified claims of his vassal, Charles, fraught as these were with danger to the Church. Nicholas had put an end to Charles's dominion over Upper and Middle Italy and had offered opposition to his wide-reaching political ambitions, thus securing the freedom of the Church which had been greatly imperilled by Charles and his far-flung schemes. Martin IV., on the contrary, yielded to all Charles's wishes, and the latter accordingly set about making himself predominant in the western world. The path of his ambition was a rigorous one, stained in many places with blood, but Charles was determined to follow it. Already his bold schemes extended to Constantinople. Once master there, he could establish the universal monarchy which had been the aim of the Hohenstaufen. The latter had been opposed in their plans by the Popes who thought, and rightly, that such an imperial sway over the whole world would be a danger to the liberty of the Church. Now Charles of Anjou, who had been called in by the Pope to displace the Hohenstaufen, was working unremittingly but cautiously to establish a world monarchy. Already he was signing himself Charles by the grace of God King of Jerusalem and Sicily, Duke of Apulia, Prince of Capua, Senator of the Eternal City, Prince of Achaia, Count of Anjou, Provence, Forcalquier and Tonerre. He had succeeded not only in

extending his own dominions, but also in establishing valuable and extensive connections.

As Rudolf of Habsburg had definitely renounced his claim to Sicily, Charles had nothing to fear from Germany. Indeed, the German King actually became connected with him by family ties when a marriage was arranged between Clementia, a Habsburg princess, and Charles's grandson, Charles Martel. This gave the Angevins not only a new and valuable connection, but also a substantial increase in their dominions, as the princess was to bring the kingdom of Arles with her as dowry. Moreover, Charles Martel might possibly succeed to the throne of Hungary. The closest family ties, which he made use of to the full, bound Charles to France. In Italy, even in the territories not directly subject to him, the Guelf party were on his side to a man; finally, the Pope himself was his willing tool in political matters. His influence also extended to the Balkan peninsula, and even the Emir of Tunis paid tribute to him, while the Dukes of Antioch and Armenia and the Khan of Tartary sued for his favour. If he could be successful in gaining Constantinople the world monarchy would be an accomplished fact. During the negotiations for unity between Rome and Byzantium carried on by the Popes from Gregory X. to Nicholas III., Charles had had to suspend his plans of conquest in the East, but he succeeded in turning Martin IV. against the idea of union, and in driving the Pope to an open breach with Michael Palæologus. On November 18, 1281, the Pope once more excluded the Greek Emperor from the communion of the Church and anathematized him. When this had happened, the road was open for Charles's eastern conquests, which actually acquired an air of righteousness since he was waging war against an enemy of the Church.

Hitherto his preparations had been conducted with some secrecy, now they went forward quite openly, especially in Achaia and Epirus. The necessary funds were supplied by ecclesiastical tithes from Sardinia and Hungary which had been granted to him for a term of six years. But while he was engaged in preparations for a great campaign, the whole situation was completely and suddenly altered by the Sicilian Vespers.

The term "Sicilian Vespers".

The expression "Sicilian Vespers" dates from the end of the fifteenth century. Pandolfo Collenuccio used it first in his *History of Naples*, printed in 1539.[1] The name has persisted down to the present day, although even in the nineteenth century scientific investigation showed its historical inaccuracy. Any connection with Church vespers is as unfounded as is the leading rôle ascribed to John of Procida who became a legendary hero of conspiracy. In actual fact, the Sicilian Vespers was no long-plotted conspiracy but rather an outbreak of a people long held down by force, who could no longer endure the harsh rule and the arbitrary and stupid treatment meted out to them by the foreign rulers of their country. Villani, and later on Flavio Biondo, who died in 1463, turned this into a tale of a conspiracy and alleged that the ringing of the bell for vespers— hence the name—was the signal for the slaughter of all Frenchmen throughout the island.[2]

Date of the Vespers.

In spite of all that has been written about the revolt in Sicily, the facts have not even yet been entirely cleared up. Even as regards the date unanimity is lacking. One source gives Sunday, March 29 ; seven give Monday, the 30th ; eight, Tuesday, the 31st ; and one puts the date as late as April 1.

Amari, and more recently Cartellieri,[3] select Easter Tuesday, March 31, and they are probably right, for

[1] *Cf.* Amari, *Sulla orig. della denominacione " Vespero Siciliano "* (Palermo, 1882).

[2] *Cf.* Cartellieri, p. 222.

[3] *L.c.*, p. 208, n.

this date is given by Bartholomew of Nicastro, who
was in Messina, only some 155 miles from Palermo.
Since he occupied an important municipal office he
would undoubtedly have been in a position to inform
himself accurately regarding an event which had fundamental results for Sicily, and he would certainly not have
forgotten the date of such a decisive occurrence. The
Parma annalist is the only contemporary source
who tells us the time of the rising. According to his
story, the people of Palermo proceeded to the fair green
after their midday meal. From the description given by
Bartholomew of Nicastro it may be assumed that the
revolt broke out during the afternoon. Within a few
hours all the French who were at the green or in the
town had been killed and " in midnight darkness " the
justiciar, Jean de Saint Rémy, fled from Palermo.

There are four principal versions of the origin and
development of this short and bloody revolution. One
describes a long-prepared conspiracy preliminary to the
massacre, organized by John of Procida, a nobleman
of Salerno, who had been physician and confidant of the
Emperor Frederick II. and the latter's son Manfred.
Loyal to the House of Swabia even in its downfall, he
fought for Conradin and was deprived of his estates
after the latter's tragic death.

When a Frenchman violated his wife and daughter and
struck down his son who had tried to protect them,
John left his home in 1279, devoting himself hence-
forward to vengeance on the French. He went to
Manfred's daughter, Costanza, Queen of Aragon, who,
with her husband, King Peter III., received him with
kindness and respect, and set himself to win over Costanza
and her husband to a campaign of revenge for the shameful fall of the Hohenstaufen and the injury done to himself. At his own expense and on his own responsibility
he strove to clear the road for an invasion of Sicily by

Peter. But all these tales of his activities are purely legendary.[1] The only important service which history records of him is the alliance which he brought about between Peter and Michael Palaeologus. Undoubtedly he was in Sicily a loyal comrade and adviser of Peter and his wife, as he had been to the latter's father, Manfred. But history knows nothing of the leading rôle in the Sicilian uprising which was attributed to him at a later period. Even Ranke emphasizes the fact that an artificial stimulus would be out of the question in such a passionate outburst of popular excitement.

The second version, resting chiefly on the testimony of Bartholomew of Nicastro, describes the people of Palermo as enjoying themselves on the fair green near the little church of St. Spirito when a Frenchman named Dronet arrived with an armed retinue to search the people for arms. A girl, who was accompanied by her brother and her lover, had to submit to a personal search, during which she fainted, whereupon one of the bystanders snatched a bayonet from a Frenchman and stabbed the latter, crying out " Death to the French ! " This is described as the occasion which caused the people's wrath to overflow. The account given by Bartholomew has a distinctly poetic and romantic character, and is clearly influenced by the story of the fate of Virginia.

A third version, put forward by Saba Malaspina, gives a description similar to the foregoing, but more collected and dispassionate. Malaspina, too, should have had good information about the matter, since he lived at the Curia, and the Pope assuredly received an exact account of what had happened. His version runs : the people had collected outside the city, drawn to some festivity. Some Frenchmen mixed with the

---

[1] Giovanni Villani is principally responsible for the legend.

crowd and behaved in an aggressive and unbecoming manner towards the women, whereupon the Sicilians gave loud expression to their displeasure. The French, unaccustomed as they were to any resistance, concluded that the unwonted courage displayed was probably based on the possession of hidden arms, which the people were forbidden to have. Immediately they began to search for these weapons, but a shower of stones met them, and, accompanied by cries of "Death to the French", the massacre began.[1] This report does not err on the side of unduly favouring the French, but censures their harshness openly.

The fourth version agrees with the Venetian, Marino Sanudo the Elder, in ascribing the revolt to a new and particularly oppressive tax which Charles of Anjou had levied for his contemplated campaign against Constantinople. A rumour got about that anyone who did not pay would be branded as slaves had once been and as cattle still were branded for identification, and that the branding irons were actually being manufactured in Palermo. This degradation to the social level of slaves and the implied equality with domestic animals produced a terrible sensation among the populace. When the French again provoked the people by a search for arms, during which they also gave offence to women, the long suppressed rage of the people broke out, and with the cry of "the stammerers must die"—the French were commonly so called because of their defective pronounciation of Italian—popular justice established itself. Desclot mentions in another connection (*Crónica del Rey en Pere*) the proposed branding of the defaulting taxpayers.

All accounts agree on the point that insults offered

---

[1] Amari concludes that the correct version is a combination of the second and third.

to Sicilian women brought existing bitterness to a head, and most of the chroniclers are at one in regarding the Sicilian Vespers as a divine judgment for the arrogance and tyranny of the French. Even Saba Malaspina of the Curia does not differ from the others in this view.

The attitude assumed by the Pope must be regarded as mainly contributory to the growth of the legend of a conspiracy plotted by John of Procida. In his first statement on the occurrence the Pope declared that King Peter of Aragon had been for a long time making preparations to conquer Sicily ; that Peter's campaign in Spain had been only a blind to conceal his real intentions ; and that he had systematically stirred up the people through his agents. The Pope calls him a child of lies, and goes on to say that Peter could make no claim as Manfred's heir, seeing that Manfred was excluded from the succession by his illegitimacy in the first place and, in addition, by the excommunication first of Frederick II. and later of himself. Peter's activity in Sicily, where he had stiffened the backbone of the rebels, was the cause of the uprising, and the Pope mentioned as significant the fact that the people of Messina had been at first prepared to negotiate with the papal legate, but had refused all negotiations once King Peter arrived. However, the view put forward in this statement [1] of the Pope's is demonstrably incorrect. Probably it was based on accounts sent to the Curia by friends of Charles of Anjou. In reality it was the Sicilians who first appealed to the Pope, offering to submit to him absolutely on the sole condition that no foreigner should be placed over them. Only when the Pope rejected their embassy and demanded unconditional submission did the harassed islanders turn for help to the King of Aragon. There can hardly be any doubt that the incorrect account in the papal brief

---

[1] *M. G. H., Ep.*, ii, 1296.

contributed considerably to building up the legend of the conspiracy led by Procida.

Another statement made by the Pope, that Peter had conquered Sicily by force of arms and to the accompaniment of bloodshed, gives a completely false picture, for the islanders had joyfully welcomed Peter as a deliverer when the Pope had refused to help them. It is equally false to describe Peter, as was done in the papal brief, as a persecutor of the Pope and of the Church.[1] His campaign in Sicily had not the smallest connection with a struggle against the papacy or the Church. He was merely endeavouring to extend his power at the cost, not of the Church, but of the oppressing Angevins.

Modern investigations [2] have made it possible to outline as follows the course which events took. In accordance with an ancient custom the people of Palermo were wont to go at Easter to the Church of Santo Spirito and to celebrate there on the green the annual parish fair, and this was done on Easter Tuesday, March 31, 1282. French soldiers (*servientes*) who were also present, participating in the games and dances, offended against propriety by giving open expression to their lewd desires, and thus provoked the anger of the young men of Palermo who quickly expressed their views, going so far as to utter threats against the strangers. The French, unaccustomed to opposition, suspected that the people were showing courage because they had arms secretly and in defiance of an express prohibition. To test the

Incidents of the revolt.

---

[1] ". . . Et ut nihil omittat ad persecucionem nostram et ipsius ecclesiæ intentatam, ad pacificum statum Urbis patrimonii b. Petri aliarumque terrarum ipsius ecclesie subvertendum et partes easdem a nostræ obediencie debito avertendas, sicut ex multorum fida relatione percepimus nunc per nuntios, nunc per literas, variis machinationibus nititur et nisibus fraudulentis insistit, ut nos et ipsam ecclesiam iniquitate conculcet."

[2] *Cf.* in particular Cartellieri, *l.c.*, p. 138 ff.

matter they proceeded without delay to search the people, and with that the patience of the Sicilians was at an end. Rage against their oppressors dammed up for years now burst its banks. Hand-to-hand fighting began, and before long could be heard through it the cry " Death to the French ". Like wild-fire the words were taken up, and when the Frenchmen present on the green had been struck down, the raging mob, which had now let loose its anger and tasted blood, rushed into the city and slaughtered all the French whom they could find. No distinction was made as regards non-combatants ; men and women, old men and children were slain ; even the French clergy were not spared. Nor was any mercy shown to unborn children. It is reported that even Sicilian women who were expecting the birth of children by Frenchmen were massacred after fearful tortures and their babes destroyed. Lust for blood had taken possession of the people, and the frenzied Sicilians bathed their hands in its streams. All the chroniclers describe with horror the cruelties indulged in when the popular anger, stemmed for years, had once broken out.[1]

Palermo establishes a republic under the suzerainty of the Church.

Immediately, in the night of March 31—April 1, the people of Palermo held a conference to decide on the next step to be taken. Their decision, fixed as it was while they were still fresh from the events of the day, is of great importance in helping us to a true appreciation of these events. They established a republic under the suzerainty of the Church and elected Roger de Magistro Angelo as their leader with Henry the Bavarian, Nicholas of Ortoleva, and Nicholas of Ebdormonia as councillors.[2]

---

[1] Cf., in addition to the chroniclers already mentioned, Ricobald of Ferrara (Muratori, Script., ix, 142 ; Annales Januenses, 294).

[2] Bartholomew of Nicastro reports this in his chronicle (chap. 14) : ". . . Cum autem cives ipsi de statu civitatis ipsius salubri disponerent, nomen Romane matris ecclesie invocantes, statum communem firmant et vexillum imperialis aquile, quod semper cives ipsi consueverunt

No more convincing proof could be offered of the fact that in Sicily there was no question of a revolt against the Church or the Pope, but solely of liberation from the oppression of Charles of Anjou. For the people while still fresh from frenzied deeds of bloodshed did not declare the overlordship of the Chrch at an end, even though the Pope despite their entreaties had failed to protect them against the foreign ruler, but on the contrary they declared expressly that they were under the supremacy of Rome. The course followed proves also that the Sicilian Vespers was not the work of the King of Aragon, for if that were so, he would assuredly have taken steps to have himself at once proclaimed King of Sicily, instead of permitting a decision favourable to the Curia to be reached. On the other hand, one cannot go so far as to say that Peter's friends were not working on his behalf, with or without his knowledge, even though our sources of information make no mention of such a plot. But quite definitely there can be no question of an artificially worked up revolt.

Peter kept his plans too secret to risk the preparation of a popular insurrection, for an agitation involving a whole nation cannot be kept secret. If perhaps Byzantine gold and Spanish encouragement were not entirely absent from the fight for freedom, the origin of that fight was nevertheless the systematic oppression year by year of a free people, an oppression which ultimately drove the Sicilians into a war of liberation. A direct intervention on the part of Peter was not necessary, for time was on his side, and in all probability the events of Easter, 1282, were not even very opportune for him.

gerere feliciter cum tubis, et cimbalis erigentes, Rogerium de Magistro Angelo concivem eorum in capitaneum et alios in suos consiliarios procrearunt . . ."; and again in chap. 22, "Felices cum Christo aquilas nostras ereximus, decernentes vivere in communi."

Allies
sought.

The first task of the newly elected leaders was to establish Sicily's restored freedom on a secure basis, because if nothing else was clear, this much was, that Charles of Anjou would stop at nothing to re-establish his rule over Sicily and that this would then be even harsher than it had been previously. Allies were sought on all sides. Tried troops marched through the country under the banners of the republic and the Church, on the latter of which were depicted the keys of St. Peter. They issued a general appeal to fight for freedom and the casting-off of the foreign yoke. Everywhere republics were set up which declared their readiness to follow the lead of Palermo and to submit themselves to the direct supremacy of the Church. Thus the revolt extended throughout the whole island, being still associated with the persecution of all Frenchmen who could be found. We learn of a massacre at Forli on May 1, 1282, in which some two thousand French under Johannes de Appia were slaughtered after being enticed there by a stratagem of Guido of Montefeltro. But our sources also report cases where Frenchmen who had behaved justly were spared. Thus the Knight William was allowed to depart freely from Calatafimi because he had earned the respect of the people by his just demeanour. Estimates of the number of the French who were killed vary between eight thousand and twenty thousand.

Messina
joins the
movement.

At first the island seemed at one in rejecting the French dominion, and it was a bitter disappointment to Palermo when Messina dissociated itself from the revolt. The situation thus created was all the more dangerous because at the same time the Curia rejected the embassy sent from Palermo to offer subjection to the Holy See on the sole condition that the French rule over Sicily should cease. The Curia demanded unconditional submission, and, when this was refused, preparations for the punishment of the rebels began.

Charles of Anjou also advanced with a portion of his fleet against Palermo. Then it was shown—very opportunely for Palermo and for the Sicilian cause— that the movement which had developed in the island was indeed a national one. For the people of Messina, against the wishes of their leaders, insisted on associating themselves with Palermo and the national movement. On April 28, Bartholomew of Maniscalco hoisted the city flag with the Cross as a symbol of the establishment of the republic. On the following day Baldwin Mussonus was elected leader by the assembled people and elders. Rainald de Limogiis, Nicolaus Saporitus, Peter de Ansalono, and Bartholomew of Nicastro— already mentioned as a chronicler—were appointed as a council of advisers. Simultaneously the republic was solemnly inaugurated under the protection of Jesus Christ and the Church of Rome. This established the unity of Sicily, and French sway over the island came to an end within the space of one month.

It is interesting to notice the position taken up by the clergy in a situation which must have been embarrassing for them. On the one hand, as patriots they must have rejoiced to see their native land freed from foreign oppressors ; on the other, the Pope was commanding a complete return to the old conditions and a re-establishment of Charles as King. We have only the scantiest information as to the steps taken by the Sicilian clergy. But one conclusion at least may be safely drawn, namely, that the clergy adopted a very reserved attitude. Certain prelates, it is true, took the popular side, because they found it impossible to condone the tyranny of the French, but even these do not appear to have come into the open. Probably they limited themselves to an avoidance of anything which might hinder the struggle. A few leading personalities among them took their places definitely

Attitude of the clergy of Sicily.

on the side of the people in their struggle for freedom. These included the archbishops of Monreale and Messina, the latter of whom in particular gave express recognition to the new popular government as the only lawful one.

The fight was not to be decided merely by a contest between Peter of Aragon and Charles of Anjou.   The whole world looked on with interest, and both parties were concerned to draw other elements into the struggle. First of all, each party sought to win the Pope to its side.

Attitude of Martin IV.

If Martin IV., who, in his devotion to Charles, was devoid of any will of his own, had not been called to guide papal policy, the decision would certainly have been different.   The fulfilment of his predecessor's wishes was now offered to him freely :   the direct subjection of Sicily to the Pope with a consequent increase in the political and financial power of the Curia.   With the Angevins confined to Naples, and Sicily united directly with the papal State, it would be easy to hold in check the ambitions of the house of Anjou.   Recognition of the freedom from harsh oppression won by Sicily would have been a human act as well as a wise one, and one inspired by a wide vision of Church policy.   The Pope justified his support of Charles on the grounds of the latter's model faith and fidelity to the Church.[1]

From the very beginning Pope Martin showed a lack

---

[1] In the credentials which accompanied Sabinus as legate to Sicily after the Sicilian Vespers the Pope wrote : ". . . Hoc enim est regnum ecclesie Romane peculiare precipuum, cui presidet rex devotus ipsius ecclesie filius et pugil intrepidus, regnum ipsum sua potenti strenuitate liberans et defendens de manibus impiorum ac ad eiusdem exaltationem ecclesie conservans et protegens, superna benedictione perfusus, cuius tota domus regia sincere fidei clareque devotionis titulis insignita et aromatibus imbuta virtutum in gremio dicte sancte Sedis et nostro predilecta incumbit." From this the Pope deduces an obligation to devote special care to the King and his kingdom. Hence, too, the decision to send one of the most eminent cardinals after the Sicilian Vespers as legate.

of independence in his dealings with this vassal, being in fact under the latter's influence, and adopted a stern attitude towards the Sicilians. Soon after his coronation the islanders, who were subject to the overlordship of the Pope, sent a delegation to ask for Martin's protection against the harsh rule of their King. The delegates, bishop Bartholomew of Patti and the Dominican Bongiovanni, were only allowed to voice their complaints against Charles of Anjou in the open consistory in Charles's presence. Not only did the Pope refuse to hear their plea, but he even allowed Charles's servants to seize them as they left the palace and hold them prisoners. The bishop secured his release by bribery, but the monk died in prison.[1] A similar negative result awaited the delegation from Palermo which appeared before the Pope after the Sicilian Vespers for the purpose of declaring the submission of the Palermitans. The Pope's aloof attitude caused them to look for help elsewhere, namely to Peter of Aragon. But another opportunity was offered to the Pope to repair the errors into which he had been led by his fondness for the French : when the city of Messina joined Palermo against Charles, it declared that it did not approve of the request for aid which had been dispatched to Peter, and succeeded in inducing Sicily to swear obedience to the Pope alone and to refuse admission to any foreign prince. They wished to establish a federal State under the supremacy of the Church and were prepared to receive as the Pope's representative any person whatsoever, except Charles of Anjou. But once more this comprehensive declaration of fealty was not welcomed by the Pope, who was determined in all circumstances to maintain Charles of Anjou as ruler of Sicily without regard to the interests of the

---

[1] Mariana, *Historia de las Espannas*, xxiv, 6 ; Nicolai, *Spec. Rer. Sicul.*, i, 3 ; Muratori, x, 924.

Church as a whole. It is a striking fact that we have no information regarding these final negotiations between the Curia and Sicily. Even Saba Malaspina, the Curia chronicler, says nothing about them. One has the impression that the Curia endeavoured, without making it unduly clear, to ignore this undesired submission to the supremacy of the Church. All we know is the negative outcome of Sicily's efforts to preserve itself free from shameful oppression while maintaining loyalty to the Church.

When all means and possibilities of moving Martin IV. to sympathy and assistance had been exhausted and no success had been attained, the responsible leaders of the Sicilian liberation movement were forced in the end to turn elsewhere for help. In no quarter was this so obviously to be sought as at the court of Peter of Aragon.

Peter of Aragon and his plans for Sicily.

Peter appeared to be the most suitable person to intervene in Sicily, because, first of all, as the husband of Manfred's daughter Costanza, he might to some extent claim to be the heir to the Hohenstaufen realm. It is said, indeed, that John of Procida succeeded by his diplomatic skill in getting Nicholas III., the strong defender of papal power in Italy, to consent to Costanza laying claim to Sicily. In any case Peter had sufficient initiative and courage to extend his rule to the island. Knowing full well the resistance which would be opposed to such plans, he made his preparations with the greatest secrecy and caution. He equipped his forces, nominally to attack the enemies of the Faith in Africa and to fight in that continent for Church and Faith, taking pains that his plans for a crusade should be widely known. In

Peter asks the Pope's help for a crusade against the Moors.

September, 1281,[1] he sent William de Castelnau to the

---

[1] Muntaner (105) represents the matter as though Peter had waited until the African project was a success and had only turned to the Pope " when the King saw that the enterprise was so glorious and of such advantage to Christianity ".

Curia with the request that the Pope should place at his disposal for his projected Crusade against the Moors the tithes which had been collected in Tarragona, and that the Pope should take Aragon under his protection during Peter's absence. Further, he asked that the bishop of Valencia should be sent as legate and that the latter should announce the Crusade privileges and indulgences, and should confer them. The Pope refused these requests. He was afraid, as Peter himself correctly stated later to Rudolf of Habsburg and Edward I. of England, that the campaign might be directed against Charles of Anjou. The reason he gave, however, was that the goal to be attained was beyond the strength possessed by Aragon. What mightier monarchs had already failed to achieve would hardly be possible for Peter of Aragon. Moreover, the latter should have got the permission of the Curia before starting his preparations. Martin did indeed send a legate, not the desired bishop of Valencia, however, but Bartholomew, bishop of Grosseto, and his mission was not to preach a crusade, but to obtain information regarding Peter's plans.[1] The King of Aragon understood quite well the reasons why his request had been rejected, but was clever enough to accept the decision quietly and to maintain his intercourse with the Curia as usual. Nothing is known of the fruits of bishop Bartholomew's mission : obviously there were none.

As Peter had had no success with the Pope, he now endeavoured to gain favour with a number of cardinals, among them Gerard, cardinal-bishop of Sabina, and Hieronymus, cardinal-bishop of Preneste, whom he asked to advance the canonization of Blessed Olegarius.

Meanwhile he went on equipping his forces, and in the spring of 1282 he entered the port of Fangos. There French mission to Peter.

---

[1] Potthast, 21877.

on May 20 he received a French delegation, sent by King
Philip at the request of the troubled Charles of Anjou,
to ask an explanation of the arming in Aragon. Peter's
only reply was that his sole wish had always been to
serve God, with which oracular statement the delegate
had to be satisfied, although they communicated the
threat that France would regard these preparations as
directed against itself and Charles. To prevent an attack
on Aragon by France, now that he himself was abroad,
Peter tried to keep France occupied in watching its old
enemy England. Even while still Infante, Peter had been
endeavouring from 1273 onwards to make an alliance
with England. A marriage was to take place between
Eleanor, daughter of Edward I. of England, and Alfonso,
Peter's son and heir.[1] When he came to the throne
Peter at once set about establishing friendly relations
with England. After a short period of delay, which was
his own fault, he exerted himself with all his energies
to bring about the alliance.[2] On June 1, 1282, in the
presence of numerous trusted counsellors, among them
John of Procida, he authorized the archbishop of
Tarragona and bishop Gosbert of Valencia to continue
the negotiations with England during his absence in
the field. On August 15 the betrothal took place at
Huesca, but the marriage did not follow, for it had to
be deferred again and again because of various difficulties
that intervened. When it was finally settled in 1291,
Alfonso died during the preparations. The mere project
of the marriage sufficed to start the rumour that Peter
had worked out his scheme of conquering Sicily with the
encouragement of the King of England,[3] but we know

[1] F. Darwin Swift, *The Life and Times of James the First, the
Conqueror, King of Aragon*, Oxford, 1894, p. 298.

[2] *Cf.* Cartellieri, *l.c.*, 189, where the various sources are set out.

[3] According to the Yearbooks of Piacenza for 1282 and also
Salimbene in his *Chronica* (*Monumenta hist. ad provincias Parmensem
et Placentinam pertinentia*, iii, Parma, 1847, p. 282).

on the contrary from a letter of King Edward to Peter's wife, Costanza, that the King took good care not to espouse the cause of Aragon.[1]

Peter's cool calculations and skilful diplomacy were revealed in the preparations for his schemes. He must have guessed—or may perhaps have learned through friendly cardinals—that the Pope was determined to inflict the severest penalties on anyone who assisted the Sicilians. It followed, accordingly, that the Pope might declare his kingdom forfeit. King Peter, however, anticipated all eventualities: on January 2, 1282, in the presence of a few confidants, who again included John of Procida, he renounced all his rights as King of Aragon in favour of his eldest son, Alfonso. By this means he hoped to secure the kingdom of Aragon to his family, come what might.[2]

Peter makes further preparations.

When in actual fact Pope Martin did declare that Peter had forfeited Aragon, Alfonso was able to rely on this abdication in protesting against the grant of the kingdom to Charles of Valois.

Even when everything was ready for the departure from Aragon Peter kept his plans a strict secret, and when a start was made in the beginning of January, 1282, nobody knew the destination. Not until the fleet was on the high seas were the captains allowed to open the sealed orders to learn their goal. On January 28 Peter reached Kollo on the African coast, where he learned that circumstances had altered considerably. He had hoped on landing to find a powerful ally in Ibn Wazir, who, however, had betrayed him and had paid for his treason with his life. From the start Peter met

Departure for Africa.

---

[1] Rymer, *Fœdera*, i, 625.

[2] The documentary evidence of this renunciation has been lost. But an account of it is to be found in Zurita, *Añales de la corona de Aragon*, i (Zaragoza, 1669). The Pope also makes reference to it. *Cf.* Amari, *La guerra del vespro Siciliano* (1886), i, 275.

with stubborn resistance. All sources of information, even the *Liber Pontificalis*,[1] describe miracles of valour performed by all, but especially by the King, who is said to have carried out a regular massacre of the unbelievers. But it is not probable that Peter exposed his army to excessive risks and exertions, since even then his real goal was Sicily, and he was waiting merely for a favourable opportunity to advance thither on some good pretext. He would hardly in the circumstances exhaust his army before the decisive campaign had begun. His only reason for going to Africa was to be nearer to Sicily, and he was now waiting for a suitable opportunity to advance on the island.

Sicily asks help of Peter.

The opportunity arrived before long. On the initiative of a citizen named Hugo Talach, Nicholas Coppola was sent on April 27, 1282, as an envoy to King Peter to offer him the crown of Sicily. The King was much too cautious to respond at once, fortunately for himself. For opinion in the island changed under pressure from Messina, the citizens of which demanded and obtained that the island should submit to the Pope on the sole condition that Charles should not be sent to rule them again. Although Peter was not inclined to accept the first proposal, he nevertheless took care to maintain contact with Sicily, and even sent a delegation to the island, no doubt for the purpose principally of reporting on the situation. Meanwhile the Pope rejected abruptly the hand held out by the islanders and Charles was threatening the severest penalties. Necessity united the oppressed : early in August, 1282, the popular assembly sat in Palermo in the Church of Santa Maria dell'Amiraglio to decide on a course of action. Nicholas Specialis writes of a mysterious old man who appeared in the assembly and disappeared equally mysteriously after

---

[1] *L.c.*, 640.

having indicated King Peter as the saviour. Mediæval historians were fond of mysteries. Actually no such remarkable intervention was required in the circumstances. No other saviour was possible but the King of Aragon, who was so close at hand, and whose heroic deeds against the Moors were known to all. In addition the memory of the Hohenstaufen still lived in Sicily and Manfred's son-in-law could count on a considerable sympathy on the island. In any case the assembly agreed unanimously to invoke the help of Peter of Aragon and to offer him the crown of Sicily. A delegation, which again included Nicholas Coppola, equipped with plenipotentiary powers, set sail, clothed in black, according to Muntaner, and travelling in a vessel with black pennants and black sails. On arriving where Peter was they kissed the ground three times and approached him on their knees, crying "mercy, mercy". They based their petition on the facts that Peter was the most pious and most just King in the world ; that Sicily belonged by right to his wife ; and finally, that it was the duty of a king to stand by widows and orphans, and that Sicily was now in the position of a widow and orphan.[1]

From the beginning Peter had known that many of his nobles were not enthusiastically in favour of the Sicilian expedition. To overcome this difficulty he had, after the first delegation reached him from Palermo, sent another embassy to the Pope to ask for help in his fight against the unbelievers. Obviously Martin was less inclined than he had been before to render aid, seeing that Peter had undertaken the expedition to Africa against his wishes. Shortly after the second delegation of Sicilians reached Peter's camp, his messengers returned from the Curia with an unfavourable answer, and the situation was then ripe for the

---

[1] Muntaner, i, 54 (109).

execution of his plans regarding Sicily.   Peter explained
to his nobles that, since the Pope refused to help, it was
impossible for him to continue the fight against the
unbelievers alone ; instead of returning home, it would
be better to go to the assistance of the noble and oppressed
people of Sicily and liberate them from a shameful
tyranny.   Even though some individual grandees were
opposed to this plan and returned to Aragon, the majority
were now won over to it ; enthusiastically so indeed, if
Muntaner is to be believed,[1] many knights offering to
follow Peter to Sicily without pay. The King put himself
and his enterprise solemnly under the protection of God :
" Lord, in thy service and for thine honour I embark
on this campaign, and commit myself and my army
into thy hands.   Since it is pleasing to thee and "—
turning to his knights—" you wish it, I shall set out
for Sicily in the name of God and under his protection
and that of the Blessed Virgin Mary and all the saints."
Whereupon the knights replied, " let us cross the sea."
All then fell on their knees and sang the *Salve Regina*.
From Kollo the King sent word to Edward I. of England
that he intended to accept the proffered crown, giving
as his reasons the Pope's refusal to support his crusade
against the infidels and the poignancy of Sicily's appeals.[2]
Later on he also complained to Rudolf of Habsburg
that the Pope had nullified what would have been a
successful campaign against the unbelievers by refusing
all support.

At variance with this statement is the account given
by the Pope in his letter to cardinal John, titular cardinal
of the Church of St. Cecilia.[3] Rightly the Pope describes
the African expedition as a feint, but he also describes
Peter as invading Sicily by force of arms and attributes

[1] i, 56 (113).   [2] Armari, iii, 323 ff.
[3] *M. G. Epp.*, ii, 1294 ff.

to this invasion the obstinacy and determined resistance of the island, especially of Messina. As proof of which he mentions that before Peter's arrival the people of Messina had been inclined to negotiate with the papal legate, but afterwards had refused to do so.

The Pope even accuses Peter of bringing parts of Sicily under his sway by force of arms and bloodshed. This account does not correspond with the facts. The real reason why Messina broke off negotiations was because the Pope and Charles refused to give Sicily another King. Before Peter arrived all Sicily, including Messina, was determined to resist Charles to the last, and no stimulus from Peter was required in that regard. The Pope's account seems to have contributed substantially to the growth of the legend of Procida's conspiracy. It is interesting to note that the *Liber Pontificalis* adopts a more impartial attitude. There it is stated simply that Sicily itself summoned the King of Aragon to its assistance.[1]

In the last days of August Peter crossed from Africa. He made a successful landing at Trapani [2] on August 31, and made his ceremonial entry into Palermo on September 4 as the saviour of the island from foreign tyranny and the lawful representative of the Swabian rights. His first care was not the acquisition of the crown, but rather to bring help to the people, especially to Messina, which was being sorely pressed.

Peter in Sicily.

When the news of the Sicilian Vespers reached King Charles in Orvieto from the lips of the archbishop of Monreale, his first step was to get in touch with the Pope and make sure of his help. Martin's views being what they were, this was not difficult.

---

[1] *L.c.*, 460. ". . . Deinde tota Syzilia sic rebellans Petrum regem Aragonie in suum defensorem et dominum vocavit."
[2] *Annales Januenses*, 294.

Charles then hurried to Naples to prepare a counter-revolution. At the time he thought no doubt that the matter was a passing episode which might delay, but could not prevent, his ambitious plans to found a world empire with Constantinople as its centre. It was fortunate for him that he had been eagerly preparing an expedition against Greece, as he was now able to turn against Sicily a portion at least of the forces he had collected. He appealed also for help to the Pope and to France. His army advanced slowly on Messina, laying waste all the villages along the route. For this Messina revenged itself by burning some seventy ships belonging to Charles which were lying in the harbour. Before the siege of the city began the papal legate offered to intervene. He was received in the city with honours, but no agreement was reached, because the Pope and Charles demanded unconditional submission, while the citizens required as their one condition that the island should be ruled by an Italian. When the legate had returned without success the fight began, and it was then that the city appealed to Peter. But before he could do anything the French raised the siege and withdrew to Calabria. The fight now went on by land and water, on sea against Charles and on land against King Philip I. of France. The former campaign was led by Peter's admiral Roger de Loria, the latter by Peter himself.

The Pope's attitude.

But one more mighty still entered into this struggle, namely, the Pope. He supplied money to recruit and maintain the armies, and by granting tithes opened up sources of supply to Charles and Philip. He also made use of spiritual weapons. In a bull [1] dispatched to Palermo on Ascension Thursday (May 7, 1282) he deplored deeply the bloodshed which had taken place in that city, as elsewhere in Sicily, and commanded the inhabitants of

---

[1] Potthast, 21895.

those towns which had renounced their allegiance to Charles to return at once to fealty to Charles and the Curia if they did not wish to be excommunicated. At the same time he prohibited most strictly the rendering of any assistance to the rebels and threatened the severest penalties for any infringement of this prohibition. Not wishing to confine himself to this written statement, he sent the cardinal archbishop of Sabina, Gerard Blancus of Parma to Sicily about a month later (June 5). In his credential letters the legate's qualities were extolled, his great knowledge, his wisdom and skill, his zeal and fortitude. The Pope could ill afford to do without the legate at the Curia ; by the choice of him he gave expression to the importance he attached to the matter. Since he could not be himself in a number of places at once he wished at least to send one of his most tried councillors as a harbinger of peace. The Pope left his legate complete freedom to act in the conduct of his mission according to his judgment and conscience.[1] The bull drawn up at the time containing a list of the special privileges of the legate is more expansive than usual.[2] In addition to the general purpose of the mission it contains thirty-six special powers. He was given almost unlimited jurisdiction over the area to which he was accredited. The entire body of the clergy, of whatsoever rank or standing, without exception, was made expressly subject to him. He had the power to penalize all of them, even to send them to Rome to justify themselves, and if they did not go, to displace them and deprive them of their livings where these had not been conferred canonically and to confer the livings on

Dispatch of a Legate.

Powers of the Legate.

---

[1] *Reg.*, 270. ". . . Facias auctoritate nostra, quecumque ad honorem Dei et proximi statum illarum partium ac reformationem prosperi status regis et regni predictorum videris pertinere." Potthast, 21912.

[2] *Reg.*, 270c ; Potthast, 21913.

others. All members of the ecclesiastical estate who
resisted him could be at once deprived of office and
punished with excommunication and interdict. He
was empowered to give grants of all livings of the Apostolic
See ; he could introduce Franciscan friars for all duties [1]
and could permit them to ride with him and establish
female foundations. He had the power to induce the lay
nobility under threat of forfeiture of all church livings
to swear an oath of fealty to Charles and to renounce all
disloyalty to him. On solemn occasions he might grant
an indulgence up to one year and forty days on the usual
conditions, and in return for contributions to the Church
and the papal treasury could remit for a period of three
years ecclesiastical punishments up to one hundred days.
He was also accorded the privilege of conferring the
office of public officialatus on four persons, provided
they had passed an examination. To this was added an
extensive power of dispensation. On all places within
his accredited territory he could impose an interdict and
likewise raise it. He could give absolution for
irregularities incurred through disobedience to the constitution of Pope Innocent in the fight against the
Hohenstaufen.

He could free from the excommunication they had
incurred all clergy ordained by excommunicated bishops
other than those who had been present at Manfred's
coronation ; likewise from excommunication incurred
through supplying arms to the Saracens, and even from
excommunication arising out of simony. He could also
dispense from the irregularity of *defectus natalium* if the
father was not a priest or person in orders, and the child
had not been conceived in adultery or incest. A third
group of privileges had reference to the legate and his
retine. They could select any confessor they pleased ;

---

[1] This right is renewed in a bull of April 12, 1283 (*Bull. Franc.*, 500).

could lay claim to Church property for their maintenance and could draw on the receipts from their livings, excepting the attendance fees, and could in addition require contributions from all persons belonging to the ecclesiastical estate. The legate was empowered, moreover, to confer livings in the Sicilian churches on his followers, up to a maximum of twenty, even though the number of livings in the churches in question was restricted canonically. Simultaneously the Pope issued a rescript [1] to the lay nobles of Sicily urging them to receive his legate with all respect and to assist his efforts. In a special communication he urged the King of Sicily to further the activities of the legate. To do so was of course to the King's interest and to his interest only.

Furnished with these exceptional powers the papal legate began his difficult mission with an attempt to win back Messina to allegiance to the Pope and King Charles. Respectfully received by the city's leaders, he could not deny the justice of the condition laid down by Messina for submission. He even advocated the city's wish that in future none but an Italian should rule over Sicily.

But his efforts at peace broke on the resistance of the Pope and King Charles, who demanded unconditional surrender, which Sicily could not grant without delivering itself over to the sacrifice. Thus the fight had to go on. This resistance prevented the legate, like the Pope, from exercising any influence over further developments. He was forced to satisfy himself with the execution of certain tasks entrusted to him by the Curia, which were, however, of minor importance. In November, 1282, the Pope instructed him to give bishops to a number of churches which were vacant, likewise to appoint superiors in certain monasteries. In some cases he had to examine and test first of all the validity of the ecclesiastical election

---

[1] *Reg.*, 270a.

before conferring the necessary orders and powers.[1]
He was also entrusted by the Pope with arranging for the
renewal of the fortifications of Monte Cassino, and for
the re-fortification of the churches of Salerno and the
fortress of Olibani, as well as of other fortified places.
This work was to be executed at the expense of the King
of Sicily, who was to declare in advance in writing that
he would be responsible for all expenses.[2] In 1283
the legate had other tasks of minor importance to discharge. He is directed by the Pope (Feb. 9, 1283) to
find out why it is that a number of Sicilian archbishops
and bishops are petitioning the Pope to be relieved of
their offices. Since the Pope wishes to conform to their
desire, if there is substantial reason for it, the
legate is to investigate the matter and report to the
Pope.[3] At the same time he is instructed by the Pope
to get from the administrator of the vacant livings
in Salerno an account of his stewardship, since it is
reported of him that he is negligent regarding his duties.[4]
An essential part of the legate's mission consisted in
raising funds to cover the cost of his embassy. The
Pope allowed him to draw 600 ounces of gold from the
revenues of the Church livings vacant at the moment in
Naples, Salerno, and Chieti. Receipts were to be issued
for these sums and forwarded to Rome [5] (Feb. 9, 1283).
Late in the autumn (Nov. 27, 1283) the Pope again
gave permission to make use of 600 ounces of gold from
the vacant Sicilian livings to cover the cost of the legate's
mission.

A more important task assigned by the Pope to his
legate was that of determining what was the legal situation prevailing in the island under William II. This
followed a request to the Pope from Naples, Capua, and

[1] *Reg.*, 288–284, 295–7.   [2] *Reg.*, 275.
[3] *Reg.*, 306.   [4] *Reg.*, 308.
[5] *Reg.*, 305.

other cities for the re-introduction of the legal system of William II. Since the Pope was not sure of the details of this system he entrusted his legate to carry out the necessary investigations.[1]

The severest blow delivered by the Pope against Peter of Aragon was the legal proceedings which he brought against him and which led to Peter's deposition. In previous centuries this would have been a crushing blow, but the weapon of excommunication and release of subjects from allegiance had in the course of time been employed so often and so unnecessarily that this last resource was not enough to save his kingdom of Sicily for Charles of Anjou. The result of the case was made public in a papal bull of November 18, 1282.[2]

The papal bull of excommunication.

It begins with a history of the events leading to the rising in Sicily and the Pope's efforts to nip the rising in the bud. The failure of these efforts is wrongfully attributed by the Pope to King Peter of Aragon. With justice the Pope assumed that the King's advance in Africa had been a feint, but it was unjust to treat Peter as the promoter of the revolution, as proof of which the bull adduces that the people of Messina had at first received the papal legate cordially, but that the latter's efforts had led to no result. The bull goes on to controvert Peter's hereditary claims to Sicily on family grounds, since these were nullified by Manfred's illegitimate origin. This attitude of Peter's was, it stated, all the more contemptible since from the time of Pope Innocent III., Aragon had always been a direct fief of the Holy See and because the revolt stirred up in Sicily under the cloak of a godly campaign against the infidels had really let loose a war against the Church. Finally,

---

[1] *Reg.*, 473, 488 ; Potthast, 22081. The development of the law in Sicily will be considered in connection with the constitution decreed by Honorius IV.

[2] *Reg.*, 276.

the Pope announced once more in solemn form the excommunication which the King had already incurred, *ipso facto*, by his transgression of the veto decreed on Ascension Thursday against aiding Sicily. With this the Pope associated a further ban on acts hostile to Charles, on helping Peter or Sicily, as well as an obligation to drive Peter from the island. The bull also forbids Peter to undertake any acts as King of Sicily. All oaths sworn to him were declared null and void and the penalty of the interdict was laid down for any transgression of these commands. As the latest date for Peter's penitent return to obedience to the Pope, the feast of Candlemas Day (February 2) was fixed, April 1 being laid down for the more remote countries which supported Peter and Sicily, and May 1, 1283, in the case of Michael Palæologus.

Anyone who by the dates appointed had not sought peace with the Church and made good the harm he had done would forfeit all his property and would be shut out from the communion of the Church. Only on his death-bed would this excommunication be withdrawn and, if he should recover, the ecclesiastical sanctions would come into force again unless he made his peace with the Church within three months. In order that the Pope's decisions should be known generally he commanded that they should be affixed to the doors of the Church of St. Flavian the Martyr at Montefiascone.

This bull was largely responsible for a false view of the Sicilian Vespers. The account it gives is based on a completely one-sided and, indeed, incorrect version of what had happened, prepared by friends of Charles of Anjou. Based on this judgment of the Curia the legend of a Sicilian revolt instigated by Peter was allowed to spread and to undermine historic truth. It must be kept before our minds that in actual fact Peter did not instigate

the revolt and that he did not summon the people of
Messina to resist, but that Sicily as a whole and Messina
in particular only appealed to him when the Pope
demanded the unconditional return of the Sicilians under
the French yoke, and rejected their tendered submission
to the supremacy of the Holy See.   Since the true state
of affairs was generally known, the bull cannot have
produced much effect, and it is remarkable that even
the cardinals were not unanimously in favour of it,
for a number of them maintained relations with Peter
in spite of the ban.

Above all the Pope was concerned to deprive Peter of *Further measures taken by the Pope.*
outside help while providing Charles with the necessary
financial resources for his struggle.   As early as May 5,
1282, Martin declared in the bull of that date, that
all alliances contracted with Peter or with Sicily were
null and void.[1]   In an instruction to the bishop of Rieti
in May, 1282, the Pope emphasized that any help to Sicily
was forbidden,[2] and he was quick to translate his precept
into practice by giving an example of his determination
to take severe steps if his veto on help were transgressed.
Guido of Montefeltro and Conrad of Antioch, two
zealous supporters of old of the Swabian cause, were
solemnly excommunicated, and the judgment in their
cause posted at Orvieto.[3]   In 1283 both judgments were
renewed and confirmed and at the same time intercourse
with them was penalized by excommunication.[4]   The Pope
exerted himself with special zeal to prevent Venice from
forming an alliance with Peter.   He ordered the bishop
of Castello, whose diocese included Venice, to go thither
in person and there to assemble the clergy and people
in the Church of St. Mark or the Piazza di San Marco,
or elsewhere, to proclaim to them the proceedings and the

---

[1] Potthast, 21895.   [2] Potthast, 21907.
[3] *Reg.*, 266, 268, 277.
[4] *Reg.*, 284, 309, 461, 468, 469, 470, 483, 484.

judgment against Peter of Aragon and to explain the matter to them in the vernacular.[1] At the same time he issued strict commands to the March of Ancona not to aid Peter with its ships.[2] On November 18, 1283, he renewed these commands to Venice and Ancona and directed them also to Genoa and Pisa, forbidding even free commercial intercourse (*commercium spontaneum*), with Sicily.[3] In order to make it easy for those who had gone over to Peter to return to the Pope, he gave his representatives power in all cases where money or provisions had been supplied to the Messenians by persons who feared otherwise to be raided by Messenian ships, to remit all punishments incurred by such persons by reason of the help they had thus given. By such means it was hoped to build golden bridges across which the feet of Peter's adherents might return to the Curia.[4]

On the other hand, the Pope was doing all that in him lay to supply Charles with all things necessary for a successful campaign, and Charles was not backward in demanding such assistance. Having arrived in Rome he explained in open consistory how the Pope and the cardinals were responsible for the course of events, since it was only to fulfil the wishes of the Pope and the Curia that he had conquered Manfred's kingdom. Now, through the Pope's fault the King of Aragon had snatched Sicily from his grasp. The Pope was to blame in many respects : he had been niggardly in the assistance he gave ; he had refused to help Peter against the heathen, and, by thus making it impossible for Peter to fight for the spread of Christianity, had turned his attentions towards Sicily. Peter's appeal for help against the Moors

[1] *Reg.*, 471 (the hint about the Italian vernacular is noteworthy) ; Potthast, 22031 (June 8, 1283).
[2] Potthast, 22032.
[3] Potthast, 22077.
[4] *Reg.*, 487.

had been just and reasonable, " therefore, Holy Father, you are responsible for our misfortunes ! " Unless the Pope took speedy measures against Peter, he went on, the latter would enter Rome as a conqueror. Accordingly, the Pope should immediately decree an indulgence for all who assisted Charles against Peter ; only by this means could the latter be deprived of his allies. The Pope should also bear the entire expenses of the campaign and should summon the King of France to a Crusade against Aragon, for Peter could not be beaten until he was deprived of his own kingdom and his resources exhausted. According to Muntaner's account [1] the Pope agreed with everything that Charles had said. He even assumed responsibility for what had happened, since he had refused Peter's request for help in his war against the heathen " following his inclination rather than his judgment ". In conclusion, he consoled Charles thus : "Be comforted and of good heart, for Holy Church grants you all that you have asked." Much to Charles's relief the individual cardinals confirmed this. The chief essentials for war were then, as now, financial supplies. Already the Pope had promised Charles of Anjou for his war against Byzantium the proceeds of a church-tax, namely, the tithes of Sardinia, Hungary—if the King of Hungary agreed—and, of course, Sicily.[2] These funds were now employed against Aragon and, in addition, the Pope made an advance of other money. Baronius actually reports under the year 1283, that the Pope decided to use the Lyons tithes for Sicily when Charles was demanding help and the papal coffers were empty. He instructed Berardus the *præfectus ærarii apostolici* to get together funds up to 15,600 ounces of gold from the tithes of Scotland, Dalmatia, Sweden, Hungary, Slovenia, and Poland, whether

---

[1] *L.c.*, i, 78, p. 152.   [2] Potthast, 21879 of Mar. 18, 1282.

these were already lodged at the Curia or were deposited in banking-houses elsewhere. He also showed consideration with regard to the delivery of the moneys payable to the Curia from Sicily. Thus, he deferred until Christmas the payment of interest amounting to 8,000 ounces of gold which was due on the feast of Saints Peter and Paul.[1]

Allies were as important for Charles as funds, and in this respect also the Pope did everything possible to help. He instructed his legate Gerard to make it generally known that all who had formerly opposed Charles, but who now supported him, would be forgiven for their former error.[2] In particular Martin exerted himself to mobilize in Charles's favour the latter's most natural ally, France. Meanwhile he was still endeavouring to prevail on Peter to renounce his project, and when these efforts failed he repeated on November 12, 1282, the excommunication against the King of Aragon[3] and shortly afterwards announced through his legate Gerard that all who fought against Peter of Aragon would be granted in the event of their death in battle the same death-bed indulgences as were accorded to the Crusaders.[4]

Deposition of King Peter.

When, notwithstanding all the papal efforts, Peter's success in Sicily continued to grow, Martin proceeded to depose him. On March 21, 1283, the Pope declared that he had forfeited all rights to Aragon, and released everyone from obligations or oaths to the deposed and excommunicated king : all communities which adhered to him were laid under an interdict.[5] This measure evoked strong resistance. Even in the College of Cardinals they did not meet with unmixed approval, for certain

---

[1] Potthast, 22033 of June 8, 1283.   [2] Potthast, 21972.
[3] Potthast, 21947.   [4] *Reg.*, 301 (Jan. 3, 1283).
[5] *Reg.*, 310 ; Potthast, 21998.

individual cardinals protested against them, while cardinal Latinus and cardinal Giacomo Sabelli, later Honorius IV., did not hesitate to maintain contact with Peter even after his excommunication and deposition.[1] In Aragon itself, of course, the Pope's decrees roused still stronger objection. According to Muntaner[2] the Cortes sent a number of bishops and knights on an embassy to the Curia to complain that their king had been given no opportunity to defend himself, and to demand that such an opportunity be now afforded : he would be prepared to appear before the Pope with five or six kings as his sureties.

The report describes the dramatic scene which followed in the consistory. The Pope and cardinals did not even reply to the greetings of the ambassadors, and, on the Pope's refusing to withdraw his decrees or his judgment, one of the knights included in the delegation exclaimed : " Holy Father, it is easily seen that you are a compatriot of King Charles. His followers are listened to and supported, but no reply is accorded to the King of Aragon, who has extended the Church more than all the kings of the world for centuries. And what further conquests might he not have made for the Church if he had been supported ! " When the Pope persisted in ignoring the embassy and refused even to receive the ambassador's credentials, the latter protested in the following words : " Holy Father, since you have given us this answer, we appeal in the name of His Majesty, the King of Aragon, from your judgment to our true Lord God, the Lord of the World, and to St. Peter." They declared the Pope responsible for all that might ensue and drew up a document containing their protest.

---

[1] *Cf.* Saba Malaspina, *Liber gestorum Manfredi, Corradini, Karoli regum Sicilie* in *Cronisti e scrittori Napolitani*, vol. i (Naples, 1845).

[2] *L.c.*, 213 ; i, 104.

The Pope's only reply was to threaten excommunication and interdict on all who cast doubt on the justice of his action : " For all know, or may know, that a false decision has never been delivered by the papal court. And this decision (i.e. that against Peter) is just and will never be altered. Now go ! " King Peter is said to have received the news with the words : " Lord God and Father, I commend myself and my peoples into Thy hands and trust in Thy judgment."

France entrusted with carrying out the deposition.

King Peter's formal deposition by the Pope did not end the matter, and Martin was faced with the necessity of finding a mandatory to carry out his decision.

As might be expected, he turned to France. Shortly after the decree of deposition negotiations were opened with the King of France, Philip III., the proposal being that the kingdom of Aragon should be conferred by the Pope in fief on a younger son of King Philip, not the heir apparent. We know the conditions laid down by the Pope from two letters sent by him on August 27 and 29, 1283, to his legate in France, cardinal John, titular cardinal of the Church of St. Cecilia.[1] They were : that the territory comprised in the kingdom of Aragon should never be divided ; that inheritance should be only in the legitimate line, the eldest son coming first in the line of succession, and, if there should be no son, the eldest daughter, who if unmarried might only marry a true son of the Church, but, if married to a husband not submissive to Rome, the administration of the territory should pass to the Church of Rome until such time as he should submit, all rights reverting to the wife on his death or reconciliation to the Church, but without restitution ; even in the event of there being only one heir—or none—for both France and Aragon, the two countries might not be united, but the

[1] *Reg.*, 455, 456.

King of France might select a new candidate, related
to himself in at least the fourth degree, the selection
to be made within three months of the throne of Aragon
becoming vacant, failing which the Church should have
the right to make a free selection from among the members
of the French royal house, or, if no member of that
house be a candidate, from outside, it being laid
down, however, that Aragon should never be united
with Castile, France, England, or any other kingdom,
and that if a king of Aragon should ever succeed to
another throne, he must surrender Aragon to the
Church.

The rights and privileges of the Church and of
ecclesiastics, as well as the rights of the inhabitants,
must be preserved, in so far as they are in harmony with
Canon Law, all not in harmony therewith being declared
invalid ;   no kind of agreement or arrangement might
be made with the former King Peter without the express
permission of the Curia ;   the reigning king of Aragon
must swear the oath of fealty to the Pope in person
or by proxy within a year, this oath to be renewed within
a year of the election of each successive Pope ;   a sum
of fifty pounds of Tours should be paid as tribute yearly
on the feast of the Princes of the Apostles, the obligation
to pay beginning as soon as possession had been taken
of at least three of the Aragon crown lands, and failure
to pay within four months of the appointed date
entailing for the King the penalty of excommunication,
while the country would be laid under an interdict
after the lapse of another year and the kingdom would
revert to the Church to be disposed of freely, if the
tribute should not have been paid by September 29
in the third year ;   at each coronation the crown must
be asked anew from the Apostolic See, the coronation
to be carried out by the archbishop of Tarragona only
in virtue of special powers accorded by the Pope as

arranged between Innocent III. and Peter's ancestors when the country voluntarily surrendered as a fief to the Roman See ; only in the case of the first king should he be crowned by the papal legate immediately after the acceptance of these conditions.[1]

These provisions were to be solemnly sworn to by the King of France and the one of his sons whom he should select. If the latter was not of an age to swear, the King was to take the oath on his behalf and swear to undertake that his son should take the oath in person as soon as he was competent to do so. If the king or his son should fail to keep the oath and should disregard the admonition of the Apostolic See, Aragon should revert to the Church of Rome to be disposed of freely. The document closes with the formula for the oath.[2]

Against these conditions the King of France raised objections and put forward counter-proposals which were submitted to the Pope in twelve petitions.[3] The essential point made in them is that tithes should be granted for four years, if possible from all Christian countries, but if not, then at least from all France and from the dioceses of Cambrai, Liège, Metz, Toul, and Verdun and from the archdioceses of Besançon, Lyons, Vienne, Arles, and Aix. On receipt of the petitions Martin sent magister Ægidius de Castello, provost of Bruges, to the French Court with a detailed reply of January 9, 1284, in which some of the French proposals were accepted and others rejected. The most important of

---

[1] This is repeated in a separate document, *Reg.*, 459 of Sept. 3, 1283.

[2] Regarding this formula a note written on the margin in the fourteenth century remarks : Contrarium est verum : nam rex Aragonie non tenetur ad faciendum omagium ecclesie Romane, nisi dumtaxat ratione regni Sardinie. The earlier arrangements had ceased to have force in consequence of the conflict, but Sardinia was a papal fief.

[3] Printed in Amari, *La guerra del Vespero Siciliano*, ii, 320.

them from the French King's point of view, that regarding
the grant of tithes, was admitted almost in full, but for
a limited term, the diocese of Cambrai and the archdioceses
of Arles and Aix being excluded, and the archdiocese
of Tarentaise, with the districts of Embrun outside of
Provence and Forcalquier being substituted. As early
as September 2, 1283, the Pope called on the French
clergy to grant tithes to the King for three years for the
campaign against Aragon. This request was repeated
on May 5, 1284. On both occasions the papal legate,
cardinal John, was instructed to supervise the collection
of tithes in the non-French territories. When this matter
had been arranged, Philip of France nominated his second
son, Charles, count of Valois, as candidate for the
throne of Aragon, and on August 27, 1283, the Pope
informed his ambassador that Peter had been
dethroned and Charles of Valois raised to the throne
of Aragon.[1] Muntaner [2] reports that the elder French
prince, the heir to the crown of France, afterwards
Philip IV., disapproved of the arrangement. He did
not wish to disturb the friendly relations existing with
Aragon, and does not seem to have expected any great
success for the enterprise, for when his younger
brother went to Rome and the Pope invested him with
the kingdom of Aragon and placed the crown upon his
head, Philip is said to have given his brother the name of
the " wind king ".

Nothing decisive occurred during 1283. Once more,
on April 15, the Pope repeated the ban against Peter,
and forbade all the nobles and ecclesiastics of Aragon
to have any intercourse with their excommunicated
King.[3] Again the bull of excommunication was nailed
to the church doors of Orvieto. On May 27 the Pope

---

[1] Potthast, 22061 (Aug. 27, 1283).   [2] *L.c.*, i, iii, p. 211.
[3] *Reg.*, 460 ; Potthast, 22013.

once more drew attention to Peter's excommunication
by declaring all processes against the " rebels " in Sicily
to have the force of law.[1] When the repeated ban against
Peter did not have the desired effect, the Pope intensified
the penalties against all who maintained any intercourse with him or Sicily. He imposed a complete
boycott on the island and its inhabitants : all communication with them—even in the way of business—was
made punishable with excommunication, and still further
penalties were threatened if the veto was infringed. In
particular the city of Venice was mentioned.[2] The only
intercourse permitted was such as might eventually
be necessary for a Crusade. This bull was also posted
publicly by the Pope in Orvieto.

Combat suggested between King Peter and Charles of Anjou.   Knowing the difficulties of a campaign against Peter,
Charles tried to reach his goal more quickly by another
road. Like Peter he was regarded as one of the bravest
and most skilful knights of the time. He now made the
remarkable proposal to Peter that the fate of Sicily should
be decided in a combat with one hundred men on either
side ; saying, no doubt correctly, that the two bravest
men in the world would assuredly be found among these
two hundred knights. He suggested that the King of
England should act as judge and that the combat should
take place in the latter's territory, namely, at Bordeaux.[3]
The Pope, however, protested strongly against the proposal. As early as the end of 1282 he was urging Charles
of Anjou to abandon the idea, and he repeated this
admonition on February 6, 1283, and again on April 5

[1] *Reg.*, 467 ; Potthast, 22026.

[2] *Reg.*, 482 : ". . . Interdicimus omne commercium spontaneum,
ita quod ipsis nec ab eisdem Siculis emere aut ipsis aliquid vendere
liceat, vel aliquem cum eis contractum seu quamcunque obligationem
inire, nec ipsos scienter in suis terris seu et locis recipere vel ad dictam
insulam sponte accedere sub quocunque colore, seu vasa vel arma sive
quecumque alia illis necessaria seu utilia mittere vel deferre . . ."

[3] Muntaner, i, 73, p. 141 ; *Liber pontificalis*, 461.

in that year. On the last-mentioned date he communicated also with the King of England whom he forbade to take any part, directly or indirectly, in the project. He also demanded that the King should not allow the combat to take place in any territory subject to him. To emphasize this warning the Pope sent as legate cardinal John, titular cardinal of the Church of St. Cecilia, of whose advice the King could avail himself. The cardinal was instructed to prevent the combat from taking place in any circumstances whatever. In a proclamation of April 13 the Pope instructed his legate to loose all vows and oaths which had been taken regarding the matter, and to declare such oaths as not binding.[1] Muntaner says that in spite of the papal prohibition and although he knew that plots were being made against him, Peter daringly arrived in Bordeaux for the fight, in order to keep his word, but that Charles did not appear.

One reason probably why the Pope forbade this combat was that the outcome of it was uncertain ; for throughout he was concerned primarily to bring the Sicilian question to an issue favourable to Charles. He kept a strict watch on the observance of the interdict in Aragon, and instructed the archbishop of Narbonne on January 13, 1284, to make inquiries as to how it was being maintained and to make a report on the matter.[2] On April 6 and May 18 he re-affirmed the ban and interdict on Aragon.[3] But his main pre-occupation all the time was to gain new allies for Sicily, and as before, he looked primarily to France. He tried to hasten the negotiations for the transfer of Aragon to a member of the French Royal House. On January 10, 1284, he urged his legate, the titular cardinal of St. Cecilia,

New ban and crusade preached against Aragon.

---

[1] *Reg.*, 302, 452–4 ; Potthast, 21955, 21981, 22006.
[2] *Reg.*, 489.   [3] Potthast, 22123, 22141.

to pursue the matter zealously even if the king had not yet given the desired assurances. In another letter sent to the legate at the same time the Pope gave the legate power to require the King-Elect of Aragon to swear only those provisions affecting himself. By this means he hoped to hasten a decision even before Philip had given his consent.[1] At last, on May 5, 1284, he was in a position to hand Aragon over to Charles, the second son of the King of France. On the same day he confirmed the treaty made with the help of the papal legate between the new king and his uncle, Charles of Anjou.[2]

The Pope also strove to get Charles other allies as well as France, looking for this purpose to the city states of Italy. For example, on January 23, 1284, he directed the archbishop of Genoa to read out in his cathedral an account of the proceedings against Peter, and to admonish the chiefs and people of the city to have no intercourse and to do no business with Sicily under pain of excommunication. Similar instructions were sent to Pisa and other less important cities.[3] Hand in hand with this campaign, Charles's own efforts to secure the help of Venice went forward,[4] but the climax of the struggle was reached when the Pope resolved to announce that the Crusade privileges should apply to the war against Peter, the Christian King who but recently had fought for the Church against the Moors.

On June 4, 1284, Martin entrusted the Provincial of the Franciscans for Tuscany, Corsica, and Sardinia, as well as his legate cardinal Gerard, with the preaching

[1] Potthast, 22092, 22093.
[2] Potthast, 22131, 22132.
[3] *Reg.*, 490.
[4] Potthast, 22126.

of the Crusade against Peter, " the son of evil." [1]   The
reason he gave for this grave decision was that Peter
was leaving nothing undone to injure the papacy and the
Church :   since he had begun to rule Sicily the heretics
were being encouraged and the labours of the Inquisition
hampered, and, in consequence, the number of those
who fell away from the true faith was increasing
enormously ;   since Sicily was a point of strategic
importance for the Crusade movement, all activity on
behalf of the Holy Land was suffering and was in fact
being rendered impossible ;   a Christian persecutor of
the faith was more dangerous than an unbeliever or a
heretic who had never known the truth.   These were
the grounds put forward by Martin as forcing him to
preach a Crusade against Peter.   The indulgences granted
originally to the Crusaders were to apply to anyone

---

[1] Potthast, 22149, 22153 ; *Bullar. Franc.*, 529.   Of interest is the
fully correct announcement of the indulgence with emphasis on the
necessity for repentance and confession :   " Nos enim de omnipotentis
Dei misericordia et beatorum Petri et Pauli apostolorum eius auctoritate
ac illa, quam ipse nobis licet immeritis ligandi atque solvendi contulit
potestaten confisi, omnibus illis, qui signo eiusdem vivifice crucis
assumpto per annum in personis propriis et expensis vel in personis
propriis et alienis expensis negotium huiusmodi prosequentur, quosve
in eius prosecutione infra annum more contigerit ac illis eciam, qui
pro qualitate sui status et pro suarum iuribus facultatum ad dictum
negotium prosequendum per idem tempus idoneos miserint bellatores
aut subventionem aliam extribuerint vestro vel eorum, quibus hec
commiseritis, arbitrio acceptandam, illis quoque, qui decimam per
triennium eidem Sicilie regi concessam pro toto eodem triennie primo
anno excoluerint, illam suorum peccaminum, de quibus corde contriti
et ore confessi fuerint, veniam indulgemus, que concedi transfretantibus
in terre sancte subsidium secundum Lateranensis statuta concilii
consuevit.   Huiusmodi quoque indulgentie volumus esse participes
iuxta quantitatem subsidii et devocionis affectum omnes, qui ad
subventionem huiusmodi negotii de bonis suis alias congrue ministra-
bunt.   Volumus insuper et districte precipimus quod tam vos, quam
illi, quibus huiusmodi predicationis officium duxeritis committendum,
in premissis sitis solliciti et attentati nec in illorum execucione quisquam
vestrum alium impediat vel perturbat . . ."

who gave personal military service at his own expense or the expense of others for one year against Peter, or who helped the fight according to his means, as well as to all who paid the three years' tithes in one sum provided they repented of their sins and confessed them contritely.

Defeat of Charles in naval battle off Naples. On June 4, Pope Martin declared a holy war against King Peter, but on the very next day the latter's fleet won a decisive victory over Charles's ships off Naples. Charles's son, Charles of Salerno, was completely defeated and himself taken prisoner by the Sicilian Admiral Roger de Loria. This victory brought release from captivity to Manfred's daughter, Beatrix.

The naval battle at Naples did not end the struggle between Aragon and France, for at a synod in Paris, where cardinal Cholet preached the Crusade against Aragon, the King of France and his son took the Cross, and in the spring of 1285 France entered the campaign with considerable forces on land and sea. Thus a war began, of which the end was not then easy to foresee.[1] But the fate of Sicily had been decided at Naples. The news of the defeat, particularly of the capture of his son and heir, broke Charles's heart. Although seriously ill he summoned the estates to Melfi in December to obtain from them the necessary means to prosecute the campaign with energy. Stubborn resistance awaited him. Although the Pope, to whom he had likewise appealed, had made him a fresh grant of tithes, he felt that he would not survive to employ these funds in person. When he felt his end approaching, he saw his whole life's work in jeopardy once more and could do nothing but appeal first to the Pope to preserve his kingdom for his son, and then to the King of France to protect his French properties, since his heir was a prisoner

---

[1] *Liber pontificalis*, 461.

of Aragon. He died on Sunday, January 7, 1285, at Foggia in the palace of the Hohenstaufen, at the age of 65, having reigned nineteen years. On his deathbed he received the last sacraments and died invoking the name of Jesus.[1] His body was brought to Naples and buried in the cathedral which he himself had begun, and which was to be completed by his grandson, Robert, in 1316.

Charles is among those historical figures whose character is a matter of dispute. Some of his contemporaries indicate this by their varying opinions of him. Giovanni Villani, whose youth coincided with Charles's later period, writes concerning him : " Charles was wise and shrewd in his judgments, brave in battle, stern and greatly feared, respected by all the kings of the world, lofty in his mind, capable of and ready for all high enterprises, steadfast in misfortune, firm and reliant in keeping his promises. He was a man, not of words, but of action ; he rarely laughed ; he was as abstemious as a monk, his views were strictly Catholic, and his justice was immovable. His glance was stern, his form broad and sinewy. His complexion was of an olive hue and his nose was large. In kingly majesty he excelled all the rulers of the world. He spent little time in sleep and was wont to say that sleep was lost time. Generous to his comrades in arms, he was greedy for land, power, and money to further his enterprises. He took little heed of courtiers, jesters, and servants." [2] His opponent Peter describes him as outdoing Nero, and as more cruel than the Saracens, but nevertheless Dante, who was a Ghibelline and who lays to Charles's account the blood of Conradin and the murder of Thomas Aquinas, does not place him in hell for these crimes but pairs

Charles's death.

His character.

[1] _Lib. Pontif._, 464.
[2] _Cf._ Reumont, _Geschichte der Stadt Rom_, ii, p. 607 ff.

him in Purgatory with his opponent, Peter, who is
said to have exclaimed on hearing of his death : " the
best knight in the world is no more." No impartial
critic can deny the harshness and cruelty with which
Charles pursued his aims, but it is equally impossible
to overlook his intellectual greatness. His efforts were
inspired, no doubt, by the ambition to increase his own
power and influence and that of his house, but that should
not cause us to disbelieve the words he is reported to have
spoken on his deathbed : " My Lord and God, I truly
believe that Thou art my Saviour. I pray Thee, have
mercy on my soul. I undertook the conquest of Sicily more
to serve Thy Church than for my own advantage or for
any other worldly reason. Wherefore, forgive me my
sins." In these words he did not deny worldly intentions,
but subordinated them to the service of God. Mediæval
man was so theocentric that he could really feel that the
highest and ultimate impulse for his actions was to honour
God and serve the Church, side by side with, or
transcending, very material motives. In this Charles
may be regarded as a prototype of mediæval man, who,
remote from modern introspection and reflection, was
able to serve both God and his own self in complete
intellectual harmony and balance, and who found it
easy to regard war as a deed done in the service of God.
The conception of a Holy War, in which thousands
believed, is an incontrovertible proof of such a
psychological possibility.[1]

Measures
taken by the
Pope after
Charles's
death.

The news of Charles's death filled the Pope with deep
grief, to which he, together with the College of Cardinals,

[1] The collection of letters known as *Principum et illustrium virorum
epistolæ* (Amsterdami apud L. Elzevirium, 1644) contains (p. 162 ff.)
a letter from Charles to Peter of Aragon, as well as one from John of
Procida to Pope Martin IV. and another from King Peter to Charles.
None of these letters is genuine. They were composed by J. Donzellini
of Verona. *Cf.* Cartellieri, *l.c.*, p. 222.

gave public expression, He strained every nerve to
fulfil the last wishes of the dead King by preserving
Sicily for the house of Anjou. He did this not only
through respect for Charles's wishes, but because to
do so was in harmony with his whole policy. Even
when he was cardinal-legate he had striven on behalf
of Charles of Anjou. As Pope he had been associated
with Charles by the closest ties. Thus a collapse of the
Angevins could not fail to be regarded as a defeat for
himself. Charles had appointed Count Robert of Artois
regent until such time as his son should be free to assume
the reins of power, and the Pope now appointed his
legate, cardinal Gerard, to assist the regent. These two,
equal in status, were to restore order in Sicily. Now for
the first time the Pope decided to try reason and clemency,
a decision which, if taken three years earlier, might have
changed the whole course of Sicily's history. He caused
the island communities to be called upon to send
representatives to the Holy See, with whom he could
discuss personally the best plans for constitutional
and administrative reforms to overcome the undue burden
borne by Sicily. He ordained further [1] that everyone,
high and low, might appeal to the two regents regarding
their concerns. He also sent money to the island to
relieve the most urgent need there. But nothing could
alter the fate of the Angevin dynasty. Sicily was lost
to them for ever, and their plans of ruling the world had
come to nought, there to remain.

When Charles died, Sicily, which he had subdued at
the cost of so much blood, was in a state of disorder similar
to that in which he found it on his arrival. He had
cherished great plans and had gone forward, adding
success to success, with his eyes ever fixed upon his goal.
Even when Count of Anjou and Provence he had got

International importance of the Sicilian Vespers.

---

[1] Potthast, 22123.

a foothold in Upper Italy, as conqueror of the Hohenstaufen, he had strengthened his position there, and as Roman Senator and Regent of Tuscany had established himself firmly in Middle Italy. Southern Italy was in the hollow of his hand when he had Sicily, and he was on the point of advancing from ruling Italy to a world dominion, which was particularly feasible with a politically weak Pope such as Martin IV. It seemed that where Hohenstaufen had failed, Angevin would succeed. One great advantage to him was that the Pope not only avoided interfering with him, but actually assisted him. If Charles's plans had materialized it would have meant that the *imperium* would have passed from Germany to France, and Charles's plans may be regarded as the first effort in that direction. Constantinople would hardly have had the strength to resist Charles's political projects permanently. The Pope might perhaps have had sufficient strength to do so, but he had bound his destiny completely to that of the Angevins and supported Charles's ambitions with all the means at his disposal, blind to the dangers to the freedom of the Church inherent in an Angevin world dominion. Once more history teaches us that developments take place in a direction quite different from that which the earthly factors would lead us to expect. The change was brought about by the Sicilian Vespers, no carefully prepared and thought-out scheme, but a spontaneous outbreak of an oppressed people's hatred of its oppressors and desire for liberty. From the international standpoint the consequences of the Sicilian Vespers were important, not because they liberated Sicily for ever from foreign rule, but because they caused the collapse of French dreams of empire, which could never again be realized to the extent then contemplated. Muntaner[1] regards this as an act of

---

[1] *L.c.*, i, 90.

divine mercy. By its means the freedom of the papacy was preserved without defending itself, for the occupant of the papal throne did not realize that there was any danger. We can imagine what effect an Angevin world empire would have had on the papacy when we remember how, even in existing circumstances, Pope Martin was a mere tool in the hands of Charles and how the latter was able, even when he was a Senator of Rome, to limit the importance of the papacy. Even without a world empire, an Italy united under the Angevins would have meant the end of the liberty of the Popes, and a French empire of the world would certainly have had no place in it for a free papacy. How the papacy was affected even in spiritual matters is shown by the fact that Martin's dependence on Charles sufficed to destroy the efficacy of the weapons of spiritual jurisdiction in the hands of the pro-French Pope. For in spite of excommunication and interdict, in spite of crusades and indulgences, the Pope was not able to restore his favourite, Charles, to his throne. Lamentable and terrible as was the Sicilian massacre of Easter, 1282, it fulfilled a purpose in the development of the world. Deeds of blood must of course be condemned, but who can throw a stone at the Sicilians ? Deeds must be judged not merely impartially but also in the light of the feelings of those who do them ; only thus can they be understood. The Sicilians themselves spoke their best defence when they said to Pope Martin regarding the Sicilian Vespers : " This is not a revolt nor an ungrateful flight from the bosom of our mother, the Church ; it is a resistance lawful, according to canon and civil law. It is chaste love, protection of modesty, defence of liberty. Misery caused a final outburst of passion. There is a violence which is necessary, and it is right to protect human liberty when it is at stake. And when this violence bursts loose there is no cruelty so cruel, in order that

it may serve as a warning and a threat to evil-doers." [1]
Charles of Anjou overthrew the power of the
Hohenstaufen in blood, and in blood he established
his rule. In blood that rule was overthrown by an
oppressed nation, and it was the heir of the Hohenstaufen
who helped the enslaved people to regain their liberty.

There is indeed a majestic element in the history of
the world which causes even such events as appear to be
opposed to world discipline to serve that discipline
despite themselves.

[1] *Cf.* Reumont, *l.c.*, ii, 607.

CHAPTER IV.

His friendship with Charles of Anjou determined the tenor of Pope Martin's policy, and his relations with other states were to a considerable extent dictated by considerations of that friendship. He continued as Pope the policy which he had begun when he was cardinal, working with all the dignity of a papal legate in his native France on behalf of his country. Even then his policy was so involved with French interests that he went so far as to offer assistance to the efforts that were being made to transfer the dignity of the Western Empire from Germany to France. Charles of Anjou must have attached the greatest importance to having an Emperor agreeable to his great project, for he set himself to obtain the Imperial crown for his nephew Philip. From the beginning Charles realized that such a revolutionary idea could not be realized without the support of the Curia, so he turned for aid to his friends in the College of Cardinals, Ottoboni, the Guelf, and cardinal Simon, afterwards Martin IV. In agreement with these two, he revealed his plan to his nephew Philip, who, however, did not receive it with enthusiasm. Efforts were then made to win him over to it under the guise of a moral obligation : he was told that every prince is called upon to do everything in his power in the service of God, and that the position of Holy Roman Emperor offered the greatest opportunities in existence for such service.

Attempt to transfer the Imperial Crown to France.

271

He should think, for example, of the extent to which
he could advance the Crusade movement if he were
Emperor : France would also benefit, for then his native
country would not have to fear the Emperor as a possible
opponent. By such idealistic representations Philip
was at last moved in 1273 to send a mission to the
Curia with regard to the matter. The Pope was already
on his way to the Council of Lyons, and the French
representatives met him at Florence at the end of June.
Keeping in constant touch with the two cardinals, the
ambassadors attempted to influence Gregory X. in favour
of their project which the cardinals had already formulated
in a manner acceptable to the Pope, and which concealed the selfish aims of Charles of Anjou. However, the
Pope was already fully informed and did not allow himself
to be persuaded ; while remaining quite cordial his
attitude was unfavourable. Their friends in the Curia
obtained a second audience for the French embassy,
but without any greater success : Gregory gave no
decision, but that was tantamount to a rejection of the
scheme, for nothing short of positive support would have
held out hopes of success. Accordingly even cardinal
Simon, knowing full well that no other decision need be
expected from the Pope at the moment, gave up the idea
for the time being and advised the French delegation
to return home.

When Simon himself had been elevated to the papal
See, the suspicion grew that he was desirous of depriving
Germany of the Imperial dignity. The earlier episode
had not remained a secret, so the feeling can be
understood. It was not the first time that the Pope had
been so suspected, but suspicion had not been so strong
formerly. Frederick II. had voiced the same fear, and
after Simon had become Pope the danger was spoken of
openly in Germany. The cathedral prelate, John of
Osnabrück, felt it his duty to warn the Pope of the danger

of such a policy in a memorandum [1] laid before the Pope by cardinal James Colonna. He pointed out that the passing of the Imperial crown to Germany was as much the result of divine providence as the establishment of the *sacerdotium* in Rome and the allotment of the *studium* to France (referring to the *studium generale* of the University of Paris). Nothing should be done in the way of interfering with it, neither should the rights of the Electors be tampered with. Charlemagne had established the Holy Roman Empire with the Pope's express approval —in fact on his instructions—on a divine foundation : anyone altering that foundation would expose the Western World to the greatest dangers and would open the road for Antichrist. We do not know whether this document made any impression on the Pope, but at least no further serious effort was made. Probably those in a position to know realized the hopelessness of such an undertaking.

Martin's co-operation in the attempt to unite the Imperial crown eventually with the crown of France should not be interpreted as indicating a policy definitely hostile to Germany. He was thinking of French interests to the exclusion of all else.

In so far as cordiality towards the German ruler could be reconciled with those interests, Martin did not hesitate to be cordial. Indeed, he made determined efforts to reconcile the interests of Rudolf of Habsburg and Charles of Anjou and to bring these two together. Thus at the Council of Lyons he advocated the cause of Rudolf,[2] in whom he hoped to gain for Charles an adherent, and thus secure a firm support for Charles' future efforts.

The alliance was to be brought about by a marriage

---

[1] *De prærogativa Romani imperii*, published by Waitz in the *Göttinger Abhandlungen*, vol. xiv (1868).

[2] Böhmer, *Reg.*, 1267.

between Rudolf's daughter, Gerta, and Charles's grand-son, Charles Martel, and the matter went so far that Charles of Anjou sent representatives to Lyons where the Council was sitting to await there the arrival of Rudolf and Gerta. Rudolf, however, seems to have felt that such a close connection with Charles might be going too far, seeing that each of them had much the same interests at heart. For the present he contented himself with sending the Provincial of the Franciscans, Conrad Probus, to Lyons to negotiate with the Pope. Conrad was very well received at the Papal Court. Since the time of his election Rudolf had had certain adherents among the cardinals, notably cardinals Simon and Ottoboni, who hoped for help from Rudolf in the struggle with the Ghibellines. Negotiations fell through on account of the impossible demands of Charles of Anjou, who asked for nothing less than the cession of Piedmont by Rudolf. While not agreeing with this demand, the Pope put it forward, and any lack of enthusiasm on his part was made up for by the warmth with which it was advocated by Charles's friends in the College of Cardinals, particularly Simon. Although the negotiations came to a standstill and Gerta was not brought to Lyons, relationships remained cordial. It was generally considered that cardinal Simon had pleaded Rudolf's cause at the Council of Lyons with energy and success. When the cardinal saw no further hope of procuring the Imperial Crown for a Frenchman, he wished at least for an Emperor friendly to Charles of Anjou who would not stand in the latter's way. These conditions seemed present in Rudolf of Habsburg, who was of a most conciliatory disposition, which accounts for the support given to him by the Angevin cardinals. When Simon was elected Pope, his cordial attitude towards Rudolf of Habsburg at this time was remembered.

On that occasion the German monarch's envoys, on

their journey from Padua with his daughter Clementia, recalled Simon's friendly attitude in Lyons, and congratulated Rudolf on the ground that the Pope would undoubtedly behave to him as a benevolent father[1] might. The friendly relations between cardinal Simon and Rudolf appear to have endured for some time, since at the end of 1275 the cardinal used his offices with Rudolf on behalf of the envoy of the Margrave of Este.[2] Among the first actions undertaken by cardinal Simon when he became Pope was a renewal of the efforts to unite Rudolf with King Charles of Sicily, and his diplomacy succeeded in bringing about an agreement in May, 1281. Under date of May 25 the Pope summarized the treaty drawn up and formally signed by the two monarchs in respect of the county of Provence and Forcalquier.[3] Rudolf of Habsburg showed himself agreeable to the wishes of Charles and the new Pope, hoping thus to attain more readily to his goal, the Imperial crown, and to secure the succession of his son. With this end in view he had ceded the Romagna to the papacy without much struggle and was prepared to hand the kingdom of Arles over to Anjou. Even during the papacy of Nicholas III. these negotiations had been in progress, but the Pope died before they came to a head. For Rudolf this was unfortunate, for it led to a one-sided implementation of the treaty. Rudolf could not withdraw his consent to the wedding nor interfere with the occupation of the kingdom of Arles by the Angevins, but Pope Martin was able to defer indefinitely the advantages which Rudolf

---

[1] *Wiener Briefsammlung*, N. 166 (Mar. 5, 1281): ". . . Novissime papa creatus est dominus Symon Touronensis videlicet et vocabitur Martinus, qui vestra negotia in concilio Lugdunensi satis fideliter studuit promovere et credimus, quod circa vos et vestros pii et gratiosi patris officium debeat exercere."

[2] *Wiener Briefsammlung*, N. 155.

[3] Böhmer, *Reg.*, 1298a; *Reg.*, 11; Kaltenbrunner, 233.

was to have gained, namely, his journey to Rome and coronation as Emperor.

The treaties were indeed concluded formally under Martin—as we might expect, since they were altogether in the interest of his protégé Charles—but no word was spoken of an immediate journey to Rome or coronation. That Rudolf regarded the coronation as settled is indicated clearly by a number of circumstances, such as the remission of all taxes in Wiener Neustadt, excepting a contribution to his Roman expedition,[1] which shows that he must have counted on the possibility of visiting Rome within the next few years. A preliminary step towards it was the dispatch to Tuscany of two vicars of the Empire, bishop John of Gurk and the Imperial chancellor, Rudolf of Hoheneck. This was possible after the death of Nicholas III. While he was alive consideration for him prevented it from being done, since in 1278 he had induced the Emperor to hand over even the temporal jurisdiction over Tuscany to his nephew, cardinal Latinus. Now on the Pope's death the cities of Tuscany, in particular Pisa, sent envoys to Rudolf on August 22, 1280, to express a wish for the appointment of Imperial vicars. By his appointment of the two vicars on January 5, 1281, Rudolf satisfied this wish. He gave the vicars full powers and empowered them to take possession of all imperial properties, receive homage, punish resisters, and adopt any other measures necessary. The Imperial chancellor was given a letter of credit for 2,000 marks on the guarantee of the King and the Empire. At the same time the inhabitants of Tuscany were admonished to be obedient and respectful to the vicars.[2] It is noteworthy that the Pope and Charles of Anjou, on May 21–4, 1281, respectively, called on the lords

[1] Reg., 1270.
[2] Reg., 1252, 1253.

and cities of Tuscany to render obedience to the representatives of King Rudolf. In doing so Charles drew attention expressly to his friendship and family connections with Rudolf of Habsburg.[1] The claim on the grounds of family connection was based on the fact that the Vicars brought Princess Clementia with them to Italy. On March 22 they arrived with her at Orvieto, where they were received with ceremony by Charles's representatives. On the following day the newly elected Pope Martin IV. was crowned.

Although the relations between the Pope and King Charles on the one hand and Rudolf of Habsburg on the other were now regulated outwardly, as shown by the recommendation given to the Imperial vicars of Tuscany by the Pope and the King of Sicily, Rudolf's prospects of an immediate expedition to Rome and with it of a coronation were very small. The new Pope had no interest in the crowning of Rudolf as Emperor. Had he not when cardinal aided the endeavours to divert the Imperial crown to France ? No doubt Martin IV. attached importance to the preservation of the formal etiquette of mutual intercourse : he apprised the King of the appointment of a collector of tithes and asked for his help and encouragement ; he notified the appointments of bishops in the Empire and showed other small courtesies,[2] but the matter rested there. No word appears of negotiations regarding the coronation. It would seem in fact that Rudolf did not try to open the matter ; no doubt he realized the hopelessness of any effort. As a matter of fact circumstances were such that a visit by Rudolf to Rome was not desired by the Pope. While Gregory X. had been dealing with the question, he had been impelled by his wish to start a crusade in which he

---

[1] *Reg.*, 9 ; Potthast, 21757.
[2] Böhmer, *Reg.*, 1667, 1758, 1783 ; Kaltenbrunner, *l.c.*, 239, 253.

desired particularly the participation of the Emperor
as the temporal leader of Christendom. Such plans
were foreign to Martin IV. The only plans which he had
for the Orient were those associated with Charles and
the latter's dream of an Angevin world Empire. To
such schemes a strong emperor could only be a hindrance.
Accordingly Pope Martin did not take the smallest interest
in Rudolf's journey to Rome. In fact such a journey must
have appeared to him inopportune. This held even more
strongly when disturbances in Italy occupied the Pope
and caused him to fear that they would be strengthened by
the appearance of Rudolf in Rome. For the occupation of
the Romagna by the Church was by no means undisturbed
and violent disorders had broken out there. Under the
leadership of Guido da Montefeltro the Ghibellines
attempted to destroy the sovereignty of the Church. At
first the struggle developed unfavourably for Rome,[1] and
on May 1, 1282, the papal troops suffered a severe reverse
at Forli. Not until the spring of 1283, when fresh re-
inforcements had arrived from France, was it possible to
bring the Romagna into subjection to the papal See. One
can understand that while this struggle continued in
the Romagna Rome endeavoured to prevent the King
from coming thither, and Rudolf could advance no plea
against arguments which were based firmly on fact.
Then, even before peace had been established in the
Romagna, a more serious struggle had developed in Sicily,
and the effects of the " Sicilian Vespers " were not
restricted to the island nor to the portions of Lower Italy
belonging to the kingdom of Sicily, but extended over the
whole of Italy and involved, as already explained, both
Spain and France. Obviously, while these events were
taking place it would be most inconvenient for the Pope
and King Charles to have King Rudolf marching through

[1] *Supra*, p. 211.

Italy at the head of an army.   After all no one could fore-
tell how the King's mind might work when once in Italy.
Accordingly, the Pope was careful to avoid the least
word which might encourage Rudolf to undertake the
journey.   Even Martin, who was usually so active and
who turned in all directions to procure allies for Charles,
had not the smallest hope of inducing Rudolf to help
Charles.   Perhaps he knew that Peter was also looking for
assistance from the German King.   In the spring of 1284,
when King Peter was in the direst straits, not only
fighting against Philip of France and Charles, but also
abandoned by his own grandees, he sent one embassy
to the Queen-Mother Marguerite, Charles's old opponent,
and another to Germany.   The envoys were to justify
Peter's actions to Rudolf and to induce the latter to enter
into a matrimonial alliance.   They probably reached
Germany in the spring of 1284, but we hear nothing of any
success attained by them.   Rudolf adopted an attitude
of reserve and avoided taking sides.   In such circumstances he must himself have recognized that it
would be inopportune to go to Rome, particularly as
the Pope was absorbed in these Italian and Sicilian
problems.   At all events he made no further efforts at
this time to acquire the Imperial crown, although, of
course, not abandoning the project.   Indeed, he lost
no opportunity of considering it, and was always
endeavouring to prepare for it at least, even if he could
not execute it.   He was concerned especially with
obtaining and securing a way of entering Lombardy
and with bringing Milan to a frame of mind friendly
to himself.   For the present he satisfied himself with
dealing with points like these.   His relations towards
the Pope remained formally correct, but, compared with
an earlier period, a coldness is clearly perceptible.   On
one occasion, on January 13, 1283, the Pope urged him
to show more interest in the Holy Land, and sent him

the Italian canon, Master Aliro of the Church of St. Mark at Venice, to carry out the collection of tithes as decreed by the Council of Lyons, in collaboration with others already so engaged.[1] Among the latter was Master Theoderic of Orvieto, who had informed the Pope that the tithes collected in Germany were inadequately safeguarded. This caused the Pope to require the money to be deposited with a trustworthy Italian banking house.[2] We find only one other reference to King Rudolf when he intervened with the Pope to procure a dispensation for a marriage within the fourth degree of consanguinity. The Pope granted the request, which contained no element of the unusual.[3] As Martin identified himself completely with the interests of Charles of Sicily, the question of the coronation of an Emperor could not be arranged. It had been much nearer to solution under Popes Gregory X. and Nicholas III. than under Martin IV., the Pope who subordinated the interests of the Church as a whole to those of the French ruling house.

The Pope attempts to reconcile Rudolf of Habsburg and Philip of Savoy.

There was another situation in which the Pope essayed the rôle of peacemaker with Rudolf, but here again his attitude was so partial and hostile to Rudolf that his efforts were fruitless.

For a considerable time there had been some antagonism between the Counts of Savoy and the House of Habsburg, arising out of certain legal claims of the Empire. In the autumn of 1281 bishop William of Lausanne appeared at Constance before Rudolf to complain of Count Philip of Savoy, who was encouraging, and even inciting, the rebellious citizens of Lausanne in their struggle with the bishop. This intensified the strained relations existing between the German King

---

[1] Böhmer, *Regesten*, 1758.

[2] Kaltenbrunner, *l.c.*, 250.

[3] Böhmer, *Regesten*, 1803.

and the Count of Savoy. Two parties now set themselves
to ease the situation. On the one hand, Margaret, the
widow of St. Louis of France, who still took a keen
interest in politics, often in opposition to her son, the
King of France, attempted to move King Edward of
England to mediate between the adversaries. King
Edward did in fact yield to her representations and sent
two plenipotentiaries to mediate in February, 1282.
Both disputants agreed to nominate negotiators;
King Rudolf named bishop Henry of Basle, while Count
Philip's selection was Abbot Benno of Susa. The
negotiations took place at Mâcon, the residence of Queen
Margaret, who herself played an important part, as is
expressly stated in the documents dealing with them.
An armistice was agreed to in April, 1282, and Henry
of Basle and bishop Berlio of Belley were entrusted
with composing the disagreement. The most important
points in their solution were agreed to in writing by
Philip on June 11 in the same year, but King Rudolf
was forced to repudiate the draft treaty, since it took
cognizance only of the interests of Savoy, for the Pope
had associated himself with Margaret's efforts and
bishop Henry had offered inadequate resistance to the
combined pressure of these potentates. For example,
the draft provided not only for a matrimonial alliance
between Rudolf and Philip by the marriage of the former's
granddaughter, the younger daughter of his son Albert,
to a nephew of Philip, but further decreed a complete
renunciation by Rudolf of his rights and of the territories
to which Philip laid claim, no other claim to be put
forward until after the death of Philip. This meant
a complete, if veiled, recognition of the occupation by
the Counts of Savoy. The Pope sent a special envoy to
Rudolf to induce him to yield, but the envoy was obliged
to return empty-handed in August, 1282. By going
too far the Count of Savoy and the intermediaries failed

in their purpose and on November 11, 1282, the Count had to admit in a letter to King Edward that, in spite of all the efforts made by the Pope and the King of England, peace had not been established.

Relations with France.

Friendly relations between the Pope and the German monarch were impossible because Martin IV. did not pursue an independent policy but espoused the interests of the King of France. So much had been made clear already in the Pope's Sicilian policy, and it was emphasized by his attitude towards Rudolf of Habsburg. Martin, the former papal legate in France, had never concealed his preference for his native land. While using the sternest terms of reproach regarding the King of Aragon, he had none but expressions of the warmest appreciation for the King of France and Charles of Anjou. For Martin France was the traditional and special place of sanctuary[1]; its King was the unequalled champion in the fight for the Church,[2] and that King's actions were accorded full recognition by the Pope. Contrary to the usual custom, the newly elected Pope before his coronation promised the King of France complete support. He himself described as unique this notification of his election to the King of France, and the promises conveyed with it,[3] justifying his action by his special affection towards his well-beloved son, and expressing the hope that he might have an opportunity of proving his goodwill to the King in some special way.[4] As matters turned out he fulfilled that wish and prophecy. His goodwill towards France manifested itself, among other ways, by an

---

[1] *Solitum et speciale refugium* : *Reg.*, 272 (Dec. 13, 1282).

[2] *Singularis athleta* : *Reg.*, 455 (Aug. 27, 1283).

[3] *Singularis nuntiatio* : *Epistolæ* (Martène et Durand, ii, 1282).

[4] "Licet autem insitum nostris visceribus erga magnificentiam regiam non ignores affectum, illum tamen tibi cum plenitudine benedictionis offerimus, intendentes eundem in tuis opportunitatibus efficacius, quantum cum Deo poterimus exhibere."

abundance of favours bestowed on members of the royal
House of France, the most important of which are dated
October 7, 1281. Thus, at the request of that House,
the Pope granted its members an indulgence of 100 days
if they heard a sermon after confession. A similar
indulgence was granted to any person who, on the same
conditions, heard a sermon in the presence of the King
or Queen.[1] On the same day he granted the King and
Queen a further indulgence of one year and forty days if
they were present at the consecration of a Church.
Again, the indulgence was applicable to all present with
them at the ceremony.[2] He also decreed that alms given
by the King should be regarded as restitution for expropriated lands provided the expropriation was the work
of his ancestors and that the injured person was not
personally known to the King.[3] Of special importance
was the privilege that no person, by virtue of his own
powers or of powers committed to him, could excommunicate the King without the express mandate of the
Pope, with whom this privilege rested.[4]

Nor might any other sentence of ecclesiastical punishment be issued against him unless with the special
permission of the Pope.[5] If the King conversed with
persons under solemn ban of excommunication, but
without taking part in those persons' crimes, he was not,
contrary to the canon law of the Church,[6] to fall
under the ban. He had the right of hearing Mass
with his retinue in places under an interdict, on
condition that the doors of the Church were closed,
no bells rung, and the people under the interdict
excluded, provided that he himself was not the cause
of the interdict ; on feast days, in these circumstances,

---

[1] *Reg.*, 36.   [2] *Reg.*, 37.
[3] *Reg.*, 39.   [4] *Reg.*, 41, 46 ; Potthast, 21798.
[5] *Reg.*, 42.   [6] *Reg.*, 43.

Mass might be sung for the King on similar conditions.[1]
He possessed the further privilege of selecting from among
the secular clergy or the orders a confessor who was
thereby given power to release him from the ban of
excommunication.[2] The Queen of France rejoiced in
practically the same privileges. In her case also a general
excommunication had no effect, and a special excommunication could only be uttered on the Pope's
specific mandate. Like the King and on the same conditions she could hear Mass in places under an interdict.
Moreover, her confessor had the additional power of
dispensing her from fasting when she was ill.[3] Under the
same date the Pope informed the King that all the
faithful who after a contrite confession prayed for the
King were granted an indulgence of twenty days for each
day on which they so prayed.[4] By this means the
Pope spurred on the people of France to invoke God's
assistance for their King. A week later Martin entrusted
the Abbots of St. Denis and St. Germain with seeing
that nobody should dare to hinder the King in the
exercise of these privileges.[5] This shower of grace fell
also on the members of the royal family and the
household, for on the same day (October 7, 1281) the Pope
decreed further that the King's son Philip might also
select a confessor from among the secular clergy or the
orders.[6] The King's sister, Blanche, was also remembered.
She was permitted to visit the Cistercian monastery
Regalis Montis in the diocese of Beauvais twice a year in
the company of four women for purposes of devotion,
but she was not allowed to spend the night there. The
privileges accorded to the household related in the first
place to the enjoyment of benefices. Clergy in attendance

[1] Reg., 44.   [2] Reg., 45.
[3] Reg., 63, 66, 67, 68.   [4] Reg., 38 ; Potthast, 4795.
[5] Reg., 56 (Oct. 15, 1281).   [6] Reg., 73.

on the King were allowed to retain their benefices, except the daily attendance fees. Six clergymen in the Queen's retinue and three in that of Princess Blanche enjoyed the same privilege, but in the case of the latter the three clerics were to be named in the presence of the bearer of the privileges.[1] Every cleric in the royal household was entitled to pursue his studies at Paris while retaining benefice, again with the exception of the attendance fees.[2] They could be appointed to benefices by any bishop in communion with Rome.[3] The Queen's retinue had the right of confessing to other clergy in the absence of the priest of the parish.[4] The priests in the Queen's household and in that of Princess Blanche had the further privilege, wherever they should be, of celebrating Mass according to the ceremonial followed in the Royal Chapel at Paris, and they might not be obliged to undertake any other *officium*.[5] A week later Martin granted the King as a further grace that his clergy could not be forced either by the Holy See or its legates to assume any mission against their will unless the Pope made other regulations with specific mention of this privilege.[6] Martin actually went so far as to diminish, if the King desired it, important rights and privileges of the Church which had been stressed and emphasized by other Popes. He instructed the French bishops not to interfere with the King and his officers if they prosecuted crusaders guilty of serious crimes, despite the privileges granted to crusaders. The Abbot of St. Denis was expressly instructed to supervise the execution of this mandate, and to apply ecclesiastical punishments to any ecclesiastics who disregarded it and interfered with the pursuit of such crusaders by the King.[7] Likewise, clerics who

---

[1] *Reg.*, 49, 69, 70.

[2] *Reg.*, 48 (Oct. 10, 1281).

[3] *Reg.*, 40.

[4] *Reg.*, 64 ; Potthast, 21749.

[5] *Reg.*, 65, 71.

[6] *Reg.*, 47 (Oct. 14, 1281).

[7] *Reg.*, 51, 52.

followed worldly occupations were excluded from the *privilegium fori* and made responsible to the secular justice of the King and his officers. If they did not submit themselves voluntarily to the courts they were to be treated as if they had themselves renounced their spiritual privileges.[1] The right of sanctuary was also restricted by an instruction issued to the French bishops by Martin at the beginning of his reign : if heretics, reasonably suspected of heresy, took refuge in a church, they were to be seized regardless of the fact and treated as if they had not sought sanctuary.[2] More significant still, the King instructed his legate, cardinal John, to set aside a number of decisions of the synod of Tours (August, 1282)[3] because the King had protested against them on personal grounds. This had reference to a number of disciplinary reforms decreed at this synod by archbishop John de Montsoreau following on a visitation of the Churches of his archdiocese. Among them was one which laid down that secular authorities who oppressed Churches or ecclesiastical personages, or who interfered with ecclesiastical personages or jurisdiction, should be proclaimed in all the Churches of the archdiocese as excommunicate. The decree went even further by requiring that any person suspected of such an offence should clear himself of the suspicion. Failure to do so caused him to be excluded from the communion of the Church, the fact being notified publicly. On May 24, 1283, Martin directed his legate to amend these clauses as they gave offence to many. No one, however, could have taken offence save the King of France, but that sufficed to cause the Pope to have set aside forthwith provisions which were doubtless for the good of the Church.[4]

Financial favours to France.

In financial matters likewise the Pope was more

---

[1] *Reg.*, 53.   [2] Potthast, 21806.
[3] Potthast, 22017.   [4] Hefele, *l.c.*, 227.

accommodating to France than the interests of the Church warranted. The French treasury had not yet collected the full amount due to it from the Lyons tithes when in 1282 King Philip III. again asked for the grant of new church tithes throughout his realm for a period of three years. At first the Pope was disposed not to yield, as the occasion did not warrant his doing so. For, even if the King assisted his uncle Charles to retain Sicily, as desired by the latter and by the Curia, that fact did not constitute an adequate reason for a grant of a crusade tax. However, the Pope, while refusing, was contemplating aid of another kind for France. He informed the King in confidence [1] that he had in view a declaration deposing Peter of Aragon and the transfer of Aragon to a French prince. The execution of the papal mandate to this effect would be a suitable reason for adding to the grant of territory permission to raise tithes. When Peter had in fact been dethroned, Philip hastened to demand from the Pope an immediate grant of tithes before taking any other steps to carry out the Pope's wishes. About this time the papal camera ordered a full statement to be drawn up showing the financial relations with the French treasury. Allowing for any consideration of the interests of the Holy See, it would have been an easy matter—likewise a fair and just one—for the papal financial authorities to show in this statement that sums were due to the Holy See. In fact, however, the Pope admitted a statement in favour of France showing a sum of 121,154 pounds to the credit of that country. There was added to that during Martin's reign a sum of 54,352 pounds 7 soldi and 6 denarii for payment of troops and a loan of 100,000 pounds of Tours for a similar purpose.

---

[1] *Familiariter et confidenter.* The expression is an index of the relations between Pope and King.

In 1283 a portion of this debt was paid off, but there remained a balance of 129,077 pounds, 6 soldi and 2 denarii, which was employed chiefly in armaments for the "Crusades". This debtor relationship of the Holy See to France persisted until the fourteenth century, and frequently gave the Kings of France a convenient means of bringing pressure to bear on the Curia.[1]

Proceedings for the canonization of Louis IX.

Another example of the manner in which the Pope met half-way the wishes of the King of France was Martin's readiness to fall in with French wishes for the canonization of King Louis IX. When papal legate in France, Martin had already taken preliminary steps in the matter on the instructions of Gregory X., but the Pope had died before he had time to consider cardinal Simon's report. Martin had then referred the matter to Innocent V. and later to John XXII., but without obtaining a decision on the material he had submitted. Not until Pope Nicholas III. occupied the papal throne was the question revived, and cardinal Simon, who was once more on a mission to France, was then re-entrusted with the collection of material. But again the Pope died before an opinion could be given. The French bishops then applied to the new Pope, Martin IV., and requested him to carry through the canonization. Bishop Simon de Perruche, Martin's nephew, and the bishop of Amiens came to Orvieto to ask Martin in the name of the archbishops of Rheims, Sens, and Tours, and of the majority of their suffragans and other French prelates, to include officially in the calendar of the saints of the Church the name of King Louis IX., who, on the evidence of miracles, was already included among the princes in heaven.

Whereupon the Pope instructed the archbishop of Rouen and the bishops of Auxerre and Spoleto to investigate these miracles, either in person or by deputy, at the

---

[1] Gottlob, *Kreuzzugsteuern*, p. 123 ff.

tomb of King Louis in St. Denis or at any other place they thought proper. In doing so the Pope stated expressly that the investigations which he had himself conducted years before still held good. On December 23, 1281, he communicated this decision to the French bishops,[1] but the ceremony of canonization did not take place until 1297. Politics and material questions overshadowed the canonization of the King of France until it came as a welcome opportunity to Boniface VIII. to improve his relations with France.

Very different from the course of events in France was the development of the Pope's relations with England. The synod of Lambeth of October, 1281, best explains the situation there. Matters had been taking an unfavourable turn for the Church since 1279. A statute of that year had prohibited the further acquisition of land by the " dead hand ", particularly by that of ecclesiastical bodies. A further decree had commanded the nobility and clergy to produce before a special Royal Commission documentary proof of title to their possessions, and this had led to a number of church foundations being deprived of possessions justly acquired, but for which documentary evidence of title could not be produced. This was the final factor in causing archbishop John Peckham of Canterbury to summon to a synod at Lambeth for October 7, 1281, all the bishops within his jurisdiction, as well as various abbots and many other clerics of various ranks. The King sought to limit the freedom of this conference. On September 28 he issued a short decree to the archbishop, the contents of which were clear : " he who wished to retain his living should be careful not to speak at Lambeth on matters concerning the crown, the King's person, or the King's rule." Despite this effort at intimidation the synod took place, but it avoided any

Situation of the Church in England.

---

[1] *Reg.*, 84, 85 ; *Bull. Franc.*, 473 ; *Suppl.*, 154 ; Potthast, 21822.

criticism of the questions provoked by the royal decrees and concerned itself primarily with matters of church discipline. The results of its deliberations were embodied in seventy-two paragraphs which emphasized or in some case modified earlier decisions. The most important provisions may be summarized as follows :—

(1) The Most Holy Sacrament of the Altar must be held in greater respect. This entailed confession by every priest at least once a week and the maintenance in every Church of a locked tabernacle and a handsome pyx. The Eucharistic elements should be renewed each Sunday. At the Elevation of the Host, the Church bells should be rung so that persons not present in the Church could kneel and obtain the indulgence. The faithful should be instructed that they receive the Body and Blood of Christ under the appearance of bread, but, on the other hand, that the wine handed to them to drink is not consecrated but is intended merely to facilitate the swallowing of the Host. Parish priests may not give Holy Communion to any person unless they know that that person has prepared himself by confession. For this reason it is forbidden to give Holy Communion to a member of another parish unless with the permission of his own parish priest. The only exceptions to this are persons travelling on business and cases of urgent necessity.

(2) Priests should avoid undertaking the saying of too many Masses for individuals or families lest they should not be sufficiently available for the parishioners in general. In particular they may not accept more offerings for Masses in any year than they can undertake without detriment to their duties. It is strictly forbidden to say one Mass in return for two offerings.

(21) No religious may be the executor of a will without the permission of his superiors. Such permission may only be granted to conscientious men.

(22) It is punishable not to wear the tonsure and ecclesiastical dress.

(23) Sons of priests and of rectors of Churches may not succeed their fathers in office. If they have actually done so they are to be at once deprived publicly of office.

(24) Every person invested with a benefice by a bishop shall receive a certificate of the fact.

(25) The accumulation of benefices in the hands of one person is strictly forbidden.

(26) No one may appear as an advocate unless he has studied canon and civil law for at least three years.

(27) On the death of a bishop or archbishop every priest in his diocese shall say Mass for his soul.[1]

These synodal decrees were again emphasized and extended after the visitation of archbishop John Peckham in the summer of 1284, which had clearly shown the need for them. In particular, provisions were added regarding clerical dress, and those against concubines being kept by priests, those regarding the proper keeping of the Blessed Eucharist and the education of the clergy. The representatives of Church learning being almost exclusively Franciscans and Dominicans, these must be allowed to preach. Provisions against usury were also reissued.

The Lambeth synod terminated on October 10. On the 19th of the same month the archbishop summoned all abbots and priors who had not appeared there to explain their absence. On November 2 he replied to

[1] Mansi, l.c., xxiv, p. 405 ff.

King Edward's decree by demanding that all laws
which oppressed the Church unjustly should be repealed,
since all laws must harmonize with the papal decrees
and the statutes of the councils, as well as with the
teachings of the Fathers.   Every King is bound to
submit to the Pope and obey him, if he does not wish
to imperil his crown.   Hitherto the freedom of the
Church had been respected by all Kings of England
except Henry I. and Henry II.   Nothing is known of any
decisive results from this moderate document.

The Pope
intervenes
on behalf
of the
imprisoned
Count of
Montfort.

Within three months another synod had to be held, the
occasion being Pope Martin's summons to the English
bishops to intervene for the liberation of Count Amaury
de Montfort who was unjustly held prisoner by
the King of England.   The prisoner was the son of
that Count Simon de Montfort-Leicester who had carried
on the operations against Henry III.   He had entered the
Church and became a papal chaplain.   In 1276 he
desired to escort his sister Eleanor, who was betrothed
to Prince Llewellyn of Wales, to her bridegroom.   This
matrimonial alliance of the Montforts with Wales,
which was always prone to disturbance, was by no means
pleasing to the King, the less so as on a previous occasion
the father of Amaury and Eleanor—known as the English
Catiline—had formed an alliance with Wales against
England.   Accordingly he came to a quick decision
and took the two Montforts prisoner when on their
way to meet Eleanor's bridegroom.   Pope John XXII.
exerted himself forthwith to procure the release of the
prisoners, but without success.   In 1278 Eleanor was
released after King Edward had defeated Llewellyn and
eliminated the danger of a new revolt.   Now on
September 20, 1281, the Pope appealed [1] to the King of
England in a letter begging, as his predecessor had done,

------

[1] *Reg.*, 18.

that the papal chaplain be set free. The negotiations
with the previous Pope had not come to anything owing
to the Pope's death, and now he, Martin, was taking
the matter up and offering security that the Count
of Montfort would undertake, as had been already done
under Nicholas III., that he would never enter any
English territory without express apostolic permission,
would do nothing to help anyone else to enter England
in a hostile spirit, and would give no assistance of any
kind to anyone who was planning anything hostile
to England, its King, or its Royal House.

Martin made a simultaneous appeal to the archbishop
of Canterbury and his suffragans that they should
take steps to secure the release of the papal chaplain.[1]
This appeal led to the synod of London of February 15,
1282, at which, however, the only bishops in personal
attendance were those of London and Rochester. The
other bishops sent representatives. To support his appeal
Martin sent the papal chaplain and dean of Le Puy,
Magister Raymundus, to England.[2] These combined
efforts did indeed succeed in giving back his freedom
to the Count of Montfort. At this synod a complaint
was heard by the chancellor Simon de Micham of
Salisbury and vicar Robert of Sturminster against
the archbishop of Dublin and papal chaplain Arditio,
because the latter, as chief collector of the Lyons tithes,
had kept back their due pay from the sub-collectors.
In support of their case they cited papal decrees, but
the genuineness of these was so doubtful that the synod
decided not to give any decision but to leave the whole
question to Pope Martin.[3]

The Pope built great hopes of a crusade on the King

The King of
England's
Crusade
promises.

[1] *Reg.*, 19 ; Potthast, 21787.
[2] Potthast, 21788.
[3] Mansi, *l.c.*, p. 459 ff.

of England. When he was prince he had undertaken an expedition on behalf of the Cross and had
shortly afterwards registered the Crusade vow. There
was a widespread hope that he would succeed in conquering Jerusalem. This fact induced a more yielding
disposition towards him on the part of the Curia, but
encouraged the King on the other hand to show no
consideration to Rome.

When the opportunity arose he renewed his Crusade
vow and thus obtained from the Curia a grant of Crusade
tithes. He profited by the frequent changes of Pope as
these occasioned automatic interruptions of the negotiations. Matters continued thus until 1296, when the bull of
Boniface VIII. *Clericis laicos* caused a temporary break
and a conflict with the Curia, but till then the British
clergy had consistently paid tithes for eighteen years for
the contemplated Crusade. Edward I. was not satisfied,
however, with levying the tithes, but endeavoured to get
control of the funds collected for the Holy Land. In
1282 he forbade the exportation from the kingdom of
the proceeds of the Lyons tithes, which had been levied
for that object. Merchants and bankers who agreed
to forward the money despite this edict were threatened
with the forfeiture of their goods and even with the
loss of their liberties or their lives. The Mayor and
Corporation of London, as well as the wardens of the
Cinque Ports and other officials, received strict instructions
to seize those who defied the prohibition, and to lodge
them in safe custody. These measures were occasioned
probably by the arrival of the papal treasury official
Geoffrey of Veçano, who had been appointed by Martin
to take over the sums collected for the Crusade within
the realm of England and to deliver them to the Curia.
The King went even further. Shortly after he vetoed
the export of gold, he caused convents, Church buildings,
and other places where Crusade funds were deposited

to be entered forcibly, the seals of the coffers to be broken and the money removed. No heed was paid to the protests of the responsible custodians, and the entire sum was collected in a safe place where it was at the King's disposal.[1] These proceedings on the King's part must not be regarded as a direct contest between the King or the people of England and the Pope; they were based exclusively on the desire to keep the money in the country. They had nothing to do with principles or points of view, but rested on purely material grounds. News of the King's raids spread, as one might expect, very rapidly. Berard of Naples[2] wrote to the King to tell him that it was rumoured that he had seized the Crusade funds for his own purposes, and to ask him to write and make it possible to denounce these reports as untrue, for they could not be reconciled with the King's known zeal for the Holy Land. If, however, there should be any truth in the rumour, then he begged the King to make restitution as quickly as possible for the wrong that he had done. In that case he should also declare the reasons for his misdeeds so that the affair could be cleared up in Rome. He prayed that God might give him the grace not to be influenced by considerations of temporal success but by those of eternal salvation.[3] As a matter of fact the King decided to restore the treasures and money which had been seized, although it was stated, indeed, by the custodians that everything did not find its way back to its lawful possessor.[4]

Historical sources tell us of an attempt on the part of King Edward to withdraw altogether from the Crusade obligation which he had accepted voluntarily. He

---

[1] Raynaldus, *Annales* (year 1283).

[2] Martène et Durand, *Epistolæ*, ii, p. 1299 ff.

[3] Martène et Durand, *l.c.*, 1300.

[4] Gottlob, *l.c.*, 141.

proposed that the Pope should be satisfied if his brother
Edmund undertook the Crusade, and asked that the
Crusade tithes should be left to Edmund, who was
ready to embark on the Crusade without delay.

To put this case forward he sent the dean of York as his
ambassador to the Curia. On January 8, 1283, the
Pope replied unfavourably. He urged Edward not
to be resentful if the Pope insisted on a personal performance of his promise. If that was absolutely
out of the question, the Pope reserved his decision
regarding the tithes.[1] When in 1284 the King's life
was in the gravest danger after an attempt to assassinate
him, the Pope took the opportunity, when congratulating
him on his recovery from his serious injuries, to admonish
him to see in the occurrence the finger of God and a command that he should undertake another Crusade to the
Holy Land. In this letter the Pope applied to King
Edward epithets which he usually reserved for the King
of France : " fighter for Christ," " champion of the name
of Christ," " hero of Christendom." [2]

Zealous as Edward was to collect the Crusade tithes and
to keep them in his territory, he showed no eagerness
to pay interest on them to the Pope. Year after year he
had to be reminded of it, unsuccessfully as a rule. For
example, in a letter of August 21, 1281, the Pope ordered
the King to pay to Geoffrey, the officer of the papal camera,
the annual interest for the previous three years and for
the current year, amounting to 1,000 marks sterling.
On February 3, 1282, and February 13, 1284, the same
sum was demanded as interest.[3]

Except for Crusade plans and tithe demands there
was little occasion for dealings between England and
the Curia. On January 28, 1282, Pope Martin asked

---

[1] *Reg.*, 286 ; Potthast, 21967.

[2] Martène et Durand, *l.c.*, 1297 ; Potthast, 22193.

[3] Potthast, 21781, 21845, 22102.

the King to intervene in the dispute between Queen
Margaret of France and Charles of Sicily regarding
Provence and the county of Forcalquier.[1] The year
1283 brought an appeal from the Pope to King Edward
to prevent by any means in his power the " detestable "
combat between Peter of Aragon and Charles of Sicily
for the crown of Sicily.[2] In the summer of the
same year the Pope endeavoured to prevent Edward
from giving his consent to the matrimonial alliance
of his daughter Eleanor with Alfonso, the son of Peter
of Aragon.[3] A little later the Pope appealed to him to
intervene in Castile, for the freedom of the Church was
imperilled by the happenings there and very bad example
was being given. King Edward was to take steps
to prevent the Church's liberty from being restricted
and for the restoration of peace and order in Castile.[4]
Finally, mention may be made of a recommendation
on behalf of the Cluniac monks made by the Pope to
King Edward.[5] The Pope's remaining interventions
in English affairs relate to matters of church benefices,
either new grants or decisions in disputed cases. Once
there was a grant of an indulgence to two convents of
Poor Clares. All of these communications are of secondary
importance.[6]

Pope Martin's relations with the kingdom of Aragon Spain.
have been described in the chapter relating to the
" Sicilian Vespers ", but a consideration of papal policy
towards Spain must include some reference to Castile.
Like his predecessors, John XXI. and Nicholas IV., Castile.

---

[1] Potthast, 21844.

[2] Potthast, 22005 (April 5, 1283).

[3] Potthast, 22049 (July 7, 1283).

[4] Potthast, 22055 (August 9, 1283).

[5] Potthast, February 1, 1283.

[6] The following are the papal letters in chronological order : Potthast,
21807, 21846, 21910, 21911, 21915 ; *Reg.*, 224, 225 ; Potthast, 21963,
21964, 22013 ; *Bull. Franc.*, 511 ; Potthast, 22078, 22171.

Martin's chief concern was to make peace between France and Castile, for the war arising out of the succession after the death of Alfonso still persisted. France maintained firmly its support of the claim made by Blanche, daughter of Louis IX. and wife of Ferdinand, elder son of King Alfonso of Castile, on behalf of her two children. In the very first year of his reign Martin urged King Alfonso to make peace with France, as the war had lasted for five full years. He urged peace all the more because this war among Christian princes was nullifying his Crusade plans. The King should consent at least to a truce.[1] It is noticeable that the Pope's pleas for peace were addressed only to the King of Castile and not to the King of France. Here again Martin showed his partisanship.

During Martin's papacy the situation in Castile was further complicated by struggles within the realm itself. Alfonso's sons rose against their father and tried to secure power for themselves, whereupon the King disinherited the heir apparent, his son Sancho. The majority of the grandees of the kingdom ranged themselves on the side of Sancho. King Alfonso sought aid from Aben Yussef, the ruler of Fez and Morocco, but before the latter could send any material assistance a dispute between the two rulers brought the matter to naught. The King addressed himself to the Pope in terms of the greatest urgency, sending as ambassador to support his prayers Montaninus de Camilla, who conveyed to the Pope the King's wish that a legate *a latere* might be sent to take steps on the spot to bring the princes to submit and to deliver up the territories which they had unlawfully occupied.

In his reply of January 17, 1283, the Pope expressed his regret at being unable for two reasons to agree to

---

[1] Potthast, 21831 ; Martène et Durand, *l.c.*, ii, 1286.

this request. In the first place the ambassador's credentials were defective, as he was unable to produce any special instructions from the King on the point ; besides, before the Pope could intervene he would have to make inquiries from the bishops and spiritual nobles of the country. Until the results of these inquiries were available he could not make up his mind as to the best course to follow.[1] Martin then appealed to the bishops [2] to forward him reports on the question and instructed them to pray for a favourable outcome of the matter. The reports sent to him must have been favourable to King Alfonso, for on August 9, 1283, the Pope issued orders to the temporal and spiritual nobles of Spain that they were not to support the rebellion of King Alfonso's sons nor hinder the King in the exercise of his rights. He gave release from all oaths which might have been sworn to the sons and forbade the clergy on pain of losing their dignities and benefices to take the princes' side. The archbishop of Seville was entrusted with the carrying out of this decree.[3] At the same time the Pope called on the Kings of England and France to ensure peace and quiet since the interests of the Church were imperilled by disturbance.[4] By these means the Pope did succeed in inducing Sancho in 1284 to submit to his father, who in turn revoked the decree of disinheritance.

For a considerable time relations between Portugal Portugal. and Rome had been strained in consequence of attacks by the King on the liberty of the Church. For these attacks King Alfonso and his son Dionysius were excommunicated and the country laid under an interdict. The nobility now persuaded the King to agree to a concordat, and the Portuguese bishops requested the Pope to accept

---

[1] *Reg.*, 300.   [2] Martène et Durand, *Ep.* ii, 1292.
[3] *Reg.*, 479 ; Potthast, 22056.   [4] See above and *Reg.*, 481.

it. After a consideration of its terms and the inclusion of certain formal changes, Martin agreed to it, and on March 25, 1284, the conflict was terminated by a letter of the Pope to the bishop of Leon and the archdeacon of Salamanca.[1]

Majorca.

We have just one letter, dated February 7, 1285, to the Pope from King James of Majorca. It arises from the fight against Peter of Aragon. The Pope granted tithes to the King for three years, so that he might be in a position to lead an adequate force against Peter concurrently with France.[2]

The northern countries.

Travel conditions of the period caused intercourse with the far-off northern states to be very meagre. King Magnus of Sweden on November 22, 1281, was granted by the Pope the usual privilege of selecting his own confessor freely from among the secular or religious clergy, and this confessor had apostolic power to absolve from all sins except those reserved to the Apostolic See, and to modify vows, except the vow to undertake a Crusade and the vow of complete virginity.[3] The few remaining papal decrees relate to benefices and tithes. In 1282 the Pope appointed a small commission, consisting of a Cistercian abbot, a Dominican prior, and a Franciscan guardian, to test the canonical election of bishop Nerva of Bergen as archbishop of Drontheim.[4] On April 26 in the same year the Pope interfered in a dispute regarding the filling of the bishopric of Viborg in Finland. The chapter had chosen by canonical election Ascerus, a canon of chapter, but the Metropolitan bishop, Johannes, archbishop of Lund in Denmark, would not recognize this election and nominated the Franciscan friar Peter of Viborg to be bishop of the place. In the

---

[1] Potthast, 22119 ; *Bull. Franc.*, 518.

[2] Potthast, 22208.

[3] *Reg.*, 89 ; Potthast, 21816 ; *Bull. Franc.*, 476 ; Baronius, an. 1281.

[4] *Bull. Franc.*, 486.

interests of peace Ascerus renounced any claims he might have, but the chapter held a new election and chose one Nicholas, who, however, died at Rome before the Pope could give a decision on the dispute, whereupon the chapter elected Thrugill as bishop. Peter, the Metropolitan's candidate, made his rival a prisoner. When this happened, the Pope instructed the bishop of Ripen in Denmark to call upon Peter to release the prisoner immediately and to come himself to Rome to await the Pope's judgment in the case.[1]

Another letter directed to archbishop Johannes of Drontheim is dated May 15, 1282, and tells the archbishop to deliver to certain specified merchants of Lucca the amounts collected for the Crusade tithes.[2]

Papal communications with Poland and Silesia are likewise concerned exclusively with material questions. For a number of years Henry IV. of Breslau, Duke of Silesia, had interfered with the liberty of the Church in Breslau and with its possessions. For years he had collected tithes, besides appropriating other revenues and possessions—including entire villages—and imposed heavy burdens on the bishop's vassals and subjects. After a temporary solution in 1276 on the basis of an arbitration the Duke again attacked the Church in 1281, and was in consequence excommunicated by bishop Thomas of Breslau. Both parties turned to the Pope for a final decision, and in 1282 the bishop of Fermo, the papal legate sent for the purpose, decided in favour of the bishop. While the latter caused the decision to be published, the Duke refused to accept it. He appealed to Rome, and did not shrink from deeds of such violence that the life of the bishop was in danger, and the latter was forced to take refuge in the fortified castle of Ottmachau near Neiss. As the legate had raised the ban

---

[1] *Bull. Franc., Suppl.*, 153.   [2] Potthast, 21900.

on the Duke solely on condition that he should be
reconciled to the bishop, the latter now ordered his
clergy to recognize the continuance of the ban and to
act accordingly.   This instruction met with very strong
opposition, especially from the religious orders who
celebrated Mass in the Duke's presence.   The Pope now
appointed as judge with full powers the competent Metropolitan, archbishop James Swinka of Gnesen, who
summoned a synod of the province to meet at Lencicz
on January 15, 1285.   This synod confirmed the renewal
of the excommunication by bishop Thomas of June 30,
1284, declared the Duke guilty of a number of fresh
deeds of violence, and repeated the excommunication on
its own behalf.   But this synod was likewise unable to
bring peace to the Church, for the bishop was again
forced to flee, and retired in 1285 to Ratibor.   In 1287
the Duke laid siege to the city, whereupon the Bishop
surrendered himself, going to the enemy's camp in his
episcopal vestments and in solemn procession.   The
Bishop's magnanimity touched the Duke, who threw
himself at his adversary's feet and gave full satisfaction
for all his hostilities against him.[1]

The Pope had also to protect the bishop of Cracow.
It was reported to him that by a stratagem Lestcho,
duke of Cracow and the adjoining territories, had seize
the bishop, imprisoned him, and deprived him of his
estates.   On April 10, 1283, the Pope appointed bishop
Thomas of Breslau and bishop John of Posen to investigate
the matter, and, if the report proved true, to excommunicate Lestcho and those who had helped him.[2]

Two other documents have reference to the levying
and collecting of Peter's Pence in Poland.   They are
addressed to the temporal and spiritual nobles who are

---

[1] Baronius, an. 1284 ; Hefele, *l.c.*, p. 236 ff.
[2] *Reg.*, 317 ; Potthast, 22009.

asked to assist the collectors and to urge all persons in arrears with payments, principally the priests of the Teutonic Order, to fulfil their obligations.[1]

In Hungary, likewise, the Pope had to call the King ^{Hungary.} to order. He was informed that King Ladislaus was leading a life unworthy of a king. In fact, the papal legate, bishop Philip of Fermo, had felt himself obliged to excommunicate him and to prevent him from exercising his rights in the matter of bestowing benefices in his gift. The legate appointed to these benefices himself. Pope Martin tried to influence the King by kindness, decreeing that no prejudice was created through the filling of the benefices by the legate and that, once the ban of excommunication was lifted, the King himself could appoint suitable persons to the benefices of which he was patron as often as they fell vacant.[2] On August 30, 1282, the Pope congratulated the King on the occasion of a victory and urged him to show his gratitude to God by avoiding vice, practising virtue, and dismissing evil counsellors.[3]

Particular importance attaches to the Pope's relations ^{Byzantium.} with Byzantium. Here it was not a matter of foreign policy but one of the unity of the Church. With great difficulty success had been achieved at Lyons, and recent Popes had shown iron determination in preventing Charles of Anjou from setting out to conquer Constantinople, and from sacrificing to his personal ambition the union brought about with such pains. But with the death of Nicholas and the election of the francophile Martin the Angevins were given a free hand. Charles persuaded the Pope that the surest way of achieving a permanent union between Rome and Byzantium was

---

[1] Potthast, 22199–22201.
[2] *Reg.*, 215 ; Potthast, 21923 ; Baronius, an. 1282.
[3] *Reg.*, 216 ; Potthast, 21933.

by the complete subjection to himself of the Eastern
Roman Empire, for if he should succeed he would not
only guarantee union, but would undertake a complete
latinization and catholicization of Constantinople.
While Michael, the Greek Emperor, did the newly elected
Pope the honour of sending the Metropolitans of Heraclea
and Nicæa to congratulate him, the Pope received the
envoys coldly from the outset, and when three weeks
had hardly passed from his coronation, on April 10,
1281, he excommunicated the Greek Emperor, Michael
Palæologus, and all Greeks as schismatics. The first
solemn bull of excommunication is dated November 18,
1281.[1] The Pope allowed Charles to convince him that the
Emperor's attitude had been insincere throughout and
that he had never been in earnest with regard to union.
The ban of excommunication ended the plans for it.
Michael answered it by prohibiting the mention of the
Pope's name during Mass, and was on the point of formally
dissolving the union, but he died on December 11, 1282,
before taking a final decision. His son and successor
Andronicus made the formal breach. Immediately after
ascending the throne he declared that he had only agreed
to the union under protest and that he now wished to atone
for his weakness. He forced the Patriarch, Johannes
Bekkus, who was in favour of union, to resign. Having
sent him to a monastery, he reappointed the former
Patriarch, Joseph. The churches were solemnly sprinkled
with holy water to cleanse them from the stain of the
union, and penances were imposed on all adherents of
the union. Bishops and priests were even suspended for
months, and the two archdeacons Meliteniotes and George
Metochites, who had once attended the Pope's Mass in
Rome as representatives of Byzantium, were deprived
of office for ever.

---

[1] *Reg.*, 278 ; Potthast, 21815.

Matters became worse when it was made clear that hostilities were in contemplation against Byzantium. As early as July 3, 1281, an important treaty was signed at the papal court in the presence of high officials of the Curia in the Pope's confidence. As long as anyone could remember, Venice had been an enemy of Byzantium for commercial reasons. Now it agreed at the papal court to a formal treaty with King Charles for a war against the Greek Empire : on the one hand, King Charles and Philip the Latin Titular Emperor of Constantinople, and on the other, the Doge of Venice, by his representatives Giovanni Canis Dandolo and Giacomo Tiepolo, formed an alliance against the "usurper" Michael Palæologus.[1] Venice was to augment Charles's fleet with forty vessels. Preparations were made for the fight, and the first consignments of troops had already started when the Sicilian Vespers brought all Charles of Anjou's far-reaching plans to nought. The Pope gave moral aid at least to the fight. On May 7, and again on November 18, he renewed the ban of excommunication against the Greek Emperor.[2]

In 1283 the Emperor summoned a synod in Constantinople to end the matter. On account of illness the Patriarch Joseph could not be present, and the conduct of affairs was in the hands of the Patriarch of Alexandria, Athanasius, who was all too easily open to the influence of fanatics. The synod condemned the writings of the friends of the union. The former Patriarch, Bekkus, was summoned to give an explanation, and appeared after securing a safe conduct. He was given the lowest place in the synod, which may account for the fact that he did not venture to defend his former attitude courageously, but endeavoured instead to excuse his writings by pleading

---

[1] *Cf. Fontes rerum Austriacarum*, xiv, 287, nn. 373-5.
[2] *Reg.*, 269 ; Potthast, 21896, 21948.

the theological tendency of the time when they were
composed. He went so far as to have himself brought
before the Patriarch Joseph and to make a profession of
faith hostile to the union. He also signed his resignation.
Nevertheless, he was exiled shortly after to Prusa in
Bithynia, with the consent of the Emperor. The
opponents of the union had such influence over the latter
that he actually refused the right of church burial to his
father because of the union into which Michael had
entered. He also forced his mother to abjure solemnly
union with Rome. Nor did the death of the Patriarch
Joseph in 1283 alter the situation. George of Cyprus
was chosen to succeed him, bearing the name Gregorius,
as Patriarch. Formerly a pronounced adherent of union,
he was now equally pronounced in his hostility towards
it. At the first synod held under his presidency on Easter
Monday, 1283, the bishops friendly to union were attacked,
fanatical monks being particularly prominent in these
proceedings. A second synod confirmed the banishment
of Bekkus and his followers to Bithynia where they were
held prisoners.

Meanwhile, however, Bekkus had recovered his courage,
and nothing could move him to abandon again the line
which he had adopted of favouring unity. He died in
1298, and with him the last upholder of the union of the
Christian Churches in the East passed away.

The Pope on his side forbade any alliance with the
East, and it is interesting to notice that even at the time
Baronius criticized the Pope for this. He says that the
decree of excommunication against the Greek Emperor
had been uttered without preliminary warning, wantonly,
and in the interests of King Charles, but not in those of
the Church.[1]

Judged by the policy of his predecessor, Martin IV.'s

---

[1] Baronius, an. 1281.

foreign policy represents a retrogression. Pope Nicholas set before himself as his goal the strengthening of the independence and freedom of the Church. Martin, on the contrary, looked to France for the salvation of the Church and attuned his entire policy to the furtherance of French schemes, particularly to the support of the plans of Charles of Anjou for a world empire. It was well for the Church that these plans did not succeed, for their success would have involved the gravest threat to the freedom of the Church. Thus Martin IV.'s foreign policy shows very clearly that the direction of the Church rests not in the hands of the Pope, but in those of Him who said : "I am with you all days even to the end of the world."

CHAPTER V.

IN his conduct of the internal affairs of the Church
Martin IV. followed traditional lines. His policy was
characterized by a pronounced degree of favour shown
to the mendicant orders. Where possible, preference
was shown to French elements, and an opportunity in
this regard was afforded by the creation of cardinals
which took place within a few weeks of Martin's coronation : the exact date cannot be determined. One source
gives the date of the coronation as March 23, but this
is highly improbable. Other witnesses mention March 29,
others again April 12. In any case the creation of cardinals
must have been complete by the beginning of May.
In all Martin appointed seven cardinals, of whom four
were French, one English, one a native of Lombardy,
and only one an Italian proper. The sole Italian, who was
made a cardinal-deacon, was Benedict Gaetani, who later
became Pope Boniface VIII. The reason for his election
was no doubt the personal merits of the young priest,
but perhaps Gaetani's political opinions also helped.
Martin was personally acquainted with him, as they had
travelled together on his first French embassy, and
it may have been as a result of the influence then exercised
on young Benedict by the practised diplomat that the
former became a friend of the French and an adherent
of the French party in the College of Cardinals. Whether
that is so or not his friendship for the French decided
his elevation to the cardinalate. In him the Pope

Creation of Cardinals.

nominated an Italian, but an Italian who would take the French side in the College. The Pope's personal predilection was shown when he confirmed the new cardinal in his rich benefices as early as May 6, 1281.

The first person on whom Martin conferred the cardinal's hat was Bernard de Languissel, archbishop of Arles. The other Frenchmen who were raised to that dignity under Martin were Jean Cholet, Gervaise de Glincamp, archdeacon of Paris, and Gaufridus de Barro, dean of Paris. The Englishman was Hugh Atratus of Evesham, and the remaining nominee was the Lombard Count Glusianus de Casate.

In his policy towards the religious orders the Pope developed a pronounced tendency to favour the mendicant orders. This preference was, in part at least, well founded, as at the time the orders had the greatest vitality and were best fitted in the stress of the period to act as guardians of the Church. The privileges which Pope Martin accorded to the mendicants related primarily to the power of hearing confessions and preaching, and of appointing syndics to protect their material interests. They are set out in the bull *Ad fructus uberes* of December 13, 1281. There it is laid down that the General and Provincials of the Franciscans may appoint suitable friars, tested by the heads of the order, to hear confessions and to preach. Only once a year are the faithful obliged to confess to the priest of the parish in accordance with the decrees of the fourth Lateran Synod.[1] In the bull *Exultantes in Domino*, dated January 18, 1283, the Pope alleges that the procedure of recourse to Rome in cases where the Franciscans suffer injury in their secular rights and possessions is a much too involved one and is often an inadequate remedy. Therefore he gave the General of the Order,

Policy towards the Orders.

Mendicant Orders.

---

[1] Potthast, 21821, 21836, 21837 ; *Bull. Franc.*, 480.

the Provincials of the Order, and the Guardians the power
to appoint secular syndics to administer the property
of the order. Lest these should acquire power over the
order and act to its detriment rather than to its
advantage, as had frequently happened with the wardens
in the old orders in former times, whose functions had been
similar, the heads of the order were given the right
to dismiss these administrators at any time and appoint
others in their places.[1] Strong opposition was aroused by
the former of these two wide-reaching privileges. The
campaign against it was headed by the University of
Paris [2] and the French clergy generally, but in other places
also, in Vienna for example, attempts were made to
interfere with the exercise by the Franciscans of such
fundamental privileges. In the early part of July,
1282, archbishop William of Rouen and bishop William
of Amiens wrote to the archbishops of Rheims, Sens,
and Tours, urging them to define their attitude to the
mendicants' privileges : provincial synods should be held
to consider how to overcome the danger to the Church
involved in the breaking up of the parish organism ; the
results of the various synods should then be considered
in a conference of bishops of the Metropolitan Sees
with the assistance of experienced canon lawyers, and
decisions taken as to the best means of carrying them out.
Nothing is known of the success of these admonitions,
and there are no clues in the synodal archives preserved
which might lead to our knowing whether the synods
were actually held, but we do know of a special mission
sent to the Curia to obtain an interpretation of the
privileges favourable to the secular clergy. Its efforts
met with no success, for the report that the Pope shortly
before his death had limited the privileges as requested

[1] *Reg.*, 249 ; Potthast, 21976 ; *Bull. Franc., Suppl.*, 156.
[2] *Chartularium universitatis Parisiensis*, ii, 1, 539, 543.

is denied by the Franciscan Richard de Mediavilla.[1] The struggle was to continue for decades and resistance to the privileges was particularly strong in Vienna. The Prior of the Dominicans and the Guardian of the Franciscans complained to the Pope that the parish priest of Vienna and his vicars were preventing the mendicant friars from making use of the papal privileges, and were even doing so in a manner which caused serious scandal among the faithful. To make matters worse, the parish priest took his stand on an agreement between the bishops of Salzburg and Passau, which laid down that the mendicant friars should be obstructed in their use of the privileges. On receiving this complaint the Pope wrote to the bishop of Passau giving him strict instructions to compel the parish priest and his vicars to make good the injury they had done, and to make use if necessary of canonical penalties without right of appeal. Simultaneously the Pope instructed the bishop of Olmütz to verify whether his orders had been carried out in Vienna.[2]

In Italy also the mendicants' privileges appear to have provoked resistance, for the bishops of Castello and Chiusi were entrusted by papal letter with protecting the Franciscans in their enjoyment of the papal privileges.[3] At times the Pope used severe penalties to compel respect for the privileges he had granted. One case is known where the authorities of Parma restricted the Dominicans in the exercise of their rights and privileges. The cardinal of Ostia, the papal legate, excommunicated the chief citizens and laid the town under an interdict. Even when the city submitted to this pressure, Martin summoned those responsible to appear before him to give

[1] Cf. *Archivium Franc. Hist., Revue trimestr.*, 1925, pp. 28, 298 ff.
[2] *Bull. Franc.*, 482 ; *Suppl.*, 154 ; Potthast, 21847.
[3] *Bull. Franc.*, 483, 484 ; *Suppl.*, 154, 156 ; Potthast, 22052.

an account of themselves.[1]   In cases, however, where
it was shown that the mendicants had overstepped their
rights, the Pope acted sternly. For example, we hear
of a complaint sent from Urbino by the papal legate
Bernard : the mendicant friars of that city took their
stand on papal privileges which permitted them to
celebrate Mass on certain feast-days even during an
interdict, but did not confine themselves to the terms
of that privilege. On the contrary, they continued
to celebrate Mass for ten days after the feast—even
beyond the octave—and while the privilege only allowed
them to say Mass within closed doors, so that the people
could not assist at it, the mendicants circumvented
this provision by cutting large openings in the doors
through which the faithful could see and hear the celebration of Mass. The Pope empowered his legates to put
a stop forthwith to these abuses and to punish the
offenders by an interdict.[2]

Another conflict involved the mendicant friars of the
dioceses of Milan, Como, and Brixen, and concerned the
right of the bishop to visit the monasteries of the
mendicant orders. While the bishops insisted on this
right, it was questioned with equal insistence by the
Franciscans. Both parties appealed to Rome. Pope
Nicholas appointed a commission of cardinals to consider the legal position, but, for some unknown reason,
the case dragged out slowly. Pope Martin extended
the commission, but as late as 1285 the mendicants
requested him to arrange that the testimony of
some aged brothers who might possibly die soon, but
whose evidence was of value, should be taken down in
writing. The Pope appointed to hear their testimony
a small commission, consisting this time not of cardinals

---

[1] *Reg.*, 130.
[2] Potthast, 22084 ; *Bull. Franc.*, 513 ; *Svppl.*, 156.

but of mendicants, and instructed it to report the results
to himself immediately,[1] but he too died before he could
give a decision.

One of the first decrees of the Pope regarding
the mendicant friars followed the lines of canon law
and laid down that it was forbidden for members of those
orders to transfer themselves to any other order with
the sole exception of the Carthusians. Any attempt
to act otherwise was punishable with excommunication.[2]
Very frequently, much more so indeed than members
of other orders or secular clergy, the Franciscans were
entrusted with special missions as arbitrators or investi-
gators.[3] Not seldom, too, they were appointed to
bishoprics and archbishoprics. The first such nominations took place in December (on the 23rd), 1281, and were
to the episcopal Sees of Gnesen and Ragusa. On one
occasion the new bishop was even exempted from the
necessity of first obtaining the permission of his superiors
in the order ; this was in the case of the Franciscan
Leonard, appointed bishop of Tricarico.[4] In such cases
more than once a special papal decree restored the liberty
to bequeath property by will : the papal chancery had
already evolved a special formula for the procedure.[5]

A number of privileges were granted to the convents
of Poor Clares. The majority confirm them in their
possessions or protect them against attempted aggression.
Grants of indulgences also figure among them.[6]

Papal favours were extended also to the other orders. The old
Numerous privileges were issued to the Benedictines, Orders.
Cistercians, Canons Regular, Templars, etc., as well

[1] *Bull. Franc.*, 528.
[2] Potthast, 21773 (July 30, 1281).
[3] E.g., *Reg.*, 312 ; *Bull. Franc.*, 505, 508 ; *Suppl.*, 153–8 ; Potthast, 21989, 21991, 22001, etc.
[4] *Bull. Franc.*, 524 ; *Suppl.*, 157.
[5] *Bull. Franc.*, *Suppl.*, 153.
[6] E.g., *Bull. Franc.*, 471, 473, 508 ; *Suppl.*, 156, 157.

as to female orders in which vows, privileges, and in
particular exemptions are confirmed or newly declared,
or which place the houses of the order under papal
protection.[1] Among those so favoured the Benedictines
are the first, standing next to the mendicant orders in
the number of privilege grants issued to them.   To
a number of their abbots, including the Abbot of Tours,
the Pope granted the right of wearing *pontificalia* ;
in other cases he gave power to the Benedictines to consecrate the sacred vessels for their monasteries and the
neighbouring churches.[2]   In individual cases he also
granted an indult for celebrating the offices of the Church
behind closed doors during an interdict,[3] or he provided
service tithes for the monasteries.[4] He even granted
the Abbot of St. Martin of Tours the power to punish
with ecclesiastical censure all who assailed overtly the
abbot's property.[5] In another case he prohibited the
issue of an ecclesiastical censure against a religious house
without the express permission of the Holy See.[6] The
Abbey of Cluny was the object of special solicitude. He
endowed it with privileges, providing for the preservation of its property, and decreed that no abbot might
alienate for any purpose, even a church purpose, moneys
or properties intended for the convent.[7] St. Denis,
however, was the foundation on which the greatest number
of privileges, and the most far-reaching ones, were
bestowed. It already stood above its fellows by reason
of the fact that its abbot was appointed as procurator

[1] E.g., Potthast, 21748, 21749, 21751, 21752, 21762, 21763, 21764,
21778, 21779, 21780, 21817, 21838, 22072, 22194 ; Martène et Durand,
ii, 1300 ; *Bull. Franc., Suppl.*, 157.

[2] *Reg.*, 229, 316, 339, 376 ; Potthast, 21929, 22046.

[3] Potthast, 21876, 21893.

[4] Potthast, 21893.

[5] Potthast, 21857.

[6] *Reg.*, 378 ; Potthast, 21861.

[7] *Reg.*, 257, 265 ; Potthast, 21983.

of church property in France, the Abbot of St. Germain assisting him (July 7, 1282).[1] The abbot for the time being of St. Denis was given power to free from all ecclesiastical punishments all persons within his jurisdiction and, if himself a priest, to give the tonsure and minor orders to the members of the monastery and to consecrate church vessels.[2] Another indult forbids all church dignitaries, even a papal legate, to impose ecclesiastical penalties on the monastery without express papal permission and grants the monastery a number of minor financial advantages.[3] It is characteristic that the largest number of privileges, and the most important, were directed towards France.

Not only the religious orders, but numerous temporal Privileges. and spiritual princes, enjoyed ecclesiastical privileges. Mention has been made already of those granted to the members of the French Royal House. Of privileges granted to bishops—and occasionally to canons—the greater number had reference to the right of executing a will freely.[4] The first of the kind was granted to bishop John of Gurk on July 25, 1281. It grants freedom to bequeath by will all property not received through the Church. From the Church's chattels at his disposal during his lifetime he is to provide for his funeral expenses and for the payment of wages due to his servants, whether they are his relatives or not, but this provision is not to deprive the Church of what it needs. Other privileges were frequently combined with this one. For example, the archbishop of Dublin was granted (March 1, 1284), together with the right of bequeathing freely, the power to release the members of his diocese from excommunication incurred through non-payment of crusade tithes, as soon as they had discharged their obligations ; likewise

---

[1] *Reg.*, 125, 124.
[2] *Reg.*, 122, 123 ; Potthast, 21865.
[3] *Reg.*, 146, 147 ; Potthast, 21886.
[4] *Reg.*, 12, 13, 17, 21, 91, 186, 217, 246, 335, 383, 421.

the right to dispense two clerics from the *defectus natalium* in order that they might be admitted to Major Orders and to appoint three persons as *tabelliones*. Finally, he was accorded the important privilege that no one could impose ecclesiastical punishment on his diocese or its members without the express permission of the Pope.[1] A similar privilege, as already mentioned, was granted occasionally to princes and also, it is interesting to note, to the *podestà*, council, and municipal assembly of Perugia.[2] Other privileges accorded to individual bishops the right to wear the *pallium*. In two cases the Pope sent the *pallium* in accordance with earlier privileges, which he ordered, however, to be examined, and once he sent it to bishop James of Otranto without the previous issue of a *privilegium*.[3] As a reward for special zeal he granted the archbishop of Bourges the right of filling canonries and other benefices falling vacant in his diocese with persons who appeared suitable to him without regard to existing statutes.[4] Analogous to the confirmations of property and grant of papal protection to monasteries were similar marks of papal favour shown to bishops and towns. We have preserved for us two such confirmations of property issued to archbishop James of Upsala [5] in regard to an estate presented to the Church, as well as a papal protection *privilegium* issued to Rimini.[6]

Dispensations.

A considerable number of papal favours related to dispensations, mainly of impediments to marriage due to consanguinity. In all the many cases where they were requested, such dispensations were granted when

[1] *Reg.*, 422.

[2] *Reg.*, 106.

[3] *Reg.*, 369 ; *Bull. Franc.*, 526, 527 ; *Suppl.*, 157.

[4] *Reg.*, 347.

[5] Potthast, 21746, 21777.

[6] Potthast, 22183.

relationship existed only in the fourth degree.[1]   We
know of dispensations granted to Sweden and Denmark,
as well as to Italy, France, and Germany.   King Rudolf
of Habsburg [2] appears once as a petitioner, likewise
the King of England.   In the case in which the
latter intervened the Pope was even prepared to give
a dispensation for a relationship in the third degree
provided that the contracting parties took an oath that
their marriage would put an end to an enmity of long
standing.[3]   In other cases the Pope refused a dispensation
when the relationship was in the third degree, as in the
betrothal of Sancho, son of King Alfonso of Castile.
He also refused a dispensation in these circumstances
to a daughter of the King of Castile.[4]   Possibly the Pope's
political opinions were not devoid of influence in these
decisions.

A few dispensations were concerned with irregularities.
In these cases the petitioner was the King of France,
at whose request the Pope dispensed Henricus de
Vizilliaco, papal chaplain and treasurer of the Church
of Lodi, from an irregularity arising from an injury
to the eye with resulting partial blindness : if chosen
as a canon the bishop of Paris was given power to grant
him a dispensation.   In another case the Pope granted
a dispensation to Radolf, rector of the Church of Britwell
in the diocese of Lincoln, from the defect of illegitimacy
when he was appointed archdeacon.[5]

In the question of accumulating property Pope Plurality of
Martin showed the greatest tolerance.   The first and Benefices.

---

[1] *Reg.*, 6, 35, 170, 171, 232, 263, 337, 398, 404, 438 ; Potthast,
22173, 22189, 22190 ; *Bull. Franc.*, 491 ; *Suppl.*, 155 ; Baronius,
an. 1284.

[2] *Reg.*, 398.

[3] *Reg.*, 404.

[4] *Reg.*, 303 ; Potthast, 21971 ; Baronius, an. 1283.

[5] *Reg.*, 181 ; Martène et Durand, ii, 1290.

probably the most extreme case of plurality of benefices which he approved was that of his former secretary, Benedict Gaetani, who was to become Pope Boniface VIII., and who possessed rich benefices in Italy, France, and England. All regulations prescribing residence, all oaths registered, all penalties of excommunication, and all suspension attaching to the non-fulfilment of the residence obligation were declared inoperative and revoked. Only the attendance fees were kept from him, but with that exception he received all the revenues, even if he were non-resident. The only obligation imposed was that he should provide that the cure of souls in the various districts was not neglected.[1] It is of course superfluous to mention that even with the best possible intentions Benedict Gaetani would not have been in a position to supervise the cure of souls by the representatives he appointed since the benefices lay so far apart. Bishop Burchard of Metz also enjoyed a considerable number of benefices ; he held the cathedral provostships of Liège and Utrecht, as well as additional benefices in the dioceses of Liège, Cambrai, Sens, and Utrecht.[2]

The Pope showed particular consideration to his chaplains in this matter. One of them held canonries and benefices in seven churches.[3] To another he sanctioned, in addition to a provostship in the diocese of Terouanne, further benefices in the dioceses of Cambrai and Liège, in so far as these were not concerned with the cure of souls.[4] In addition, we find many privileges granted for the combination of two benefices,[5] sometimes indeed with a limitation of period.

Thus, bishop Johannes Valentinus of Dié was permitted to hold for three years the Benedictine monasteries of

---

[1] *Reg.*, 15. [2] Kaltenbrunner, 248.
[3] *Reg.*, 208. [4] *Reg.*, 201.
[5] *Reg.*, 209, 233, 262, 264, 355, etc.

the diocese of Langres, of which he had been superior up to the time of his election as bishop, and to continue to rule the monasteries, both spiritually and financially, because the bishopric he had taken over was heavily in debt.[1] In England the opposition to excessive accumulation of benefices seems to have made itself felt, for archbishop John Peckham of Canterbury, notwithstanding a papal dispensation from the residence obligation, deprived the papal chaplain Theodosius de Camilla without more ado of certain benefices which he assigned to other priests. Thereupon the Pope instructed his Nuncio in England, Magister Geoffrey of Veçano, to call upon the archbishop and the clergy concerned to restore the benefices to the papal chaplain within a fortnight.

In one case there was a mere release from the residence obligation, when Pope Martin revoked that obligation for William Durandus, dean of Chartres, contrary to the statutes of the chapter, according to which such a dispensation might not be granted nor might a general dispensation be availed of. This was done in recognition of services rendered to the Holy See in order to make it possible for Durandus to continue at the Curia or to proceed to any place in the Pope's service.[2]

In general, faithful service to the Holy See was rewarded by Martin with the grant of benefices, and for this purpose the numerous reservations of spiritual benefices were useful. A considerable proportion of the documents issued by the papal chancery were concerned with reservations and grants of benefices. If a benefice fell into the Curia through the death of its occupant,[3] if any difficulties arose as to the choice of a new occupant,[4]

---

[1] *Reg.*, 264.
[2] *Reg.*, 10.
[3] *Reg.*, 2, 132.
[4] *Reg.*, 92, 328 ; *Bull. Franc., Suppl.*, 154, 155 ; Kaltenbrunner, 235.

or if the person first chosen did not accept the benefice,[1] the fact was availed of by the Pope to reserve the benefice. In addition he made general reservations of all benefices in extensive districts ; for example, all bishoprics and abbacies in the kingdom of Sicily. If the Pope felt any doubts as to election procedure, he ordered a verification of the canonical election,[2] which might result in a refusal of recognition and the nomination of a new bishop by the Pope.[3] But if the Pope held the canonical election to be in order he confirmed the choice.[4] If a reservation was not admitted the Pope was able to insist on it. The reservation of the bishopric of Gurk had not been brought to the notice either of the chapter or of the archbishop of Salzburg, and when it fell vacant the chapter and the archbishop elected a dean of the cathedral of Regensburg named Conrad and requested the Pope to confirm their choice. The latter, however, annulled the election, taking his stand on the reservation, and the bishop-elect was forced to renounce all rights. The Pope then instructed the chapter to propose a suitable candidate, and when Conrad's name was put forward as a mere suggestion the Pope nominated him as bishop of Gurk.[5] Likewise, in the case of the reservation for John Marli, chaplain of the cardinal-bishop of Sabina, of the next canonry to become vacant in Cambrai, the Pope intervened when the reservation was disregarded and took steps to see that the vacancy was filled in accordance with the reservation.[6]

[1] *Reg.*, 93, 94, 126, 252 ; *Bull. Franc., Suppl.*, 155, 157. But when the bishopric of Wexio in Sweden fell vacant by the bishop's resignation, he ordered a new election in a letter to the archbishop of Upsala (*Reg.*, 83).

[2] *Bull. Franc.*, 492, 502, 510 ; *Suppl.*, 158.

[3] Potthast, 21916.

[4] E.g., Potthast, 21826, 21951 ; *Bull. Franc.*, 506, 513 ; *Suppl.*, 154.

[5] *Reg.*, 174, 340 ; Kaltenbrunner, 240.

[6] *Reg.*, 387.

Pope Martin was watchful to prevent any alienation of Church property. Persons who laid hands on it or who injured the Church were laid under ecclesiastical punishment until they made good the damage they had done.[1] He took similar action against abuses within the Church when such were brought to his notice. It has been pointed out already that he did not tolerate abuses even when committed by the Franciscans whom he so favoured, and that he caused the evasion by them of the Urbino interdict to be at once stopped and punished. He summoned to Rome the Franciscan Peter, who was bishop of Viborg in Finland concurrently with Ascerus, for an investigation of the proceedings which had made him a bishop. This matter concluded by the eventual deposition of Peter under Martin's successor, while Ascerus resigned voluntarily.[2] In the early part of his reign he intervened on behalf of the unjustly banished bishop Bernard of Vicenza and insisted on the reinstatement of the bishop in his dignities, and on the punishment of the guilty persons.[3] Likewise, when it became known that abuses had crept into the Church of Sta. Maria Rotonda at Rome, he had them stopped at once by his representative.[4]

Pope Martin and his predecessors transferred to the inquisition a part of their jurisdiction, namely, decisions in all cases concerned directly or indirectly with matters of faith. He issued an instruction to the archbishops and bishops of France not to hamper the inquisitors in the exercise of their functions.

They had instructions from him to proceed against all persons guilty or even suspected of heresy, likewise against converted Jews who had fallen away again from

[1] Potthast, 21742, 21743, 21765, 21767, 21771, 21835.
[2] *Bull. Franc.*, 526.
[3] *Reg.*, 16.
[4] *Reg.*, 312 ; *Bull. Franc.*, 505.

the Faith. The Pope even suspended the right of sanctuary in the case of persons who fled to a church solely to escape the arm of the inquisition.[1] We have another edict of the Pope's in which he commanded the *podestà* of Viterbo, Annibaldus de Annibaldis, to assist the Inquisitor, Friar Angelus de Reate, in all matters concerned with his office (February 26, 1284).[2] On the other hand, however, he wished the Inquisition to avoid anything in the nature of unnecessary severity. The authorities at Florence complained to the Pope that the inquisitors were seizing property in cases where no heresy was known, where no trial had taken place, and when the suspicion of heresy had arisen after the property had passed into other hands. The Pope decreed that in future property could not be expropriated if it had been acquired in good faith from other persons without the new owners being aware of heresy on the part of the former possessors. Only if heresy was suspected at the time of the transfer of the property, or if the property had been given away by a person suspected of heresy in order to avoid forfeiture, might it be seized.[3]

Theological studies.

Another way to preserve the purity of the Faith, the positive way, lay in the direction of encouraging the study of theology. We know of no great papal provisions intended to direct theological study into new avenues, or even to advance it especially, but certain significant decrees of the Pope make it possible to draw conclusions as to his attitude. He maintained the privilege by which a cleric was entitled during the period of his studies to enjoy the fruits of his benefice without fulfilling the residence obligation. In his very first year he renewed

---

[1] *Reg.*, 77 ; Potthast, 21806 ; *Bull. Franc.*, 472 ; Baronius, an. 1281.

[2] *Bull. Franc.*, 526 ; *Suppl.*, 157.

[3] *Reg.*, 203 (November 22, 1282) ; Potthast, 21950 ; *Bull. Franc.*, 497 ; *Suppl.*, 155.

this privilege for the University of Paris.[1] Further, he instructed the archbishop of Toledo to hand over to his canon Ferrandus Roderici, who was at the Holy See and desired to study theology, all the revenues of his benefices.[2] He interested himself also in the advancement of learning in Rome. From the middle of the thirteenth century onwards interest had been taken there in the cultivation of legal science, although this study was forbidden to the clergy. Chairs were established for canon law and civil law which were occupied by the most learned men of the period. In 1265 Charles of Anjou endeavoured to establish a University at Rome, but these efforts were not successful until the Papacy of Boniface VIII. Nevertheless the attempt deserves recognition. To the university of Oxford Martin granted the privilege that no member of its *civitas academica* might be summoned, even by a papal legate, before a court outside of Oxford because of a contract concluded within the town, provided that the person concerned gave satisfaction to justice at Oxford, and unless the Pope in a particular case decreed otherwise, with specific mention of this privilege.[3]

On one occasion circumstances forced him to concern himself with the university of Bologna. The students of that university had presented a number of petitions to the city authorities and had bound themselves on oath, that if these petitions —which related mainly to privileges—were not acceded to by the feast of St. Michael (September 29) they would leave the city and for five years would not attend the *studium generale* of Bologna. Among other things the petitions demanded that any incursion on the university's privileges by the city should be compensated by a fine of 1,000 pounds.

[1] *Reg.*, 48 ; Potthast, 21802 (October 10, 1281).

[2] *Reg.*, 227 (August 29, 1282).

[3] *Reg.*, 23.

Further, the city was asked to undertake not to interfere with the teaching activities of any of the professors unless the students consented. These two demands were rejected, the first because no one would be responsible for the fine, and the second because the city reserved to itself the right of calling on any professor to discharge his duties as a citizen if the good of the city demanded it. Although the greater part of their demands had been acceded to, the terms of their oath compelled the students to leave the city. To save injury, either to the students or the town, Pope Martin empowered the Prior of the Dominicans and the Guardian of the Franciscans in Bologna to release the students from their oath.[1]

It is interesting to read that the Pope also issued a *privilegium* for the establishment of a grammar school at Hamburg. As a rule it was only the *studium generale* which depended on a papal indult, but in this one case the Pope granted full powers to Johannes de Luneborch and other parishioners of the Church of St. Nicholas in Hamburg to establish there a *schola artis grammatice* for children.[2]

Liturgy.

In the domain of liturgy Pope Martin was likewise satisfied to continue the tendencies he had inherited. It may be assumed that he was interested in reviving the veneration of the saints as he sent a valuable reliquary of St. Mary Magdalen to the Church of Sens and granted an indulgence for reverence paid to it. The most important effort he made was that to extend the Roman rite to the whole western world. He gave power to the chapter of St. Martin of Tours to follow the Roman procedure in the *divinum officium* in so far as it seemed desirable to them. But they were on no account to adopt it exclusively; certain feasts were to continue to be

---

[1] *Reg.*, 226 ; *Bull. Franc.*, 495 ; *Suppl.*, 155.
[2] Potthast, 21769 (July 7, 1281).

celebrated in the traditional manner, notwithstanding the adoption of the Roman ritual.[1] Further, on March 1, 1284, at the request of the King of Sweden, he gave permission for the use of the Roman rite at the celebration of the church *officium* in the royal chapel.[2] These papal decrees have interest as showing clearly that the use of the Roman liturgy was extended not only because of pressure on the part of the Curia, but that in fact permission to use that liturgy was regarded as a distinction and a privilege for which Kings pleaded on behalf of royal chapels and outstanding monasteries.

The entire inner life of the Church went on under Martin IV. in great peace and without any revolutionary innovations. The Pope was so much absorbed in foreign politics that he could not direct his attention primarily to the domestic conditions of the Church. Moreover, no occasion arose calling for the devotion of particular attention to church matters. Events went on slowly as they had been going, and Martin IV. did little to interfere with their march.

---

[1] Potthast, 21850 (February 13, 1282).
[2] Potthast, 22106 ; Baronius, an. 1284.

CHAPTER VI.

THE CRUSADE MOVEMENT. CRUSADE TAX. CRUSADE PLANS.

POPE MARTIN IV. inherited the crusade idea from his predecessors. The Council of Lyons had determined to enlist the whole West in the service of the Holy Land, the first step in that direction being the creation of the financial organization necessary to such a campaign.

The Lyons Tithes. At that Council an immense taxation network had been created, to extend over the whole of Europe from Portugal to Poland, Sweden, Iceland, and Greenland. With the exception of a few orders the tax was to apply equally to all the clergy and was to be levied in all countries on identical principles. Pope Gregory X. informed Pope Martin, then cardinal Simon de Brion, that the decision regarding the tithes had been adopted unanimously by the Council, and other reports speak likewise of a general agreement.[1] According to the Council's plan the amounts collected were to be devoted exclusively to the Holy Land, and this is the only conceivable explanation of the approval given to the acceptance of such a severe burden by the clergy. It is easily understood that this agreement was converted into violent opposition when it became known that the funds were being used for quite different purposes.

A vast army of officials had to be enrolled to collect the tax. Each country had its own collectors and sub-collectors ; if there was resistance, excommunication and interdict were invoked to compel payment, and it must be conceded that these spiritual penalties lost their

---

[1] Cf. Raynaldus (an. 1274) ; Potthast, 20884.

terrors mainly because they had become a formal process in the execution of papal taxation policy. The papal chancery was chiefly occupied in appointing collectors and their subordinates, in issuing constant instructions to them to be more prompt in collecting and forwarding the tithes by threatening excommunication and interdict, or by using their powers to raise the ban when the amounts were paid.

Germany was strongest in opposition to the payment of the tithes as soon as it was known there that the money was not being devoted to the Holy Land. Under Pope Nicholas III. numerous cathedral chapters took their stand on that fact and refused payment because of it. Archbishop Conrad of Magdeburg (1266–77) went further and organized a formal opposition at a provincial synod. On his initiative it was decided that no member of the province should pay the Lyons tax on threat of immediate excommunication, loss of benefice and incapacity to obtain further benefices. When this reached the Pope's ears he instructed the collector of the district, Rayner de Oria, a canon of Liège, to investigate the occurrence reported. If the facts proved to be as stated, in order to check the spread of such blasphemy he was to announce the excommunication of all con- cerned and order them to appear in Rome within two months to receive suitable punishment. The bishops were to be instructed to appear in person ; the others could be represented by proxy.[1] At the same time the Pope ordered that the collector should issue a final admonition to the archbishop of Cologne, Siegfried of Westerburg, who had hitherto refused to deliver the tax paid by others and deposited with him, or to pay his own tax, and who, although excommunicated, continued to celebrate Mass. If the archbishop did not fulfil his obligations within

Resistance to the tithes.

_____

[1] *Reg.*, 152 (May 12, 1282).

six months, he was to be ordered to appear before the Pope.[1] The collector also received papal instructions to deal with the bishop of Meissen, Witigo of Wur (1262–93), who had been excommunicated as early as 1277 for refusing payment of tithes. He was now again admonished to pay his own taxes and to influence the prelates and abbots of his diocese to do likewise on threat of the reimposition of the ban of excommunication.[2] Steps were also taken against the bishop of Osnabrück, Conrad of Rietberg, who had used the tithes for diocesan purposes. In the Pope's name the collector demanded from him the restoration of the money within a month, otherwise he would be excommunicated, suspended, and summoned before the Apostolic See.[3] In the same month (May) the Pope sent more stringent instructions to the collector, whom he seems to have thought dilatory. He pointed out that the decrees of his predecessor, Gregory, left the payment of the crusade tax to the conscience of all functioning prelates, and that accordingly numerous prelates of the ecclesiastical provinces of Cologne, Bremen, Magdeburg, and of the town and diocese of Kamin had had the temerity not to pay the tithes or to pay only part of them. Likewise some of the sub-collectors had refused to give an account of their collections and various persons with whom funds had been deposited refused an account of those sums. All such persons had already incurred by their disloyalty the punishment of excommunication decreed by the Council of Lyons, and this penalty had been expressly pronounced also by the papal collector. Now the Pope ordered Rayner to apply again to all persons who appeared suspect and particularly to all who were known to be in

---

[1] *Reg.*, 155 (May 13, 1282).

[2] *Reg.*, 152 (May 12, 1282).

[3] *Reg.*, 154 (May 12, 1282). *Cf.* also Baronius, an. 1282 ; Kaltenbrunner, 244–6.

default, urging them to do their duty and to do it within a period to be fixed by him. All who submitted and paid or delivered the money were to be released from ecclesiastical punishments, but were to have a suitable penance imposed on them, especially if they had celebrated Mass notwithstanding excommunication. Those who did not obey were to be again laid under ecclesiastical censure, and if that did not avail within a month they were to be ordered to appear before the Apostolic See either in person or by proxy, there to receive suitable punishment. The collector was to report to the Pope immediately what steps he had taken and their result.[1]

When the foundations had been thus laid for an efficacious collection of crusade funds, the Pope instructed his collector a few months later to transfer immediately from the proceeds the sum of 8,000 silver marks to a Florentine banking house which was frequently entrusted by the Pope with the administration of financial matters.[2] But all this pressure, all this severity ordained by the Pope, and all these ecclesiastical punishments did not avail to bring in the tax fast enough. A year after receiving the Pope's orders, the collector was still unable to transfer the sum demanded to the bank and he had to accept a severe reproof, together with new commands, accompanied by a threat of effective punishment, if he failed to produce the amount required.[3] No doubt the Pope's dissatisfaction with him was the reason why Rayner appealed to the cardinal-deacon James of St. Maria in Cosmedin to be relieved of his office.[4] As there was question at the moment of collecting the new tax in the border dioceses on the western frontier of the Empire for France's campaign against Aragon, it probably suited the Pope to entrust the collection to some one

---

[1] *Reg.*, 157 (May 22, 1282).   [2] *Reg.*, 220 (October 1, 1282).
[3] *Reg.*, 410 ; Kaltenbrunner, 258 (November 10, 1283).
[4] Kaltenbrunner, p. 263 ff.

who had fully proved himself. Moreover, it became possible to concentrate the collection to a greater extent. A number of collectors were engaged in Germany, apart from the army of sub-collectors. Rayner de Oria, the Liège canon already mentioned, was in charge of the ecclesiastical provinces of Cologne, Bremen, Hamburg, and the diocese of Kamin ; Master Roger, canon of Verdun, who had been appointed by Gregory X., operated in the archdiocese of Trier and Metz, with Aliron de Riccardis, canon of St. Mark's of Venice, as assistant. The latter supervised the archdiocese of Salzburg and the dioceses of Prague, Olmütz, Eichstadt, and Bamberg, all belonging to the province of Mainz. His activity in the Alpine regions is described for us in his own *Liber decimationis* written in 1285.[1]

On July 10, 1282, Roger was replaced by Theodericus, prior of St. Andrew's in Orvieto, who was probably in the Pope's personal confidence, but Canon Aliron was confirmed in his post as assistant, as when Roger held the office. When Rayner fell out of favour and asked to be relieved of his office, the Pope entrusted Theodericus —many months after Rayner's petition, it is true—with the tithe collection in the ecclesiastical provinces of Cologne, Bremen, Hamburg, and the diocese of Kamin (November 27, 1284). Later, but not under Pope Martin, he was commissioned also for Aliron's district, so that from 1289 or 1290 onwards he was the sole collector for the German Empire.[2] He seems to have possessed particular aptitude for his office. He drew the Pope's

---

[1] *Cf.* Steinherz, *Mitteilungen der österr. Instituts für Geschichts-forschung*, vol. xiv, p. 50 ff. ; *Programm des fürsterzbischöflichen Privat-gymnasiums Colleg-Borromäum*, Salzburg, 1887. Mention may be made here also of the published authority concerning the Swiss tithes, viz. *Fontes rerum Bernensium*, iii, 387.

[2] Sources of information regarding the collectors are : *Reg.*, 222, 428 ; Potthast, 21918 ; Kaltenbrunner, 203 ff., 242.

attention immediately to the fact that it would be of great advantage to his labours if he could be specially recommended to King Rudolf of Habsburg. The Pope yielded to his wish in the matter without delay, and repeated the recommendation when his collection area was extended.[1]

Rudolf's position was made difficult by the fact that the Pope in agreeing to French wishes for tithes for the Aragon campaign, had included in 1284 the western border dioceses of Liège, Metz, Toul, Verdun, and the archdioceses of the kingdom of Arles, namely, Besançon, Lyons, and Vienne, while Arles and Aix were excluded as belonging to the domain of King Charles. These dioceses of the Empire, as well as the French Church, were burdened by decree of Pope Martin with the payment of tithes for four years. Dissatisfaction became general in Germany when it became known that these tithes were not to be used for the Holy Land or any other struggle against the infidel, but to support King Philip of France in a war against King Peter of Aragon. Most exasperating of all, German territory was being taxed for the advantage of France and of Charles of Anjou and to the detriment of Peter, who was husband of Costanza, the Swabian Emperor's grand-daughter, and who desired to avenge the deaths of Manfred and Conradin, to snatch Italy from the grasp of the Angevins and to restore it to the descendants of the Hohenstaufen. Sympathies were, naturally, on Peter's side, and the Germans were most unwilling to pay taxes to be used against him ; their bishops and clergy could never be induced to regard Philip's campaign as a " crusade " ; and from all the districts concerned, from Liège to Basle, petitions poured in to King Rudolf asking him to procure relief. Rudolf's hands were tied

---

[1] *Reg.*, 245.

because of his aspiration to the Imperial Crown. In unison with the princes of the Empire he lodged a protest with Pope Martin against the collection on German soil of tithes to be used against Aragon, but when the Pope wrote him a mollifying letter he allowed the collection to proceed. A further protest lodged with Martin's successor Honorius IV. was likewise without avail.

German hostility to the tithes was heightened by the conduct of the collector, Theodericus, who informed the Pope that the moneys collected in Germany were not safe there, and that underhand attempts were being made to apply them to purposes other than help for the Holy Land :   accordingly, it would be desirable to transfer these funds elsewhere. Pope Martin responded of course to this stimulus and ordained that the collection should be removed from Germany without delay and delivered to the bankers in Florence, Siena, Lucca, or Pistoia.[1] One can understand that great bitterness was aroused in consequence throughout Germany, all the more as the sums of money in question were considerable. It is known, for example, that in the archbishopric of Salzburg alone Aliron collected 2,800 kilograms of fine silver in the years 1282–5 [2] ; that bishop Henry of Basle was obliged to levy 600 silver marks from three citizens of the town in order to be able to pay the tithes ; that Aliron certified the receipt from the bishop of Passau of a first instalment of the six-year crusade tithes amounting to 600 talents of Passau pence. The cathedral dean and the prior of St. Alban's in Basle appointed 18 silver marks as the tithe contribution of the cathedral chapter of Strassburg, which he released from the ban incurred through non-payment. From Provost Conrad of Rans-hoven Aliron received two pounds of Regensburg coins

---

[1] *Reg.*, 244 (January 13, 1283) ; Kaltenbrunner, 284.
[2] Steinherz, *l.c.*, p. 50 ff.

and six of Salzburg coins as a first payment, amounting to one-third of the sum due. Bishop Leopold of Seckau ordered the churches of Gradwein, Strassgang, Graz, Vorau, and Pettau to deliver 10 silver marks " before next Sunday " to the abbot of Admont or his representative, this amount to be deducted from the total crusade tithe, and the bishop ordered his commands to be fulfilled under penalty of excommunication.[1] From all this the fact emerges that the contributions by bishops and chapters, and also by individual canons and churches, were large, and that the obligation to pay quickly under threat of severe ecclesiastical punishments constituted a heavy burden on the clergy. It is intelligible then that the collectors, and still more the sub-collectors, with whom individuals had to deal, were anything but popular. Berthold of Regensburg, who himself preached the Crusade even before the Lyons tithes were introduced, described the Crusade fund collectors contemptuously as " penny preachers ".[2]

Regarding England, like Germany, there exists a large body of material relating to the collection of the Crusade tithes. There, too, the collectors were changed from time to time. In 1274 the papal chaplain, Raymundus de Nogeriis, and the Dominican John of Darlington were appointed collectors-general. The former had previously had duties in England in 1272 as representative of the papal camera ; the latter, well known for his theological and philosophical writings, had been made archbishop of Dublin by Pope Nicholas in 1279, that See having been vacant for nine years. Even after this appointment matters underwent no change there, for in the beginning John was prevented by his duties as collector from taking up residence. In 1277 Raymundus was

The tithes in England.

---

[1] *Wiener Briefsammlung*, n. 240.
[2] Gottlob, *l.c.*, 194.

summoned to the Curia to give an account of his collection
and was entrusted thereafter with other church business,
his place in England being taken by another papal
chaplain, Master Arditio, primicerius of Milan, who was
likewise created bishop—of Modena this time—on
December 23, 1281, the creation entailing, of course, no
obligation of residence.[1] Master Geoffrey de Veçano,
canon of Cambrai and official of the papal camera, appears
in 1282 as an assistant, at first with limited powers.
On March 7 of that year he was entrusted with the
collection of crusade moneys, due by reason of vows,
oaths, or discharge from vows in England, Wales, Scotland,
and Ireland. When it proved impracticable in the course
of time to keep the archbishop of Dublin out of his diocese
indefinitely, Geoffrey was assigned to him on October 7,
1283, to help in the collection so that John could take
up residence in Dublin.[2] On two occasions the archbishop of Canterbury gave expression to hostile and
unfavourable criticisms of Geoffrey. These criticisms
were not concerned with the latter's work as collector,
but with the assignment to Geoffrey by the Pope of other
tasks on behalf of the Church. In a letter to the Pope
the archbishop accused Geoffrey of opposing him in his
efforts to free England from lay and non-resident holders
of benefices and alleged that Geoffrey had shown himself
to be unfitted for the task entrusted to him by the Holy
See, especially as he appeared to have no knowledge of
the law. In a letter addressed at the same time to the
cardinal of Tusculum, the archbishop went so far as to
describe Geoffrey as a wolf appointed to judge shepherds
and to denounce him as his own open enemy.[3] In spite
of this Geoffrey continued as collector until 1288. Not

[1] Potthast, 21827.
[2] Potthast, 21862, 22066, 22069 ; Reg., 385, 386.
[3] Regesta episcopi Jo. Peckham, ii, 598, 468 ; 600, 469.

until the reign of Pope Nicholas IV. were the Bishops of Winchester and Lincoln entrusted with the tithe collection. As sub-collectors we hear of one Simon of Micham, chancellor of Salisbury, and Robert, vicar of Sturminster in the same diocese.[1]

In England, too, the Pope caused the collection campaign to be pushed forward with the greatest vigour. When in October, 1281, the collectors asked him for instructions regarding certain poor female orders, the members of which were so poor that they must have depended on begging but that some of their relatives supplied them with the bare necessaries of life, the answer given by the Pope was that the usual regulations were to apply.[2] In these circumstances one can understand Martin giving orders that various prelates who had not carried out the tax arrangements should be dealt with with all severity and ordered to appear before the Apostolic See, unless they paid within three months.[3] At the end of a year the collectors were ordered to forward the entire amount collected to a Florentine house by a messenger approved by the Pope.[4] Perhaps the Pope was so quick in ordering the dispatch of the money because he knew the King of England's ambition to acquire it for his own purposes. Already in the reign of Pope Gregory, King Edward had made representations that the tithes of England, Wales, Ireland, and Scotland should be put at his disposal for his projected Crusade. The King of Scotland had also pleaded for the tithes of his kingdom and had been actually promised them by Innocent V. When Edward's request was not granted, he chose the direct method and caused the proceeds of the tax to be taken by force from its custodians and deposited where he thought fit. Thereupon the Pope demanded that the money should

[1] Potthast, 21811.   [2] *Reg.*, 32 ; Potthast, 21804.
[3] *Reg.*, 29, 33.   [4] *Reg.*, 219 (October 1, 1282).

be returned in full, and instructed the primate at the same
time to use his influence with the King to that end.[1]
Ultimately the King had no alternative but to obey the
Pope and endeavour—unsuccessfully, however—to obtain
permission to retain the taxes in England.[2]

Scotland. Scotland had its own collector in the person of
Baiamundus de Vitia, canon of Asti, but he was subordinate to Geoffrey. At first the collection there seems
to have proceeded without difficulty. Pope Martin
instructed Baiamundus to remit the first moiety for the
first year to the same Florentine bank which has been
already mentioned, and in doing so expressed the hope
that the King would not object. In fact the latter did
as the Pope desired. It would appear that at this time
the collector hinted that the funds were insufficiently
safeguarded in Scotland, whereupon the Pope informed
him that he had recently made special representations
to the King, urging him to undertake a Crusade. If he
agreed, permission was given to retain the tithes, with
the exception of the first instalment already forwarded,
and to deposit them in a safe place according to his
judgment. If, however, the King did not take the desired
decision, the collector was to transmit the entire taxes
without delay to the bank mentioned and forward an
exact account to the Holy See.

Norway. In Norway the tax arrangements encountered an
obstacle which at first seemed insurmountable. Affairs
of state were carried on there by a regency on behalf of
the young King Eric II., and a double avenue was available to obstruct the payment of tax, indeed to make it
impossible. To a great extent the tithes were paid in
kind, and it was out of the question to remit these
payments to Italy. Accordingly, the Pope ordered the
collector, archbishop John of Drontheim, to convert the

[1] Potthast, 22047, 22048.   [2] Potthast, 22143.

goods into money as best he could and to deliver the
amounts received for them to a Lucca banking house.[1]
Against this procedure the regency issued a double
prohibition : on the one hand it was forbidden for laymen
to give silver, in particular specie, to the clergy, thus
making it practically impossible to barter the goods for
silver coins ; in addition, it was prohibited to export
gold or silver. The Pope appealed to the young King to
revoke these two decrees.[2]

This campaign against the crusade tax in Norway had
a far-reaching background. In 1280 a struggle had
developed around clerical privileges based on a concordat concluded three years earlier. The government
wished to make laity and clergy equally liable for war
taxes, a wish which was opposed by the clergy, led by
the archbishop of Drontheim and the bishops of Oslo
and Hamar, who claimed tax exemption for the clergy
on the basis of the concordat. The government was
in a position to exert pressure in this matter by preventing the collection of the crusade tithes in the kingdom,
and in fact the tithes were not handed over until
the struggle between Church and State ended in 1286.
The question of the immunity of Church property from
taxation, which was later to provoke the serious conflict
between France and Pope Boniface, was not resolved. The
clergy retained their privileges, without official recognition
of these, however, by the State, and the decrees were
revoked which had prevented the payment and remittance
of the crusade tithes in Norway throughout the whole
of Martin's reign.

The collection in Sweden and Denmark was supervised Sweden and
for seven years by Master Bertrandus Amalrici. When Denmark.
he became bishop of Arles in 1282, Pope Martin entrusted

---

[1] *Reg.*, 119, 161 ; Potthast, 21858.
[2] *Reg.*, 120 ; Potthast, 21859, 21860.

the collection to the bishop of Aarhus. In 1285, at the beginning of the reign of Pope Honorius, a former parish priest of Castiglione in the diocese of Arezzo named Huguitio was given charge of the collection in Sweden, Denmark, and Norway, and held the office for ten years. In these countries the ban of excommunication was also invoked for dilatory tithe payers.[1]

Luxemburg. Of interest is a statement by Count Henry of Luxemburg that his father had been empowered by the Holy See to withdraw and retain the sum of 15,000 pounds from the proceeds of the crusade tithes in the towns and dioceses of Cambrai, Verdun, Toul, Metz, and Liège. No other trace could be found of this privilege, so the Pope on October 1, 1283, instructed bishop Remigius of Chalons-sur-Marne to call upon Count Henry to appear, either in person or by proxy, at the Curia, bringing with him the necessary documentary proofs so that the matter could be investigated. The Pope declared that an examination by the bishop of Luxemburg was not enough, which throws a significant light on the relatively high standing in criticism of the papal Curia. It was considered feasible to conduct there authenticity tests which could not be conducted outside of the Chancery.[2]

Portugal. Archdeacon Gerard of Braga in Lusitania wielded the office of collector in Portugal. On November 11, 1282, a Franciscan named Monaldus was sent by the Pope to obtain from the collector in the presence of a number of creditable witnesses an account of his operations, and to procure the delivery to the bank with which the Pope dealt of the entire amount collected. Two statements of the proceedings were to be drawn up, of which one was to be left to the collector and the other, signed by all present, forwarded to the Pope. It would seem that

---

[1] Potthast, 21790 ; Gottlob, *l.c.*, 108.
[2] *Reg.*, 247.

Brother Monaldus' task was not too simple, for it is only in the year 1285—on February 21—that we hear of his sending 6,000 gulden to the bank. The Pope certified the due receipt of that amount.[1]

Master Gerard of Modena is known to us as collector for Poland and Hungary. Earlier, in 1275, he had been appointed to collect Peter's Pence and other ecclesiastical dues. When he became bishop of Cajazzo in 1283 he grew careless in his tax collection and was therefore replaced, on January 9, 1285, by Johannes Muscatæ, archdeacon of Gnesen, whose place was taken in 1287 by canon Adam de Polonia of Cracow.[2]

Poland and Hungary.

There were fewest difficulties in collecting the tithes in France and the kingdom of Sicily, since those kingdoms derived most profit from them and the money remained in the country from which it was drawn. Pope Gregory X. had granted Philip of France for outlay on behalf of the Holy Land one half of the entire amount collected as crusade tax in the first year. On the basis of this grant payments were made to Philip again in 1281 and 1282 from the crusade funds collected. The amounts collected in France remained there, deposited in Paris with the Templars, and the Pope could only draw on them with the special permission of the King on a promise of repayment. The statement of accounts drawn up by the Pope and the King in 1283 with regard to these funds showed entirely to the King's advantage.[3] That large sums were in question in France also can be seen from the fact that the Cistercians, whose contributions were made in a lump sum, had to pay an annual amount of 8,000 pounds.[4]

France.

In Sicily there was a similar situation. On March 8, 1282, Charles of Anjou was given by Pope Martin a grant

Sicily.

[1] *Reg.*, 242 ; *Bull. Franc.*, 496, 530 ; *Suppl.*, 155.
[2] Potthast, 22198 ; Gottlob, *l.c.*, 108.
[3] *Reg.*, 81 ; Kaltenbrunner, 238 ; Gottlob, 1259 ; Cartillieri, *l.c.*, 68.
[4] *Reg.*, 54, 55.

of the entire tithes of Sardinia and Hungary for six years, as well as all receipts from pious bequests and legacies and amounts paid in return for release from vows in the entire kingdom of Sicily, in Provence, and Forcalquier during the same period.

Supervision was in the hands of the archbishop of Rouen in France and of the bishop of Cassano in Sicily. The latter received instructions from the Pope on April 5, 1282, again to urge all defaulters in Sicily, who were of course automatically excommunicated, to pay and, if they did so, to release them from the ban. Those who did not respond to the appeal should be excommunicated by name and ordered to appear before the Pope within a month. In fact the Pope complained that the Sicilians were particularly remiss in paying the crusade tax, and attributed that fact to the excessive consideration shown by Gregory X.[1]

Methods of collection.

In saying this he indicated the great difference between the methods by which he himself collected the tax and those followed by Gregory. The latter made the payment of the tax an obligation of conscience, but did not attempt to exercise any outward supervision over the fulfilment of the obligation. Martin, on the other hand, set a gigantic machine in motion and exercised a strict control over the methods of collection and also the methods of payment. Collectors were either obliged to appear before him, and give an exact account of their operations, or else to answer to a representative of the Pope, giving detailed documentary proofs for everything.[2]

Even in the case of poor monasteries, requests for abatements were refused, the only exceptions known to us

---

[1] *Reg.*, 7, 116, 140.
[2] In addition to the various cases enumerated, see, for example. *Reg.*, 7, 8.

being in France, where the collector, the archbishop of
Rouen, is instructed not to apply for crusade tithes
to the canons and permanent chaplains of the Church
of St. George at Chartres, as their revenues did not
exceed 15 pounds. Other clergy in France received similar
dispensations,[1] but everywhere else payment was
demanded rigorously. For no other crime were so many
sentences of excommunication issued as for non-payment
of church taxes, above all crusade taxes. These exclusions
from the communion of the Church fell on holders of high
ecclesiastical office and on entire religious communities,
or were at least threatened.[2] Examples are Siegfried
of Westerburg, archbishop of Cologne, the Patriarch
Pantaleon of Constantinople, and his vicar-general who
had done nothing to deserve it. The Patriarch had preferred to send the tax direct to Rome, instead of paying
it to the collector, the archbishop of Crete, whereupon
the latter had announced the excommunication of the
Patriarch and of his vicar-general. When the bearer
of the taxes had sworn that the Patriarch had fulfilled
his obligations, the Pope caused the clerics to be freed
from the ecclesiastical punishment imposed on them.

In the matter of the crusade tax the case of the town
of Brixen stands apart. The *podestà*, the city captain,
and the municipal authorities had decided that all
disputes in church tax matters requiring a decision
should be dealt with by the civil courts, before which
ecclesiastics could not appear even as witnesses. By
this means the city and its citizens sought to insure
themselves against harsh dealings on the part of the papal
collectors. But they reckoned without the Pope, who
compelled them to withdraw their decision under threat

---

[1] *Reg.*, 409.
[2] *Reg.*, 25, 86, 151, 164, 368 ; Potthast, 21813, 22191 ; Kaltenbrunner, 237.

of excommunication for the civic officials and interdict for the city (June 4, 1282).

The only people outside the jurisdiction of the collectors were the Cistercians, who instead were obliged to contribute a fixed sum, which was distributed among the individual monasteries.[1]

Although constant use was made of ecclesiastical punishments against those unwilling to pay, Pope Martin went so far in addition as to invoke the aid of the secular arm of justice in cases when spiritual punishments failed. He sent specific instructions to ten archbishops and their suffragans to invoke the help of the State if they did not succeed by means of spiritual punishments in extorting the payment of the crusade taxes.[2]

Administration of the funds.

At first the funds were kept and administered in the countries where they were collected, but the Pope's experiences in this regard were in truth unhappy. Mention has been made of the seizure of the money by the King of England. Reports were received from the collector for Germany that many persons were only awaiting an opportunity to lay hands on the money. In France the collections had been entrusted to the Templars for safe keeping, and early in 1283 the Prior of the Templars was obliged to inform the Pope that a member of the order named John de Isca had run away, taking with him 11,000 pounds from the proceeds of the crusade tax. The Prior pleaded that the Templars were not in a position to make good the loss immediately, unless by delivering themselves into the hands of usurers, and the Pope, out of regard to the services to the Holy Land rendered by the Paris Templars and the Order generally, and in view of the the lack of enthusiasm shown for the Crusade —to which the Pope sorrowfully testifies—decreed on

[1] Potthast, 20905, 21012.

[2] *Reg.*, 20 (January 30, 1283).

January 11 that one half of the amount should be paid by the feast of St. John the Baptist and the remainder a year later. The collector, the archbishop of Rouen, was entrusted with seeing that the Pope's orders were observed and was instructed to obtain guarantees for punctual payment.[1]

Experiences such as these impelled the Pope to appoint another way of holding the funds in future, namely, to give control over them to influential merchants, corporations, or banks. At first three great houses were chosen in Florence, Pisa, and Lucca ; in Siena the local funds were left to a merchant company of the town. If a statement made by Baronius relating to 1284 is to be believed, misappropriations were not unknown in these banks either. If that is so we can better understand the established fact that from July, 1283, onwards Pope Martin concentrated the funds in the house of Thomasius Spillatus and Hugo Spina of Florence, of whom he stated expressly that no doubt could be entertained of their honour. From that date all collectors were instructed to forward the taxes to the Florentine house— even the French funds were to be remitted.[2] The administration of the money by great commercial houses with branches in all important centres had of course great advantages, including ease of exchange, swift and safe remittance, the possibility of obtaining loans easily in advance against remittances to arrive later from remote countries. Although such an intention or wish was not present, this employment of the banking houses to handle the financial affairs of the Curia contributed considerably to strengthen European finance.

Much bitterness was provoked by the fact that this tax, collected by methods of all kinds to finance a crusade, *Employment of the funds.*

---

[1] *Reg.*, 204.

[2] *Reg.*, 4, 350, 400, 414, 433 ; Potthast, 22168, 22214 ; Kaltenbrunner, 263, 264, 268 ; Böhmer, *Regesta imperii*, 1758.

was not applied to a crusade, but to quite different purposes. Gregory X. had initiated this action and had been followed by John XXI. and Nicholas III. Now Martin in his turn used the crusade tithes for the wars in the Romagna,[1] for Sicily, for the Angevins, and against Aragon.

On December 13, 1282, the Pope asked the consent of the King of France to the withdrawal through his legate of the sum of 100,000 pounds of Tours from the Temple funds in Paris for the conduct of the campaign in the Romagna. At the moment the Church was without the funds necessary therefor, but the Pope undertook to return the amount when possible.[2] We know, too, that in the year 1283 alone, no less than 76,210 gold pounds [3] were expended by Petrus de Romanis in enlisting French troops. Twenty-five years later the French treasury claimed the sum of 54,352 Tours pounds, 7 soldi, and 6 denarii spent on troops and their pay, sent in 1282–3 to the Romagna at the request of Pope Martin.[4] In 1285 Pope Honorius mentions 400 pounds of Tours lent to French troops in the Romagna.[5]

In support of the Angevins in Sicily the papal coffers had been completely emptied as early as 1283. The Prince of Salerno was given 5,000 ounces of gold to make preparations for a landing on the island and later received "a much larger sum" [6] to buy or hire ships in Venice ; again, 15,000 ounces of gold were paid out to the prince in Rome by the Florentine banking house of Bonaccorsi from the Pope's account. In return the bank was given a bill on the church tithes. On February 13, 1284, the prince gave a receipt for 10,000 ounces of gold, given to him on loan supposedly. In an account

---

[1] Muratori, *RR. II. SS.*, viii, 1141.
[2] *Reg.*, 272.
[3] Theiner, *Cod. dipl.*, i, 279.
[4] *Recueil des hist.*, xxi, 531.
[5] *Reg. Honorius IV.*, 470.
[6] Raynaldus, an. 1283.

drawn up by the French royal treasurer, Adam de Dussiaco, for the period September, 1283, to the end of February, 1284, there appears an item of 16,319 ounces of gold received by the Pope as crusade tithes and used in the campaign on behalf of the Angevins.

Under the date April 23, 1284, Martin announced to his legate the dispatch of an *ingens pecunie quantitas* to be given to the Prince of Salerno as a loan from the Pope. Three days later the prince confirms the receipt of 15,608 ounces of gold, Church tithes, from the Lucca banking house entrusted by the Pope with collecting the money : he asks the Pope to credit the bank with that amount.

In a papal brief dated July 25, 1284, instructions are given to Berardus, prefect of the Apostolic Camera, to withdraw 15,000 ounces of gold from the tithes of Scotland, Denmark, Sweden, Hungary, Slovenia, and Poland, and to hand them over to John de Tomasis Spiliati and his company for King Charles of Anjou for the protection of his territory.[1] That this was done is shown by the general account rendered by Gerard of Modena, as well as those of archbishop Bertrand Amalrich of Arles, tithe collector for Denmark and Sweden. Both of these countries supplied large sums for the war in Sicily, but in Scotland resistance was encountered, for the King prevented the exportation of the money. On the other hand, we read in the report of the collector for Hungary of a further loan of 16,000 ounces of gold granted by the church of Rome to the Prince of Salerno to which Hungary was to contribute from the Hungarian crusade tithes. In addition Hungary contributed to Sicily from a church collection 732 ounces and 26 taren of gold, and again 53 ounces and 28 taren. King Charles himself is supposed to have received from the Curia as early as 1283 sums totalling 23,393 ounces and

---

[1] Raynaldus, an. 1283 ; Potthast, 22168.

14 grains of gold.[1] Further assistance to the Angevins from the Church and the Pope was represented by the prolongation in 1294 by the Pope for two years of the tithes of Sicily and Provence granted by Gregory X.   To the Count of Artois, the regent of Sicily during Charles's absence and after his death, Martin gave financial assistance to the amount of 100,000 pounds of Tours, but there is no means of determining whether this sum was a gift or a loan.   All we know is that during the regency the Sicilian crown received from the Holy See loans amounting in 1306 to 366,000 ounces of gold.[2]

Remunera-
tion of the
collectors.
A portion of the proceeds of the crusade tax was required for the staff employed in the collection, for as a general rule the collectors had been directed since the Council of Lyons to deduct their maintenance from the proceeds of the tithes.   It would seem that in the beginning the Pope considered that the collectors should be compensated for their labours merely by personal exemption from the payment of tithes, but from the first this scheme met with difficulties. The archbishop of Dublin asked the Pope what he should do, since many of the taxgatherers were so needy that they could not devote themselves to the collection without special recompense.   To this the Pope answered that the same rules applied to Ireland as to other countries : collectors were themselves absolved from the obligation to contribute, but no further payments might be made to them.[3]   Six weeks later, however, on November 1, 1281, he instructed the Archbishop to pay to the sub-collectors from the proceeds of the tax the sum of three shillings a day, the amount promised them.[4] As an exception, power had been already given in the beginning of September for the collector to withdraw

[1] Raynaldus, an. 1283.   [2] Gottlob, *l.c.*, 118–22.
[3] *Reg.*, 31 (October 15, 1281).   [4] Potthast, 21811.

from the tax revenue a fixed sum for his maintenance. We learn, for example, that the Pope continued the newly nominated bishop Peter of Rieti in office as a collector, and that he allowed him to take up to two gold florins a day for his maintenance, so that he could devote himself to the collection with still greater zeal.[1] Before long a general regulation was adopted which permitted every sub-collector to take for himself the sum of three shillings daily from the revenues of the collection. Theoderic and Aliron, the collectors in Germany, were allowed five shillings a day because of the heavier expenses entailed in that country. Even then, however, they seem unable to manage, for on December 13, 1283, the Pope granted these two a sum amounting to 18 pounds a year[2] to be paid in monthly instalments in addition to the regular five shillings a day. This was done because of the numerous journeys they had to undertake, the great distances which they had to cover in order to supervise their staffs and subordinates, and because of the high cost of food. About a year later he increased the daily allowance of the collector Theoderic, because of the high prices ruling in Germany.[3] Collectors who had their activities rewarded by appointments to bishoprics were obliged to pay crusade tithes on the benefices they received, and were allowed to deduct only so much as they had been obliged to pay from their benefices during their period of office as collectors. This recalls definitely the fact that at first the collectors' sole recompense was their exemption from the tithe payment. Accordingly, it was regarded in their case as a privilege that, having been formerly in possession of benefices on which as

---

[1] *Reg.*, 28 (October 7, 1281).

[2] *Reg.*, 429 ; Kaltenbrunner, 261.

[3] Feb. 2, 1284 : " quod in istis provinciis habeantur ad presens victualia more solito cariora."

collectors they had not to pay, they were not obliged to pay in retrospect. Those unable to pay were given a period of grace up to three years.[1]

Towards the end of his life the Pope made efforts to obtain control of the entire proceeds of the tax for his own purposes. It stands on record that on February 13, 1285, he issued instructions to the Polish prelates,[2] if to none others, to pay *procuratio* again to the papal collector, John Muscatæ. The sum fixed was 16 Tours soldi. In addition the prelates were to provide a safe conduct for the papal collector. This new imposition on the clergy could not be established universally and the crusade revenues continued to be reduced by the amounts necessary for the maintenance of the collectors.

The crusade tithes collected under Martin IV. by the employment of all the powers at the disposal of the Church did not help in any way to secure the Holy Land for Christendom, but they did contribute largely to damage the prestige of the Church. Nothing was heard of help for the Holy Land, but demands for money were all the louder for that. The Pope also issued instructions that clerics in drawing up their wills should bequeath legacies for a crusade. If anyone left his property for pious purposes generally, the residue, after due demands had been paid, was to be employed likewise for the Holy Land.[3] To the Pope's honour it must be stated that he himself left 2,000 Tours groschen from his property for the Holy Land.[4]

Crusade prospects.

Nothwithstanding all these financial exertions nothing whatever was done on behalf of the Holy Land during the pontificate of Martin IV. It must be granted that conditions in Europe were not at all favourable to a crusade, but they might have been more favourable

---

[1] *Reg.*, 428.
[2] Potthast, 22210.
[3] *Reg.*, 76, 79 ; Potthast, 21796.
[4] *Reg. Hon. IV.*, 471.

if the Pope had not complicated them by his unremitting and one-sided intervention on behalf of French interests. The German monarch Rudolf was demobilized in Germany ; Charles of Anjou was combating the revolt in Sicily ; the King of France was instructed by the Pope to lead a campaign in the interests of his family against Aragon ; in Italy the city states were fighting with one another, if not involved in the struggles of the kingdom of Sicily. The King of England alone was free to act, but he had no serious thoughts of undertaking a crusade : he made sure, however, to secure the proceeds of the tithes. Previous to the Sicilian Vespers, Charles of Anjou had proclaimed his intention of leading a crusade, not so much, however, because he wished to help the Holy Land as because his ambition was to found a world-wide empire and to latinize the western world for political reasons. These plans, which would certainly not have redounded to the advantage of the Church, were shattered by the rising in Sicily.

While it is granted that the Pope was responsible only in part for the unfavourable conditions present in Europe, it must be said that the responsibility for squandering the crusade funds rests entirely on his shoulders, and there only. That responsibility was all the greater because he opposed stern denials to rumours of the misapplication of the funds and complaints based thereon. He put himself right to some extent no doubt by having a crusade preached against Sicily and Aragon, thus justifying himself in using the money as it was received for a " crusade ". But the decrees of the Council of Lyons had appointed the tax specifically for the Holy Land. In reality the immense sums which flowed in for the protection of the Holy Land were used to protect French interests and to strengthen the international position of France and of Charles of Anjou.

The Pope even went so far as to diminish crusaders'

privileges, when requested to do so by the King of
France. Among those privileges was a provision that
persons guilty of a crime should be acquitted of their
guilt and exempt from punishment if they atoned for
their misdeeds by taking part in a crusade. Pope Martin,
however, decreed, in a *privilegium* issued to France
in the very first year of his pontificate, that the King
and his officers had the right to proceed against such
persons even though they had taken the crusade vow.
He instructed the archbishops, bishops, and other prelates of France not to obstruct the King or his officials
in the execution of such proceedings. In addition he
instructed the Abbot of St. Denis to impose ecclesiastical
penalties on all Church dignitaries who interfered with
these privileges of the King of France.[1] Apparently
the Pope anticipated that this diminution of the crusade
privileges in favour of the King would be ill received,
since he made provision immediately for dealing with
resistance to it.

In his crusade policy, as in everything he undertook,
the Pope could not restrain his partiality and preference
for France, and it is beyond doubt that this weakness had
particularly unfortunate results for the Church as a whole.
Martin cannot be freed of the heavy responsibility of
misusing the ecclesiastical jurisdiction for secular ends,
but there is no means of determining in how far he
realized either the responsibility or the misuse. One
thing is at least certain, that the few years of his
pontificate were enough to bring excommunication and
interdicts into still greater contempt among wide circles
than had been done already by earlier misuses of those
powers. For now they were degraded by being used
almost exclusively as weapons of the financial authority.
Nothing, nay, less than nothing, was done for the Holy

---

[1] *Reg.*, 51, 52 (October 7, 1281).

Land, for the contributions made by Christendom on its behalf were employed for other purposes by the Pope, so much so that his successor was faced with empty coffers at home and a perilous situation in the Holy Land.

One other result should be mentioned in passing. The exceedingly skilful administration of these funds by the Pope, with the help of great commercial and banking houses, contributed substantially to stabilize financial institutions in the western world.

CONCLUSION.

IN the midst of his struggles, with his plans and projects unfulfilled, Martin IV. was called to depart from this life.   On Easter Sunday, March 25, 1285, he celebrated High Mass solemnly ; on the same day a violent fever seized him.   His physician did not recognize the disease, nor realize the danger ; indeed he was quite confident that there was no danger of death, although the Pope knew himself to be seriously ill.   Three days later, on Wednesday, March 28, Martin succumbed to this short but severe illness.   He died towards midnight, the lateness of the hour accounting probably for the confusion which makes some writers give the date of his death as March 28 while others state the 29th.[1]

After his death miracles are said to have taken place at his bier before his burial.   In particular cures of the sick are mentioned, but our only source of information on the subject is the *Liber Pontificalis*.[2]   Martin had expressed a wish to be buried at Assisi, but as he held a reputation for sanctity among his friends in Perugia they did not wish his body to leave the city.   On April 2 he was interred in Perugia.   As has been described, that city had been obstinate in its resistance to the Pope, and had been reduced to submission only a short time before his death and burial there.   Even the orders of his successor Honorius to the civic authorities of Perugia to allow of the transfer of the remains to Assisi [3]

---

[1] *Liber Pontif.*, 465 ; Potthast, 1794 ; Pertz, *Mon. Germ. Script.*, xix, 29.

[2] *L.c.*, 464.

[3] *Reg. Honorius IV.*, 270 ; Potthast, 22361.

were unsuccessful. Since the year 1295 an urn on a
pedestal in the Cathedral of St. Lorenzo in Perugia encloses
the ashes of Martin IV. and of the greatest Pope of the
Middle Ages, Innocent III.

One tomb unites two men who differed fundamentally
in their outlook : Innocent III., champion of the rights
and liberties of the Church, protagonist of the idea of the
universal monarchy of the Church, which is ruler of all,
Innocent III., who forced the King of France to conform
to Christian morality ; and Martin IV., the Pope who was
dominated by France and who placed the universal
Church at the service of French ambitions of conquest.

It may well be that Martin found it hard to die. He
saw the world devoid of peace, and that he was not
without responsibility for the fact. With foreign help he
had indeed succeeded in reducing the Romagna, but Italy
was none the less in a blaze. The Ghibellines whom he
had combated so rigorously were not crushed ; Peter
of Aragon scorned the excommunication and interdict
uttered against him, and the exploitation of these weapons
had robbed them of their efficacy ; Sicily sought unremittingly to be at peace with the Pope, but the
unsuccessful character of its approaches to its overlord
forced it to help itself otherwise. When the Pope showed
that he would consider no ruler but the Angevins, the
Sicilians had no alternative but to oppose their wishes
to his. It is of interest to notice that this was probably
the first occasion on which a people determined its fate
with complete freedom. But that free decision was not
taken until it had been forced on the Sicilians. Their
fixed determination was to submit to the Pope and to
ask him to appoint another ruler over them, but they
wished to exclude their former ruler, Charles of Anjou.
Because the Pope insisted on Charles, the Sicilians were
compelled to fight for their freedom.

The fight ended with a serious defeat for the Pope and

a victory for the islanders, who were really fighting in a just cause. But the dream of a victory in the Holy Land was shattered abruptly by the "Sicilian Vespers". However, a victorious advance by Charles of Anjou through Constantinople to the Holy Land would have been no blessing for the Church. It would merely have made the French masters of the world for the time being at the expense of the Church and its liberty.

After a restless life, without having attained any decisive success, Martin IV. ended his earthly career. He shows himself as a man not lacking in goodwill, but unable to resist the pressure of outside influences. His life is characterized by the fact that his friends attempted to weave around him a halo of sanctity while his opponent Dante places him in hell, there to suffer for his sins. In reality he was a man who had all the qualities and weaknesses of the average man. He certainly took pains to give of his best to the Church and to serve it with all his power. If he did not always select the best method of doing so, that must be regarded as one of those dispensations of Almighty God by which He desires to show humanity that earthly power cannot overthrow the Church even when a weak and inadequate representative guides its destinies on earth. The divine power of the Church is most manifest when its earthly power and human resources are least obvious.

HONORIUS IV.

Sources and Bibliography.—In general our sources of information concerning the pontificate of Honorius IV. are identical with those relating to his immediate predecessors, in particular, Martin IV. To them must be added the Papal Registers which have been edited in full and have been accessible to all since 1888 (*Les Registres d'Honorius IV.*, publiés par Maurice Prou, Paris, 1888). In a detailed introduction M. Prou, the editor, subjected the registers to a critical examination. A monograph by B. Pawlicki is based on this work (*Papst Honorius IV.*, Münster i. W., 1896), but does not make use of all the material available at the time.[1] In many respects historical research has advanced since it appeared, and although I have, of course, made use of Pawlicki's work, the present monograph will be found, I hope, more exhaustive.

Contemporary sovereigns were the same as those cited for Martin IV.[2] The most important material used is set out at the beginning of the present volume and is cited merely by catch words in the footnotes.

[1] *Cf.* O. Redlich, *Regesten des Kaiserreiches*, p. 452.
[2] See p. 167.

CHAPTER I.

ELECTION.   PERSONAL DETAILS.   CHARACTER.   PREVIOUS
CAREER.

FEW papal elections have been carried through as calmly
or as quickly as that of the successor of Martin IV.
At the time the contrary might have been anticipated.
Martin had unduly strengthened the French element in
the College of Cardinals, thus giving that element an
exceptional degree of influence over the pending election.
On the other hand, it might have been assumed that the
excessive and partisan favour shown to French interests
would produce a determination in the minds of the
opposing party not to allow the election of a second such
Pope in any circumstances.   Everything seemed set
accordingly for a prolonged and exciting election.

Election.

Exactly the opposite occurred, and the Church remained
but four days without a visible head.   On the day after
Martin's funeral the cardinals entered the conclave, and
on the following day, on the first vote taken, the cardinal-
deacon Giacomo Savelli was chosen Pope.

At that time the College of Cardinals consisted of
eighteen members, six of them cardinal-bishops, six
cardinal-priests, and six cardinal-deacons.   Three were
absent on business as papal legates : Gerhard, cardinal-
bishop of Sabina, as legate and regent in Sicily ; Jean
Cholet, cardinal of St. Cecilia, as legate in France ; and
Bernard, cardinal-bishop of Porto, as legate in Upper and
Central Italy.[1]   On April 1 the fifteen remaining cardinals,

[1] That the last mentioned was not in Perugia may be deduced from
a letter addressed to him by Martin IV. on March 21, 1285, but not
registered as a bull, so that it was not dispatched until after the election
of Honorius (*Reg.*, 9).   The legate was then at or near Bologna.

as prescribed, attended the Mass of the Holy Ghost in Perugia, where the late Pope had died. The remainder of the day was devoted to preliminary discussions which cleared the ground to such an extent that on the following day, April 2, Giacomo Savelli, cardinal-deacon of Sta. Maria in Cosmedin, was unanimously elected Pope.

A careful examination of the circumstances explains this expedition. A cardinal who had the interests of the Church at heart, no matter how dear France was to him, could not have wished to continue the policy of Martin IV. For to continue it would be tantamount to a great effort to destroy the Church. Accordingly, even the French party in the College of Cardinals must have desired a man possessing the skill and courage to change the policy pursued previously and to follow once more a Church policy instead of a French one. Since it was certain that attempts would be made by various sections, above all by the Angevin section, to influence the election, the electors hastened to present the world with an accomplished fact. In addition one man among the cardinals stood out—not physically, but all the more intellectually — as a particularly suitable choice. Salimbene [1] no doubt merely voices the general feeling of his time when he describes Giacomo as the first among the cardinals. His character and his earlier work appeared to guarantee that he would be a shepherd to the whole Christian world. The only dissenting voice is that of an anonymous and hostile Franciscan who ascribes the election of Giacomo to chance. He writes [2] that the cardinals were split into two camps, one of which put forward a candidate which the opposite party, it was thought, could not possibly accept, namely, the crippled Giacomo. But, as this nominee belonged to the opposite

---

[1] *Chronicon Parmensis* (Parma, 1857), 332.
[2] *Continuatio anglica fratrum minorum brevis* (*M. G. SS.*, xxx, 714).

party, he is supposed to have been accepted by it, and the aged cardinal, contrary to all expectations, was elected. The inaccuracy, not to say nonsense, of this account is clear from the fact that the situation described had developed in the discussions which had preceded the election and that, accordingly, either party would have been in a position to alter its plans and to give its votes to another candidate at the first ballot. Besides it is impossible to think anyone so clumsy as to nominate a candidate whom he does not wish elected, particularly a candidate from among his opponents, who are thus enabled to have their candidate elected without difficulty by merely agreeing.

It would certainly be correct to assume that the personal qualities of the newly elected Pope determined his selection. The cardinals must have wished that the Pope should be a Roman and a member of an influential Roman family, so that order might thus be restored in Rome and in the papal states by the employment of influence and of material advantages. By their quick choice the cardinals fulfilled a desire of the German monarch before they were aware of it, for after the death of Pope Martin, Rudolf wrote to the cardinals that the thought of the Church being deprived for long of its shepherd filled him with care and anxiety. He begged them fervently to give the world a new spiritual head, unanimously and as quickly as possible. Before the letter containing this request could reach the cardinals, his wish for a speedy and a harmonious papal election had been accomplished.

Personal particulars. The new Pope was born in 1210, and belonged to the influential noble Roman house of the Savelli. His father, Luca Savelli, a Roman senator, had died in 1266. His mother was Joanna Aldobrandesca of the house of the Counts of Santa Fiora. His paternal great-uncle was Pope Honorius III., after whom he selected the name of Honorius IV. His brothers were Giovanni Savelli, who died in 1279 as *podestà* of Orvieto, and Pandulfo, who was a senator of Rome when Honorius IV. became Pope. He had one sister, Mabilia, married to Agapitus Colonna. The family had rich estates, owning extensive properties in the Latin hills and in the region of Civita Castellana, in addition to lands in Rome on the Aventine, where the Pope too erected his new residence, as well as palaces and fortresses in that district which was called in consequence Vicolo de Savelli.

It is an interesting and significant fact that at all times the family had been faithful to the cause of the Guelphs and the Angevins. The Pope's two brothers had fought at Tagliacozzo under the banner of Charles of Anjou and the personal bravery and determination of Giovanni di Savelli had preserved Rome from falling into the hands of Pietro di Vico, Manfred's follower. This personal attitude of the family explains why the Pope, who was otherwise so mild, would not yield an inch in the Sicilian question, although as a skilled diplomat he must have known that there was no possibility of holding a position which was in fact already lost. No doubt, being a man with a strongly developed feeling for the law, he was deeply influenced by the desire to maintain the law.

Very little is known of his youth or of his life before he became Pope. He spent a number of years in Paris studying, as we learn from an observation which he made incidentally and which suggests that he had been there for several years, and that even in his old age he liked to think of those days.[1] During this period of study he held a benefice in the Church of Chalons-sur-Marne,[2] availing himself of a general indult of the

Education and development.

---

[1] *Reg.*, 267. ". . . olim, dum nos minor status haberet, in eiusdem studii laboribus observati de illius dulcedine libamina grata libavimus per plures annos . . ." [2] *Reg.*, 767.

University of Paris.   This fact, too, he recalled gratefully
throughout his life.   He wrote [1] that he had not merely
derived material advantages from this Church, but had
also attained there to his first step in ecclesiastical
advancement—a canonry—and that as his advance
in the hierarchy had begun in that Church, it was only
just and proper that he should distinguish it with privileges
and marks of favour.   This was no mere vague
intention ; it was carried out.   A whole series of privileges
which he granted to the Church in question are a proof
of it. [2]   In addition, he held a benefice as rector of Berton
in the diocese of Norwich up to the time when he was
chosen head of the Church. [3]

The only other reference we have to him is in regard to
his appointment as cardinal-deacon of Sta. Maria in
Cosmedin by Pope Urban IV. in 1261. [4]   What a high
opinion that Pope held of the cardinal's abilities is shown
by the fact that he contemplated appointing him to
a post of the highest importance at a very critical time.
Manfred's troops menaced Rome and the Pope was
without funds.   In this dangerous situation the Pope
considered the nomination of Giacomo Savelli as papal
prefect in Tuscany and commander of the papal troops. [5]
In the succeeding years we find the cardinal-deacon of
Sta. Maria in Cosmedin participating in a whole series
of events of prime importance.   When Charles of Anjou
landed in Italy to take possession of Sicily, he was one
of the deputation of cardinals who in Rome invested
Charles on behalf of the Pope with the fief of the
kingdom of Sicily (July 28, 1265). [6]   In 1272 he was a
member of a commission of six cardinals to whom by

---

[1] *Reg.*, 569.   [2] *Reg.*, 21, 185, 308, 499, 569, 470.
[3] *Reg.*, 422.   [4] Raynaldus, an. 1261.
[5] Martène, *Thesaurus novus anecdotorum*, ii, 84, 56.
[6] Martène, *Thesaurus*, 220 ff. ; Raynaldus, an. 1265.

way of compromise the election of a Pope was entrusted after an interregnum lasting almost two years.[1]

As a matter of course he took part with the other cardinals in the second general council of Lyons of 1274, and was one of those in attendance on the Pope at the solemn opening of the Council. On one occasion he is mentioned as a witness at the taking of the oath by the representative of Rudolf of Habsburg and before long he made the personal acquaintance of that monarch, for he was among the cardinals sent to Lausanne by Gregory X. for the first peace negotiations opened with a German King since the great struggles with the Hohenstaufen.[2] The further conduct of those negotiations was committed by Hadrian V. to him, together with the cardinal-archbishop of Sabina and cardinal-deacon Giovanni Orsini. The object of these conferences was not alone the imperial coronation, but more particularly the formation of an alliance between Rudolf of Habsburg and Charles of Anjou. The meeting with Rudolf took place in Viterbo, but the early death of the Pope prevented any decision.[3] When the negotiations were at last concluded under Pope Nicholas III., Giacomo was again present as a witness when Rudolf's representative, the Franciscan Conrad, took the oath and swore that the German King would restore all the rights of the Church.[4] His employment in these negotiations with Rudolf is an indication that he did not belong to the French party in the College of Cardinals, which was opposed to any arrangement with the Habsburg King.

We have no information regarding his activities in later years. This may be due in part to his physical ailments which hindered his appearance in public, for

[1] Raynaldus, an. 1271 ; *M. G. SS.*, xviii, 554.
[2] Raynaldus, an. 1274 ; Mansi, *Conc. collectio*, xxiv, 66.
[3] Raynaldus, ann. 1276, 1277.
[4] Kopp, *Geschichte der eidgenössischen Bünde*, i, 1, 220 (Leipzig, 1845).

contemporary authorities inform us that during those years his hands were crippled, and so crippled were his feet that he could not walk, or even stand upright without support.

He had to sit in a chair while celebrating Mass and at the Elevation of the Consecrated Elements his hands were raised by a mechanical contrivance.[1] If, in spite of this, the cardinals decided to elevate this physically hampered man to the highest post in Christendom at a particularly critical time, his mental qualities must have been all the more vigorous and remarkable. Doubtless Martinus Polonus [2] had good authority for his statement that the Pope had been chosen for his " wisdom, goodness, and simplicity of manners ". His whole pontificate is characterized by understanding, kindness, and benevolence, by which he achieved incomparably more than he could have done by unyielding harshness. As a matter of fact, in the one field where he showed himself unyielding, namely, that of overcoming the Sicilian troubles, he achieved no success ; whenever he acted with leniency he succeeded in restoring order. The English Franciscan already referred to reproaches him for being harsh towards the poor and kind towards the rich and powerful, basing the statement on the Pope's kindness in giving dispensations from canonical impediments and for plurality of benefices, but the reproach is certainly unfounded. Obviously dispensations allowing for the combination of a number of benefices had reference to the richer clergy, but the Pope did not forget the Franciscans either, even if he did not heap favours on them as his predecessor had done. That he did not drew on him no doubt the ill-will of the Chronicler.[3]

---

[1] Muratori, *Scriptores*, ix, 727 ; in the *Continuatio Anglica* (*M. G. SS.*, xxx, 114) the chronicler inserts the ugly satire : Ponitur in Petri monstrum mirabile sede Mancus utraque manu, Claudus utroque pede.

[2] *M. G. SS.*, xxii, 482.

[3] On other occasions, too, Franciscans frequently spoke of him in

When news of the election reached Rome, great joy was expressed. Spontaneously the Romans elected Honorius as a life senator and appointed a deputation to convey the news to him and to invite him to come to Rome for his coronation and to remain there.[1] The newly-elected Pope showed great pleasure at this and promised to hasten to Rome without delay,[2] but for some unknown reason his departure was delayed for several days, for the date of a letter shows that he was still in Perugia on April 25. His solemn consecration and coronation took place on Trinity Sunday, May 20, 1285,[3] after he had been ordained priest the day before by the cardinal-bishop of Ostia. As his motto he chose a phrase typical of his disposition : *Pars mea Deus in sæcula*, " The Lord is my portion for eternity." In his announcement of election *urbi et orbi* he likewise gave expression to this humble confidence. Taking as his text the dictum of St. Paul (1 Cor. i, 27 ff.), he points out that God often chooses the weak for the purpose of showing that it is He Himself, and not mankind, who rules the Church. In an election announcement addressed to individuals he combined the announcement in every case with a request for prayers and assistance.[4]

He accepted the Romans' invitation to establish his residence in their city and built himself a dwelling on the Aventine. During the summer months he resided in Tivoli, probably in order to avail himself of the sulphur baths of Aquæ Albulæ.

a hostile fashion. Hampe, for example, reports a lampoon which must refer to him.

> O Pater Honori
> Patris non vivis honori
> Desine vade mori
> Dabimus cathedram meliori.

[1] Vitale, *Storia diplomatica de senatori di Roma*, 194 (Rome, 1791).
[2] *Reg.*, 825 ; Potthast, 22226.
[3] Prou, *Reg.*, introductory chapter ii ; Pawlicki, 13.
[4] Potthast, 22232, 22231 ; *Reg.*, 472.

CHAPTER II.

CONDITIONS IN ROME AND THE PAPAL STATES, AND IN
ITALY GENERALLY.

Rome.

I N Rome the election of a Roman in the person of Giacomo Savelli had been hailed with enthusiasm. The name Savelli was well known. The father of the newly-elected Pope had distinguished himself as a senator and at the time of the election his brother exercised senatorial office. When the Romans had put an end to the Angevin regime after the Sicilian Vespers, Martin IV. had been obliged to recognize the fact. He then appointed Pandulf Savelli senator with Peter Annibaldi, and Pandulf, although physically infirm like his brother, understood how to exercise his rule, as his father had done in peace and prosperity.

When the news reached Rome that the brother of their excellent senator had been chosen head of the Church, it was no wonder that he too was elected without more ado as a senator for life. As early as April 5, 1285, Honorius returned thanks for the honour thus shown to him and promised to come without delay.[1] His arrival was, nevertheless, delayed for a few weeks, but the Pope remained in Rome almost constantly during his two years' reign and lived on the most cordial terms with the citizens. He immediately confirmed in office the two nominees of his predecessor, who understood so well, especially his brother, how to maintain peace and order in Rome. Although Pandulf Savelli had conducted the city's affairs with such distinction and although the people appreciated him, he did not prolong his term of office.

---

[1] *Reg.*, 825 ; Potthast, 22226.

According to the rules laid down by Nicholas III., the term of office was to be but one year. When the year expired in the summer of 1285, the Pope made no exception in his brother's case, but called Orso Orsini and Nicholas Conti to the office of senator.[1] He himself hardly ever interfered in civic matters. Under his reign Rome enjoyed complete peace, the streets were safe, and the nobles did not dare to indulge in excesses or disorders. Not content with establishing his own residence on the Aventine—he moved there as soon as the buildings were ready in the autumn of 1285—he tried to get the district populated once more. He had houses built and roads laid out in order to draw thither a section of the city's population. However, the lack of water prevented these efforts from having permanent results, and it was not long before ruins were the sole testimony to a Pope's hopes.

As in the city, his efforts in the papal state were directed to establishing peace so much needed. Martin IV. had of course been successful in crushing the most serious revolts, but there was nothing in the nature of real internal peace, and this was not established until the leader of the Ghibellines submitted completely. As soon as Honorius was able to detach his former supporters, open and secret, Guido had no alternative but to yield. He delivered to the Pope his faithful city of Urbino and sent his son as hostage. At the Pope's command he himself had to go into exile and retired to Asti in Piedmont. In Urbino the fortifications were levelled and the most important Ghibelline families were exiled like Guido. Otherwise the Pope was not severe, and his wise moderation contributed more than anything else to the establishment of peace. He instructed William Durandus, rector of Romagna, to allow persons formerly exiled for rebellion to return to their estates.[2]

Government of the Papal State.

---

[1] Pflugk-Harttung, *Iter Italicum*, ii, 619 ff. ; *Reg.*, 927.
[2] *Reg.*, 224.

As a testimony to his successful activity in the Romagna he appointed William Durandus bishop of Mende. At first the Pope instructed the new bishop to arrange for the administration of the diocese in his absence, since he himself was indispensable in the Romagna. Not until four months had elapsed was he ordered to arrange for his consecration.[1] Then the Pope appointed his own cousin, the Proconsul Peter Stephani, as Count of the Romagna and the Massa Trabaria. A document relating to the Romagna was addressed to the latter as early as January, 1287.[2]

For the entire papal state the Pope's policy was based on the principle of using gentle methods to the utmost. He withdrew the ecclesiastical penalties imposed for political reasons by his predecessor : the cities of Bologna and Cesena were freed from the interdict which they had incurred through supporting Guido di Monte-feltro.[3] Rollandus de Ferentino, papal chaplain and rector of the Duchy of Spoleto, was empowered by the Pope to take back the cities of Cesena, Visso, and Spello into the communion of the Church from which they had been cast out by Martin because they had disobeyed him during the struggle between Perugia and Foligno.[4] A whole series of other towns were released likewise from the penalties imposed by Martin.[5] Even Viterbo, which Martin had never been able to forgive for the attack on the conclave by its citizens, was taken into favour again. This city appealed to the Pope, and its appeal was heard, although it did not escape punish-ment, for it was compelled not only to raze its walls and fortified towers and build a hospital at its own

[1] *Reg.*, 285, 286, 511.
[2] *Reg.*, 723 ; Potthast, 22549.
[3] *Reg.*, 224.
[4] *Reg.*, 23, 835 ; *cf. supra*, pp. 213 ff.
[5] *Cf. Reg.*, 129, 496, 686, 864.

expense, but it also had to sacrifice its political independence.

It lost its separate jurisdiction, and the Pope reserved to himself the appointment of its *podestà*. In addition a number of castles had to be handed over to the Orsini. The price thus paid for remission of ecclesiastical punishments was certainly a high one, and the once flourishing city never completely recovered.[1]

Open resistance to papal rule was offered only by the town of Jesi in the March of Ancona. The lords of that city, the three brothers Simonetti, had been zealous partisans of Guido di Montefeltro, but recognizing the hopelessness of further resistance to the Pope, declared themselves ready to submit. Pope Honorius accepted their submission and appointed a relative of his own, Nicholas Boccamazzi, as *podestà*. The Simonetti were not prepared to give up their power, and opposed the new *podestà* by force of arms, going so far as to plunder benefices of the Church, such as Villa Ripa and Collemanto. Thereupon the Pope ordered Godfrey of Anagni, rector of the March of Ancona, to advance against the city, and called upon the towns of Genoa and Osimo to support the rector. This sufficed to bring the city to reason. It submitted finally, but was sentenced by the Pope to pay in atonement a fine of 5,000 pounds of Ravenna. The new rector of the March, the bishop-elect of Jorea, was to collect the fine.[2]

Thus, under the rule of Honorius, the papal States presented the unusual picture of perfect peace, such as was known but seldom either before or after. Firmness and strength of purpose, combined with leniency, brought the territory the peace it so needed—unfortunately, however, for the short term of two years.

---

[1] *Reg.*, 485, 486, 487, 927 ; Ciampe, *Croniche e statuti della città di Viterbo*, p. 375 (Florence, 1872).

[2] *Reg.*, 839, 840, 896.

If the Pope's principle in the papal States was one
of not interfering unduly, but of leaving the towns as
free and independent as possible, he applied this principle
of non-interference even more generally in his dealings
with the remainder of Italy. He intervened only when
invited to do so, when there was question of revoking
penalties imposed formerly, or—and in this case very
firmly—when the rights of the Church were attacked.

It must be reckoned as a success for the Pope that
he was able to attain peaceful relations with the mighty
city of Venice. Martin IV. had imposed a ban on the city,
because it had refused to bring aid to Charles of Anjou,
and had even expressly forbidden its citizens to take part
in the war. Those who disobeyed this civic instruction
were severely punished. When Honorius assumed control
of the Church the Doge sent three delegates—his own son,
Andreas, Leonardus Venerius, and Nicholas Faletrus—to
ask that the ban be raised. The ambassadors declared that
the veto on taking part in the Sicilian war had not been
directed against the Church, but had been issued solely
in the interests of the city, to save it from harm ; moreover, the city disclaimed for the future all hostility
against the Church. Honorius was satisfied with this
declaration and required only that it should be entered
on the city's records, that all measures against those
who had aided Charles of Anjou should be revoked,
and that these persons should be compensated for any loss
they had suffered. When Venice had done this, Honorius
empowered the Ordinary, the bishop of Castello, to free
the city from the interdict. Thus peace was fully established between the Pope and the powerful city.[1]

Chroniclers also report an intervention of the Pope
in the bitter struggle between the republics of Genoa
and Pisa. This struggle was for pre-eminence and prestige.

---

[1] *Reg.*, 479, 486 (August 5, 1285) ; 315 (March 18, 1286).

The Tuscan towns, which for commercial reasons desired
to weaken Pisa, entered into an alliance with Genoa,
and in its extremity, according to Salimbene,[1] Pisa
appealed to the Pope for help.

All that can be established on documentary evidence
is that Pisa's domestic politics underwent a change at
this time. Whereas formerly the Ghibellines had led
the city, these were now overthrown. Count Ugolino
della Gherardesca became *podestà*, and he, by his influence,
was able to detach most of the Guelf towns from the
league against Pisa. That the Pope, as reported by
Salimbene, threatened excommunication against all who
continued hostilities against Pisa, cannot be proved
from documents, and in any case does not accord with
the Pope's general policy. It is quite true that the Pope
had a disagreement with Genoa and laid that city under
a ban, but this was for other reasons than Genoa's fight
with Pisa. It arose because the Genoese had captured
Neapolitan vessels which maintained commercial relations
with Pisa, and had imprisoned the crews. As suzerain
of Naples the Pope sent a friendly bull to Genoa
demanding that interference with trade should cease
and the loss suffered by the Neapolitans made good.
Apparently Genoa did not accede to this request, and
was accordingly laid under an interdict.[2]

A second occasion also arose to intervene in Genoa.
In 1270 the Guelfs had been driven from the city and
in 1277 sentenced to perpetual banishment. They now
appealed to Pope Honorius to intervene on their behalf.
The Fieschi family complained especially that they had
been deprived of their rights over Sestri and Lavagna,
which belonged to them, and that payments were being
demanded of them for which they were not liable, while
their revenues were being kept from them and their

---

[1] *L.c.*, 339.　　　　[2] *Reg.*, 364 (May 13, 1286).

possessions occupied by strangers. The Pope entrusted the investigation of the case to cardinal Gervasius of St. Martin, and on July 23, 1285, through the archbishop of Genoa, he summoned the city to send representatives to the Curia to settle the affair.

In this case, however, the Pope was not able to attain any really permanent success by his intervention.[1] In Pistoia likewise he tried to mediate between Guelfs and Ghibellines, but it is easily understood that it was not always possible to bring to an end by one stroke enmities which had lasted for decades. The Pope lacked the power to enforce peace.

His efforts to establish peace.

In many cases, however, he attained complete success in bringing about a reconciliation with the Church, thanks mainly to his understanding tolerance. Guido di Battifolle, count palatine of Tuscany, was accused to the Holy See of complicity in the murder of the bishop of Silva, the ambassador of King Alfonso of Castile. After a thorough investigation his innocence was established, and the Pope accorded him permission to rebuild his castle of Gangaretum which had been destroyed by the people of Florence.[2] Honorius also caused the restoration to the noble Guido Novelli of a number of castles which the owner had been forced at one time to deliver to the Angevins.[3] The Margrave of Montferrat had made a prisoner of the bishop of Tortona when that town was captured in 1284. During the siege of Sorti the imprisoned bishop was brought before the city walls to induce the surrender of his relatives who were defending the town. When the surrender did not follow, the Margrave's soldiers killed the bishop, and for this the Margrave was excommunicated. He appealed to the Pope for release from the ban, and his request was granted

---

[1] Cf. Pawlicki, p. 97 ff.

[2] Reg., 172.

[3] Reg., 55.

on condition of his performing a severe penance.[1] Thus
the Pope showed leniency in so far as the interests and
rights of the Church allowed it.[2] If these were infringed,
however, he knew how to fight obstinately in their
defence, as was experienced by the cities of Florence
and Bergamo. A democratic regime had been introduced
at this time in a number of cities from which the old
ruling families had been driven, and in many places the
new system deprived the clergy of their rights and
privileges. In Florence and Bergamo the privileges
enjoyed by the clergy as such were abolished without
more ado and the clergy put in the same position as
other citizens. They were made subject to secular
jurisdiction and could even be subjected to corporal
punishment. It was also forbidden to bequeath legacies
to the Church. Honorius was firm in resisting such
excesses of democracy, and he was successful in bringing
about the repeal of these anti-clerical laws.[3]

His attitude in the Sicilian question was diametrically Kingdom of
opposed to his usual leniency and tolerance. On this Sicily.
point he clung steadily to the position taken up by his
predecessor Martin IV., and rejected every attempt at
conciliation, short of complete surrender. This attitude
is intelligible from two points of view. It has been
indicated already that the Savelli family was on the side
of the Angevins, and assisted them from the moment
they had taken possession of Sicily, and it can well be
understood that Giacomo Savelli could not and would
not abandon his family tradition on becoming Pope.
The cause for which the members of his family were
prepared to shed their blood, even sacrifice their lives, was
sacred to him ; he would have regarded it as treason
if he had abandoned it, and treason not merely to sacred

[1] *Reg.*, 228. [2] *Cf.* also *Reg.*, 123.
[3] *Reg.*, 167, 714.

family ideals and to the Angevins, to whom his family were bound by the closest ties of loyalty, but above all treason to the Church. Sicily was and remained a papal fief, and the changes which had taken place in its government had developed without the Pope's consent, in fact against his express wishes, and without regard to ecclesiastical sanctions. One of the Church's rights had been thus invaded and the Pope's leniency invariably vanished when such a right was in question. Accordingly, placed as the Pope was, only one attitude was possible for him in the Sicilian question : an unyielding insistence on the rights of the Church, and with it indirectly an absolute adhesion to the Angevin rights over Sicily. Thus, the Sicilian policy of Pope Honorius was not in contrast to his usual attitude, but was a logical development of his political principles. The only thing which may cause some surprise is that such a skilled and wise diplomat should have taken no account of the earnest efforts of the Sicilians to alter their intolerable situation with the knowledge and consent of the Holy See, and of the fact that they had only acted independently when those efforts failed to overcome the resistance of Pope Martin. He might have considered that the outbreak against the Angevins was not the result of a conspiracy, nor a struggle against the Church, but an unpremeditated outbreak of long restrained wrath on the part of a southern people. Such reflections come easily to one who considers the situation after the lapse of centuries ; obviously they were not so clear and apparent to contemporaries and those who played a personal part in these events.

Another difficulty must also be considered. In the College of Cardinals there was a French majority which had to be considered by Honorius. Having already acted against their wishes in resuming negotiations with Rudolf of Habsburg for the latter's imperial coronation, he could not afford to embitter and alienate

the majority of the cardinals by an abrupt abandonment
of the Angevins and their historic rights.   Had he done
so the consequences in the College of Cardinals would
have been unhappy.   These circumstances must also be
taken into account by anyone who wishes to understand
Pope Honorius' policy in Sicily.

In the early months of the new Pope's reign the Development of the situation.
campaign of Philip III. against Aragon, desired and
directed by Martin IV., became a reality.   It was to
decide the fate not only of Aragon but of Sicily.   In
the summer of 1285 Philip crossed the Pyrenees at the
head of his troops with the papal legate at his side as
an indication that the campaign was a Crusade.[1]
Honorius approved of this step, for, when Rudolf of
Habsburg appealed to him to remit the tax being levied
for it in the western dioceses of the Empire, he rejected
the request firmly and deliberately on the ground that
the campaign being conducted by the King was one
which in the Pope's opinion was in the interests and,
in fact, in the service of the Church.   Again, when
King Edward of England approached Honorius for help
in his efforts to promote peace between the two warring
monarchs, his mission was unsuccessful.   The Pope
refused on the grounds that, on the one hand, the King
of Aragon deserved punishment, and on the other, he
could not check Philip in the midst of his successes,
seeing that the latter had accepted the labours and
expenses of this campaign in the service and at the
request of the Church.   When the fight ended with
Philip's death, the Pope extolled the dead King for
giving his life in the service of the Church and accorded,
therefore, an indulgence to all who prayed for the repose
of his soul.[2]

Nevertheless, the war ended otherwise than it began,

[1] *Reg.*, 234.   [2] *Reg.*, 591.

and differently from the expectations expressed by the
Pope in his letter to the King of England ; it ended
in the defeat of Philip, in a rout rather than a retreat.
But it cost both antagonists their lives. The King of
France fell a victim to the plague which had broken
out among his troops, and King Peter of Aragon died in
consequence of a wound received during a sortie at the
siege of Gerona. As King Charles of Sicily had died
earlier, an entirely new situation was created.

Peter of Aragon died on November 11, 1285. On
his death-bed, urged by his confessor who threatened
otherwise to refuse him absolution, he is said to have
sworn a declaration to make good the damage done to
the Church and to renounce his claims to Sicily. On
December 15 news of his death reached his son James,
who was ruling Sicily in his father's absence. Without
regard to his father's last promise or to the Pope, he
assumed the succession to the throne of Sicily and had
himself crowned King in the cathedral at Palermo on
February 2, 1286, in the presence of numerous temporal,
and also spiritual, princes. Not until afterwards did
he send two ambassadors, Gilbert de Castelleto and
Bartholomew de Neocastro, to the Pope to ask for the
latter's *ex post facto* sanction to his accession. It was
obvious that the Pope would reject such an arrangement.
He could do nothing else, for it represented beyond any
doubt a clear infringement of the rights of the Church.
Sicily was unquestionably a papal fief, and an assumption
of sovereignty without the consent of the suzerain was
definitely a breach of the law.[1] The Pope rejected the

Accession of King James.

---

[1] An account of this mission and of the speeches exchanged is found
in a report of one of the envoys, Bartholomew. However, this account
is true to the spirit of its time, and does not adhere strictly to historical
truth. It must be accepted with reserve, especially as regards the
text of the speeches delivered. Printed in Muratori, *Scriptores*, xiii.

embassy and, on April 1, 1286, he extended the excommunication declared against the dead King Peter to his son James and the latter's mother Costanza. With that the Pope's attitude was declared unequivocally. In the short period intervening between May 3 and November 18, 1286, he issued four further bans against both.[1] He declared the coronation invalid, and Bartholomew of Neocastro maintains that the Pope tried to draw Sicily away from Aragon and, even while the war between Philip and Peter was in progress, sent two monks, Perronus de Aydona and Antonius de Monte, to abbot William de Maniachi with a letter promising release from the ban of excommunication to all who reconciled themselves to the Church and entered its service,[2] this being an attempt to withdraw the Sicilians from the House of Aragon. No trace of such a letter is to be found in the Pope's *Regesta*. The authority for its existence is a partisan of Aragon, and it is to be used accordingly with the greatest discretion. Such a procedure is not in harmony with the Pope's frank disposition. Perhaps the doubtful communication is to be connected with a letter of the Pope's to his legate and regent in Sicily, Gerhard, in which he empowered the latter to free from the ban of excommunication those who, despite previous adherence to Peter, now admitted and regretted their error. This power of remission was stated expressly not to apply to the islanders,[3] but we can quite well believe that individual preachers, with or without the legate's knowledge, invited the people of the island to abandon Aragon, holding out to all who did so hopes of being released from the ban. But a papal campaign on these lines

---

[1] *Reg.*, 494, 768, 807.

[2] Muratori, *Scriptores*, xiii, p. 1112.

[3] *Reg.*, 477.

is hardly credible. In any event, even according to
Bartholomew, the efforts in Sicily were a lamentable
failure. They only attracted a few people who held
secret conferences in Messina regarding future developments ; these meetings becoming known, all those who
took part in them were arrested before any further steps
could be taken. The two monks were sent back to
Naples—which appears to be a proof that the proceedings
emanated from the legate, not from the Pope—some
of their companions being held prisoners while others
were executed for participation in a conspiracy. The
report states further that Abbot William was sent to
the papal court after a short imprisonment. Perhaps
the Sicilians expected that the Pope would view them
more tolerantly because they had not punished the
responsible clerics more severely, but had merely deported
them from Sicily. However, the Pope's attitude in
the matter was so fixed that nothing could affect it.

Honorius called on James and Costanza, the two rulers
of the island, to leave Sicily before the Feast of the
Ascension. When they did not obey, all places where
they sojourned were laid under an interdict. The bishops
who had attended the coronation were summoned to
Rome to explain themselves.[1] But excommunication
and interdicts had been used too often, especially against
dilatory tax-payers, and they had ceased to have much
effect. Neither the new king nor the bishops took any
notice. On the contrary, James proceeded from the
defensive to the offensive. The dreaded Admiral Roger
de Loria visited the French coast with his fleet, and at
the same time Bernardo da Sarriano, acting on his orders,
landed on the Roman littoral, plundering and burning
Astura. This particular place was chosen because the
government of Astura was in the hands of a son of that

---

[1] *Reg.*, 768, 807.

Giovanni Frangipani who in the past had taken Conradin prisoner when in flight after the battle of Tagliacozzo, and had delivered him up to Charles of Anjou. Now the son had to suffer for the father's deeds and lose his life during the sack of Astura (September 4, 1286). The Pope's answer to this defiance was an ineffectual excommunication and a threat to remove the bishops from rank and office unless they appeared at the Holy See before *Lætare* Sunday [1] (March 16, 1287).

One European monarch, King Edward I of England, exerted himself honourably to bring the Sicilian confusion to a conclusion acceptable to all parties. Personal motives may possibly have weighed with him, but beyond question the chief incentives to his noble efforts were his desire for unity among Christians and his interest in the Holy Land. Even under Martin IV. he had initiated an attempt to restore peace, but it was doomed to failure from the beginning. Prospects improved when Pope Honorius, skilled in diplomacy and independent in policy, was elected. As soon as the King received intimation of the election he at once sent an envoy to the Head of the Church to convey his congratulations on the election and, at the same time, to implore the Pope's co-operation in establishing a just peace. At the moment the Pope felt himself unable to accede to the request because as the King of France had just achieved his first successes in Aragon " in the service of the Church ", he did not wish to interfere with him. He permitted, however, that emissaries of the King of England should be sent to Charles II, who was a prisoner, for the purpose of negotiations, without regard to the interdict in Sicily.[2]

Circumstances changed when the struggle between Philip III. and Aragon took a course unfavourable to

England's mediation.

---

[1] *Reg.*, 806, 807.   [2] *Reg.*, 938 ; Rymer, *Fœdera*, i, ii, 239.

France. There could no longer be any question of hampering Philip, and the Pope now urged Edward not to slacken his efforts for peace,[1] admitting while so doing the difficulties, which were serious.[2] These difficulties were not raised by Charles II, who was ready to renounce Sicily in exchange for his liberty, but by the Pope and the cardinals, who believed that in no circumstances could they abrogate the Church's rights, and who, being more Angevin than the Angevins themselves, would not allow Angevin rights over Sicily to be infringed. While the children of the imprisoned prince and the barons and prelates of Provence and Forcalquier were calling out for peace ; while Charles II himself formally renounced Sicily, the Pope stood firmly for Angevin rights over Sicily. Thus there developed an episode which was almost grotesque when Charles II, who had declared early in 1285 that he was prepared in return for his release to renounce Sicily, signed a treaty in Barcelona on February 27, 1287, at the instigation of his friends and followers. By its terms he renounced all claim to Sicily and the adjoining islands, to the bishopric of Reggio, and to the Tunisian tribute, in favour of James of Aragon and his heirs. He further declared himself ready to use his influence with the Pope to induce the latter to take cognizance of this renunciation and to raise the ecclesiastical punishments incurred by the late Peter of Aragon and his wife and son. This treaty was to be stabilized by a double marriage, and Charles was to be set free as soon as the Pope gave his consent. Meanwhile hostilities were to be merely interrupted by an armistice. Charles sent an embassy to Rome to procure the Pope's consent to the treaty and thus gain for him his freedom, an assumption rejected angrily by Honorius who declared

[1] *Reg.*, 920.　　　　　[2] *Reg.*, 944.

his astonishment that Charles should be willing to betray
to rebels the rights of the Church and of his own house.
He declared not only that the treaty of Barcelona was
null and void, but likewise any other treaty bearing on
the matter, declaring that there was only one basis
on which peace could be concluded with Sicily—unconditional submission to the judgment of the Church.
As a consolation he conceded to the imprisoned prince
the privilege of having Low Mass celebrated for him
and his family by his own chaplain in spite of the interdict
imposed on the country.[1] Before any further decisions
could be taken the Pope died.

Thus his rigid adherence to a legal position prevented
him from bringing the matter to a termination. Still
less was he able to set at naught or cry a halt to a movement which had already made history. Sicily remained
lost to the Angevins ; but no agreement was reached
until 1302 under Pope Boniface VIII.

Sicily remained lost to the Angevins, despite the Sicilian
assistance, not moral only but financial, given to them by tithes.
the Pope, who indeed financed the war. Martin IV.
had applied to Sicily [2] most of the money raised for the
Holy Land, and in addition had granted to Charles of
Anjou for three years tithes from Italy, Corsica, and
Sardinia, to enable him to recover Sicily. He was not
able to issue regulations for the collection of these tithes,
as he died soon after granting them. Immediately
after he assumed office Honorius arranged for the
collection. Italy was divided into five tithe districts
and collectors appointed for each.[3] Further, the Pope
issued exact instructions as to the methods of collection.[4]
They are based on earlier models. The first unified

[1] *Reg.*, 813, 814 ; Potthast, 22581, 22582.
[2] *Cf.* p. 346.
[3] *Reg.*, 12. *Cf.* also *Reg.*, 36, 38.
[4] *Reg.* 60.

code of regulations for the collection of tithes dates from 1267 and relates to a three years' French tithe under Clement IV. Gregory X. adapted it for the Lyons Crusade Tithes, and with but few alterations it was issued by Honorius in 1285. Of the fifty-three individual rules, the following deserve mention : Religious houses which serve the poor or sick are exempt, as are female houses the members of which live on charity, and clergy with an annual income not exceeding seven pounds of Tours. Detailed rules are given for the assessment of benefices and the amounts to be paid. Tithes need not be paid on outlay essential to the maintenance of the benefice holder, but must be paid on outlay which was merely useful. Payment must be made on stole fees and bequests but not on " *pitantiæ* ", which were additional grants, nor on special offerings intended for particular purposes, nor on offerings for candles and the like, nor on sums given for the maintenance of Church fittings and furniture. Also exempt from tithes were offerings given to bury the poor when these were collected from the laity. Payments made by a parish priest to his curates might be deducted from the tithe assessment, but not amounts used for their maintenance. Attendance fees were assessed for tithe payment. Whether the tithe should be paid at once or in instalments was left to the judgment of the tithe-payer, but if he decided on payment in one sum that decision remained fixed and was registered by the collector.

Payment had to be in cash.[1] Any person who knowingly and deceitfully paid less than he was liable for was visited with excommunication. But the secular power was to be invoked only in case the offender was so obstinate as to be unaffected by ecclesiastical punishment. The names of excommunicated persons were to

---

[1] A decree which no doubt strengthened the financial position.

be read out every Sunday with ringing of bells and
this was to continue until they had paid their debts.
Release from punishment was not to take place until
the debt had been paid in full. In doubtful cases of
small importance the collectors could decide themselves ;
serious cases were to be referred to the Holy See. In
addition to the general exemptions the Pope arranged
for abatement or exemption in special cases, in particular
in the case of members of certain orders.[1] Exemption
was frequently associated with proof that these orders
used their funds for the sick and the poor. As regards
the collector's remuneration the Pope arranged that
the collector might deduct one golden florin a day and
that the sub-collectors should be exempt from the
obligation of paying tithes while engaged in collecting
them.[2]

If the efforts of Pope Honorius to recover Sicily for
the Angevins were hopeless and doomed to failure, his
legislative activity on behalf of the south Italian portions
of the kingdom was important and successful, and in
fact had decisive effects on future developments. In
this respect the Pope's attitude was diametrically opposed
to that of Martin IV.

Legislative measures regarding the Kingdom of Sicily.

Martin IV. had given Charles of Anjou unlimited
authority over Sicily. Charles had one thought only
in mind, to create a world empire for himself. His rule
throughout the kingdom was relentless and quite
unnecessarily severe, although he was less to blame in
that regard than his officials, who had formerly been
enterprising knights in his country, and who, having
nothing to lose in Sicily, wished to amass fortunes there
as quickly as possible, being, moreover, men with no
sense of justice or righteousness. While Martin IV.

Situation in the kingdom.

[1] *Reg.*, 207, 258, 304, 498, 541, 749.
[2] *Reg.*, 12.

regarded the Sicilian Vespers as the outcome of a conspiracy, Honorius admitted[1] that the reason for the
Sicilians' revolt was to be found in "excessive
oppression". When accepting the fief, Charles of Anjou
had undertaken to avoid all oppression, to abolish abuses
disadvantageous to the people which had arisen in the
course of centuries, and to restore the law to the status
it occupied under King William II. († 1189), who was
greatly revered by the Sicilians. He made no effort
to carry out these promises. Some of the Popes had
reproved him for this,[2] but Martin IV. had no word of
censure for him. Even when Charles, impelled by
circumstances, took some steps towards giving the
people justice, the Pope did not approve of it.

Charles of Anjou was much too astute a politician
not to realize the seriousness of the situation when the
Sicilian revolution broke out. He knew, too, where
the movement had its roots, and was determined
to remove the causes of dissatisfaction in order
to prevent a spread of the revolt to the mainland.
The necessity to do so became more acute when Peter
of Aragon took immediate measures to set aside the
excessive burdens borne by the people of the island
and to restore the laws as they had been under
William II. Charles saw himself obliged in consequence to root out the abuses which had acquired
the force of law in the administration of the kingdom.
On June 10, 1282, he issued fifty-eight decrees at Naples,
intended to alleviate the worst hardships and to assure
to the people their fundamental rights.[3] When his son,
Charles of Salerno, succeeded, he, too, continued what
had been so happily begun. He assembled the temporal

---

[1] *Reg.*, 96.
[2] *Cf.* Raynaldus, ann. 1266, 1268.
[3] *Constitutiones regni utriusque Siciliæ*, p. 307 ff. (Venice, 1580).

and the spiritual nobility of the kingdom and the representatives of the towns on the plain before St. Martin's in Calabria in a parliament, where the privileges of each order were guaranteed and their duties determined harmoniously. In part the arrangement was intended to be merely temporary, for he undertook to revive the rules that had existed under William II. To do so it was necessary to discover first what the position then had been. It was decided that the individual cities should send expert envoys to Pope Martin IV., and that in this way the old rules should be re-established by the Pope. A number of cities did as arranged but the Pope refused the task which had been assigned to him. He was more concerned with the interests of the House of Anjou than the Angevins themselves. Clearly he feared lest the rich revenues of the kingdom should be too much curtailed, for a diminution in the rights of the Church or a financial sacrifice on the part of the Pope was not in question. Without investigating the legal position under William II., he dismissed the envoys with the remark that it would be impossible to determine what the conditions under William II. had been, and that one should not act hastily or lightly in such an important matter : a decision on the question should be left until later.[1] This was tantamount to postponing reform until the Greek Kalends.

In this way Martin had actually obstructed the making of laws which would be in favour of the oppressed people. He satisfied himself with instructing his legate to determine what were the rules of William's laws in matters of taxes and dues, and this did not lead to any practical result. Not until the dying King of Sicily, feeling the weight perhaps of his responsibility for his kingdom and filled with anxiety for his realm if the reforms should

---

[1] Potthast, 22042 (July 1, 1283).

not be established, appealed again to the Pope to carry
out those reforms, did Martin decide to summon representatives of the Sicilian towns to consider a reform
in the laws relating to taxes and dues. Before he could
do more death robbed him of the opportunity to make
good his earlier delays.

Steps taken
by Pope
Honorius.

This was the position when Pope Honorius assumed
control of the Church. He departed from Martin's
line of conduct and exerted himself to restore order and
justice. After a zealous study of the matter and in
consultation with the cardinals, he issued two bulls
on September 17, 1285, which regulated the legal position
in the kingdom of Sicily for the immediate future, and
influenced it for a considerable time to come. One
of these [1] bulls is practically a repetition of a part of the
laws of the assembly of Calabria, arranged in seventeen
sections : it guarantees to the various ranks of society
their rights and privileges. The second [2] also reproduces
many forgotten provisions of earlier collections of laws,
particularly those dating from the reign of William II.
It consists of forty-five ordinances intended to protect
the people from self-seeking oppressors and from depriva-
tion of their rights by officials. In terse sentences the
Pope develops his political philosophy in an introduction :
every community must be founded on justice and peace,
which are themselves most closely connected and either
of which is impossible without the other. Likewise
the policy of the authorities towards their subjects
must be dictated by justice. When the authorities
once depart from this position the thrones of monarchs
begin to totter. No doubt a popular uprising against
injustice can be crushed by force for a while, but its
strength will be all the more primitive when sooner or
later it overflows, and it will then carry everything before

------

[1] *Reg.*, 97.   [2] *Reg.*, 96.

it. Sicily was the best example of this thesis. The
people of that country had been oppressed since the
time of Frederick II., and the position had become worse
under the Angevins. Hence, revolt had broken out
there.[1] The Pope now desired by the issue of his forty-five
ordinances to help to restore justice and peace.

The historical title by which this important decree
is known is " Constitutio super ordinatione regni Siciliæ "
or else " Provisio (Ordinatio) super bono statu regni
Siciliæ ". The most important regulations included in
it are the following :—

The *subventio generalis*, a levy collected by the King,
was in future to be collected as of old on four occasions
only, and not more than once a year nor beyond an
amount fixed by the Pope. The four occasions were :
(1) to equip an army for the necessary protection of the
country in case of war or rebellion at home ; (2) to ransom
an imprisoned sovereign. In these two sets of circumstances a levy might be made up to 50,000 ounces of
gold. The remaining occasions were : (3) to arm a son
or other near male relative of the King ; or (4) to marry
a daughter, sister, or other near female relative of the
King. In the former case the amount allowed was
12,000 ounces of gold, in the latter 15,000. The allevia-
tion which this implied may be understood when we read
that Ameri [2] calculated the amount levied by this tax
in 1276—a year of peace—according to the material
in the Naples archives, to be more than 60,000 ounces
of gold. Later the assessment increased steadily.

---

[1] This admission by the Pope is significant as being in opposition
to his predecessor's view. According to Martin, the whole thing was
a trumped-up revolt, a *coup* of Peter of Aragon. (*Cf.* p. 229.) On the
other hand, it is remarkable that the Pope did not draw the inevitable
conclusions from this admission, to abolish the unjust Angevin regime
which had been swept away by the will of the people, and to make
peace with Aragon, which was the mere instrument of the popular will.

[2] *La guerra del Vespro Siciliano*, i, p. 79 ff. (Milan, 1886).

Other State contributions were in a similar way regulated and reduced to reasonable dimensions. Compensation payment for an unsolved murder, which in such cases had to be paid by the community where the murder took place, was fixed, that for a murdered Christian being double the amount for a heretic.

The constitutions provide also that the King may issue a new coin only once and that such issue be of full value. By this means trade and commerce were protected from injury through the arbitrary issue of debased coinage.

Exact and moderate fees were fixed for the services rendered by officials. Of importance was the determination of feudal succession and the regulation of feudal relations generally, and another important moral provision was the abolition of all marriage prohibitions issued by the King. For the future the marriages of the nobility were not to require the King's consent.

The rights and duties of vassals were also set out clearly. Investigations arising from complaints might only be carried out in the presence of the accused, unless the latter remained absent obstinately and wilfully. He must be informed of the points in the accusation and given an opportunity to defend himself. Any person whose rights were interfered with had the right of appeal to the Holy See. No person could be prevented from making use of this right or suffer any injurious consequences through availing himself of it. In the last provision the Pope reserved expressly to the Holy See the interpretation of any possible doubtful cases. These constitutions were signed by the Pope and fourteen cardinals.[1]

Of the seventeen provisions of the second bull, which concern the rights and privileges of the estates,

---

[1] *Cf.* Prou's introduction, *Reg.*, pp. xxxiv–xlviii.

particularly those of the clerical estate, the following
deserve mention :—

Clerics may not be summoned before a secular court,
except in fief matters where it is provided for expressly
in a convention between the King and the princes of
the Church. The right of asylum must remain sacred,
save in the cases excepted by the common law. The
houses of ecclesiastical personages might not be requisi-
tioned without their consent by officials, nor might
official business be carried on therein without their
express permission. Lay persons might not interfere
in church elections, conferring of benefices, or other
spiritual matters of any kind whatsoever, nor in the
proceedings of the ecclesiastical courts, save in so far
as patronage rights or other special rights so ordain.
Ancient rights of the Church and of spiritual persons
must remain intact. The Church's right to inherit is
stated specifically, and spiritual persons and institutions
are entitled to insist on the payment of debts due to
them. Jews who are vassals of the Church may not
have incumbencies imposed on them, nor any other
particular duties.

The bull is likewise signed by the Pope and the
cardinals. The Pope ordered the two regents, the count
of Artois and the legate, to have the constitutions
announced solemnly in all the towns,[1] and Raynaldus
states in his *Annals*[2] that count Robert administered
the oath to the two constitutions to all officials. Honorius
even laid down severe ecclesiastical punishments for
disregard of these regulations.

During his pontificate they were unquestionably
valid State laws, but when Charles II came to the throne
on his release from imprisonment, he asked the Pope's
successor to repeal the ecclesiastical penalties provided

---

[1] *Reg.*, 98. [2] Sub ann. 1285.

for a breach of the constitutions. Pope Nicholas, while
not setting the constitutions aside, did actually abolish
the ecclesiastical penal sanctions. After that certain
provisions which were inconvenient to the king were
no longer observed, while he took his stand on others
as being papal decrees, when they were to his advantage.
If the constitutions had full and unrestricted legal force
for but a short time, nevertheless their importance
for the development of the administration of the kingdom
remained. It is significant that King James included
many of the provisions in the constitution which he drew
up for the kingdom.[1] Honorius himself contemplated
a certain limitation on the force of these laws, for he
decreed expressly that the alleviations which they
contained could not be claimed by apostates or rebels.[2]

The issue of these two constitutions was the most
important act performed by the Pope as suzerain of
Sicily. His remaining decrees were in line with his
usual tendencies, namely, to preserve peace by the
exercise of leniency. He empowered the legate to remit
the ecclesiastical punishment incurred in cases where
persons who had once assisted Peter of Aragon had since
returned to obedience to the Church.[3] This instruction
was hardly an attempt to draw the Sicilians away from
Aragon by promises and leniency: it was rather a
manifestation of the Pope's policy of remitting punishments which had lost their justification and of exercising
leniency instead: as soon as penance and atonement
has taken place, an ecclesiastical punishment has no
longer any inward justification. On the other hand,
he acted with the utmost severity against all ecclesiastics
who had associated themselves with the anti-Angevin
movement. For example, he issued orders to Bishop

---

[1] *Cf.* Giannone, *l.c.*, iii, 106.

[2] *Reg.*, 99. *Cf.* Potthast, 22289–93.

[3] *Reg.*, 282, 290, 477.

Paschalis of Larino through his Metropolitan, the archbishop of Benevento, to appear within a month before the Holy See to justify himself, as he was alleged to have instructed the members of his diocese to rise against the rule of the Angevins.[1] But he was ready to forgive even serious crimes as soon as the evil-doers had atoned for them and asked him for absolution. He gave proof of this by releasing Henry of Castile and Riccardus Annibaldi from ecclesiastical punishments. The former had been a zealous partisan of Conradin whom he had received at Rome when he was a senator. Taken prisoner at the battle of Tagliacozzo, he had since remained imprisoned and excommunicated. The Pope, however, now absolved him after he had done penance. The second-named had been *podestà* of Viterbo and as such had interfered in the papal election of 1280–81 : he had also been guilty of numerous offences against the Church and its priests. He, too, was now released from punishment after he had visited the principal churches at Rome as a penitent, going barefoot as a sign of penance and with a rope around his neck.[2]

As in the papal States, the Pope was able to re-establish peace and order in southern Italy. He himself described his task as follows : " Not alone among the powerful and the great, but also among all other degrees of the kingdom of Sicily should there be an absence of disorder and strife, and all methods must be employed to maintain peace and harmony." [3] This he succeeded in doing in an exemplary fashion, but peace did not continue for long when his reign ended, a proof of the fact that it was the consequence of his methods of governing.

No change deserving of mention took place in the Curia.

---

[1] *Reg.*, 468.

[2] Pawlicki erroneously represents these two persons as one (p. 47 ff.).

[3] *Reg.*, 556.

administrative machinery of the Curia under Honorius.
The head of the papal chancery was the same as during
the previous pontificate, namely, Master Petrus Peregrossus of Milan.[1] He is noteworthy for the severity
with which he visited forgeries of papal bulls. On hearing
of one such case he ordered the evil-doer to be sent
prisoner to the Curia.[2]

Tabellium.　　Pope Honorius conferred the office of *tabellio* [3] to
a far greater extent than his predecessor had done.
In eighty-five cases he himself appointed *tabelliones*, and
in twenty-eight cases he gave others powers to appoint
suitable men to the office. Usually permission was
given for one or two appointments ; power to make
six was given only in the case of the papal legate to
Germany. Of the nominees, eleven have been shown
to be laymen ; the rest were Franciscans. As an
examiner of qualifications we find in the beginning
Nicholas of Terracina, who had also acted under
Martin IV. from July 31, 1285, or it was usually the
papal chaplain Hugolinus of St. Michael, but sometimes
another papal chaplain, Pandulf de Suburra, or Master
Peregrinus de Andirano, Master Johannes, Rogerius de
Salerno, the papal chaplain Master Garsia, and on one
occasion the vice-chancellor Peter of Milan himself.
The other examiners were probably also, in the main,
officials of the papal chancery. While Martin gave power
to confer the office of *tabellio* but once on a person who
was not a bishop, we find three cases during the much
shorter reign of Honorius, namely, the Provincial of
the Dominicans in France, the Inquisitor Philip of
Mantua, and Geoffrey of Veçano.

　　To sum up, the Italian policy of Pope Honorius IV.

---

[1] Potthast, 22227.

[2] *Reg.*, 493.

[3] *Cf.* p. 220.

may be described as clear-sighted and wise, tolerant and social. By the exercise of those qualities he succeeded in securing peace and order in Italy, to an extent unknown before or after these decades. Only in the island of Sicily, where the Pope departed from his usual maxims of government, did he leave matters in a state of disorder to his successor.

CHAPTER III.

POLICY OF POPE HONORIUS OUTSIDE ITALY. GERMANY.
ENGLAND. FRANCE. ARAGON. CASTILE. HUNGARY.

THE foreign policy of Pope Honorius was dictated by
the interests of the Church. Whereas Nicholas III.
had not been able to suppress his feelings as an Italian
and Martin IV. had definitely remained a Frenchman,
Honorius made an honest effort to determine his political
position entirely as the weal of the Church demanded.
In this he resumed the political tendencies of Gregory X.
His entire foreign policy was based on an endeavour
to unite firmness and gentleness in a sound conservatism.

Relations
with the
Empire.

His relations with Germany stood naturally in the
foreground of his political interests. While Martin
reigned, the efforts of the German monarch, Rudolf of
Habsburg, to be crowned emperor were doomed to failure.
Honorius, on the contrary, adopted from the beginning
a friendly attitude towards Rudolf, and he could afford
to do so without any fears for the Church. Under
Martin France had become paramount and the papacy
was dependent on it. Centralizing tendencies in France
strengthened the realm more and more, and Church
independence became of necessity more and more
doubtful. Co-operation with Germany on the other
hand offered a certain counterpoise to this and did not
signify danger to the Church. For the Empire had been
gradually breaking up since the time of the Hohenstaufen. Centrifugal force was growing stronger and
stronger ; the development of territories with State
jurisdiction and the aggrandizing policy of the individual
princes left the Empire weak and innocuous.

The matter which Honorius had to deal with first

was not new to him. Together with cardinal Bertrand
of St. Sabina and Giovanni Orsini, he had been entrusted
by Hadrian V. with the negotiations regarding the imperial
coronation of Rudolf. This fact was bound to influence
Rudolf to send an embassy to the Pope immediately on First
his election. It was headed by Henry of Klingenberg, Embassy.
the Royal Protonotary, and its mission was to convey
to the Pope the congratulations of King Rudolf on his
election, and to assure him that Rudolf was prepared
to be helpful to the heirs of King Charles I. of Sicily,
among whom was his own son-in-law. At the same time
it was to request a favourable decision in the matter
of the filling of the archbishopric of Mainz, and the
revocation of the decree ordering tithes to be collected
for France against Aragon in the dioceses on Germany's
western frontier. Finally, Henry was probably entrusted
with giving expression to Rudolf's view regarding the
Imperial Coronation.

Only in the matter of remitting the Aragon tithes
was the Pope disobliging, and in that he took his stand
on the fact that King Philip's campaign had been undertaken on behalf of the Church. In all else he showed
himself most cordial, as Rudolf had hoped. In his
reply, dated August 1, 1285,[1] he thanked the King for
his exertions on behalf of the Church and of the heirs
of Charles of Anjou, and he promised to fill the Mainz
vacancy in a manner that would satisfy him. Probably
the Pope himself did not see quite clearly in the matter
at this time, for the legal position had not yet been
clarified. Archbishop Werner had died at Mainz on
April 2, 1284, and a double election followed. One
section of the Cathedral chapter elected the provost of
the chapter, Peter of Reichenstein; the other section
chose a cousin of the deceased archbishop, prebendary

---

[1] *Reg.*, 476 ; Potthast, 22276.

Gerard of Eppenstein, archdeacon of Trier. Both applied to Pope Martin for a decision and the latter had authorized cardinal-deacon Benedict to investigate the whole matter. His investigation had not been completed when this first embassy of Rudolf's arrived. The latter had accordingly to be satisfied with the Pope's assurance —which, however, in itself was very valuable—that the Pope would appoint a bishop pleasing to him, if investigation should show that the nomination lay with the Pope. King Rudolf's great interest in the matter can be simply explained in the light of the fact that the archbishop of Mainz as chancellor of the Roman Empire was one of the most influential of the electors. In view of his efforts to preserve the crown in his family the filling of this electoral position was a matter of the utmost importance to him.

Second
Embassy. The negotiations carried on by the Royal Protonotary regarding Rudolf's journey to Rome and his coronation as Emperor must have been successful, for as early as November, 1285, we find Rudolf arranging to send another embassy to the Pope from Lausanne. The credentials are dated November 22.[1] Among the ambassadors were Magister Lupold of Wiltingen, William of Befort, Peter, the provost and bishop-elect of Mainz, and the knight, Marquard of Ifenthal. At the same time the king began his preparations for the journey to Rome. He first appointed the papal chaplain Percival Fiesco, count of Lavagna, to be vicar-general of Tuscany. The choice fell on him because he had been for a long time in intimate contact with Rudolf and with the King of England, and above all—as brother of Pope Hadrian V.—with the Curia. In him Rudolf thought he had found a man who would also be *persona grata* in Rome and who would find it all the easier on that account

---

[1] Redlich, *Reg.*, 1949, 1950.

to establish order in Tuscany, as was essential to the march to Rome.[1]

The delegation sent to Rome had the double mission of having a date fixed for the coronation of the Emperor by the Pope and of obtaining sanction for financial assistance to carry out the march to Rome. It was obliged to return without having attained these objects, why is not quite clear. It is surmised that the members of the delegation had not been selected with sufficient care, and this surmise finds support in a hint given to Rudolf by cardinal Uberto as early as November, 1274, a hint which was not sufficiently heeded at the time. In accordance with the Curia usage, the cardinal had written to the King that in the matter of the imperial coronation he should send an embassy of distinguished men, of high spiritual and temporal rank and dignity, in keeping with the importance of the occasion and Roman usage. This hint had certainly not been regarded in the appointment of the delegation led by the Cathedral provost. Perhaps, too, the latter may have in some way aroused antagonism in Rome and made himself *persona ingrata,* which would also explain why the Pope did not select him when filling the Archepiscopal See of Mainz. It is also possible that the powers with which the delegation was endowed were inadequate.[2] In any case the only result was that the King had to send a fresh delegation.

About two months later Rudolf once more dispatched an embassy to Rome, this time from Augsburg. As its head he selected the very skilful Henry of Isny, bishop of Basle, a Franciscan, said to have been at one time Guardian in Lucerne and as such formerly confessor

Third Embassy to Rome.

---

[1] Redlich, *Reg.,* 1951.
[2] Pawlicki's view, that the delegation had no powers, is in contradiction to the fact that the credentials exist in the Vatican Archives.

to count Rudolf of Habsburg and his family. Absolute
proof of this cannot be produced,[1] but in any case he
knew Rudolf before he became King and, according to
the Königfeld Chronicle, he appears to have played some
part in Rudolf's elevation.[2] He had been a member
of the delegation which Rudolf had sent to Pope
Gregory X. nine months after he became King. At
that time he was Lecturer in Theology at the Franciscan
monastery at Mainz. Other members of the delegation
were the Vice-Chancellor, Henry of Klingenberg, who
had successfully led the first embassy to Honorius,
and the Count Palatine Protonotary, Provost Albert of
Illmunster. We can see that this time the ambassadors
were chosen with much greater care and regard to rank
and position. The main purpose of the mission was
to have a date fixed for the coronation, but it was also
entrusted with bringing the question of the vacancy
in the Archepiscopal See of Mainz to a satisfactory issue,
with procuring the dispatch of a papal legate to Germany,
and with achieving agreement regarding the Imperial
Vicariate of Tuscany. In the event of Percival not
being acceptable to the papal court, bishop Henry was
to treat with Orso Orsini or cardinal Matteo Orsini
regarding the filling of this office.[3] On February 1 the
credentials of the ambassadors were drawn up, as well
as a number of recommendations to the notable cardinals
and officials of the Curia, and also to the cities of
Lombardy, Tuscany, and the Romagna, as well as the
Margraves of Este and Ancona. The credentials
addressed to the Pope empowered " his dear prince
and privy councillor, bishop Henry of Basle " to give

---

[1] Cf. Eubel, *Historisches Jahrbuch*, ix, p. 393 ff.
[2] Eubel, *l.c.*, 396.
[3] Cf. Redlich, *Reg.*, 1973, 1974, 1951 ; Hampe, *Histor. Viertel-
jahresschrift*, iii, 540.

the sworn undertakings required by the Pope as a preliminary to the coronation of King Rudolf as Emperor.[1]

This embassy was entirely successful, more so indeed
than Rudolf himself had anticipated, in consequence no
doubt primarily of the skill and charm of the leader of
the delegation.[2] He procured the agreement of the
Curia to the nomination of Percival as Imperial Vicar
of Tuscany, and the Pope called on the inhabitants of
Tuscany to obey the Imperial Vicar (May 17, 1286).[3]
But its greatest success was the decision regarding the
filling of the Mainz See. Bishop Henry was commissioned by the King to recommend Henry of Klingenberg, a member of the embassy, to the Pope for some
high church dignity on the grounds of his capacity and
his services.[4] Beyond a doubt this was a modest way
of putting him forward for the position of Archbishop
of Mainz. To Rudolf's great astonishment, no doubt,
the Pope appointed, not Henry of Klingenberg nor
either of the two candidates who had been selected
previously, but no other than the leader of the delegation,
bishop Henry of Basle. On May 5, 1286, Pope Honorius
informed King Rudolf that the two candidates elected
in the dual election had renounced their claims and that
he had appointed bishop Henry of Basle, in spite of his
resistance,[5] archbishop of Mainz, because of his remarkable
qualities and services, and had given him the *pallium*.
The Pope requested the King to grant his protection to
the new archbishop and his church. No request made

[1] Redlich, *Reg.*, 1972–82, 1986–8.
[2] A letter from Bishop Henry to King Rudolf apprising the latter
of his success is not genuine, but merely a *tour de force*.
[3] *Reg.*, 912 ; Potthast, 22416. *Cf.* Ficker, *Forschungen zur
Reichs- und Rechtsgeschichte Italiens*, 4, 488.
[4] Redlich, *Reg.*, 1992.
[5] Redlich, *Reg.*, 2021 : ". . . quamquam tanti oneris et honoris
subire sarcinam formidando nostro in hac parte proposito importune in
quantum licuit restitisset . . ." Potthast, 22439.

by the Pope could have been more welcome to Rudolf. It put his closest confidant thus into the most influential position in the Empire as chancellor and elector. By doing this Honorius expressed his goodwill towards Rudolf and the German Empire more clearly than he could have done by lengthy declarations. It showed, too, that he was interested in strengthening the German Empire, for it was a powerful support for the King to have in the See of Mainz such a trusted and reliable friend. In order to compensate the two former candidates the Pope appointed the Cathedral Provost, Peter of Reichenstein, who had been recommended by Rudolf, to the position formerly held by Henry of Basle, giving him power to have the higher orders conferred by any bishop within the prescribed interval—up to then he had been merely a sub-deacon. On May 19 he gave a dispensation regarding plurality of benefices to the second candidate, Gerard of Eppenstein.

It was equally important for the King to have a date fixed for the imperial coronation. On May 31, 1286, Honorius informed King Rudolf that he had appointed February 2, 1287, after consultation with the cardinals ; this represented a mutual support of *sacerdotium* and *imperium* on the one hand and, on the other, it accorded with the urgent request put forward by the Archbishop of Mainz on behalf of the king. At the same time he notified the electoral princes of the date, and about two months later (on July 22) he called on them to furnish Rudolf with financial assistance for his imminent journey to Rome.[1] While fixing a date for the coronation he appointed, in accordance with " repeated pressing requests " of King Rudolf, the cardinal-bishop John of Tusculum as legate to Germany to advise King Rudolf

---

[1] *Reg.*, 550, 551 ; Redlich, *Reg.*, 2023 ; *Reg.*, 806 ; Kaltenbrunner, 311 ; Potthast, 22465, 22466.

regarding his expedition to Rome,[1] and at the same time as legate to Bohemia, Poland, Pomerania, Kashubia, Prussia, Livonia, Russia, Denmark, and Sweden. He instructed and exhorted the spiritual and temporal dignitaries of those countries to receive the legate well.[2]

John de Boccomati, cardinal-bishop of Tusculum, was the only cardinal appointed by Honorius, and was related to him personally. Honorius had the highest opinion of him and described him on occasion as a man of proven discretion and one of knowledge and efficiency.[3] He also appointed him his executor.[4] It was certainly a proof of his goodwill that he should appoint a man whom he respected so highly as legate to Germany. He endowed him with extensive powers and privileges, particularly as regards dispensing power,[5] such as we have seen given to Martin's legates. He was given the right of demanding *procuratio*, and the legate made use of this power, such an extensive use indeed that it caused the first dissatisfaction in Germany. Honorius took some pains to avoid excessive burdens. In order to save the dioceses on the western border of Germany from a double levying of *procuratio* he instructed his legate in France to omit for one year the collection of dues from the German dioceses within his jurisdiction, the following dioceses being mentioned expressly : Liège,

---

[1] In the reign of Nicholas III. Rudolf had succeeded in getting a legate appointed to Germany, the Cardinal-Priest Hieronymus of the church of St. Pudentiana being contemplated for the position, but the matter did not come to a head owing to the death of the Pope. It throws a significant light on the relations between Martin IV. and Rudolf that the sending of a legate was never mentioned between them. Not until Honorius was Pope did the King take the matter up again— this time with success—a success, it is true, other than that hoped for and desired by him.

[2] *Reg.*, 770 ; Potthast, 22467–9.

[3] Theiner, *Cod. dipl.*, 292.

[4] *Reg.*, 823, 830. For his other offices *cf. Reg.*, 344, 351, 363, 373.

[5] *Reg.*, 772–805 ; Potthast, 22470–2.

Metz, Toul, Verdun, Basle, and Cambrai. It is significant that in this list the Lorraine bishoprics are mentioned, but not those of Burgundy, with the exception of Basle, for which Bishop Henry had obtained relief when in Rome.[1] This consideration was not particularly appreciated in Germany, but was taken rather as a matter of course. The *procuratio* was felt rather keenly and the legate took more pains to make it so than one might have expected. In this John showed his character to be different from that given to him by the Pope. It must be admitted frankly that his methods contributed to increasing dissatisfaction in Germany.[2] He did not leave the Curia until August, when he proceeded with a great retinue to Milan and across the Alps to Basle. At once he laid claim to the grant of *procuratio*. These burdens were felt all the more because the people were unaccustomed to them, for no legate had been in the district for decades, since 1254–5. On September 24 and 25 he demanded from the bishops of Breslau and Brandenburg within a month 150 marks each and 110 marks from the bishop of Olmütz, immediate payment being required under threat of suspension and excommunication. Similar demands were presented to other bishoprics and monasteries. For example, 10 marks were claimed from the poor monastery of Schliersee in Upper Bavaria and the religious there in consequence were forced to sell a mill.[3]

An evil reputation as an exploiter of the German Church thus preceded the legate when he decided to move on from Basle, where on September 17 he consecrated Peter, provost of Mainz cathedral, as bishop.

[1] *Reg.*, 770 (May 31, 1286).
[2] Jordanus of Osnabrück says of him: ". . . culpa sua totam Teutonicam provocavit . . ." *M. Oe. I. G.*, 19, 671.
[3] Stenzel, *Urkunden des Bistums Breslau*, 231; Riedel, *C. D. Brandenburgensis*, i, 8, 174; *C. D. Moravie*, iv, 324.

In the beginning of November we find him in Colmar and on the sixth of the month in Strassburg. On the 20th he was issuing documents from Speyer. There he was visited by King Rudolf, who had wished for some time to establish contact with him, particularly because the fixing of the date for the imperial coronation was very urgent. Internal disturbances within the Empire had delayed him for so long. First he had to combat Count Eberhard of Wurtemberg, then to deal with the rebellious bishop of Speyer, whom he besieged for weeks in Lauterburg, and then, having taken the city, banished him from the Empire. While this was going on, the rebellion in Swabia broke out afresh and Rudolf was forced to return there and besiege Count Eberhard in Stuttgart. Without subduing the latter he made peace merely because he was unwilling to defer any longer his meeting with the legate.

On November 25 Rudolf entered Speyer, when it was much too late to adhere to February 2 as the date of the imperial coronation, for it was only now that discussion began of the preparations, including the financial preparations. The result of the discussions was the decision to summon a national council to meet in Würzburg [1] in March, 1287, which would also be regarded by the King as a parliamentary assembly. Rudolf now fixed his hopes on Würzburg. He was interested in the imperial dignity less for its own sake than because the possession of the imperial crown would make it possible for him to envisage the preservation of the crown in his family, which was the dearest wish of his heart. It is not in accordance with the facts to maintain that he then aspired to establish constitutionally the hereditary

Meeting of King Rudolf with the Legate at Speyer.

---

[1] Redlich, *Reg.*, 2051. When Pawlicki assumes that the convocation of a national council in Würzburg had already been decided in Rome, he goes too far. At that time the situation was not sufficiently developed to make such decisions possible.

succession of his house. Such bold plans were not for him ; he was far too practical a politician. What he wanted was to see his son selected as King of Germany during his own lifetime. That would secure at least the next step in the succession, but the essential preliminary to this according to previous usage was his own coronation as Emperor. Not until that had taken place could the election of a new King with the right of succession to the imperial dignity ensue. The further postponement of the imperial coronation meant a postponement of his aim. Now, however, Rudolf had hopes that in the assembly at Würzburg he would be able with the legate's help to get an assurance at least from the electors. It may be assumed that Bishop Henry had given expression to the King's wishes when on the delegation to Honorius and that, in view of the Pope's attitude towards Rudolf, he had obtained an understanding of and approval for them. The legate, too, was probably instructed accordingly, and thus Rudolf really had reason to hope for a favourable development of his plans and desires.

These plans did not remain hidden from the temporal and spiritual princes of the Empire. The rumour was passed round that Rudolf, with the legate's help, was trying to establish an hereditary kingdom in Germany and to deprive the electors of their privileges.[1] With this went the fear which had never been quite stilled since the days of Frederick II., and which had been roused afresh by Martin IV.,[2] the fear that the papacy would divorce the imperial crown from Germany. And the princes were expected to finance this attack on their rights ! The rumour indeed ran that the

[1] *Annals of Worms.* M. G. SS., 17, 77.
[2] *Cf.* Jordan of Osnabrück, *De prærogativa Romani imperii* (Waitz, *Göttinger Abhandlungen*, xiv, 1869).

legate would fix a large tax for the expenses of the journey to Rome. Collectors were still travelling through the country collecting the Lyons Crusade tithes, and to these were added the legate's *procuratio*. According to fourteenth-century sources of information every papal legate at this time was entitled to receive one hundred gold florins a day from the date of his appointment, and to allot this amount among the various monasteries and churches. As we have seen, John was making full use of this right. Now a further tax still was contemplated.

When early in December the legate in Worms summoned the National Council for the third Sunday in Lent (March 9, 1287), and King Rudolf called a meeting of the Reichstag at the same time and place, both hoped that the regeneration of the German Empire would result. It was to be a magnificent assembly. All the German prelates were summoned, and every chapter was to send two representatives. Rudolf made provision to secure peace and order in Würzburg, in view of the fact that some time previously bitter dissension had broken out between the townspeople and the clergy. The civic authorities were endeavouring to annul the clergy's privileges ; in particular they required the clergy to assume the same burdens as the laity. In the course of the dispute the city was laid under an interdict, which inflamed the popular wrath and led to the clergy being either driven from the city or imprisoned. Now King Rudolf gave orders to release the prisoners, readmit the banished clergy, restore order in the town, and make preparations for the Reichstag.[1]

The convocation of the council was the signal for the launching of a campaign against it in Germany. The prelates were determined to prevent any further financial Counter-campaign of the Bishops.

[1] Redlich, *Reg.*, 2056.

burdens being imposed under any circumstances whatever. One ecclesiastical prince, archbishop Siegfried of Cologne, had the further intention of bringing the King's political plans to naught. Probably he felt obliged to represent the interests of the German electors, and he was the only possible representative, for the See of Trier was empty and the archbishop of Mainz was such a close confidant of the King that he represented the views of the latter rather than those of the electors. The non-clerical electors were all closely related to the King. Siegfried feared that the election of Albert as King during his father's lifetime would mean the end of free election by the electoral princes. Accordingly, he launched his counter-campaign. Early in 1287 he assembled the clergy of the archdiocese of Cologne for the purpose of making an appeal to the Pope against the papal legate. The appeal was on these lines : the German Church was in difficulties ; in Cologne, for example, the Church had been plunged into absolute penury in consequence of the collection of the Lyons tithes.[1] Notwithstanding this fact the legate to Germany was demanding *procuratio* and his emissaries were collecting it with wanton lack of consideration. In addition, the legate had summoned all ecclesiastical dignitaries to a meeting in Würzburg on March 9, an inconveniently near date. To go there would entail further heavy expense and would be difficult as far as Cologne was concerned, because to reach it the only route was through territory at enmity with Cologne. Although the legate maintained that he had been sent to strengthen the imperial power, the conviction was held generally throughout Germany that his intention was to make Germany a hereditary kingdom

---

[1] Incidentally an attack is made on the use of the tithes for purposes other than the Holy Land, when the Archbishop says the tithes were supposed to be intended for the Holy Land : " ut prima facie credebatur, licet forte alius eventus sit secutus."

and thus separate it from the Empire with which it had always been inalienably connected. Thus he contemplated the extinction to a certain extent of the second light of the world, the imperial dignity, and the curtailment in the most severe fashion of the rights of the German electoral Princes. Further, it was generally known that he wished to impose yet another tithe payment on Germany for a number of years. In such ways as these the legate was exceeding all bounds of justice and was doing untold injury to the Church. Despite all requests he had not yet stated what his powers were. In order to save the Church and the country from immeasurable injury, from excommunication and interdict, the Church in Cologne was appealing to the Apostolic See. The archbishop and chapter of Cologne confirmed this with their seals.[1]

The Cologne chapter now sent this very effectively drawn appeal to the other churches in Germany with the request that they should associate themselves with it. In view of the feeling in Germany at the time it must have met with approval everywhere. We know that in Austria and Styria at the end of 1286 or the beginning of 1287 the prelates applied to Duke Albert for redress against the high dues payable to the legate. If their application was unsuccessful, the Austrian and Styrian prelates said they would be forced to appeal to the Pope. As one can understand, Duke Albert took no steps: to do so would have been indirectly against his father's and his own interests. And accordingly the archbishop of Salzburg and his suffragan-bishops of Freising, Regensburg, Passau, Brixen, Gurk, Chiemsee, and Seckau did in fact appeal to the Holy See against the legate's unbounded demands for *procuratio*. Later on the

---

[1] Redlich, *Reg.*, p. 447 ; *M. Oe. I. G.*, 12, 649 ff. ; A. Dopsch in the *Festgabe für Büdinger*, 213 ff.

archbishop of Gnesen and his suffragans appealed in the same sense to the Curia.[1]

Archbishop Siegfried of Cologne had thus placed himself at the head of the dissatisfied Church, the dissatisfied country, and, above all, the dissatisfied princes. Archbishop Henry of Mainz could not oppose him openly, for the bitterness was such that to do so would have destroyed his influence and made him useless to his King. The elector of Cologne was probably concerned in the first place to frustrate the holding of the Council. He himself and the prelates who had declared themselves in agreement with his appeal decided not to attend the Council in the belief that it would then be made void. But the preparations were too far advanced, and accordingly Siegfried decided to attend and to state his case there, knowing well that he would not stand alone. By this means he hoped at least to thwart Rudolf's plans ; in this he succeeded to the full.

The National Council of Würzburg.
The Council and the Reichstag were summoned by the legate and the King respectively for the third Sunday in Lent, March 9, 1287. At the time appointed there appeared the King, the legate, and a large number of prelates and princes. The archbishops of Cologne, Mainz, Salzburg, and Bremen were present, as well as the majority of bishops from southern and central Germany, and a number from the north. The archives mention the bishops of Passau, Gurk, Lavant, Brixen, Trent, Freising, Regensburg, Eichstädt, Bamberg, Würzburg, Olmütz, Chur, Constance, Augsburg, Basle, Strassburg, Toul, Metz, Paderborn, Verdun, Hildesheim, Naumburg, Merseburg, Meissen, Brandenburg, Lübeck, Pomerania, and Sammland, as well as many abbots and prelates of the chapters.[2] Among temporal princes

---

[1] Stenzel, *l.c.*, 327 ff.

[2] These names can be determined from the letters of indulgence issued at the time and quoted by Hartzheim in his *Concilia Germaniæ*

mentioned are the following : the Duke of Bavaria
and count palatine of the Rhine, Duke Albert of Saxony,
Duke Henry of Brunswick, Margrave Henry of Hochberg,
Counts Albert and Burchard of Hohenberg, the Duke of
Teck, and many others. On Lætare Sunday, March 16,
1287, the proceedings were solemnly opened by the
legate.[1] The first business session was held on the
following Tuesday, March 18, and there the legate, with
the entire agreement of the princes of the Church who
were present, proclaimed forty-two constitutions directed
against abuses and evils in the Church.[2] They dealt
with the manner of life of the clergy. Unnecessary
bination is forbidden, as is the giving away to relatives
of Church property. The age of twenty-five is fixed as
the minimum for obtaining a parochial benefice, and the
accumulation of benefices is prohibited. It is laid down
that no one may accept a benefice from a layman ;
that when a benefice falls vacant presentation by the
patron must take place within a month, otherwise
the right of presentation is forfeited. Laymen may
not accept ecclesiastical benefices on pain of *ipso facto*
excommunication. Offences against the clergy and
forgery of papal documents are made liable to severe
penalties. The constitutions were accepted unanimously
and without any difficulty being raised.

On March 24 King Rudolf renewed for the whole
Empire the laws imposing public peace.[3] Complete

(Cologne, 1759 ff., iii, p. 734 ff.) and from the lists mentioned in Rudolf's
Regesta. According to a document communicated to " Thuringia
sacra " (Frankfurt, 1737), p. 593, seven further bishops were present.
This would bring the total number of bishops to thirty-six. *Cf.* also
Redlich, *Reg.*, 2063.

[1] *Continuatio Vindob.*, M. G. SS., xi, 714.

[2] *Cf.* Redlich, *Reg.*, p. 450 ; Hefele, *Konziliengeschichte*, vi[2], p. 246 ff. ;
Labbé, *Concilia*, xi, 2, 1319 ; Hardouin, *Collectio conc.*, 7, 1132 ; Hartzheim, *Conc. Germ.*, 3, 725 ; Mansi, *Conc. ampl. Collectio*, 24, 849.

[3] Redlich, *Reg.*, 2064, 2070.

peace still reigned in Würzburg. On March 26 the second session of the Council took place, and at this session the legate's financial demands on behalf of aid for Rudolf's journey to Rome were put forward. Regarding the extent of those demands accounts differ. Some actually mention one-fourth of all revenues for four years ; others state one-tenth. This was the signal for the opposition. The procurator of Cologne read out the full text of the appeal to Rome against the legate.

Uneasiness seized the assembly until bishop Conrad of Toul, wearing the habit of the Franciscans, mounted the baptismal font in order to be better heard, and in a stormy speech protested against the legate's conduct, carrying all present with him in a storm of applause. The bitterness almost culminated in a personal attack on the legate, who left the cathedral. The news of what had happened spread quickly, and the sparks ignited in the cathedral became flames. The mob surrounded the legate, who had to be protected by the King from physical violence. According to a Viennese authority a nephew of the legate and another Roman were killed, but this does not seem correct.[1] Either way, however, the legate's position was completely undermined. Under royal protection he left Würzburg and was in Worms on April 7 and in Metz on the 17th, where he remained until June, interfering in a Dominican dispute and thus fanning the flames of hostility against himself in those circles, hostility reflected in the chronicles of the time. Although his mission ended with the Pope's death on April 3, 1287, he continued to exercise his functions and

[1] The chief sources of information regarding the Würzburg Council are : *Annales Osterhov.* (*M. G. SS.*, 17, 550) ; *Annales Wormat.* (*SS.*, 17, 77) ; *Continuatio Vindob.* (*SS.*, 9, 714) ; *Continuatio Ratisbon.* (*SS.*, 17, 416) ; *Flores temporum* (*SS.*, 24, 249) ; Sifrid von Balnhusen (*SS.*, 25, 711), with which *cf.* Redlich, *Reg.*, 452 ; Eubel, *Hist. Jahrbuch,* 9, 437 ff. ; 661 ff.

rights, and as late as September, 1287, he was demanding
—that apparently being for him the most important
part of his office—a sum of 1,500 marks as *procuratio*
from the ecclesiastical province of Mainz. Small wonder
that a sigh of relief went up when he left Germany
that month, and that Gottfried of Emmingen expressed
the hope that in accordance with the general wish he
might never return. The enraged people of Strassburg
compared the legate to the beast of the Apocalypse.[1]

Some authorities mention that the legate removed
the bishop of Toul from office. This is incorrect. He
excommunicated the bishop, who was obliged to go to
Rome to justify himself, but we find him in later years
still bishop of Toul, where he died highly revered in 1296.

Rudolf had hoped that his wishes and plans would
find their fulfilment at the Würzburg Council ; instead,
this, the last of the German Councils, became in its
disgraceful termination the grave of his hopes. Siegfried
of Cologne's opposition had been completely successful,
helped by the legate's stupidity, which was calculated
to make him as unpopular as possible. Even though
Rudolf had not intended to convert Germany into a
hereditary kingdom, his efforts to have Albert chosen
as King and as his own successor at Würzburg or shortly
afterwards had failed. This setback which Rudolf
received in Germany was all the more fateful because
the Pope, who was well-disposed towards him, died
immediately afterwards, and because in the last week
of Honorius' reign the situation in Rome changed, and
changed to the disadvantage of Rudolf. Early in 1287
the King had again sent an embassy to Rome to ask
that a new date be fixed for the imperial coronation,
as February 2 could not be adhered to,[2] and that the
new date should be as soon as possible. Meanwhile,

---

[1] Böhmer, *Fontes*, i, 125 ; *M. G. SS.*, 17, 129.
[2] Redlich, *Reg.*, 2051, 2224.

difficulties had arisen in Rome in which Rudolf was in
no way involved. Towards the end of the Pope's reign
former rivalries revived in the college of cardinals, in
particular the rivalry between the Orsini and the Colonna.
Since the days of Pope Nicholas III. the Orsini had been
friendly to the King of Germany, and on that account
Rudolf thought of appointing an Orsini ultimately as
Imperial-Vicar of Tuscany. This friendship between
Rudolf and the Orsini caused the Colonna to oppose
the Pope's accommodating attitude towards Rudolf,
and the result was that Honorius hesitated about fixing
the new date. Cardinal Hieronymus of Præneste, who
as Nicholas IV. was to succeed Honorius, and who had
friendly relations with Rudolf previously when he was
general of the Franciscan Order, advised the ambassadors
not to press the Pope, in view of the feeling in the Curia.
Then Honorius died before a date for the imperial
coronation had been appointed, and the lengthy
interregnum which followed prevented all further
negotiations. Accordingly, the fulfilment of Rudolf's
immediate plans was once more brought to naught by
the Würzburg Council and the death of Pope Honorius IV.
In spite of his views—and although his choice of a legate
was unfortunate, it was well meant—the Pope was
unable to bring papal relations with Germany to a conclusion satisfactory to both parties. The cross-currents
in Germany, and finally, too, in the Curia, were too strong
for the wishes of the two highest powers in the western
world, the Pope and the Emperor-elect, another indication
that the zenith of the " Middle Ages " was past.

England.

King Edward I. of England played an important part
in the Pope's foreign policy. From the very first,
when communicating the news of his election as Pope,
Honorius had asked him for his help.[1] English conditions, however, were not in question so much as two

[1] *Reg.*, 828 ; Potthast, 22231.

enterprises which the King was supposed to favour, namely, a Crusade,[1] and the restoration of peace between France, Aragon, and the Pope. Conditions in England were not such as to require further papal interference. In the early part of Honorius' pontificate a synod was held at London, presided over by archbishop John Peckham, which rectified various abuses which had crept in and condemned a number of heretical propositions. But the matters dealt with by this synod were not of prime importance, and the synod's decisions were the end of them. The filling of the archiepiscopal See of Dublin passed off, too, with difficulty, so that all the Pope had to do was to give the bishop-elect power to have himself consecrated by any English or Scottish bishop in union with Rome, and to send him the *pallium*.[2] A new privilege was granted by Pope Honorius to King Edward, and an important one, namely, a general dispensation for his children from possible impediments to marriage because of consanguinity in the fourth degree. By doing this the Pope gave away a powerful weapon in foreign policy, for the circumstance that the ruling houses were closely related, and that consequently marriages of their members required a papal dispensation, made it possible for the Pope to influence new marriage relationships of the dynasties. We can understand then why the Pope attached to this privilege a request that it should not be used in such a way as to harm the Church. The King was asked not to allow any of his children to marry anyone who had offended against the Church.[3]

On one occasion the Pope addressed an admonition to England, not, however, to the King but to the bishops. In England the Jews enjoyed great freedom, which

---

[1] See the chapter which deals with the Crusades.
[2] *Reg.*, 44–6 (June 11 and 12, 1285).
[3] *Reg.*, 932, 944 ; Potthast, 22487.

resulted not merely in their oppressing the Christians, but, and more important, in the fact that they attempted to win Christians over to Judaism. Chronicles report that in this they met with surprising success. A Dominican monk, named Robert of Reddinge, had associated with Jews and finally took the step of conforming to Judaism. As a Jew he took the name Aggæus and married.[1] This was, of course, an event in the Christian world. Further, contrary to the laws of the Church, Jews took Christians into their service and interfered with them in their religious duties. From this close association between Christians and Jews unlawful unions were formed.[2]

The Pope expressed his surprise that the English Bishops had not long since set themselves against such things in accordance with the regulations of the Church. In consequence he found himself compelled to issue strict orders [3] to the effect that this association of Christians with Jews should be prevented by stern spiritual and material penalties, and that all other necessary steps should be taken to end such a state of things.[4] These,

---

[1] Florentii Wigorn., *Chron.*, ed. B. Thorpe, p. 214 (London, 849) ; Grätz, *Geschichte der Juden*, vii, p. 199 ff. (Leipzig, 1863).

[2] The Pope expresses the matter thus in his Bull to the Bishops (*Reg.* 809, November 18, 1286) : " sicque, dum oportunitas suggerit et pravis actibus tempus favet, Judeorum mulieribus christiani et Judei christianorum feminis frequenter infausto commercio commiscentur."

[3] " per apostolica scripta districte precipiendo mandamus."

[4] The Pope's observations on the Talmud in this letter to the English bishops are interesting. He writes : " (Judei) etenim librum quendam maligna fraude compositum habere dicuntur, quem Thalamud vulgariter nuncupant, abhominationes et falsitates, infidelitates et abusiones nultimodas continentem. In hoc quippe libro dampnabili suum continuant studium et circa ipsius nepharia documenta ipsorum prava sollicitudo versatur. Illius insuper doctrine letifere proprios ab annis teneris filios deputant, ut eius venenosis pabulis imbuantur, eosque instruere ac informere non metuunt, quod magis in libro contentis eodem, quam expressis in lege Mosayca credi debet, ut iidem filii Dei

however, were only episodes in English history. Of incomparably greater importance were the efforts of the King of England to restore peace and unity among the Christians of the West. If there was little prospect of inducing the Pope to recognize what had occurred in Sicily, King Edward hoped at least to be able to bring about peace between France and Aragon and between Aragon and the Pope. In this the ideal aims for which Edward strove coincided with English interests which were not served by an increase in the power of the House of Valois.

Like Philip III., Peter of Aragon had fallen a victim to the French campaign against his country. His death led to an important decision, that to divide Aragon from Sicily. While James, supported by his mother Costanza, assumed the governance of Sicily, Alfonso succeeded his father in Aragon. James was well aware of the hopelessness of attempting a reconciliation with the Pope. He snapped his fingers at excommunication and interdict and had himself crowned king, surrounded by the ecclesiastical dignitaries of Sicily, who also disregarded the papal edicts. It was different with Alfonso. With the finest tact he avoided everything which could irritate the Pope. He even wrote to the Pope asking to be excused for not being able to send an embassy to the Holy See on his father's death and promising to do so in the immediate future. The Pope on his side reacted to this tactful gesture. While excommunicating James and his mother Costanza, he decreed that the cause against Alfonso should be deferred until the Feast of the Ascension.[1] Nevertheless, he adhered to the

---

filium fugientes per devia infidelitatis exorbitent et ad veritatis semitam non accedant." It must, however, be remarked that the Pope was just enough to protect the Jews when they were wrongfully oppressed, as, for example, in Sicily. *Cf. Reg.*, 97, § 16.

[1] *Reg.*, 495 (April 11, 1286).

original condemnation and to the transfer of the crown, for on April 30, not quite three weeks later, he empowered the papal legate, cardinal John, to suspend all persons who had sworn fealty to Alfonso of Aragon and to summon all ecclesiastical persons and all corporations to deliver up to the King of France or his deputy all castles and fortified places which they held on the French frontier.[1] One may fairly assume that this decree was promulgated under pressure from the legate and the King of France. It had no practical political results. That the Pope had not in the short interval changed his attitude towards Aragon is clear beyond doubt from the fact that he took no steps against Alfonso when the period of grace expired on May 21. While he issued a new decree of excommunication against James of Sicily on May 23, 1287, he again deferred the case against Alfonso because the latter had sent word that the projected embassy had only been prevented from setting out [2] by unfavourable circumstances.

Meanwhile the King of England was working hard to find some basis of agreement. While the Pope maintained an attitude of reserve he continually urged the King not to relax his efforts. As early as May 5 he praised Edward's zeal.[3] While too cautious to state his position precisely in writing, he declared himself ready to explain it verbally to a representative of the King. This caution is intelligible in view of the strong pro-French party in the College of Cardinals, which of course was by no means in favour of a peace with Aragon.

The verbal negotiations must have been satisfactory, for King Edward decided to deal personally with the princes concerned, hoping in this way to make better headway. At Easter, 1286, he committed the Government of England to his relative Edmund and set sail

---

[1] *Reg.*, 392, 393.   [2] *Reg.*, 769.   [3] *Reg.*, 920.

for France with a considerable retinue. Alfonso had already sent an embassy to empower him to negotiate with France. After prolonged negotiation an armistice was agreed to between France and Aragon on July 25. It was to last from August 22, 1286, until September 29, 1287, and included also Alfonso's uncle the King of Majorca who was an adherent of papal foreign policy.[1]

The agreement which brought it about provided for the Pope's sanction. To obtain this the King sent an embassy to Honorius consisting of Hamon de Joeles and Rudolf le Allemand. They carried a letter which asked in the most polite form for the Pope's consent, appealing to Christian charity, pointing to the example of the Good Shepherd who leads back the lost sheep, and, finally, emphasizing the advantages which would accrue to the campaign on behalf of the Holy Land.[2] At the same time he appealed to the cardinals, asking them to be favourable to his request and to use their influence with the Pope on its behalf.[3] Honorius agreed to the armistice, and retained one of the envoys whom he desired to consult further regarding the position.[4] He went even further and yielded to King Edward's request that he should send envoys. While stressing the seriousness of the question at issue and the caution with which it must be handled, he sent representatives, nevertheless, to watch over the Church's interests during the negotiations. He gave no particular powers to these representatives, but they were fully informed as to his wishes and intentions. He selected for the mission Boniface, archbishop of Ravenna, and Peter, archbishop of Monreale, both of them persons of importance, and instructed them to endeavour to secure the acceptance of certain papal conditions, which, however, were not set

[1] Rymer, *Fœdera*, I, iii, 8, 11, 12, 15.
[2] Rymer, *l.c.*, 13. [3] Rymer, 14. [4] *Reg.*, 950.

out in writing, but, if that proved impossible, not to
break off the negotiations in consequence.[1] Meanwhile,
at Christmas of 1286, King Alfonso's emissaries had at
last come to the Pope. They apologized on behalf of
their master because they had not been able to come
sooner on account of the war, and begged the Pope to
recognize the two brothers as Kings of Aragon and
Sicily respectively. In return Charles II would be
released from captivity. The Pope did not enter into
the points affecting Sicily beyond a reproof to the effect
that the King's goodwill must be questioned, seeing
that he was constantly dispatching troops to Sicily and
that he held Charles II unjustly in captivity. He also
stated formally that Alfonso had no right to Aragon,
which belonged to Charles of Valois, the brother of the
King of France, but that notwithstanding this he was
prepared to give recognition to Alfonso if the latter would
submit to the Church. Early in January the emissaries
returned, taking with them a letter of safe conduct
from the Pope. This did not mean that negotiations
were broken off, for on the contrary the messengers
brought with them a safe conduct for a new delegation
to be appointed with more extensive powers.[2] Parallel
with these happenings King Edward's negotiations went
forward. Through a confidential messenger King Edward
informed the Pope of the course matters were taking,
and received from Honorius positive encouragement
to continue his efforts for peace. The papal envoys,
who had in the interval gone back to Rome, were sent
off again, with new instructions probably, to the resumed
negotiations and were instructed to stand by King Edward
at all times with assistance and advice in his efforts for
peace.[3]

---

[1] *Reg.*, 950–4 ; Potthast, 22525, 22526.
[2] Muratori, *Antiq.*, iv, 1014 ; *Reg.*, 810, 811.
[3] *Reg.*, 966 ; Potthast, 22576, 22583.

About this time Charles signed the Treaty of Barcelona pledging himself to renounce Sicily and to strengthen the reconciliation by a double marriage : James of Sicily wedding Charles's eldest daughter and Charles's eldest son taking as wife Isalanda of Aragon, the sister of James and Alfonso. This was intended to overcome the obstacle to Alfonso's negotiations with the Pope, which arose from the latter's adherence to the Angevin rights over Sicily and his branding of every departure therefrom as a positive injustice to the House of Anjou. A voluntary renunciation of Sicily by Charles II. would make this attitude impossible and would open the road towards general peace. Philip IV. was satisfied with the arrangement, as he had but little interest in Aragon and was more concerned with strengthening his own position in France by increased centralization. The effort at peace, however, collapsed because of the Pope's absolute adhesion to the Angevin rights, even in opposition to the representative of those rights. While the Angevins themselves renounced their rights, the Pope refused to acknowledge that renunciation. New paths to peace had accordingly to be explored, but before they could be entered, or indeed found, the Pope died. A solution of the Aragonese question was thus also prevented by the unconditional and rigid adherence of the Pope to the formal rights of the Angevins.

With France the Pope stood on the most friendly France. footing. Like his predecessor he showered privileges on the Royal House. In a general ordinance he gave the King permission to avail himself of every privilege granted by a Pope to any of his predecessors. The people were to be encouraged by indulgences to implore Divine protection for their sovereign—every one who prayed for the King was granted an indulgence of twenty days, and for every Paternoster said for the soul of Philip III. an indulgence of ten days was given. These indulgences were issued for a term of ten years. But the pious French were moreover to be encouraged by indulgences to give the King something more earthly, namely, taxes : all who paid the Aragon tithes in one sum were to receive an indulgence equal to that granted to Crusaders. In this the Pope indicated that the war against Aragon was regarded by him as a holy war.

Privileges.

Privileges granted to the King were as follows : a Low Mass or a *missa cantata* might be celebrated for him before daybreak ; no legate might excommunicate or suspend him without express papal powers for the purpose ; no interdict might be laid on his court chapel ; in places under an interdict Mass might be said or sung for him within closed doors ; he could enter female religious houses, but might not eat or spend a night there ; six clergy sent by him to Paris to study might remain in possession of their benefices, as if resident. Finally, all the faithful who heard a sermon in the presence of the King and Queen were granted an indulgence of one hundred days. Similar privileges were accorded to the Queen. If she could not conveniently (*comode*) be present at a church for Mass, she could have the Holy Sacrifice celebrated for her in any decent place. She could choose her own confessor who would then have power to dispense herself and her retinue even from vows. No legate could excommunicate her without the express instructions of the Pope. She could be present at Mass behind closed doors in places subject to an interdict. She could visit convents with two or three gentlemen and six ladies of her household. The faithful who attended Mass in the Queen's presence on Holy Days received an indulgence of ten days, and one of twenty days if they heard a sermon.

Further privileges were granted to the retinue of the King and Queen. Six clergy in the King's household and four in that of the Queen were allowed to enjoy all

the revenues of their benefices, just as if they resided
in them. The household could choose their own con-
fessors on condition that once a year they confessed
to the priest of the parish. If they were in orders they
could be ordained by any bishop in union with Rome.
Canons and chaplains of the Royal Chapel were exempt
from all church taxes and *procuratio* ; they were permitted
to adhere to the liturgy prescribed in Paris. The abbots
of St. Denis and St. Germain du Pré were appointed to
protect the royal couple in the enjoyment and peaceful
possession of their privileges.[1]

Moreover, the Pope increased the powers of the legate
to France so as to make it easier for the people to procure
dispensations. The legate was authorized on certain
conditions to grant release from excommunication, and
in twenty cases to dispense from *defectus natalium*,
as well as to modify vows, excepting the three vows of
chastity, the Crusade, and of entering a religious order.[2]

In spite of this shower of favours which fell on France
the young King was by no means forward in showing
favour to the Church. Rather did he reveal an attitude
of absolutism in matters of church property and the
legal position of the clergy. This was particularly
apparent on an occasion when the Countess of Chartres
had quarrelled with the dean and chapter of that city
regarding property and rights. The Countess appealed
to the King for a decision, and he, avoiding the
ecclesiastical courts, brought the accused clergy before
the King's court. The chapter took its stand on its
legal status and asked the Pope to protect its rights.
Honorius interfered and demanded that the King should
have regard to the privileges of the clergy, but Philip
took no notice. He forbade the Church tenants to

Attitude of Philip IV. of France.

---

[1] *Reg.*, 374–91, 395–7, 591, 650–4, 658, 663 ; Potthast, 22422,
22423, 22504.

[2] *Reg.*, 481–3.

render any services to the chapter, thus attempting to paralyse its economic operations, and instructed royal officials to seize the Church property on behalf of the Crown. Thereupon the Countess had the clergy seized, imprisoned, and condemned to death. When the Pope heard of this he reproved the papal legate in France severely for allowing such things to happen without taking steps to prevent them. He ordered redress to be demanded immediately from the King and the Countess, and, if this was not at once granted, that he himself should be notified without delay so that he could intervene in person. Honorius could not conceal his astonishment that a grandson of the saintly Louis IX. should disregard the freedom of the Church.

He had already had occasion in another matter to admonish the King to restore the property of a monastery to its rightful owner.[1] These incidents appear in their true light when it is recalled that the Pope not only showered spiritual favours on France and its royal house, but that he helped that country financially by a further grant of tithes for the Aragon war, and that he also favoured France politically, and adhered so rigidly to French interests that he allowed a sound compromise in Sicily and Aragon to be nullified on account of those interests. The true character of the unscrupulous absolutist, Philip IV., who used the Church only as a tool and despised it when it suited him, showed itself quite clearly in the very first years of his rule over France.

Castile. In Castile the Pope showed no quality but that of benevolence. He instructed his legate Gerard to raise the ban of excommunication incurred by Henry, son of Ferdinand of Castile and adherent of Conradin, for inflicting injuries on two cardinals, but not until he had atoned for his conduct. A few weeks later he empowered the archbishop of Toledo and the bishop of Burgos to

[1] *Reg.*, 253, 604.

raise the interdict imposed by Pope Martin IV. in consequence of the revolt against King Alfonso.[1]

King Ladislaus of Hungary by his behaviour caused Hungary.
the Pope much anxiety. He was married to Elizabeth,
a sister of Charles of Anjou.

Internal dissensions with the nobility who were
quarrelling regarding the succession to the childless King,
and external disturbances caused by Tatar attacks
forced the King to establish contact with the Cumans
resident in Hungary who were more heathen than
Christian, and with their aid to ward off internal and
external difficulties. This association was personal as
well as political. The Queen was older than Ladislaus
and exercised considerable political influence. She was
probably exercised to secure the succession in Hungary
to a member of the House of Anjou. These circumstances
estranged Ladislaus from his wife. Taking a quick
decision, he had her imprisoned in 1285 and thereafter
associated with Cuman women on a forbidden footing.
The matter did not come to the Pope's ears until the
spring of 1287. Immediately he intervened in accordance
with his duty as the guardian of Christian morality.
He wrote to the King admonishing him that his life was
unworthy of a successor of St. Stephen, and demanding
that he should abandon his alliance with the Cumans,
release Elizabeth and take her to himself as his wife
in accordance with the commandments of God. At
the same time Honorius instructed archbishop Lodomer
of Gran to preach a Crusade against the Cumans unless
they desisted from oppressing Christians and to grant
the Crusade indulgences to those who took part in this
holy war. Further, he ordered the archbishop to force
the King to resume marriage relations with his lawful
wife, making use if necessary of ecclesiastical punishments. Honorius appealed, in addition, to Rudolf of

[1] *Reg.*, 319, 808 (March 8, 1286, and November 7, 1286).

Habsburg for help to the archbishop of Gran in his mission.[1] These papal bulls are dated March 12, 1287, but do not appear to have been sent. In the *Register* there is a marginal note on one of them to the effect that after it had been sealed and registered it had been taken back for alteration and had not been registered again.[2] As identical bulls were dispatched by Nicholas without mention of the fact that Honorius had already dealt with the matter, it may be assumed that the Pope's death prevented the dispatch of the bulls. This view is supported by an observation of Pope Nicholas IV. to the archbishop of Gran that Honorius had already sent him a bull in this connection, but that it had not been dispatched because of the Pope's death.[3]

To sum up, it may be said regarding the policy of Pope Honorius IV. that he honestly endeavoured to put the interests of the Church first. Even where he showed himself implacable on behalf of the Angevins he was convinced that the rights of the Church which he had to defend were identical with the interests of the House of Anjou. He did not attain great success in any field, seeing that the time allowed to him for his labours was short indeed. There remains to his honour the testimony that he did not pursue a Roman, nor a French, nor a German policy, but a Church policy.

[1] *Reg.*, 761, 762 ; Redlich, *Reg.*, 2063 ; Potthast, 22585–90.

[2] *Reg.*, 761. " Ista littera postquam fuit bullata et regestata, fuit remissa domino et postea mutata sed nondum remissa ad regestam."

[3] Theiner, *Cod. dipl. Ungariæ*, i, 359 : ". . . sed earum missionem illo morte prævento subsecutam non esse."

CHAPTER IV.

CREATION OF CARDINALS—THE RELIGIOUS ORDERS—
QUESTIONS OF CANON LAW AND DISCIPLINE—ADVANCE
OF LEARNING.

FOR reasons of Church policy Martin IV. had greatly Creation of Cardinals.
enlarged the College of Cardinals : Honorius IV., on the
contrary, created but one cardinal. In December, 1285,
he appointed his relative archbishop John of Monreale to
be cardinal-bishop of Tusculum ; otherwise no creations
took place during his pontificate. This single appointment was not dictated by Church policy but rather by
a touch of nepotism which also became apparent in the
filling of other positions. As papal legate to Germany
cardinal John has been mentioned already.

Opinions differ regarding the Pope's attitude towards The religious Orders.
the religious Orders. He is accused on the testimony
of Salimbene and various other Franciscan chroniclers
of being an enemy of the Orders, and is even credited with
contemplating a revocation of the privileges bestowed
on the mendicant Orders. The privileges were to have
been withdrawn, it is alleged, on Maundy Thursday.
News of the step contemplated was communicated to
the mendicant Orders by their protector, Cardinal
Matteo Rosso, who declared himself unable to avert
the threatened danger. In answer to the prayers of the
members of the Orders, however, God prevented the
project from maturing, for the Pope died on the appointed
day.[1]

This invention was well calculated to impress mediaeval
readers, who would be greatly edified by God's intervention on behalf of the mendicant Orders, and whose

[1] *Chron.*, 371, 378.

confidence in those Orders would be thereby increased.
No doubt the fable was composed for that purpose.
There is no evidence whatever of any hostility on the
part of the Pope towards either the Orders in general
or the mendicants in particular. The fiction is best
controverted by a short summary of the marks of favour
bestowed by Honorius on those Orders. In the very
first year of his reign he confirmed the Franciscans and
Dominicans in the privileges already granted to them in
their entirety.[1] In addition certain important privileges
were given particular confirmation, such as the privilege
that Provincials of the Order could accord permission
to preach to suitably educated members of the Order,[2]
and the Dominican Indult of celebrating Mass, receiving
the Sacraments and saying the Divine office during an
interdict, provided that it was done behind closed doors,
all others than Dominicans being excluded.[3] Members
of the mendicant Orders were appointed by Honorius
to bishoprics, including sees as important as Mainz
and Florence.[4] We find them as tithe collectors[5];
the Inquisition was entrusted to them exclusively[6];
again and again they acted as the Pope's representatives
in the exercise of his jurisdiction. They were entrusted
with the examination of bishops-elect, of abbots and
abbesses in regard to canonical qualifications, and with
confirming or annulling elections accordingly.[7] In various
other matters also they represented the Pope, especially
in investigations preliminary to the grant of dispensations,
the power of dispensation being thus placed in their

---

[1] *Reg.*, 203, 204 ; Potthast, 22329, 22330 (Nov. 20, 1285).
[2] *Reg.*, 889 ; Potthast, 22371.
[3] *Reg.*, 260 ; Potthast, 22287.
[4] *Reg.*, 320, 500, 536, 738, 830, etc.
[5] *Reg.*, 12.
[6] *Reg.*, 103, 173, 358, 713 ; Potthast, 22307, 22322.
[7] *Reg.*, 2, 64, 143, 165, 251, 460, 581.

hands.[1] Of his own accord the Pope prescribed the Franciscan rule for various religious bodies, and appointed mendicants as superiors of convents of women.[2] He even made Franciscan monasteries independent to a great extent of the Ordinary of the place, for he gave permission to Franciscans and Dominicans to have the foundation stones of churches and of churchyards consecrated by any bishop in union with Rome if the Ordinary would not or could not undertake the consecration. The same held of the consecration of completed churches.[3] On one occasion he instructed the bishop of Tivoli to allot a church in his town to the Dominicans, as they were without one.[4] If needful, he protected mendicants when their rights or privileges were invaded by the secular or ecclesiastical authorities. For doing so he summoned the bishop of Zamora to Rome to justify himself, and he likewise summoned through their bishop the authorities of Parma to Rome because they had offended the Dominicans.[5] He caused certain monasteries abandoned by other Orders to be given or sold to them, the proceeds to be used for the Holy Land.[6] He even helped them with indulgences, which he granted for a visit to their churches or for an alms given to build a church. In both cases the indulgence was for forty days and could be obtained on the usual condition of a good confession.[7]

This rich treasury of privileges bestowed on the mendicants by Pope Honorius disposes of the fable that he did not favour those Orders. It is true, no doubt, that he did not employ them to the same extent

---

[1] *Reg.*, 24, 93, 94, 144, 148, 150, 228, 257, 259, 532, 561, 634, 635, 639, 642, 675, 744.

[2] *Reg.*, 170 ; Kaltenbrunner, 292.

[3] *Reg.*, 223, 956 ; Potthast, 22334, 22352.

[4] *Reg.*, 90.   [5] *Reg.*, 147, 370.

[6] *Reg.*, 77, 81–4, 294.   [7] *Reg.*, 681, 918.

as his predecessor Martin, who used them almost exclusively as his plenipotentiaries and who entrusted to them a large number of episcopal sees. Honorius usually made use of bishops in the former case and in the latter appointed members of the chapter to bishoprics, while not, however, excluding the mendicant Orders from these marks of his confidence. It can hardly be doubted that in this way he was more true to the intentions of the founders of those Orders as well as to the hierarchy of the Church.

For it is certain that neither St. Francis nor St. Dominic founded his Order that its members might hold visitations of the clergy, still less become Bishops. Possibly the remarkably non-committal attitude of the University of Paris towards the privileges of the mendicants [1] caused the Pope to be rather cautious in his attitude, since he had the highest regard for that University since his student days. Even this diminution in marks of favour was sufficient to excite certain over-zealous mendicants, this being the best proof that it was wrong to employ the Orders in important positions so extensively as Martin had done, for they then adopted the attitude that an omission to do so was an injustice and a reason for representing the person responsible as blameworthy.

Other Orders also experienced under Honorius the protection and favour of the Church. In the first months of his Pontificate he issued a large number of confirmations of privileges previously granted to religious orders. Benedictines. The Benedictines were especially favoured. Apart from the general confirmations [2] of privileges, a number of abbots were given the right to wear pontificals and to bless Church vessels, as well as the right to give the Cluny. pontifical blessing after solemn offices.[3] Cluny and its members were granted numerous privileges : first a

---

[1] *Chartularium Univers. Paris.*, ii, 11, 539 (December, 1286).
[2] *Reg.*, 879, 939, etc. [3] *Reg.*, 42, 91, 288, 520.

confirmation of all earlier privileges and rights, and with
it an express prohibition on restricting them.   Honorius
ordained that without powers from the Pope no person
should impose an ecclesiastical punishment on a Cluny
foundation, and that punishments imposed by bishops
without papal sanction were null and void.   All purchases,
sales, and other business transactions effected without
the knowledge and consent of the Superior-General of
the Order were invalid.

The abbot was given power to issue dispensations to
members of the Order.   Individual monasteries were
granted special indulgences available to all who confessed
their sins there.   Finally, the Pope instructed his legate
in France that the forty Cluniac monks who were studying
in Paris and had a house there should have the right to
a bell with which to summon the brethren to prayer,
and also the right to establish a burial place of their
own adjoining their chapel.[1]   The Abbey of St. Denis
was specially distinguished with privileges.   It, too,
received a general confirmation of all former privileges
and, in addition, the special favour that these privileges
did not lose their efficacy through non-use.   The
abbot of St. Denis was empowered to grant an indulgence
of ten days on the usual conditions for attendance at
pontifical ceremonies.   He was permitted to confer
minor orders in places within his jurisdiction and to
consecrate Church vessels as well as Churches which
had been desecrated.[2]

Cistercian monasteries were granted a renewal of papal   Cistercians.
protection and a special reduction in Church tithes.
For example, the tithe collector for Sicily was ordered
to assess the monasteries conscientiously and then to
prescribe a lump sum which might be paid in instalments.[3]

---

[1] *Reg.*, 402–12, 415, 464, 923 ; Potthast, 22431, 22432, 22436, 22447.
[2] *Reg.*, 845, 914–16, 922, 967, 971.
[3] *Reg.*, 15, 266.

Carthusian monasteries in general were exempt from the yearly payment of tithes on all possessions which they had built with their own hands.[1]

To Benedictines and Augustinians who had got into financial difficulties he gave permission to take possession of and to use for the purposes of the Order up to a certain amount restitution moneys which could not be applied to the purposes for which they were intended, because the injured person was unknown or not available.[2] The hermits of St. Augustine received the privilege of holding a solemn service even during an interdict in their own churches and oratories on the Vigil and Feast of their founder, St. Augustine. No limitations, such as closed doors or the like, were attached.[3]

Like the other Orders the Premonstratensian Canons received a renewal of all their privileges.[4] Honorius introduced a sound principle by striking out in the case of a foundation of canonesses in the diocese of Liège a condition that none but ladies of noble family could be received there.[5] His chief favours fell to the Orders of knights and hospitallers because of his interest in the Crusade movement. This led not merely to a confirmation of all their privileges, including those which had not been availed of, but they also were granted monasteries abandoned by religious communities, and received the right to retain for five years restitution money up to an amount of 10,000 silver marks, in cases where the lawful owners were unknown or unavailable.[6] The Humiliati were accorded the favour of making use of the Roman liturgy everywhere ; they were exempted for the year 1285 from the obligation of summoning a general chapter. They also received a number of financial favours, such as reductions in diocesan dues

---

[1] Potthast, 22245.
[2] *Reg.*, 298, 300.
[3] *Reg.*, 538.
[4] *Reg.*, 875 ; Potthast, 22346.
[5] *Reg.*, 148.
[6] *Reg.*, 151, 625, 728, 842, 856, 857, 924.

and a reduction in the Sicilian tithes. Of particular interest is the papal decree that a general of the Order elected unanimously might assume control of the Order without awaiting confirmation of election by the Apostolic See.[1]

Among the newer Orders, the Order of the Brothers of the Apostles was dissolved, in accordance with the directions of the Council of Lyons, as it was not free from heretical tendencies. A direction was issued to all Princes of the Church not to recognize or suffer the Order, but to call on the brothers to lay aside their habits and join another religious community if they wished to follow a monastic life.[2] He confirmed, on the contrary, the Carmelite Order, which as a new foundation had not Carmelites. received recognition from the Council of Lyons, a decision being left instead to the Holy See expressly. He instructed the bishops to allow the Carmelites to carry out their spiritual exercises without hindrance, in so far as they obeyed the laws of the Church. He even allowed them, like the older mendicant Orders, to celebrate Mass behind closed doors during an interdict and gave them permission to exchange their remarkable striped habit for a white one.[3]

He adopted with particular affection another newly Williamites. founded religious community, the Order of St. William (Williamites). They traced their foundation to St. William, Duke of Aquitaine († 1156), and they had received sanction from Innocent IV. Honorius confirmed all their earlier privileges and took them under his special protection. He handed over to them a number of abandoned Benedictine monasteries, as well as the monastery which he had founded when cardinal in Albano in honour of St. Paul. To the old privileges he added

[1] *Reg.*, 134, 540, 541, 910 ; Potthast, 22489.
[2] *Reg.*, 310 ; Potthast, 22391.
[3] *Reg.*, 305, 870 ; Potthast, 22387.

new ones : extensive powers of dispensation from
excommunication and interdict, protection for the
religious habit of the order, protection of its property
in the event of excommunication. Without express
papal approval the Order could not be subjected to
ecclesiastical punishments.[1] Thus Pope Honorius showed
himself a father and friend to all the Orders of the
Church. He was able, however, to make use of the
Orders in such a way as not to provoke the just displeasure
of the secular clergy by a one-sided favouritism.

Benefice administration.
The centralization of ecclesiastical administration
by an extensive reservation of benefices was as pronounced
under Honorius as in the pontificate of his predecessors.
Almost every page of the papal registers testifies to it.
Honorius also prolonged the reservation of all benefices
in the cathedral churches of Sicily, and this gave him
the desired opportunity of providing meritorious officials
of his Chancery and other officers of the Curia with
benefices. In this way he appointed as bishop of Patti
the papal chaplain Pandulf, who often acted as examiner
for the *tabellio* office and was probably an official of the
papal chancery.[2]

Dispensations.
Honorius was specially generous in the matter of
granting dispensations. Attention has been drawn
already to the reproach of the English Chronicler that
he was harsh towards the poor but gracious to the rich,
whom he dispensed willingly from the prohibition against
plurality of benefices and also from canonical impediments.[3] That dispensations were granted only to the
rich is certainly an exaggeration, but dispensations
obviously cost money and the poor could not apply

[1] *Reg.*, 67, 373, 435–41.
[2] *Reg.*, 323, 490.
[3] *M. G. SS.*, xxx, 714 : " . . . pauperibus erat honorosus et divitibus
gratiosus, quia super pluralitate beneficiorum libenter dispensavit et
de irregularitatibus quacumque ex causa contractis divites absolvit."

for them to the same extent as the rich, who had the
necessary sums at their disposal. This may have made
it appear that the Pope was more yielding to the rich
than to the poor.

Dispensations allowing the simultaneous occupation
of a number of benefices were too numerous for the good
of the Church, but it should be pointed out that in very
many cases Honorius expressly restricted the number
of benefices which could be so held to two.[1] Among
those to whom dispensations were granted was the
future Pope Boniface VIII.

Another dispensation which had an unfavourable effect
on the Church was that from the requirement of ordination as priest, or consecration as bishop, of benefice
holders. Councils and synods strove to check the abuse
of benefice holders not receiving the necessary orders, but
entrusting the exercise of the office to a deputy who was
usually poorly remunerated. The Council of Lyons
had decreed specifically that parish priests should be
ordained priests within a year. In 1286 the synod
of Bourges ordained that they should not draw revenues
before their ordination ; until then the yield of the
benefice should be employed for the Church as seemed
best to the bishop. Such decrees remained purposeless
when dispensations allowed them to be ignored. Moreover, in hardly any case can a really valid reason for
such a dispensation be found. How far things were
allowed to go will be appreciated when we read that
the bishop-elect of Metz, Burchard of Hannonia, asked
and received from Martin IV. a dispensation allowing
him to defer his consecration for three years. At the
end of that term the dispensation was prolonged by

---

[1] In the following list of references the asterisk denotes limitation
to two benefices: *Reg.*, 4, 10, 27, 54, 208*, 261*, 279, 287, 317*, 318,
442, 447, 457, 525*, 542, 687, 701, 711, 751*, 764*, 822, 945, 946
(Boniface VIII.) Kaltenbrunner, 306, 310.

Honorius for a further year.   The bishop-elect of Cambrai
was dispensed from being consecrated for a year and a
half.   Johannes Gregorii was appointed priest of the
church of Zatch in the diocese of Prague.   His appointment was canonically perfectly in order, but he did not
permit himself to be ordained for four years afterwards
although drawing the revenues of the benefice.   He then
received from the Pope a dispensation allowing him
to retain these revenues.[1]

Dispensations from canonical impediments are
particularly numerous, especially from the *defectus
natalium* arising from illegitimacy.   Among those so
favoured was a nephew of Rudolf of Habsburg, named
Rudolf of Dietikon, canon of Constance.   A general
power of dispensation for twenty cases was given both
to the legate to Germany and the legate to France.[2]
In one case a layman asked to be dispensed from the
moral defect adhering to him in consequence of his
illegitimacy, so that he might be admitted to all secular
offices and honours.   His request was granted.[3]

Honorius granted frequent dispensations from
matrimonial impediments, mostly for cases of consanguinity in the fourth degree, and on one occasion
in the third degree.   In this case the bride was a widow.
Twice the impediment was one of spiritual relationship
and twice it arose from a promise of marriage and
betrothal.[4]   Especially remarkable was the privilege
given to King Edward by which a general dispensation
for marriage within the fourth degree of consanguinity
was given to his children, with the addendum that the
partner to such a marriage should not be an enemy of

[1] *Reg.*, 212, 421, 742.

[2] *Reg.*, 243, 245, 250 (Rudolf's nephew), 279, 293, 313, 465, 481, 507,
537, 557, 648, 672, 678, 684.

[3] *Reg.*, 523.

[4] *Reg.*, 109, 206, 232, 256, 259, 268, 273, 283 (3° !), 292, 431, 458, 512,
561, 634, 635, 639, 642, 668, 722, 744, 817, 908.

the Church.[1] On two occasions King Rudolf intervened to obtain marriage dispensations, stating that his ambassador, bishop Henry, would explain the case verbally.[2]

The endeavour to alleviate hardships as far as possible led the Pope even to break through an interdict. He gave the people of Milan an indult for five years allowing them to have Requiem Masses said in cases of death even during an interdict. Moreover, he instructed the clergy of Liège not to withhold the sacraments of Baptism and Extreme Unction from the people after the clergy had left the city, and laid it under an interdict at the end of 1284 or the beginning of 1285 as a protest against the excessive taxation of food by the oligarchical city council.[3] The same benevolence moved the Pope to extend to the nobility in general favours which had been restricted previously to members of the princely houses. In one case it was a matter of free choice of a confessor ; in another, permission for a family to take with them a portable altar and have Mass offered for them by their chaplain in all becoming places.[4]

As in his foreign policy, so likewise in his internal administration, the Pope's benevolence came to an end when Church rights were impaired or serious infringements of discipline took place. While Martin had usually entrusted Franciscans to carry out local investigations on his behalf, Honorius on occasion commissioned bishops to do so, but usually summoned the offenders to appear in person before the Holy See. A considerable number of bishops were thus summoned to answer to the Pope,[5] as in the case already mentioned of the bishop

Removal of abuses.

[1] Potthast, 22460, 22461.
[2] *Reg.*, 1991, 1996.
[3] *Reg.*, 497 ; Kaltenbrunner, 314.
[4] *Reg.*, 534, 535.
[5] *Reg.*, 127, 128, 139, 147, 166, 533, 543, 547, 555, 577, 586, 633, 737, 763.

of Toul after the Würzburg National Council. He
likewise summoned civic authorities before his judgment-
seat when they had interfered with the rights of the
Church. An example has been mentioned already in
the case of Parma for the affair of the Mendicant Friars ;
the proud city of Florence was also summoned before
the Pope.[1] His justice was so far-reaching that he did
not except his legates and representatives when complaints which appeared well founded were received
regarding them. Count Adenulf complained that he had
been unjustly condemned and deprived of his property
by the two Regents of Sicily, whereupon the Pope
summoned the latter and all who had received the goods
in question before his judgment-seat at Rome. As,
however, the absence of the two Regents from Sicily
would have been inconvenient, they were ordered not
to appear in person but to send a representative with
full instructions.[2]

Honorius issued a bull against an evil which had crept
into the Church in France, where a considerable number
of clergy engaged openly in commerce. Honorius warned
all the archbishops and bishops of France to take pre-
cautions to prevent clergy from engaging in secular
pursuits, and to leave commerce in particular to the
laity.[3]

Another decree of the Pope appears worthy of mention.
In it he gave power, contrary to all rules of canon law,
to Ægidius, archbishop of Sens, to confer Holy Orders
in all dioceses without the consent of his suffragans
when on a visitation of his ecclesiastical province.[4]
If such powers were given widely they might have led to
serious consequences. The precedent was not followed,
however, and we have no means of ascertaining whether
it was the result of peculiar circumstances.

[1] *Reg.*, 167, 370.   [2] *Reg.*, 759.
[3] *Reg.*, 394.   [4] *Reg.*, 53.

The Pope showed in a variety of ways his interest in the advance of learning and the development of culture. Of special importance and of far-reaching influence was his revocation of the constitution of his revered great-uncle Pope Honorius III. which prohibited the clergy from studying law. He was influenced in this by the distinguished canonist, Bindus of Siena, who was Professor of Civil Law in Rome at the papal law school, and at whose request he allowed the attendance at his lectures of the clergy, excepting bishops, abbots, and members of religious orders, for whom the prohibition still held.[1]

A dispute between the rector and the chancellor of the University of Paris provoked the intervention of the Pope. As the University developed, the importance of the rector of the four student nations had increased more and more until he overshadowed altogether the chancellor of Notre Dame, who had been previously the head of the University. Matters went so far that the institution allowed the rector of the University, who really only belonged to the least of the faculties, the arts faculty, to summon the chancellor through his beadle to attend meetings of the four nations under threat of compulsory suspension of his lectures, if he did not appear. When the chancellor did not yield, the rector carried out his threat and forbade the students under penalty of expulsion to attend the lectures or disputations of the chancellor. The latter complained to Pope Martin IV., but the University also lodged a complaint against the chancellor, who, however, died before the affair was investigated. His successor, Nicholas of Nonancourt, took the matter up, but the University took no further steps regarding its complaint. At once Honorius took the side of the chancellor. This innovation, when contrasted with circumstances in his

---

[1] *Reg.*, 168 (Oct. 18, 1285).

student days, appeared to him quite revolutionary.
He suspended the rector's decisions and ordained that
for the present the chancellor should remain in the
enjoyment of his former rights. At the same time,
however, he commissioned the papal legate in France
to endeavour to establish an accord between the
University and the chancellor. If he did not succeed
within four months, both parties were to appear either
in person or by proxy before the Holy See so that the
Pope might give a final judgment in person. His reign,
however, was too short to carry out this intention.[1]

He had likewise to arbitrate in a second dispute. Side
by side with the *studium generale* there was an arts
faculty attached to the Church of St. Geneviève, which
had its own chancellor. This chancellor wished to
compel the Paris canons who were students to do like
other students and pay weekly into a common fund,
probably for the benefit of the burses, two Paris soldi.
The canons refused, appealed to the Pope, stating that
the burses were no concern of theirs, that they lived
privately in hostels, and that they were accordingly
not liable for this payment. The Pope accepted their
point of view and the canons remained exempt from the
obligation of payment.[2]

The Pope's interest in the study of oriental languages
was noteworthy. It is incorrect to assume that a learned
institute for oriental languages was established at Rome,
such as had existed formerly at Seville,[3] but Honorius IV.
sent clergy who had command of Eastern languages to
Paris—as Innocent IV. and Alexander IV. had done—
not for the purpose of teaching languages there nor of
continuing their linguistic studies, but that they might

---

[1] *Reg.*, 267 ; *Chartularium univ. Paris.*, i, 639–42 ; Bulæus, *Historia univ. Paris.* (Paris, 1665), iii, 480.

[2] *Reg.*, 906.

[3] Denifle, *Geschichte der Universitäten*, p. 495 ff.

study theology and then work in the East on the foreign missions. Accordingly, his reason for cultivating Eastern languages was primarily ecclesiastical rather than scientific. The Pope instructed the chancellor of the University to provide for these theological students.[1]

On one other occasion Honorius had to take action in connection with the University of Paris, this time through concern for the Faith. Among the most distinguished teachers of the Paris *studium generale* was the Augustinian hermit Ægidius Colonna, who had himself been a pupil of St. Thomas. He was well known as the teacher of the future King Philip IV. and as the author of the work *De regimine principum*. In a theological dispute with the archbishop of Paris he had defended theses of which the Pope did not approve. In the dispute Ægidius appealed to Honorius for a decision. Honorius remained firm and succeeded in inducing Ægidius to withdraw, which he did in the presence of the assembled professors of the theological faculty.[2]

Having surveyed the entire internal church administration of Pope Honorius, we cannot claim, any more than in the case of his predecessor, that it in any way indicated new lines of development. He continued in the paths of his predecessors, but lacked the strength to put down with a strong hand the abuses which had crept in. Thus plurality of benefices went on, and the spiritual office was further degraded to a matter of material interests. But personally the Pope strove honestly to serve the Church and to represent its interests. It was not lack of interest, still less lack of goodwill, but excessive benevolence exclusively which prevented the Pope from carrying out reforms which had already become needful.

[1] *Reg.*, 274 ; Potthast, 22355.   [2] *Reg.*, 35.

CHAPTER V.

WHEN Honorius became Pope he was confronted in the
Holy Land with a most critical situation ; and in the West
with coffers which, despite the Crusade tithes, were empty.
The immense sums which had been contributed had been
completely exhausted by his predecessor in a manner
which no impartial person can justify, namely, in restoring
order in the papal States and, even more, in benefiting
the Angevins and the interests of France.

Crusade tax.   Accordingly, the new Pope's first efforts had to be
directed towards procuring the most important Crusade
requirement—money. From the first moment of his
reign he set himself therefore to collect the Lyons
tithes zealously. He regularized collection methods and
arranged for punctual remittance of the funds, but,
even so, the collection was not pressed forward as it
had been under Martin. The number of bulls issued in
connection with the tithes was also considerably smaller.
Honorius also employed the punishment of excommunication as an executive method, but not with the same
ruthlessness as Martin. Further, in a few cases he
reduced the amount payable, and the Carthusians
received exemption from Crusade dues in so far as they
concerned property which they cultivated with their
own hands. The Hospitallers were also released from
the obligation to pay tithes in cases where they used
their means on behalf of the poor and the sick. Honorius
also warned the collector in Prague not to press the
archbishop and clergy if they were really unable,

because of the uncertainty of their means, to pay the tax.[1]

The head collectors in most countries were the same as those who had functioned under Martin IV. In Germany the Pope confirmed Theodoric of Orvieto, recommended him anew to the German King, and asked for a safe conduct for him.[2] In Norway, Denmark, and Sweden we make the acquaintance of a new collector, Huguitio, who held office for more than ten years, but the difficulties of conveying the tithes from those countries to Rome remained as before. Another appeal was addressed by Honorius to the King not to obstruct further the export of the tithes, and to revoke the prohibition of the sale of specie and silver. This time it was successful. The method of transmission is interesting and affords an illuminating instance of the difficulties of making calculations in a variety of coinages. Along with the money, which amounted to 520 silver marks, the new collector sent to the papal camera a lump of lead, under his seal, weighing one Norwegian pound. The difference between the Roman and the Norwegian pound was then determined in the presence of a representative of the camera, the bankers with whom the Pope dealt, and the bearer of the money. It transpired that, according to Norwegian weights, a mark was lighter by a quarter of an ounce and four grains than a mark according to Roman weight.[3]

In Scotland, likewise, the Pope endeavoured to overcome the difficulty of exporting the tithes.[4] In Poland the collection of the church tax for Rome had to be reorganized : for years neither tithes nor Peter's Pence

[1] *Reg.*, 61, 211, 242, 337.

[2] *Reg.*, 114–16 ; Redlich, *Reg.*, 939 ; Kaltenbrunner, 278.

[3] *Reg.*, 214, 217, 218, 220, 221, 247, 248, 249 ; Potthast, 22343, 22349, 22350 ; Munch, *Pavelige Nuntiers Regensskaps og dagböger* (Christiania, 1864), p. 12 ff.

[4] *Reg.*, 66 ; Potthast, 22252.

had been paid there. Now Honorius recommended
Johannes Muscatæ, the collector, to the archbishop of
Gnesen, all other ecclesiastical dignitaries, and also all
the princes and potentates of the country, requesting
a safe conduct for him. The collector's mission was to
re-establish the collection of church dues payable to
Rome ; in particular, those who had collected moneys but
had not forwarded them were to be compelled, with the
help of the bishops and archdeacons, to make restitution.[1]

The collector's remuneration varied. As a general rule
it was limited to a simple exemption from personal
payment, but the head collectors were allowed special
financial payments. Johannes Muscatæ drew sixteen
solidi a day, Huguitio eighteen, and the English collector
three shillings.[2] The honorarium was, it will be seen,
a considerable one.

Again, the administration of the funds [3] was entrusted
to banks, even to a greater extent than in Martin's
pontificate. Frequent letters regulated relations between
the collectors and the bankers, whom the Pope particularly
recommended to the goodwill of the King of England,
and whom he supplied with letters of protection.[4] The
number of banks with which Honorius had dealings
increased. The most important were those which had
done most of the business under Martin IV., namely,
the Florentine company of Thomas Spillati and Lapi
Ugonis Spina, as well as the commercial houses of Abbati

---

[1] *Reg.*, 194–8 ; Potthast, 22256, 22257.

[2] *Reg.*, 199, 214, 334, 336, 469 ; Potthast, 22258.

[3] For the collectors' reports *cf.* Munch, *Pavelige Nuntiers Regensskaps
og dagböger* (Christiania, 1864) ; *Liber decimationis diocesis Constantiensis*
in *Freiburger Diozesanarchiv* I, and the sources cited under Martin IV.

[4] *Reg.*, 43, 125, 183, 184, 186, 192, 193, 218, 219, 222, 331, 332, 470,
471, 519, 520, 553, 609, 617, 618, 621, 640, 766, 832 ; *cf.* also Jordan,
La Saint Siège et les banquiers italiens (Proceedings of the third International Catholic Congress, Brussels, Sept., 1894. Published Brussels,
1895, vol. v, pp. 292–303).

and Baccarelli, Lambertutii de Fliscobaldis (or Fresco-
baldis), Petrus Foresii, and also the Siena company of
Bonaventura Bernardini, that of the Ammantani of
Pistoia, and, finally, that of Aldobrandus Bruneti.
Representatives of these concerns are found in many
countries, and their work was facilitated by the letters
of recommendation and protection given to them by the
Pope. It is beyond question that papal finance was a
very important factor in the development of banking.

The yield of the tithes was not the only source of
supply for the projected Crusade, and Honorius in
particular exerted himself to tap new sources. He
exhorted the clergy and the laity to leave legacies to
be used for the Holy Land ; frequently the contribution
of a sum of money for the same purpose was imposed
as a penance. Finally, Honorius decreed that the
property of dissolved Orders should be sold and the
proceeds devoted to the Holy Land fund.

Under Pope Honorius the Crusade idea was resuscitated. Crusade
His policy made it possible to envisage at least the union plans.
of all Christendom for the liberation of the Holy Land ;
under his predecessor the idea had been stifled by political
interests. As soon as he ascended the throne Honorius
approached the King of England with regard to a Crusade ;
and even in Germany the possibility of one was considered, as is clear from the fact that endowments were
made to advance the *passagium manifestum*, the *publica
transfretatio*.[1]

The King of England was the bearer and the support
of the Crusade ideal. In his youth he had demonstrated
that his zeal for the liberation of the Holy Land was
genuine, and if he was then obliged to return home on
his father's death to assume the reins of government,
before achieving any great success, the firm resolution
of his soul persisted in the hope that as King he would

[1] *Cf. Regesta Boica*, iv, 777.

take the field again with a larger force and would attain
greater results.   He was, however, so much absorbed
by affairs of State, especially by the disturbances in
Wales, but also by new political tasks and interests,
that he no longer needed to seek in a foreign country an
outlet for his energies.   In fact, during the first years of
his reign he could not have found time for such things.

His interest persisted in one aspect of the matter,
the collection of the tithes.   His coffers had been emptied
by wars, particularly the long campaign in Wales, and
the tithes appeared most desirable so that he could
have money in his hands once more.   As early as the
Council of Lyons [1] Gregory X—of whom he was a personal
friend since his Holy Land days—had made him a grant
of one-tenth of all the Church revenues of England,
Wales, Ireland, and Scotland.   The amounts were not
to be paid to him until he was preparing to go on the
Crusade, but Pope Nicholas III. had gone so far as to
pay over to him immediately a sum of 25,000 marks from
the moneys collected, in order that he might equip a
Crusade expedition, on the express condition, it is true,
that the money was to be paid back in full if the promised
Crusade did not materialize.   This sum was evidently
too small in King Edward's view, for he then forbade
the export of the collected tithes.   The veto was
occasioned mainly by the recrudescence of war in Wales.
The King actually seized the tithe deposits throughout
the country.   At first Pope Martin reproached him for
this attack on the rights of the Church and the injury
to Church property, but when the King again pledged
himself to the Crusade, Martin granted him the tithes
collected in England, Ireland, Wales, and Scotland and,
in addition, the proceeds of the collection during the
three succeeding years, provided that he should take the
Cross before the following Christmas, and should advance

---

[1] Rymer, *Foedera*, i, 173.

on the Holy Land within five years at most. The King desired further concessions, but the Pope died without granting them.

Honorius was acquainted with King Edward when the former was a cardinal, and was inclined to be accommodating towards him in so far as this was compatible with the Church's interests, but he was obliged to reject some of the demands which had been made to Pope Martin. The King wished to have command of the Crusade, but the Pope saw clearly that this would cause difficulties and jealousies among the other princes. Accordingly he refused the request, reserving the decision regarding the supreme command to himself personally when the time should be ripe. Edward demanded also an extension of the usual Crusade tithes for two years on the ground that the yield of the tax up to that time was inadequate for the necessary preparations : the Pope explained that he would not give a decision on the point until he saw the first preparations for a crusade being made, but in compensation he granted Edward what had been so far collected in tithes in Scotland. Even then Edward did not make up his mind to carry out his promise. On the contrary, having been obliged to promise Martin that he would take the Cross before Christmas of 1284, and that he would carry out the Crusade within five years, he now asked Honorius for permission to defer the date until the Feast of St. John the Baptist. The Pope fixed the Christmas of 1285 as the latest date for taking the Cross, thus extending the period for six months longer than the King had requested, but in return he desired to fix a date for the initiation of the Crusade. Soon after he postponed the date of taking the Crusade vow until Whitsun of 1286, and finally until June 24, 1287. Honorius was able to justify these extensions, as conditions were not yet such as to give a prospect of really uniting Christendom for a decisive struggle with the Orient. In fact the Pope would have missed the King very much as a mediator in European affairs. King Edward made use of this compliance to extract further concessions. In 1286 he presented five petitions regarding the Crusade to the Pope through his representative ; to these the Pope replied in a bull dated June 17, 1286. Edward had asked the Pope to compel all those who had ever taken the Cross to take part in person ; but a decision on this point was deferred by Honorius. Secondly, he asked that the Crusade should be preached in all Christian countries ; to which the Pope agreed if it were done within the period fixed originally by Edward to elapse before the Crusade. Thirdly, Edward requested the tithes of all countries, the princes of which were not participating in person in the campaign ; but on this point, too, the Pope reserved his decision, being far too wise not to foresee that the majority of the princes would refuse to hand over their tithes to England, and not wishing, on the other hand, to deprive Edward of his hopes in the matter, and thus destroy his interest. Finally, he asked for the English tithes for seven further years. Honorius granted them to him for six years in all, and at the same time decreed the Feast of Whitsun in 1290 as the latest date for the Crusade, demanding that Edward must make up his mind before February 2, 1287, whether he was ready or not.

Honorius did not live to see this Crusade ; in fact it never materialized. It may be assumed that for some time King Edward himself had not seriously considered undertaking the Crusade, for his plans to subdue Scotland were absorbing him too much. The tithe payments, which were being granted to him continually in virtue of his Crusade vow, supplied him with the funds necessary to finance this very prolonged war. It never occurred to him to repay the tithes.[1]

[1] *Reg.*, 14, 478, 943, 969, 973.

King Rudolf sought to serve the Crusade idea in a
strange fashion. He could not even contemplate leaving
his country and fighting in the Holy Land, for conditions
in the Empire rendered a long absence on the King's
part impossible. There was no possibility of doing
anything until he was crowned Emperor and his son
elected as German King. On the other hand, the Crusade
vow he had taken at Lausanne ten years earlier worried
him. In this dilemma he attempted to improve matters
in the Holy Land by peaceful negotiations. In the
summer of 1285, simultaneously with the Genoese and
the Greek Emperor Andronicus II, he sent a delegation
to Egypt to Sultan Malik al Mansur (Kilawun). References
to this have been preserved in the writings of the Egyptian
historians Nuweiri (end of the thirteenth century),
Makuzi († 1333), and others. According to these accounts
the envoys reached Cairo on November 6, 1285. Their
leader was probably the famous Dominican Burchard
of Berge Sion, noted for his travels in Palestine and
Egypt. They appeared before the Sultan bearing rich
gifts of ermine and sable skins, gold embroidered silk
tissues, fine linens and satins, in all thirty-two loads
from Rudolf alone. The other envoys brought similar
gifts from their masters. The Sultan had followed
uninterruptedly in the victorious path of his predecessor,
and in the spring of 1285 had conquered two of the
strongest Christian strongholds in Syria. Rudolf realized
the purposelessness and impracticability of the Crusade
to which he was vowed, and hoped to attain more by
peaceful methods than by a Crusade doomed to failure
from the outset. Probably the purpose of the mission
was to obtain more protection and guarantees for the
inconsiderable remnants of Christian territory on the
coast of the Holy Land. The mission, however, did not
attain any success worth mentioning : it was too late

to prevent the doom of Palestine and the kingdom of Jerusalem.[1]

It is obvious that in these circumstances an alliance offered to the Pope by the Tatar Argoun for a joint campaign against Egypt [2] could avail nothing.

Pope Honorius' Crusade plans did not advance beyond the collection of funds, but at least he desired honestly to employ this money genuinely for the advantage of the Holy Land. But already the West as a unit had ceased to exist, and consequently unified action was no longer possible. The Pope alone remained as the last evidence of the great Western idea, but the idea itself was no longer understood and its expression found no echo. This was the cause of the collapse of the Crusade scheme ; the Pope was in no way responsible.

[1] *Cf.* Karabacek, *Eine Gesandschaft Rudolfs von Habsburg nach Ägypten* (*Österreichische Monatsschrift für den Orient*, 1879) ; Redlich, *Reg.*, p. 426.

[2] *Reg.*, 489. The almost unintelligible Latin deserves mention.

CONCLUSION.

DEATH OF THE POPE.   ESTIMATE OF HIS REIGN.

HONORIUS was a sick man even when he assumed the
dignity and burden of the papacy, and the mighty tasks
he undertook wore him out.   He held his office for barely
two years, dying on April 3, 1287, on the Aventine,
according to all the chroniclers.   We must assume that
his death was sudden ; possibly it was the result of a
stroke of apoplexy.

He died on Maundy Thursday, and on Good Friday his
mortal remains were laid in St. Peter's close to the grave
of Nicholas III.   His brother Pandulf it probably was
who caused the sculptor Arnolfo to carve the stone
statue of him which stood over his tomb.   Later Pope
Paul III. had his remains removed, together with the
statue, to the Sabelli family vault in Sta. Maria of Ara
Cæli, where they were laid in the grave of his mother,
Vana Aldobrandesca of S. Fiara.

In his will,[1] which he had made when a cardinal-deacon
and confirmed when Pope, he appointed as sole heirs
his brother and nephews, or their male descendants.
To their female descendants he left legacies.   In the
event of no male descendant being alive at the time of
his death his estate was to go to the Church, which should
then pay specified legacies to relatives.   A portion of
the proceeds of the chattels was to be used as a foundation for the benefit of his soul.

---

[1] *Reg.*, 823, 830.   It is interesting to note that the will, as confirmed
by the Pope, is drawn up like that of a private citizen, not in the style
of the Papal Chancery.   It is witnessed by a " notarius vocatus et
rogatus ".

Times were critical when Pope Honorius assumed the leadership of the Church, which had been shaken to its foundation by the consequences of the Sicilian Vespers. It was surely a great achievement for the aged Pope that he was able during his brief pontificate to turn the development of European history into more peaceful paths : that he did so is a proof of his diplomatic skill. His tendency was to allow leniency to bear sway in his domestic and foreign policy. Where he used this weapon to the full he met with most success; where he felt himself obliged to be more stern in defence of the Church's rights, success was denied him. In the inner life of the Church greater strictness might perhaps have achieved more than excessive compliance and kindness. But who will dare to censure a Pope for being kind ? Therein he but acted in accordance with his greatest model.

INDEX